Gutter to the Stars

Memories of a Post-Grunge Drifter (A Gen X Tale of painful lessons and redemption)

Latimer Redlance

Stacks Publishing

Copyright © 2025 by Latimer Redlance. All rights reserved.

ISBN (print edition): 978-1-7636793-5-1
ISBN: (eBook): 978-1-7636793-4-4

Latimer Redlance has asserted his rights under the Copyright Act to be identified as the author of this book. The information in this book is based on the author's experiences and opinions.

This book is a work of memoir, reflecting the author's personal experiences and perspective. While the author has strived for accuracy, the events are presented as he remembers them. The author and publisher disclaim any liability for errors or omissions. The author has changed some names and identifying details to protect the privacy of individuals involved.

The publisher specifically disclaims responsibility for any adverse consequences which may result from the use or publication of the information contained herein.

No part of this work may be reproduced, stored in a retrieval system or transmitted in any form by any means, electronic, mechanical, photocopying, recording, or otherwise, without written permission of the author, except in the case of brief quotations embodied in critical reviews.

Any person who does any unauthorised act in relation to this publication may be liable to criminal prosecution and civil claims.

For rights and permissions, please contact:
Stacks Publishing
PO Box 676
Claremont WA 6910
Australia

To my Mentors:

Jack K
Hunter S
Charles B
Kurt K
Jim M

The light that burns twice as bright burns half as long- and you have burned so very very brightly.

Introduction

This is an inspirational book. It follows my life as I batter my way from the freezing gulf islands of 80s Canada, to the wilds of the bush of 90s rural New Zealand and onto the mean streets of early 2000s Sydney. This is a nostalgic trip for all of us who grew up in these times and want to go back and relive it. This book is your time machine. I have finally written all the stories of my crazy life experiences.

I have told these tales at parties and bars over the last 20 years. This book is a culmination of a hard and exciting life well lived.

It exists to inspire a new generation to BURN MAN BURN.

These stories will solve your pain. A wise hippie once called me LAST BEAT.

Am I?

You decide.

These stories will help you lead a fuller richer life—and everyone loves a redemption story.

No one really likes the stories where the kid is abused, gets addicted, becomes a crook, and then dies or just kind of rots along screaming at things in the street.

I now work with addicts and the incarcerated. I know what it's like to have that life, and it's not cool or badass. It's proper fucked. Fucked

Introduction

beyond the imaginings of any pampered suburbanite. This does not mean it's not funny to write about though.

I was born in Canada in the winter of 76. Shit went sideways fast.

Welcome to the beginning of my life, to my first real, distinct memory...

Six years old. So full of life and hope. I don't have too many interesting memories before this time, at least nothing that stands out. After this particular incident, everything else is remembered in clear detail.

I think at this instance I decided that if I was going to survive, I would have to start paying attention. Luckily I did. I lived and I can now tell the tales.

I'm shit at writing fiction. What I'm best at is describing how things went down.

And so, as one of my Mentors once suggested to me, when I exclaimed that life was getting too intense, "Buy the ticket, take the ride... and if it occasionally gets a little heavier than what you had in mind, well... maybe chalk it up to forced consciousness expansion: Tune in, freak out, get beaten."

I now like to think of my stories as educational trials delivered to me by life, and I have documented all these wonderful times of my personal growth, so that others may be entertained from the stories I gathered on the rough roads I traveled.

And so we begin...

Chapter 1
BAD MAN JAN (Awakening the bad kid)

SO THERE I WAS, A YOUNG MAN…

I was six and we were on the run from my Dad…

A trifecta of bad things had hit our family unit, which was composed of my Mother, myself, and my 4-year-old sister…

I was being taken care of by my mother's friends, Jan, and his wife for a weekend. They were nice enough…

I was on an island off the coast of British Columbia while my mother and sister were on the island of Vancouver, in a town called Nanaimo.

It was a horrendous snowy winter.

An 80s Canada, it was a "homeless people frozen dead on the sidewalks while uncaring rich 80s stock-market fat-cats stepped over the bodies, sort of winter…"

My sister was in the car of our babysitter, Noni—A large, older woman with big hair and a high squeaky voice… Her little dog, Tippy, jumped up and got in the way of the driving…

The car crashed…

My 4-year-old sister is now in hospital with a broken leg. We have no money… And my mum has to somehow work her minimum-wage hairdressing job at "Fantastic Sam's," in the town of Nanaimo, between running to the hospital every day while staying at a friend's house.

Latimer Redlance

The ferries also started a weeks-long strike that day as part of Operation Solidarity—a huge British Columbia worker's strike in 1983.

In short, I was now trapped on an island with Jan and his family.

I was stuck there for about two weeks... which of course is the equivalent of nine years in the mind of a six-year-old.

I recall Jan explaining that my sister had been in a crash and had a broken leg, and that I would be staying with them for a bit longer, because the ferries were on strike, and so Mum couldn't get back.

No problem! They ate three real meals, had a warm house and a big TV. Something that my family, at that time, didn't have any of...Remember this was 80s TV too—Quality.

I was in the daughter's room, on a mattress on the floor. She had a record player and I was hooked on the first three songs on one of the records she had— "HIT WAVE 82."

Check out this track list!:

1. Joan Jett and the Blackhearts - "I Love Rock 'n' Roll"
2. Survivor - "Eye of the Tiger"
3. Toto - "Africa"
4. Chas & Dave - "Ain't No Pleasing You"
5. Huey Lewis and the News - "Do You Believe in Love"
6. Quarterflash - "Harden My Heart"
7. Olivia Newton-John - "Make a Move on Me"
8. Elton John - "Blue Eyes"
9. Jon & Vangelis - "I'll Find My Way Home"

In the first 24 hours of Jan being called up by my mother and him happily telling her that taking care of me was no problem at all, I experienced the following awesome shocks:

The next morning, I went to my school on the school bus with the daughter... all seemed fine... but really, dark clouds were gathering...

In class, everyone was told to get out their crayons and glue for our art project. All the other parents had supplied their kids with crayons and glue, as instructed by the newsletter we brought home.

Out came the tower-shaped, turntable Crayola Caddies... (look those beauties up if you don't know what they are—boxes of super nice crayons with built-in sharpeners in the base and the silver, gold and bronze crayons), and out came the nice, white, sweet smelling glue in clean, white bottles with easily dispensing nozzles.

I got my crayons and glue out... but within a minute...

I heard, "Pooooo! What's that stinky smell!"

"OH gross! It's HIS glue."

I looked at my glue...

My glue was in a weird gunky snotty glass pot... with the lid on crooked... and a weird old wild bristly brush jammed down into a mostly-dried, stinking, gray mass. It was most likely made up of mashed-up, rotten horse testicles.

The teacher came over... and looked at my glue... then picked up my crayons.

My crayons were not the special Crayola ones... my crayons were the four-pack from that greasy Italian restaurant our uncle took us and our mum out to... where mum started crying and talking about Dad taking off... and we had to go sit in the car...

Tiny red, blue, yellow, and green paper-wrapped sticks that drew about as good as a lightly-colored candle.

Gently putting down my crayons and looking at me with sad, kind eyes, she picked up my glue pot and said, "I'm just going to put this outside for now ok? And, you can take it home with you later. I have some other spare glue you can use."

I said nothing... but I observed the other kids laughing as they watched her take my glue outside the class.

I looked at my crayons... I looked at the other kids' crayons... I looked at their glue... I looked at their awesome 80s backpacks over on the wall... I looked at my weird, old-woman's 70s vinyl handbag... that I had for a backpack...

I had a shattering moment of clarity... We were as poor as fuck.

It sort of all lined up suddenly... the weird meals, the fact the other kid's rooms were always filled with toys, while I had only a few toys in a paper bag—wack toys that were mostly from Cracker Jack boxes or happy meals.

Our car broke down a lot and was shitty and we moved around a lot and kind of always lived in weird places... or with "Aunt someone" or "Uncle someone else".

It sank in, and I started to feel a small but painful and growing sting of unfairness...

So, I get off the bus back to Jan's big flash house and, stepping off the bus into the knee-deep snow, there is giant, bearded Jan... looking stern, and kind of angry.

He sent his kid inside and bade me go with him over to his workshop where, among the sawdust and oil smells, he crouched down to face me with his freaky skinny but big, bearded face and beery breath...

He told me that I had gone into his shed and broken many of his expensive tools, and that I would have to work off the damage every day after school now.

I just stared at him at first. This was the first time in my life an adult had suddenly become an evil liar. It was hard to take in...

I protested that I had never been into his shed and had broken none of his expensive tools.

He looked gleefully angry, in a fake way, and insisted that I had indeed broken his expensive tools and that the only way to pay for them was for me to do jobs after school, as my mum had no money and would not be able to buy him new ones.

The glue. He must somehow have known about the stinky glue.

It was a setup.

I believe, even though I was only six, my mind worked very well.

I was intelligent, but of course not wise in the ways of the world... yet.

I resigned myself to my fate... and just said "OK."

Not the first time, or the last, that I would agree to some sort of bullshit in order to survive.

So every day after school I would work until dark. He had a truck full of chopped wood and I was to climb up on the truck bed, throw a piece of wood off and roll it through the snow over to the wood stack against the wall, and stack it all up.

Every day for about two weeks, as soon as one load was complete, the next day there would be another.

After I finished the first truckload, he said "You're working so well, if you keep this up I'll have to give you a raise," and laughed heartily and meanly.

I didn't even know what he meant. But as I looked at him, a new concept formed.

Hurt Bad Man Jan.

How could I hurt Bad Man Jan?

Jan was big and strong, and my mum was gone.

But at a precise moment, while rolling a log through snow with frozen, numb, little six-year-old hands, I decided I was going to get big and strong—and one day, find Bad Man Jan and hurt him real bad.

Then, I just pushed that thought away and kept rolling and stacking the wood.

There were other injustices I added to the list of painful paybacks that would be coming Bad Man Jan's way, one day.

He spanked the shit out of his daughter one day for knocking over a bunch of beer bottles that were in the hall.

Due to the fact that I had started to hate her, and because she got to go inside and watch ELECTRIC COMPANY and other cool shows and eat food after school, she had started to hate me too.

I'd see her watching me through the window as I worked in the snow, her eyes sad. I'd stare back, and then she'd turn back to the TV, the snacks, and the warm fire.

She had Survivor guilt.

Also, I'm sure her dad told her that I broke all his expensive tools...

But any time she was bad, she was spanked till she was screaming like her arms were being ripped off.

The early 80s over the knee, POW POW POW full adult-anger, bare-arse hand spanks.

I laughed in glee and happiness. That's how demented I had become.

"Think it's funny do ya?!"

I was grabbed and spanked viciously.

I did not make a sound—I was too tough and numb for that.

His wife yelled "Jan! You will leave marks!" And he stopped.

When my mother would call every few days he would tell her I was very happy and doing great and we were all having a great time, then hand the phone to me and stand right over me to make sure I didn't say anything bad.

When the family had dinner I had to get my own food from what was left in the kitchen, I wasn't given a place at the table and had to eat in the lounge by myself.

I was not allowed any of the nice desserts they had.

But he would cheerily yell out how good they were from over at the table, while I sat with my empty plate in the lounge.

Your modern mind might like to think the wife would say something—but you can't imagine the isolation of island life in 80s Canada, or how Stockholm-syndromed to fuck his crushed-down family was.

After what seemed like a year of living in a frozen, half-starved slavery hell, my mother finally showed up in her rusty, little white car.

She was met with hugs and love by them. A glazed 1000-yard stare by me. I watched their fake display of friendship, as if looking through a fun-house mirror. A huge part of me changed that day... and I decided that I was going to have to be a SURVIVOR.

If that meant being a "Bad Kid," then maybe that's what it meant.

Fuck... The... World.

That was how I saw it. As soon as I decided this, I saw that I didn't have to play by the bullshit "Good Kid" rules anymore, and this was very freeing.

I went straight over to their daughter's Advent calendar, which had only the 1st through 8th of December eaten, and systematically opened up each little door and ate the 9th through Christmas.

Like a chocolate-eating boss.

I felt happier and more fulfilled with each swallow.

I walked out of there, guts full of plasticy, Advent-calendar chocolate, and went and sat in the car, without saying goodbye.

Life went on...

STAR-WIPE TO 20 YEARS LATER

I'm a man *grown*. Lithe and strong. About 8 years of martial arts training. Years of weight lifting on top of working very physical jobs from the age of 16. Logging, Roofing, Demolition. Seasons of hunting and killing living things... cutting throats, slicing up animals.

Training to bring death.

Black leather jacket. Long black hair. Black steel-capped boots. Hands covered in hard silver rings. I've trained and brainwashed myself into a barbaric relic from an earlier time. A time when someone would have no qualms about hurting someone really badly. An avenging angel for a small child.

How much of my life, my look, my mindset had I dedicated to this moment? Only about 85% of it—super mentally healthy.

Justice had come for Bad Man Jan.

I had traveled across the world to Canada and traveled back to this tiny island. I had a balaclava in my backpack and I had a very calm, vicious silent beating planned, with a good amount of hard stomping— something Bad Man Jan would not walk away from. I didn't want to kill him. I wanted him to live out the rest of his life crippled and broken. But I didn't even know if he was still there, or alive. I thought maybe I would just go to the spot itself... and maybe some healing would take place. But on the off chance he WAS there... the balaclava to prevent identification was needed.

While on the ferry across to the island I asked a guy who looked like a local if he knew of a guy called Jan, who lived with his family on the island in the 80s. Not only did the guy know him, he hated him, and apparently so did everyone else on the island. Jan was a horrid man who had crossed everyone at one time or another.

The local gleefully told me that about ten years back, his wife had left him, taken the kids, and they all hated him. I guess he had another kid or two later on. Not long after that he rolled his truck while drunk and broke his back. Now he lives, on the welfare, by himself... miserable and in pain in his rotting, old house. I said that was sad to hear as my mother was friends with him in the 80s, and moved quickly to the back of the ferry before the guy got a good look at me.

That was interesting to hear. I wasn't sure how I felt about that.

It was early winter, with no snow yet, and I stood at the top of the driveway, looking down at Bad Man Jan's dilapidated house. I saw the shed, now sagging and crumbling... I saw a woodpile in exactly the same place. I saw a truck with wood in the back, parked right where he used to leave it for me to unload in the snow, twenty years ago. I saw Jan hunched, gray-bearded, old, wheezing, and ragged... Standing head down, leaning on his truck, looking at the wood in the back.

He grabs a piece and starts carrying it over to the wood pile... With a cry of pain, he drops it and almost goes down.

He stands there, clutching his back. I turned and walked away... As simple as that, I had decided to forgive him.

Within a few months, the rings were off, the muscles slowly going, the leather fighting jacket put away and the kicking boots replaced with soft shoes.

"Pain or damage don't end the world.

Or despair. Or fucking beatings.

The world ends when you're dead.

Until then, you've got more punishment in store.

Stand it like a man...

And give some back."

Chapter 2
MY FIRST BEST FRIEND: TARD BOY (Mongs gunna mong)

So there I was..., a young man...

I was six, and I think for some reason we were on the run from my Dad... or ... Dad didn't know where we were living right now... or he was away for a long time working... or some such early 80s packed-the-kids-into-the-car-and-driven-off-suddenly-in-the-night-with-the-kids type of explanation.

It was an interesting limbo time for me and my sister...

It seemed that my Mum would haul us about to a series of single mothers' dens throughout Vancouver.

These big-haired women always seemed to be chain-blazing smokes, with a glass of red wine in hand and harping on about some no-good man, while us kids were shuttled outside to play—unsupervised—as the mothers ranted and cackled.

By us kids, I mean the forlorn, fed-on-peanut-butter-and-white-bread spazes that were left in a sort of confused and numb suppressed grief over the "Where's Daddy?" and "Why is he such a bad man?" quandary.

I remember so many trailers, so many hours hanging with weird, sad, and angry kids whose main pastime was smashing bottles with rocks...

So many hours spent staring at sea monkeys... and so many kids' rooms that were tiny, messy, pissy-smelling hovels in these thin single-wide trailers...

That was my world...

I started recognizing that the trailer moms and kids were way worse off than the apartment kids.

That's hitting bottom. And I kind of knew it even back then.

One particular kid on one particular day sticks out in my memory.

I will never forget it. The stink of that day is in my bones.

He was my first best friend. Why my mother thought it was ok for her six-year-old to be taken care of by a nine-year-old retarded kid I will never know.

But that day changed me—my essence—profoundly.

I have no idea what this kid's name was, but he was a retard. Not so retarded that he would just shit himself and drool—but still a retard. It was like he had no filters that made other normal kids scared or worried about getting into danger or trouble. He could talk and run about and had things going on in his life—he was by no means handicapped by his retardation.

He was quite stocky and had black hair in a crude bowl cut.

I had no idea there was anything wrong with this kid, until about a decade later.

I thought he was a cool kid and had THE FIRE!

Now remember, this is the early 80s—if you were a retard, you were a straight-up retard. You weren't "Special" or "mentally challenged" or whatever the fuck autistic is. You were a fucking Mong.

There was no recourse to people who gave a fuck about your plight. You just had to harden up and become as cunning as a bastard to get by.

As soon as I was placed in Tard Boy's care, he took me to his room, and from under his mattress he produced box after box of big chocolate-covered almonds, which we fed on until almost sick.

Then in a chocolaty daze, we went outside to the parking lot of the apartment, where he introduced me to an amazing game that he had invented.

It was called "Catch the Onion."

He had procured a sack of very large onions from somewhere, and I was provided with a plastic crate. The type that holds a number of milk bottles. It has a grid-like pattern of holders for the bottles.

Anyway, the game consisted of throwing the large onion as high as possible in the air for the other guy to catch in the crate.

The trick was that as you caught this onion, or as it hit the ground, it began to fragment, and successive catches sprayed acrid onion juice into your face, making it progressively harder to catch and the game progressively harder to play.

Now remember, this is the 80s, and the onions back then were at least twice as acrid as today.

Tard Boy's slitted Mongoloid eyes gave him an unfair advantage in resisting the burning oniony spray, and I collapsed first, gasping and unable to see or breathe properly. He fed me more chocolate almonds, from his pocket to heal me up, and led me by the arm, blind and staggering down the road to a bowling alley.

The next thing I know, the lady behind the counter at the bowling alley is yelling at Tard Boy. She's yelling, "Where's the 14 dollars? You haven't been eating the almonds, have you?!! You have to sell them to raise money for your brother's hockey trip, you stupid little shit!!!"

He screamed his innocence.

I had no idea if she could see the chocolate on our faces. Perhaps the onion spray had washed it off, I don't know. But we hightailed it out of there and back to the parking lot for another game of his design, on dusk. The perfect time for his next game.

This one was called "FIRE BIN."

From the side of the apartment block, he produced a long piece of bamboo, perhaps six meters in length. A plastic garbage bin was upended, emptied of its stinking trash, and placed on the end of the pole so it could be hoisted into the air—though not before Tard Boy, in his infinite innovation, lit the edge with a big lighter. The bin started to ignite, and as it burned he lifted it skyward on the pole, to flare prettily in the evening. It dripped super-heated molten plastic, and by flicking the pole just right, he could splatter this flaming plastic onto the parked cars or the lawn or the pavement, or the side of the apartment building. I followed him, screaming in terrified glee until the entire bin was aflame and started to SLIDE DOWN THE POLE. Quick as a flash, Tard Boy flung the entire flaming apparatus into the apartment complex's pool, where it bobbed, still burning for a bit, on the surface.

All this rampaging had made us hungry, so we headed inside to demand food from our mothers. Seeing the chocolate, onion, and soot-spattered state of us, we were put into a hot bath.

While in there, Tard Boy introduced me to his masterwork.

The crowning achievement of all his moronic games. An affirmation of freedom so reckless and unqualified that it amounted to a total denial of every kind of restraint and limitation.

This game went Full Retard.

He called it "POTIONS."

And it was as brilliant as it was simple.

It consisted of emptying everything in the bathroom into the bath, starting with the closest containers and widening out in an expanding sphere until everything was in the bath with us. And every container had to be double-rinsed to make sure we got it all.

We, of course, started by squeezing the soaps to mush, including his mum's special soaps and bath gels. Then all of the shampoos and conditioners. Then the toothpaste and mouthwash. Then we sprayed out all the 80s hair mousse into a huge foamy pile. Then two packets of scented bath salts went in.

All of his brother's hair gel and shaving cream followed. All of his mum's facial products including lipsticks. Squeezing each lipstick into a mush before dropping it into the POTION.

At this point, I kind of figured that we were probably being naughty. But he didn't seem scared or worried. He seemed really happy. So I thought it must be ok…

Then in went all his mum's makeup, eyeliners, about ten bottles of nail polish plus nail polish remover, the eyelash stick weird thing with the black goo, and the makeup bag for good measure.

That was everything we could reach, so we played in that soup for a bit, till he realized there was more stuff under the sink, so in went rolls and rolls of toilet paper, toilet cleaner, a thing of bathroom cleaning powder, and a bottle of bleach.

Stirred and stirred and stirred with the pooey toilet brush.

I started to get a bad feeling. I was sitting in a bath up to my chest of a thick, multi-colored goop. The smell started to hurt my eyes.

We tried to play in the goop, but we couldn't stop coughing, and the burning of the eyes was making catching the sodden toilet rolls difficult, and the spray stung your eyes way worse than the onion.

The next thing I remember is feeling like my ass and little doodle was on fire, and soon we were both screaming.I can remember his mum coming in and screaming something at us and turning the shower on and pulling us out of the caustic soup. She tried to pull the plug of the bath, but the goop was too thick with makeup and toilet paper to go down. I think she felt helpless, so she just furiously spanked the shit out of him, which was probably her answer to anything he did.

I was washed off and dressed and we rolled out... I never saw him again. But I do still fondly remember Tard Boy, and one day plan to introduce my son to his game of Catch the Onion, which we will play in his honor.

Chapter 3
CANDY AND WINNING AT 6 (Get your Red Hots!)

When I was six, I wanted to be Eliot, the kid from ET. ET would help me escape my shit life and find candy. I didn't have a bike he could make fly... but I imagined he could make a big cardboard box fly about with us in it. I kept one in my bedroom closet with a pillow and a blanket in it, in my wardrobe ready for us... in case he rocked up, so we could take off at a moment's notice.

As a child, I had slanty eyes. That's some good old-fashioned Fetal Alcohol Syndrome. Many 80s kids had these slanty eyes and elf-like features. I found this feature hot in girls as I grew up. Later in life, I noticed that the more redneck the girl's parents, the more elf-like she was going to look. Girls from regular or rich families had round faces and round eyes. I never put it together until I read a medical book on child development with pages and pages of pictures of us elf kids.

I love writing sad stories about my abandoned Gen X 80s childhood, and you like reading them, probably because we are fucked in the head from that childhood.

In all my childhood, the most common feeling I remember was hunger.

My mum was always on the run, and we were moving from place to place, hiding from my dad, in a classic 80s spousal abuse kids-packed-into-the-car-and-driven-off thing.

No one wanted to really help us or get in on our business, because it was the 80s and clumsy women walked into doors all the time back then. The most my mother did to reach out for help was to pound wine with other bashed single mums and join them in shrill, tearful rants while us kids were sent outside in bare feet to smash bottles in alleyways.

So... this story is about three amazing moments that I lie back and remember to this day. These memory moments from my childhood gave me such feelings of pleasure and happiness that I feel their glowing warmth right now.

THE CINNAMON RED HOTS.

I was 6, it was 1983 and I was with my Dad. Before my mum fled, there were a few times I somehow wound up with him driving about Vancouver in his blue GMC pickup. I do remember him having to go to a courthouse. "Your insane mother is divorcing me," he said before leaving me in the truck for an hour. I spent a lot of time sitting in that truck.

Anyway, one time we went into a mall. And he let me go in! I was never allowed to touch anything or go into any of the stores with him. Probably because I liked to touch things in the stores.

He made me stand outside this supermarket when he went in. I was not to move from that exact spot! I remember it all so perfectly. I stood there quietly, ignored by other mall people.

Next to me was one of those candy machine things that you put a coin into and turn a metal dial and candy comes out a chute.

I was never, ever allowed any. I had asked and been yelled at so many times for asking that I now looked upon these machines with a terrified reverence.

I checked the candy chute slots... praying... nothing... of course... there never is... I smelled my fingers. Wow... candy. I lived in a candy-less void. Candy cost money. "We have no money, because of your father."

I heard my mother say this every six minutes. Dad had the money, but I guess that had to be spent on beers and gas and going to parties, because that's all I saw him do...

I turned away dejected... but then... spied a tiny silver disc... some yards away...

My super powerful super-squint elf eyes spotted the Canadian dime.

I rushed over and grabbed it. The surge of happiness I felt blew fuses in my brain.

My heart pounded and the mall took on a sparkling, Christmassy look and feeling.

The machine candies were 10 cents!! I ran over and with shaking hands carefully put that 10-cent piece in. I cranked the handle ever so slowly to maximize the candy output, rocking the machine with my other hand as I had seen some big kids do once.

A bounty of Red Hots poured out. A pile of small, round cinnamon candy.

Ingredients:

- Corn syrup
- Natural and artificial flavors
- Acacia (Gum Arabic)
- Confectioner's Glaze
- Carnauba wax
- Corn starch
- White mineral oil
- Red 40

You gotta get that white mineral oil in ya! And Red 40 for your tweaking.

I loaded them all into my pocket and put one in my mouth. I started freaking out.

If I was caught with these, it would be bad.

I came up with a plan. By carefully only eating one at a time and stashing it up between gum and cheek, it would happily burn away there, providing me with the triple whammy of corn syrup, white mineral oil and Red 40 till it was totally absorbed. No one would know. I was in a state of total bliss.

My sugar-starved kiddie brain was just baking in those toxins.

My Dad came out of the store and I followed behind him to the truck. We rolled out onto the mean streets and highways of Vancouver, 1983...

Soon he started sniffing the air. "What's that sweet smell?" "Dunno Dad." Cue confused face. "I don't smell anything." He continued smelling the air and barking questions about the smell...

I continued my confused pantomime gaslight until he was sure he was going insane. He settled on the fact that it must be a factory baking cakes. At that point, I agreed that I did smell it.

I secretly ate every single one of those red hots over a period of days.

And to this day, cinnamon tastes like victory to me.

THE RING POP

I'm 6, I was somehow at a high school baseball game, in Nanaimo, Canada. Wandering alone about the place. Always on the lookout for dropped money or food.

I found a baseball on the ground! My candy-dreaming brain instantly came up with a plan to trade it for candy at the concession stand. I ran to the food, candy, hotdog, and coke-selling concession booth.

"Hi! I found this baseball! Can I swap it for some candy?"

The teenage girl stared down at my hopeful face and said, "Um, ok... you can have a Hot Lips or a Ring Pop." Now, I knew *all* the candies. I had spent hours in stores studying them on their racks. I had spent many years watching my rich cousins consume them, while I piteously begged for scraps... even, to my shame, grabbing and chewing second-hand gum they had thrown to the pavement a few times.

Hot Lips were gummy cinnamon lips. Fucking weird... but cinnamon. Cinnamon was victory... but... the legendary Ring Pop, both fashion accessory and candy, was the right choice.

"Ring Pop!"

I got my Ring Pop and put it on. WOW! FUCKING GRAPE! OH MY GOD. I hid under the grandstand and sucked it nonstop. Heaven. Bliss. I cruised about with it... sucking on it till I almost pulled my teeth in. I still only got halfway through. I found the uncle and his kids who had taken me to this game, and I hid the Ring Pop in the foil packet and stashed it in my pocket.

I finished it up over the next few days, anytime I was alone.

On the toilet, backing out tiny hungry kid poops. In the bath. Sneaking out of the house, and anytime in bed once the lights were out. I kept the ring and the packet, which I licked clean and continued to sniff until all traces of the grape particles were gone. To this day, that fake grape tastes like victory to me.

THE CRACKERJACKS

Same time period. I'm 6 or so and with my mum in our beat-up old car. We are in Nanaimo, B.C. Mum has to go into a bakery for some reason… to get a cake for someone, I think.

It's hot, so it must have been summer. I have to stay in the car. But I want to go into the bakery to see the cakes and donuts. I beg and beg. NO! I have to stay in the car. I realize now this is because I was a fucking maniac. I would talk to everyone. I would touch everything. I would ask millions of questions.

Once at 5, at a restaurant when my parents weren't looking, I wandered off and made friends with another family. I convinced them to order me a kid's pizza. I was eating fries off their plates and chatting to them when I was finally found. The pizza was delivered to our table and I ate it happily while being yelled at for annoying those poor people. I would go on to annoy many poor people throughout my life.

Pulling this sort of shit is why I had to stay in the hot 80s car and cook like a roast goose.

So I'm in this boiling car, looking out at the cakes and treats in the bakery window. Vacillating between misery, numbness, and hunger. Suddenly, my mum comes out with something in her hands. She opens the door and gives me a box of Crackerjacks. "The ladies in the shop bought you this."

WOW. I stared at the box, stupefied. I had had one Jack of the Cracker once before. A girl at my school had dropped one. I remembered the taste as if it were yesterday.

Now a whole box WITH A PRIZE INSIDE!!!

I carefully tore it open. The caramel popcorny smell hit me. I could feel the sweet sugary goodness all the way to the back of my brainstem. I dug in for the prize. It was a green plastic whistle. I whistled the shit out of that whistle. I had it for years.

I was so hungry I ate everything in one go as fast as I could, but I chewed everything really well. Then I sat in the car happy, blowing the whistle. When my mother got in the car, I kept blowing the whistle. I was warned that the whistle would be going right out the window if I blew it one more time.

To this day, caramel corn tastes like victory to me.

Chapter 4
SHORT McDONALD'S TALE FROM MY BADASS PAST (A Grade A Bullshit Situation)

In 1983, when I was 6, my sister and I were living with my wealthy logger uncle and his wife and four kids in Nanaimo, Canada. My mum had dropped us off to stay there as she was on the run from my dad and couldn't hide very well with us slowing her down.

This was a "Grade A Bullshit situation," according to my aunt, and she and her demented four spoiled brats tormented the fuck out of us.

But the best torment came when they got to go to McDonald's every Saturday and get anything they wanted.

On the first trip, I mistakenly said I wanted a Big Mac and a Hot Cherry Pie!

All the brats turned on me and explained that me and my sister would only be getting a hamburger (not even a cheeseburger) because we were poor and our mum was "Who the fuck knows where!" They had obviously heard their mum say this line... as it was an oft-repeated favorite of theirs.

And so it was we got a dry-as-fuck hamburger each time. I would try to enjoy it as my evil aunt would chain-blaze smokes and glare at me from under her scary brown mop of a perm.

Fast forward 40 years and I'm writing this in my beautiful house where I live with my beautiful kids and wife, doing quite well... loved by my friends... feared and respected by my enemies...

I could probably buy a McDonald's franchise if I wanted...

And the cousins... jail... alcoholism... heavily medicated with psych drugs... welfare... 7 kids to five different dudes... fat... sick...

So you know what... I just want to say thanks!

Because without people like them trying to smash me down, I never would have fought so hard to survive. Bring on the beatings!

A word from my hero Al Swearengen:

"Every fuckin' beating I'm grateful for. Every single fucking one of them. Get all the trust beat outta you. And you know what the fuckin' world is."

Chapter 5
PASSING THE CHRISTMAS DIVORCE TEST (I was my own Dad's Wingman)

As I write this, on my wall to the right of me is a picture my son drew for me at school. A picture of him happy and smiling with a belly full of pizza and a heart full of love for his caring parents.

Stable at 6... secure, happy. He's never seen his father hit his mother or raise his voice, or disappear for weeks on end to do the traditional 70s bad dad, booze, coke, and hookers thing.

I was reminiscing about something that happened to me on Christmas Day, 1983. I was thinking about how smart I must have been as a young child.

I think the insanity of my childhood environment made me super wise and cunning, as I have detailed in other stories...

Sadly, this wisdom and cunning seem to have tapered off over the years as I was engulfed by middle-class Mercia softness in my thirties... losing the battle to comfortable clothes around 2007...

So I write this bloated with Christmas snacks, in sweatpants, in my office with my double screens and my kids' pictures on the wall... as the rest of my happy family sit on the couch watching some happy Christmas movie on the giant TV in the happy lounge of the happy house in comfortable Mercia Suburbia.

I couldn't do that. I just can't. I did my best. I did the present opening and the happiness and the saying nice things, but then the essence of it drove me in here to write this... to dig up something dark...

The soil of the Gen X man's heart is stony... but he grows what he can and he tends it...

So I was six and my parents were fully split.

My sister was four, and she had gone from Canada to New Zealand with my mother. I was going onward to there as well, but with my father. This was so he could break the news to me on the way...

We were going through Hawaii. A full day stopover.

A perfect place to drop the divorce bomb.

It was weird being with my Dad. For the first time in my life that I could remember, he seemed focused on me and really happy.

Coming from winter in Canada, Hawaii was very real, bright, and hot. We went to Waikiki Beach and bought bathing trunks right in the store. This blew my mind. The air and sand were hot, and the water was bath-warm. That blew my mind too!

I had lived in Canada my whole life. I had not really experienced much "hot."

He put me up on his shoulders and fell into the water. He threw me in the air and I landed in the sparkling warm water, gleefully laughing.

This was amazing and such connection and fun. This I had never experienced with my mostly absent father. I felt a little bit of hope and healing.

But it was a build-up to a trick...

He suddenly turned to six-year-old me in the water... looking serious... my 29-year-old dad... it's 1983, he's tanned, strong, young, and muscled from years of logging old-growth 1,000-year-old redwoods out of northern B.C... has a cool Tom Selleck mustache, bless him...

"Mate... well... your mother and I still love each other, but we aren't going to be together anymore. We are having what's called a separation. Your sister is going to be living with your mother... but who do you want to live with...?"

I was so fast...

"You, Dad! I want to live with you!"

I was born cunning. I believe everyone has a magic power. Mine is cunning.

Later in life, every shaman and medicine man I met would tell me my spirit animal is the raven. Always only after less than 20 minutes of chatting to me... They must be talking to each other, these guys...

The raven signifies mystery and divination, trickery, stealth, and the attraction to the magical or mystical ways.

When I was 5, I was at a kid's birthday party. We were all playing baseball, and his mum had set up the food and the cake on the park picnic table. We were happily playing when I heard screaming from the picnic area. I looked back and saw a flock of about 20 sneaky ravens absolutely DESTROYING the cake. Like, standing in it, flapping and squawking and pecking up huge mouthfuls. White icing flying up all over them, going nuts.

I burst into laughter. The birthday kid burst into tears.

I bonded with ravens. I was going to be like them. I was going to sneak about in life and suddenly eat up people's cakes. This was the prophecy of my spirit animal. I knew the raven's ways as if born to them...

I digress...

"You, Dad! I want to live with you!"

He smiled, looking happy but also a tiny bit sad.

"I know, mate, but... you can't... I don't think it would work. I have to go and work at the logging camp and it's no place for kids." (Whiskey – hookers – coke...)

I made myself sadder...

"Dad, I would be good. I would hang out at the camp and watch TV, and we could be together."

"Oh... well, I know you want to, but I think it's really best if you live with your mother for now, but I will see you soon." (a year)

"OK, Dad." Cue slumped shoulders...

I had passed the test.

Like fuck I wanted to live with my hard-partying dad who just wanted to be free! I didn't want to cock-block my old man. We would both hate that. I wanted to be with my mum who was on her way to being hooked up with a new life by her millionaire father, in single-mum, urban-mansion, fine-wine resting time.

And so it was that I swam and laughed with my dad on that

wonderful Christmas Day in '83 at Waikiki Beach, and life went on. We went our separate ways and all was well. He thought his boy wanted to be with him and got to go off feeling good. This is a secret I have never told until now, and like every wack life experience of mine, is now a story to entertain you.

Chapter 6
SKULL CRUSHERS IN THE GOTH BASE (Goth Boss in the Bat Cave at 7)

I WAS 7. IT'S 1984. WE HAD FLED CANADA, AND MY RICH grandfather had set my mother, my sister, and me up in a nice place in a flash suburb of Auckland called Bucklands Beach.

The parents were divorced and out of control, living their best boozy 80s single-parent lives, and so it was time for me to embrace my CODP (Child of Divorced Parents) essence and start really acting up.

The first naughty thing I did was start stealing white chocolate skulls filled with some kind of yummy, weird red goo. These were called Skull Crushers. There was a store down the road from our house, and I would go in there and chat to the store owner until he had to talk to a customer. When he was dealing with them, I would grab one Skull Crusher and pocket it.

I would say goodbye and then flee back home.

Back home, I had a secret hidey hole.

It was a small cupboard in the wall of the lounge. I could almost sit up in it.

For some weird 70s reason, it was carpeted in thick green shag-pile green carpet. Into my Goth base, I had brought a number of pumpkins, some scary toys (rubber spiders and snakes), and a red candle.

I would light the candle and sit in there embracing the Goth essence of the pumpkins, red candle, and spiders. I was Goth to the bones… and was later in life to be deeply mashed into this subculture.

I would then draw the stolen skull candy out of my pocket and nibble away at it till it was gone, sucking down the yummy, red, bloody fake-raspberry goo center.

The combination of the oxygen deprivation from the lit candle in the sealed space and the toxic chemicals in the colorings and flavorings of the bright red candy blood goo in the skull would send me to the fucking moon. Pupils like dinner plates, man.

I would wait till I was, for lack of a better term, off-my-fucking-face fucked up, blow the candle out, and stagger outside to vibe man, vibe.

I now work in natural health, and I know exactly what was happening. I definitely had an extreme red dye allergy. My hippy mother ensured I had a very healthy diet, devoid of sugar and toxins. This gunge hit me like a brick.

Symptoms of Red Dye Allergy:

- Faster pulse
- Significant drop in blood pressure
- Dizziness
- Fainting
- Lack of sleep
- Poor concentration
- Hyperactivity
- Hypersensitivity
- Hyperfocus

So to me, it was drugs for sure. I was hooked and stole one skull a day for many days.

One day, my father suddenly turned up after a year of being absent… the last time I saw him was when I passed the Christmas Divorce Test over in Hawaii. He seemed wild and crazy. It was a shock to see him again after so long.

He had a cool, low-slung truck and was in full party mode. For some reason, he came and picked my sister and me up and drove us out to a farm where a bunch of his mates lived. He went inside to the kitchen to pound beers and blaze weed with his pals; my sister and I were left to roam free.

We roamed about the farm for a bit, and then we started hanging out inside, keeping to the lounge at the back of the house... soon I began sneaking into the bedrooms...

In some guy's bedroom, I saw it.

A jar by the bed full of money.

Many of us have the experience of stealing coins out of change jars, I'm sure.

This jar was piled high with silver. My blooming criminal addict brain immediately presented me the task of getting that money, so I could buy a shit ton of skull candies and fuck myself up good in my secret Goth base.

I looked around for something to carry the money in and spied a folded-up handkerchief.

Nabbing this, I loaded a good whack of the 50-cent and 20-cent coins into it, and twisting it about, snuck out of the house.

My sister saw me sneaking with something bulging in my pocket and said, "What's that?"

Me: "It's some money. I'm going to buy a present for Mum with it."

Her: "Don't tell Dad!"

Suddenly, I heard a yell. That froze us to the core.

"DON'T TELL DAD WHAT?!"

It was our Dad, and he had come out to take us home, and I was snapped.

He saw the rolled-up stolen money, and there was a shocked look as he realized that I had become a "bad kid"—the type forged in the fires of inattentive divorced 80s parents.

He snuck the money back inside into the jar... And we rolled out.

I remember him ranting on about stealing being bad, but I was just so mentally smashed from being caught at that point and super sad for my little sister who was crying her eyes out in the back.

My Dad had the scary burnt-leaves-and-beer smell fuming off him and was red-eyed and ranting. Everything was spiraling down into a black abyss. He stopped the truck at the gate at the end of the farm. It was always my job to open the gates. Opening fucking gates was the bane of my life.

I opened the heavy metal door of the truck and…POW!!! Suddenly got such a shock I was blasted into near unconsciousness. What the FUCK? I struggled back to life, head buzzing, heart pounding. Later I found I had even pissed myself a bit.

"THAT'S GOD PUNISHING YOU FOR STEALING!" yelled my Dad.

Those words went into my brain like a javelin.

I mentally snapped and went totally numb. On opening the truck door, I had touched it —with its bare metal handle—to a high-powered electric fence.

I sat there, fucked. God *was* punishing me. My sister's crying. Dad's crazy. Mum's crazy and sad. Everything is shit.

The world was pretty black.

We were taken home, and my father made me tell my mother what I had done.

I was numb. I didn't care. He blamed her for being a shit mother and said that's why we were spoiled, shit kids. He took off and wasn't seen again for ages.

I went to my room and drew pictures of ET flying away with me in a cardboard box, because I didn't have a bike he could magic up in the air.

I stopped stealing, dismantled my Goth base, and started doing much more wandering about in a confused daze of suppressed grief, being very careful not to touch things.

I did, however, eventually come right. Come out of apathy, get mad at the world, and start stealing and acting up again.

Chapter 7
BOARDING SCHOOL SAGA (Forging the weapon of me)

So there I was, a young man.

A weaselly little sprog of ten years, with a head full of Elves, witches, and goblins.

I was off to boarding school as a punishment for being a useless little silver-tongued bastard, who apparently had no discipline and could not see a task through to completion. (Overheard my mother telling a friend on the phone.)

My mother was sending me off to learn manners, discipline, and the gritty value of hard work... Or, now that I'm a grown man and thinking on it, it could have been just the fact that she had the money, and it seemed like a vaguely good idea and took care of the problem of taking care of me, so she could take off overseas.

If she had known it would only teach me stealth, deception, the intricacies of blackmail, and deep and encysted feelings of hatred she may have spent the 30 grand on a new car instead.

When people ask me what it was like at boarding school at 10 years old, I say

"If you can imagine Harry Potter... well basically exactly like that but with no magic or monsters. And instead of magic and monsters, just arbitrary punishments and random beatings, to punctuate ungodly amounts of schoolwork."

It took a little while for what small fuzzy child-like exterior I DID have, to be seared away, exposing a blackened iron core.

I will now detail the principal incidents of that searing.

I was in the dormitory on the very top floor of the school's main ancient building. It was called Crows Nest and it housed 14 of us 10-year-old's and one Prefect.

A Prefect was a 12-year-old who was in charge of us and could order us about and recommend detention if we misbehaved.

You had a tiny cubicle that housed your clothes, bunk bed, and a very small amount of possessions. You were allowed one poster or calendar. You were teamed up with another kid who they made sure had a completely incompatible personality to yours.

I did not have a bunk mate. And thus I was very lucky and was allowed to shiver, cold, and crying alone in the darkness with homesickness and hideous dread without anyone on the bunk above to hear my piteous whimpering.

After a while something inside me died and I couldn't cry anymore. I had gone totally numb and I would fall asleep to the sounds of other little abandoned ten year old's crying silently, alone in the darkness. This was soothing and made me feel good. Like I was a brave warrior like in the fantasy books I fanatically read to escape reality.

Our lives were a regimented system, only slightly harsher than a prison camp. The lights were blasted on at 6: 30 am accompanied by the shout "UP AND SHOWERS BOYS". Then you had to frozenly rush down four flights of stairs to the showers which were in a large concrete basement.

It was always damp, cold, and smelt like piss and naked shamefaced embarrassment.

A Tutor, or a Matron supervised the showers:

Tutors—The tutors were young men in their 20s who were given free room and board in exchange for a few shifts of giving us brats detentions, tormenting the fuck out of us, and generally making sure we didn't kill each other or destroy school property.

Matron—the Matrons came and went, they were "nurses" who were in charge of our health and ranged from kindly powder-smelling old fat women to young motorbike-riding, long legged and redheaded vixen nurses, who smelt sweaty, and who the older kids talked about in a gross way. For some strange reason, I had to get naked in front of these gals, and have my balls felt by them (for health reasons)

Anyway, as I was saying; a Tutor, or a Matron, supervised the showers, and you stood chilled and shivering in line until ushered into the gray-tiled concrete bunker with 15 shower heads attached to the ceiling. There you and 14 other boys would stand in a weak spray of water which was only slightly warmer than the frozen dungeon this ordeal took place in.

I found out in Year 2 that the reason the showers were cold was that the prefects were allowed to get up early and have their showers first.

They made sure they used up ALL the hot water, which was just awesome.

You got one minute and then you were off to "dry" yourself with your damp and pissy-smelling towel.

After about three months of this, I started getting harsh redness and itchiness on the sides of my feet and legs—in my teen years, my medical knowledge increased and I correctly diagnosed this ailment in my memory as chilblains. By then I was not suffering from such ailments as I had stopped living like a poor orphan from the streets of Victorian London and the knowledge was of no use to me.

After showers, we would flee back to our rooms to dress in the scratchy wool short shorts and a gray cotton shirt that was our perpetual clothing. Long-legged pants were not allowed. Thus clothed we would shiver and shake down to the dining room. Even on the hottest of summer days the hallways and cloisters had a chill to them that was never refreshing. I guess it was because it was New Zealand where outside of one mild summer month, the temperature ranges from tolerably brisk to freezing and miserable.

Once in the dining hall (which we called The Barn) we would get our breakfast. Usually a large dollop of gray porridge. It tasted pretty rough, but if you mixed enough sugar with it you could gag it down with a cup of tea.

Then it was off to school. Just a short walk along another freezing cloister.

What can I say—This was probably the best school in New Zealand; all the best teaching equipment, we learned poetry and grammar, we studied a lot of world history, made small chests of drawers in the wood shop, and did pottery. Each night after dinner we did an hour of homework back in the classrooms. In all, we got about nine hours of schooling a day and were made to play sports after school which, combined with the harsh gym classes, turned us each into intelligent little machines that could run, jump and kick a ball.

While the rest of New Zealand's ten-year-old's were crammed into classrooms of 50 and reduced to screaming imbecility through the making of potato cut-out prints and the eating of paste, we were learning by rote, poetry such as the anthem of the American Revolution —Paul Revere's Ride; instilling within me a red hot hatred for the British, and a deep and probably unhealthy identification with the early American patriots.

You know the rest. **"In the books you have read, How the British Regulars fired and fled, How the farmers gave them ball for ball, From behind each fence and farmyard wall, Chasing the Redcoats down the lane, Then crossing the fields to emerge again. Under the trees at the turn of the road, And only pausing to fire and load...."**

That's from the poem Paul Revere's Ride... in case your education skipped early American poetry.

The deep hatred for the Redcoats that was growing within me was magnified and frenzied by another poem we had to learn by rote a few weeks later- this was called The Highwayman. (1906 - Alfred Noyes)... I always felt that I was a bit of a Highwayman and I identified unhealthily with the Highwayman in the poem.

When the bastard Redcoats capture his woman (the Landlord's daughter) and she kills herself I start looking for my silver pistols and when they shoot me down on the highway, down like a dog on the highway and I lie in my blood on the highway with a bunch of lace at my throat, I start firing and don't stop until I have turned the head of every Redcoat into a canoe. In my ten-year-old daydreams…

So yes… 10 years old … in class imagining I'm shooting British infantrymen in the head… If I had just had Minecraft when I was 10 instead, I might have turned out ok…

Reading the poem would reduce me to tears and little clenched fists of fury and I would be too emotional to continue and so would just stand at the front of the class with my head down unable to utter another stanza.

I would be allowed to go outside to "calmly gather yourself". I was not asked to read that particular poem in front of the class again.

But I still know it all by heart. And here's a bit:

"A red-coat troop came marching- Marching-marching-
King George's men came marching, up to the old inn-door.
They said no word to the landlord, they drank his ale instead,
But they gagged his daughter and bound her to the foot of her narrow bed;
Two of them knelt at her casement, with muskets at their side!
There was death at every window; And hell at one dark window.
Back, I spurred like a madman, shrieking a curse to the sky,
With the white road smoking behind me and my rapier brandished high!
Blood-red were my spurs in the golden noon; wine-red was my velvet coat,
When they shot me down on the highway, Down like a dog on the highway, And I lay in my blood on the highway, with a bunch of lace at my throat."

Lacking any silver-butted pistols or smooth-bore flintlock musket of a large caliber, or Red coats to shoot I had to be content with making a tiny blow gun and needles from the poisonous spines of a cactus that grew next to the gym, and secretly shooting homemade darts into the other kids. But that is another story.

Anyway, it is not the purpose of this tale to talk about the emotional content of the history lessons I received, or my bitter hatred of all things under King George's failing British Empire, nor the mundane meanderings of eating, showering, or sleeping.

The purpose is to amuse the reader with the crazy things that happened at boarding school when I was young. And now I will begin.

THE WHACK

Days at boarding school were spent trying to avoid being beaten by larger kids, or to avoid getting caught and then beaten by the Housemaster for beating younger kids.

The Housemaster was the big boss. The twisted old disciplinarian that ran our section of the school . Basically exactly like Hagrid from Harry Potter, but instead of helping kids and being kind, he relished in beating kids and inflicting degrading and brutal punishments....

It was a shit-rolls-downhill, passing-on-the-hate bullying system that these days you only hear about in legend.

I am a bard of such legends.

Do not think for a moment that the threat, and actual eventuating of vicious beatings, deterred me from doing weird and naughty things.

Hell no.

It just made it all the more exciting and it made me much more covert and cunning.

THE WHACK

My first introduction to the real importance of not advertising one's insanity was only two weeks into my stay.

It was Saturday night and the whole school of boys aged 10-12 were allowed to sprawl on cushions and watch some G-rated movie on the small TV in the common room. You were also allowed to use two dollars of your allowance to purchase a small amount of candy which had to be eaten by the time the movie was over. If you were caught with any candy when it wasn't Saturday night you were beaten.

I had been naughty, but not naughty enough to warrant a beating (I was still warming up). I had purposely stood on the vacuum cleaner cord as another kid vacuumed the common room, causing it to pop out. So I had to sit outside the House master's office and read a book with other bad kids, instead of watching the movie and eating treats.

The whole dorm of the 11-year-old kids had been banned from the movie, for some infraction... I did not know what, but they were allowed to stay up in their dorm as there were too many of them to crowd around the office.

I saw two kids come down from the dorm and then go into the Housemasters' office. Then they went back to the dorm, running with excitement! Then the entire dorm, but for the two kids, came down and lined up outside the door looking kinda sick and fearful.

What had happened was, a few kids in the dorm had somehow snuck some candy and they shared this with the others. Two kids didn't get any so they told on the rest. Now all those kids who ate the candy were getting a caning.

Life can't get fairer.

They would go into the office and close the door behind them and then there would be a loud and sharp smacking sound and the kid would come bolting out – red-faced and staunchly go straight to the bathrooms to cry tears of deeply alone hopelessness.

I had to find out more. So I LISTENED at the door! I heard the gruff voice say " Stand on that spot and touch your toes". Then I would hear the WHACK!!.

I would jump back to my seat and a teary kid would come out.

I managed to hear three before some kid told on me. I heard him telling on me and *as* he told, I detachedly realized I was listening at the door.

I felt weak and sick. I just staggered back and stood in the middle of the hallway staring at the door. The room took on a goldfish bowl effect and things became dreamlike and unreal. I felt like fainting and shitting myself at the same time.

The door opened and the kid looked at me and smiled a teary-eyed evil smile. Behind him was the stern housemaster.

"Come in here" he announced.

The room was in the classic New Zealand post-WW1 style, decorated in the 30s. Due to the thrift and economics of the place, it would of course remain unchanged until it was dust.

Floral patterned carpet, thick brown curtains. Leather-covered chairs and the smell of neglect and fear. He was entering my name into a ledger.

Name, amount, and reason for the punishment.

Under the reason section he wrote: "Idiocy".

I stood on the spot I was told to (a large red flower in the carpet), touched my toes, and received THE WHACK.

I didn't cry. I was too tough for that shit. I just went outside and sat down, getting a few impressed raised eyebrows from some of the other kids.

I started pondering how I better lift my game and become more covert as an operating basis.

It was called THE WHACK.

Kids would say " I just got THE WHACK" or "James got THE WHACK last night and cried for ages" or "I heard the whole class is going to get THE WHACK!!".

It was so terrifying and encompassing that it was afforded FULL CAPS. When you said it you said it with respect.

When you said it, you stopped what you were doing, opened your eyes wide, and said it slowly.

It was never laughed about unless you were taunting an enemy as in "Ha Ha you're going to get THE WHHHAAAACCKK and it's gonna hurt like a bastard and you're gonna cry for mummy like a little baby!".

We often would pretend that we knew that someone was going to get THE WHACK for something they had done, that they did not think the housemaster knew about. We would tease the person to the point of terror, convincing the guy that his crime had been reported, and soon the call would come. Once a guy got so scared and overwhelmed with dread that he went and handed himself into the housemaster, telling the housemaster that he was there to get THE WHACK for stealing a granola bar from another kid.

He got THE WHACK sure enough. To this day that poor bastard doesn't know that we never told on him.

THE WHACK came in three forms. There was Sloppy Joe. He was

a well-worn old slipper and was used for first-timers, small kids, or minor offenses, he was a friend you could trust, and he didn't make you cry unless it was with relief or unless you were one of the frail weak children who were crying most of the time anyway.

There was Claudius. He was a large, old, and dangerous-looking Roman sandal. He had a lot of weight. He was an uncaring disciplinary menace that you couldn't predict and it was he who was used the majority of the time. From his efforts, hard crying and sometimes little screams were assured unless you were really hardened. When he hit you it sounded like a pistol going off behind your head and he sometimes would knock you to the ground. He was experienced.

According to legend, he had been delivering THE WHACK since the school opened in 1936.

Then there was THE CANE.

THE CANE was so scary that just the mention of it could cause a kid to cry and shake. I know one kid who ran away because someone told him he was going to get THE CANE.

THE CANE was a brutal cane made of rattan and was used only for the worst of crimes.

I once saw the toughest kid in our part of the school crawling on his hands and knees along the hallway, white and ghost-faced, dribbling and gasping like something from a horror movie. He crawled along about 10 meters of the hallway into the bathroom where he spewed on the floor and then lay screaming, for about 2 minutes.

All because of "Six of THE BEST".

THE BEST referred to the hardest most punishing hits that the tough, cricket-obsessed Housemaster could deal.

Six blows of the cane was the maximum allowed by the New Zealand legal system.

Surviving six of the best put you into such a legendary status that it was almost worth it.

The Housemaster once told us that any kid caught wandering around after lights out would receive Six of THE BEST.

I'm pretty sure this way he could just go home and pound his fat cow of a wife, instead of sticking around to make sure no one got out of bed.

THE BEST was only delivered with THE CANE. The above kid had received six of THE BEST for mooning the Housemasters' spoiled bitch daughter.

I could see why the housemaster delivered this only late at night or when the school was empty.

Everyone else was at the chapel for Sunday church while this happened and I was the only one who saw him in his sorry state.

He told me later that if I told anyone that I saw him crying after the cane, he would "Crush my balls like grapes".

I received THE WHACK three times a term for my two-year indenture, for a total of 24 WHACKS in all.

The majority of my WHACKS were administered for hurting other kids.

I had to punish the guilty as I will detail later.

I had a friend who would wait outside the office when I was getting THE WHACK. He would taunt me with "You're gonna cry, your gonna cry—your crying I can see it! You're crying!" When I wasn't crying.

However, his taunting would kick the loneliness of being 10 and abandoned to an uncaring world, in on me, and more often than not I would head to the bathrooms to cool my hot burning ass cheek in the sink with the cold tap on full blast, then crawl into my locker and shut the door after me so I could be alone in a dark little misery hole; not crying but definitely mentally damaging myself by pushing the emotions down.

One day the time came for my taunting friend to get THE WHACK and I saw him looking around to make sure I didn't see him going into the office to receive it. When he came out I was standing RIGHT THERE. With a big evil and satisfied smile on my face. He said "SHUT UP!" and burst into tears of loneliness and pain.

That made me feel good.

At some point, not long after getting THE WHACK for the first time, I bent my mind to activities of cunning and evil. Almost as if there is something to the theory that being beaten as a child is bad for your psyche... there might be something to that... but no matter...

Latimer Redlance

One of the bad cunning and evil things I did was an act of such betrayal and trickery that I hold it as one of my greatest achievements.

I was up in Crows Nest with a friend called King (we were all referred to by our last names). No one else was about and King opened up the bottom drawer of a Prefects bunk. Revealing a huge bag of candy and packets of chips and bars of chocolate!

He said, " Let's take these!".

I put forward that we take most of them but also take some down to the Housemaster saying we heard the Prefect eating them at night. That way one of our enemies would get THE WHACK and we would get treats AND the smug satisfaction of bringing doom to an oppressor. So we did that and the prefect got two of THE BEST, which made him lie on his bed, face in the pillow, for about an hour crying.

Then I made sure that King kept all the candy hidden in his drawer and I ate none.

The next day I went to King's drawer, and stole most of the treats, and hid them in a hollowed-out section of my mattress where no one would find them. I then told the Prefect that King had stolen *his* treats and had then told on *him*, precipitating the Prefect getting THE WHACK.

I showed the Prefect where King had hidden the lollies. In a rage, he swiftly ate the small number of treats I had left in King's drawer and then when King came up to the dorm he hit him in the head with a tennis racket. King tried to fight but the Prefect was stronger. King went flying back to the wall from a flurry of nasty punches to the chest. The Prefect then flipped him to the ground, and followed up by body-slamming him, with both knees, to the back. When King could breathe again he started screaming so loudly a Tutor came in and took them both down to the housemaster.

Where they both got three Claudius WHACKS.

I hid under my bed eating the lollies while this happened.

That made me feel good.

Why did I just turn around and betray my good friend King?

I had even been to his house on the weekend and stayed over and played Operation! and we had ridden bikes like happy kids, not a week before.

The simplest answers are usually the right ones.

Like any animal put into a cage and beaten I had gone fucking nuts.

I fell in with a couple of guys whose situation was the same as mine.

Sent to boarding school for becoming too tricky and evil, and once there, the beatings and abuse broke the last rungs off the sanity ladder.

We took being naughty to a new level. We only talked about our crimes with each other. We weren't cruel to those who didn't deserve it and we weren't random in our mayhem. What we did was done for personal thrills or carefully calculated to punish the guilty.

Any den of rouges needs a hideout and we had one. Underneath one of the school buildings, there was a room. A small dank smelling concrete basement that had been walled up and forgotten. No one had been down there for decades when we found it. We entered through a tiny boarded-over window that was near the ground behind a small hedge.

We found this secret window when hiding behind the hedge one day.

We stashed candles in there and stole a cushion each from the common room to sit on.

I have no idea how many hours I spent in that dark hole whispering to my friends but we all took on the smell of the place after a while.

We would get dry grass from the mowed lawn. We would roll joints of this with small rectangles of paper we tore from a bible that we stole from the chapel.

We would blaze these down in our den. Sometimes we would blaze up to ten in an hour and emerge from our den reeking and red-eyed. Giddy from smoke inhalation, we would get rid of the smell by running across the field or, we would time our blazing to before sports or swimming, so we would be able to change. If told we smelled like smoke by a quizzical student we would say we had been playing by the incinerator, but we were pretty careful.

We would get the day students (they are kids who don't board at the school) to buy us lollies and powdered drink mix. More often, we didn't have money so we would do school work for them. I would write stories for them, or poetry, which was sometimes required as homework—working by stolen-chapel-candlelight. They could then copy my work into their book before school. This would be worth at least a big packet of drink mix or a good round lolly bag.

We wouldn't eat the powdered drink mix or drink it. We would create lines of it on our books and snort it up our noses with a handmade, nicely decorated paper tube. This would give your brain a shock, and after a while, yummy lemon-lime-tasting snot would be running down the back of your throat.

One day we came to our hideout and the window had been closed off with a bolted-on metal cover. The groundskeeper had locked us out.

My two friends, now unable to find mental relief in smoking grass, and snorting lines of powdered drink mix, quickly moved on to more bizarre pursuits. Namely creeping downstairs at night to the locker room and pissing in kid's shoes and putting kids' toothbrushes up each other's asses.

I politely declined to take part in such nocturnal shenanigans, but not before taking my shoes and toothbrush upstairs with me to my cubicle.

THREE TIMES THE SKULL

So there I was, a young man.

A skinny, glasses-wearing weirdo, wandering cold cloisters.

Tormented by bigger kids, beaten ... not too badly... but enough.

Never seriously injured, but I was often threatened with a lasting injury.

The taunts, flicks, kicks, and slaps stung, and these, combined with the vicious corporal punishment being dealt out—(sometimes deserved, sometimes not), formed a powerful mixture of hate in my belly that needed release.

So that I did not go on any sort of indiscriminate rampage and get even more beatings, or get expelled, I invented the "Three Times the Skull" system.

The system was as follows:

If I was slighted by an individual, I would calmly walk up to my bedroom cubicle—sometimes holding back tears, sometimes not. I would open the secret slit of my mattress and take out a small blood-red notebook. In the notebook, I would write the offender's name, and next to the name, I would write a black skull and crossbones.

This would start a wind into the sails of my wicked pirate-style vengeance.

If you refused to share treats with me, you got a skull.

If you farted on me or hit me, you got one or two skulls—depending on the hardness of the hit or the smelliness of the fart.

If you taunted me or made fun of me, you got a skull.

If you told on me, resulting in me getting detention, that was a three-skull offense.

If you told on me, resulting in me getting THE WHACK, you immediately earned yourself ten skulls.

If I saw you bullying someone I liked, you got a skull.

And if you wouldn't get off the trampoline when it was my turn, you got a skull.

There were other one-to-three-skull offenses, but these were often decided on the spot.

The reverse was also true—if you gave me things or were kind (and you had skulls on record), I would remove skulls depending on the size of the kindness.

This was all done secretly, and I did not tell a soul of this sinister log of merits and demerits until the writing of this tale.

So what was this all about? Why all the meticulous record keeping?

I learned that I was far too impatient to wait for God or the universe to balance things out... and due to my burgeoning God Complex, it was necessary to take matters of balance into my own hands.

Well... one of two things would then happen. If you got to three skulls, I would secretly and in ninja-like style mete out what I called the Mini Punish.

But if you needed to be really brought low, I would wait until you had accumulated ten skulls, then deliver the Big Punish.

I know you want to know what happened next and which offenders I brought righteous wrath down upon, and the shape and heat of said wrath, as well as the speed at which it fell and the weight it contained...

And so I shall tell...

I well remember the glee that would rise and soar within me upon the design, development, and execution of a fitting punishment.

The time I inflicted a Mini Punish of holding in my farts and only releasing them into one offender's pillow for a period of some days. He was heard to remark that his pillow had "gone rotten somehow," and it had to be thrown away. But not before he had inhaled the lingering aroma of my reeking chuff-gas over a good series of nights.

Or the time I inflicted the Mini Punish of a urine-filled plastic bag bomb, hurled wrathfully (and secretly!) down onto a small group of three skullers from a high window.

The many Mini Punishes of telling bigger, older, more dangerous kids that I had heard the offender was calling them a faggot or saying they had AIDS. This would result in the offender being threatened or punched and often crying in terror or pain.

As a side note, for some reason back in '89, the main insult was to call someone a faggot, or to say they had AIDS. A kid could be reduced to blubbering, near-suicidal rubble by implying that they had AIDS and everyone pretending as such... and thus keeping away from them.

Social media harassment has nothing on kids deciding that some kid no one likes has AIDS and all treating them as such.

Then there was the time when a good Mini Punish went bad... I attempted to inflict the Mini Punish of hiding an offender's gym clothes so he would get detention when he didn't have them for the morning run.

While I gleefully hid his clothes deep at the bottom of the lost property bin, a Tutor was observing me. When I turned and saw him looking at me, I almost fainted dead away! My good Mini Punish had gone horribly wrong.

He strode over to the bin and liberated the tracksuit.

"MMMM ... What do you have against Jamieson?" he said, looking at the name tag.

"I was angry with him for repeatedly being mean to me—but it's ok, I'm not now," I gibbered.

"Here, I'll go give them back to him."

"Oh no—there is nothing we can do—it's in the Housemaster's hands now..." he said.

Instantly earning him the highest form of little red book award: A BIG RED SKULL WITH DAGGERS INSTEAD OF BONES, DRIPPING BLOOD, AND EXUDING EVIL RED LIGHTNING.

I think this meant that at some point in the future, I would have to kill all his pets, his entire family, and all his friends, utterly destroy everything he owned, then slowly torture him to death in the most painful way, trap his soul in a magical torture box, and then erase any record of him ever existing, in this universe or any other.

A task I am yet to complete...

He went off to give Jamieson his tracksuit, and later when I saw Jamieson, Jamieson told me matter-of-factly, "You're probably going to get three of the BEST."

This caused me to drop into quite a terrified state, and go straight to the bathroom with diarrhea.

I did receive one Claudius WHACK for what I did.

Jamieson immediately qualified for a ten-skull punish, consisting of being "accidentally" tripped down a flight of stairs a month later, while he tried to race me. He fractured his collarbone and spent three days in hospital.

As running inside was a WHACKABLE offense, he had to say he had slipped while walking.

I remember well another good ten-skull. I can't remember the name of the kid who received this punish or even what he did to me, but I bet he deserved it.

There was a tall and dangerous-looking cactus by the gym, with long purple and brown spines that would hurt like a bastard if they pricked you—resulting in swelling and pain in the pricked area.

I crafted a good blowpipe out of two straws from the cafeteria and made a poison paste by drying the greenish-yellow goop that was inside the cactus, into a horrid dark gunge. I poked tiny holes near the tip of a long and dangerous spine, to hold the poison paste better.

With my weapon concealed ninja-style, I hung around the kid and his friends, asking if they had seen the wasp that was buzzing around the area.

Of course, they hadn't, as the wasp was still within my blowpipe.

When the kid's attention was suitably distracted—WHOOOP!

Latimer Redlance

I shot the spine dart into his leg! Getting him in the kneecap! Having already freaked them with an imaginary wasp, I used the confusion of his pained cry to pretend to see the wasp, and, leaping forward, knocked the dart from his knee and cast it into the grass in the fashion of pretending to shoo a wasp away.

It didn't seem to hurt him much at first, and they returned to their playing.

By dinner time, though, he was limping slightly, and I, in my morbid fascination, was unable to leave his side.

The next day his limp was pronounced and a large red welt had appeared. By dinner time that night, the welt had redness that covered his entire knee, and he was feeling a bit weak and feverish. Getting a little worried, I had him seek the advice of the Matron.

I took him there myself, as the symptoms were starting to worry me.

Painful injury was fine, but at 10 years old, I wasn't quite ready to be a murderer.

I explained to the Matron my sighting of the stinging wasp, how the poison was probably spreading, how he must be allergic, and that hopefully, she could heal my friend.

I had started to become friends with this kid now over the day and no longer wanted him to die.

She rubbed some sort of ointment on it and sent us on our way.

Checking on him first thing in the morning revealed he had vomited over the side of the bed in the night, pooped his pajamas a little, and now had a raging fever, a purple, pus-filled knee, and the rest of his leg had swollen like an elephant's!

There were dangerous and angry-looking red lines radiating out from his kneecap like a miniature sun, and, not unlike a sun, the knee was also giving off its own weird heat!

I was starting to feel a little sick myself.

No matter what I did, I could not get myself to believe that a simple wasp had done this...

The Matron was called (not by me, as I had gone wholly unreal on the guy now and couldn't even look at him), and he was rushed to hospital.

I walked zombie-like to the cactus by the gym and rammed both of my hands into the spines, thinking that if I was somehow punished for my crime, he would get better.

I pressed the spines deep into my palms and let out little crying kiddy screams of misery and pain. Every time I wanted to pull back, I would just think of the knee and push harder.

I did this till blood was streaming out of the punctures, and the poison was making my hands feel like beach balls filled with stinging bees.

The garden began to go dreamlike, and I started blacking out from the pain, and so I pulled my hands off the spines and clasped them together in a small spray of blood, then knelt to pray at the foot of the diabolical cactus that had caused all this.

Dear GOD! If you heal him and make him better, I will always be good and never do anything to harm anyone ever again.

The kid did get better after a week in the hospital. And after a few weeks of keeping my nose clean, I forgot about my promise to God and began writing skulls in the book once more.

But I never used a cactus as a form of punishment EVER again!

Chapter 8
BREADS OF THE FAIRY (Sugary lunches)

So there I was, a young man… 12 years old. My mother always ensured that I had the most nutritious food available for school. Fruit yogurt, healthy seed-bread sandwiches with sprouts, cheese, and homemade mayonnaise. Rye Crispbread and Marmite crackers and an apple.

I would look on hungrily at the other children's lunches.

Chocolate puddings, biscuits, cans of Coke, and white bread sandwiches with margarine and filled with hundreds and thousands!

(In the UK and other Anglophonic Commonwealth countries, "sprinkles" are denoted by different signifiers. For example, "hundreds and thousands" is the most popular definition used in Britain as well as Australia and New Zealand to refer to dessert sprinkles.)

This was called "Fairy Bread."

I would try to swap my healthy lunch for their dessert-type lunch and was always met with laughter and scorn. One day I couldn't handle it anymore and I decided to just take a kid's lunch. I grabbed the kid's Coke and chugged it while keeping one leg free to kick him back with. Its sweetness made my eyes water and glaze over slightly. I had never had such goodness. Then I advanced on him and twisted the hundreds-and-thousands sandwich out of his feeble hands and crammed it into my mouth. The white bread was so soft and fluffy and the margarine was fatty and sweet. The sugary crunch of the hundreds and thousands was a delightful heavenly treat.

The other kid was bawling about having no lunch now, but I could barely hear him through my cocaine-like sugar daze. I flung him my healthy lunch and walked off.

I continued this activity, mugging the most sugary sweet lunches and giving them my lunch in exchange to stop their bleating. The kids with these yummy lunches were weak. Pinching with my strong fingers made them beg for mercy. Squeezing them made them scream like little girls and give up their lunches. If they tried to fight, they would go down in one hit. Where were the teachers? Wouldn't they stop this?

No, they were in the staff room chain-smoking and resting from the stress of trying to teach us little rhymes with hunts. This was '89 in rural New Zealand—zero shits were given.

In the beginning, the lunches had a strange effect on my super healthy body. First off, I became constipated and was either tweaking out with the shakes or feeling really tired and cranky. Sometimes I would get a tummy ache. I started getting a runny nose and a little cough. I couldn't do sports and PE as well as I used to. I stopped playing rugby at lunch times. Bright sunny days hurt my eyes, so I spent lunch times in the classrooms with other weak kids. But I still looked forward to the sweet sugary lunches of chips and cookies and cakes.

About six months of this went by...

Nowadays kids were just swapping lunches straight up with me, and physical persuasion was not needed. I went up to one of the kids who I would often torment, who had some of the yummiest lunches. I said, "Bezza, lunch! Now!" and threw him my lunch.

He looked me over for a bit and then said, "No."

I said, "What do you mean no?!" and advanced on him with my pinching, pain-bringing fingers and slap hands at the ready.

I'll bitch-slap this kid into next week for getting up in my grill like this, I thought. Possibly not those words BUT that EXACT concept. He just stood up to me. And I faltered.

He calmly said, "Do you want to see how hard I can punch now?"

I almost got a chance to say something, but my sugar-and-fairy-bread-filled brain wasn't working very well. Then I was down. I didn't even see the punch. Bright sparks exploded in my head, I was seeing hundreds and thousands before my eyes. His foot was on my chest, crushing me. I screamed like a little girl and struggled to crawl away. He put both of his strong grasping hands into my hair and pulled until tufts came out. I crawled from the classroom, dribbling and screaming to the sound of harsh laughter.

I made my way into the toilets and looked at myself in the mirror. Some skeletal kid with sunken raccoon eyes and a white sallow face with red spots looked back at me, nose running and looking pathetic. I cleaned myself up as best I could and slunk back into the class shamefaced.

I picked my discarded lunch up off the floor and for the first time in a long time, and with soft slightly loose teeth, bit into the hard brown sandwich of healing, body-toughening goodness that my caring mother had lovingly crafted for me.

I felt the strength flowing back into my atrophied stickman limbs... I looked over at Bezza chugging down his chocolate pudding dairy-based food snack...

My puffy eyes narrowed and I thought... see you in six months...

Chapter 9
THE ROUND THE PENINSULA TRIP (A school trip when I was 12)

THERE IS A PICTURE OF A BEACH CAVE THAT IS USED ON many, many desktop screens these days.

That cave is Cathedral Cove in my hometown.

That picture was a shock for me when it started staring out from office desktop lock screens.

On the clear, star-studded New Year's night of '98, I spent the night in that cave with a 33-year-old fun-time gal from Norway. (Fun-time gal: A young woman who engages in partying and romantic liaisons.)

I made it romantic as all get out, with ten tall candles stuck in the sand and a nice big blanket.

Decades later, when I saw that picture while working in corporate America and tried to tell fellow cube peeps of that wonderful night, pointing out exact areas on the screen where the good times were had, they would get uncomfortable.

But I didn't care. I wanted them to think of me and my Norway Gal every time their computer booted up... I wouldn't say Norway Gal though; I would use '90s Kiwi slang for a Nordic. "UCTEN BUCKEN."

"Yeah, me and this hot blond Ucten Buckten..."

"What is an UCTEN BUCKTEN...??" The confused Californian would ask...

"You know... a Norwegian or Swedish...

"You can't say Ucten Buckten, in America."

"But can't I say anything I like in America? Isn't that what this country is all about?

The Freedom of Speech thing?"

I act dumb; they keep explaining why freedom of speech isn't really freedom of speech...

I get them to admit that NZ is freer than America because I can say Ucten Buckten there, and people laugh instead of getting mad and giving hour-long lectures at work to the immigrants instead of making their rich boss richer like they are supposed to.

Good times...

I digress... this story is about school trips.

Mine was a rural school in New Zealand.

The school was what was called an Area School, which meant ages 5 to 17/18.

If you lived in this town from a young age you went to school all through your childhood and teens with pretty much the same people.

This created a certain demented situation where you all wind up kind of like a giant gang of brothers and sisters who mostly hate each other. Which becomes awkward when you want to start banging each other. So you mostly don't.

The girls in your class are going for guys 2–3 years older than you so you're shit out of luck anyway.

So at 12 years old, your class goes on a Lord of the Flies-ish camping trip around the Peninsula our town was on. It's a rural but super touristy place in summer.

The trip was called the "Round the Peninsula trip." Genius.

Now in retrospect, these trips were often towards the end of the year, and on any misbehavior, the culprit would be warned that they were putting their trip at risk!

If the whole class was getting rowdy, we could all be immediately smashed under control by the teacher yelling, "At this point, NO ONE in this class is going on the trip!"

Bad kids would toe the line right up to when they were ON the trip, at which point they would go all out, in an explosion of pent-up naughtiness!

I remember being a weird loner on this trip.

I had come back to this school at 12 years old just for the last few months.

And I was now a crazed mystic shaman.

The reason for this is that my mother, in her great and deep wisdom, thought it was a good idea to send me to boarding school for two years (as detailed in the Boarding School Saga Stories) while she lived in an ashram at the top of the Ganges River in India.

On returning to New Zealand she then thought it very wise to take my 10-year-old sister and 12-year-old me on a ten-month New Age journey with an American group run by a Hawaiian Kahuna and a Native American medicine woman.

A New Age super quest for rich white seekers. I found out later that this all-inclusive New Age super quest was about 100K.

I just may be getting into the "100K spirit quest journey" game one day as the guru... I'll let you know...

How this worked was that we traveled around New Zealand and Australia and lived with native tribes. In this case, the Maori of East Coast New Zealand and the Aboriginal tribes of Uluru and Mullumbimby, Australia.

Months and months of shamanic quests, sacred mountain climbs, pray fests, screaming heals, naked fire dances, sweat lodges, moonlit silent walks, solitary bush sleeps, waterfall jumps, icy river freezy plunges, and prayer stick workshops left twelve-year-old me forever changed.

All of this directly after two years of a very strict boarding school where I went from my bed to class to the rugby field on a loop. The monotony only broken by the occasional vicious corporal punishment.

By the time I got back to the human realm, I was in some kind of super whackadoodle woo-woo spiritual orbit. I had done shit and seen shit that few twelve-year-olds have, but you know what... It was a lot of fun. The food was good and the Maori and Aboriginal kids were really fun to play with.

Sometimes the adults were gone all day, so you were free to wander about in the outback and get bitten by inch-long ants. But what I really LOVED was watching grown adults absolutely lose their shit while doing these spirit quest things. The high-strung Yanks particularly.

I still find this to be one of my favorite pastimes.

But anyway... I'm at this school now and I'm as weird as fuck because I keep saying shit like "I can sense that you're crying inside, Jeremy. If you were just truthful with yourself and others you would heal."

The response to my weird shit would be "Fuck off with your faggot talk, homo!"

I learned fast to keep my stupid shaman mouth shut. I was in a new tribe now.

And so with this new tribe of kids I went on the trip. Driving in the bus to various campsites and camping.

The parents and teachers cooked for us. It was like scouts but with no activities, and the teachers and parents drinking and blazing a little weed at night. I remember a lot of beach walks and bush walks. This I was good at. I decided I was just going to spend my time hiding up trees and observing the other kids... to try to learn from their behavior and figure out how to fit in.

Two things I will never forget.

Jeremy (who I knew was crying inside) mixed up a bunch of aspirins in a bottle of Coke and drank it, in a sort of weird pill overdose fake cry-for-help thing.

He made a big deal about it and then just spewed and cried. And then faked losing his voice and became a lame mime for two days.

When some well-meaning kid told on him, the teacher asked that kid if Jeremy seemed like he was going to die...

The kid says "I don't think so..." and the teacher just shrugged.

The other crazy thing that happened on this trip was that while I was hiding up a tree, I saw one of the bigger twelve-year-olds throw something in the bushes.

I yelled down "Yo! What was that?"

And he looked up and yelled

"A condom. I just fucked Jessica."

A condom? Fucked? What the fuck is going on? Aren't we supposed to be twelve?

I hadn't gotten the memo that this was rural NZ and the Maoris grow up way faster than whitey.

I imagined this taller tough half-Maori kid on top of Jessica the tall Maori girl in one of the tents.

Having sex right after talking about the A-Team and eating burgers at the picnic table with the other kids...

Star wipe to two years later: Jessica is one of FOUR fourteen-year-old girls in my class with big pregnant bellies trying to lean forward far enough to do their maths...

One was a mentally twisted pointy-faced white girl who was always telling sexual jokes; the other three were Maori girls. They would stay in school, preggers till about seven months in, then disappear. Then a few months later they would roll up at lunchtime with the baby to show everyone.

A simpler, better time I reckon. I just was in the mash with the rest of them...

Chapter 10
EELS (Slimy and Nourishing)

Rural New Zealand. I'm 14 and trying to grow big and strong. This was not working out for me on the food being supplied by those in charge of my welfare.

There was never, ever enough food. Just nothing edible enough in the house to keep me full. And really only room in the fridge for Dad's beer.

I was basically living on the meager dinners. And even then, there was never enough because in NZ, scarcity mindset means you must ALWAYS MAKE SURE YOU NEVER cook enough food.

There must be no leftovers ever. And if you're hungry, that means you're greedy!

Fucking mental. I'm sure some Brits and Kiwis reading this grew up under the same regime.

How are you going to buy $200 worth of booze a week if you have to keep buying groceries for your hungry kids?

Anyway... I once found a way around the starvation. What kept me alive was my self-designed ENERGY POTION.

ENERGY POTION RECIPE:

- Get the huge cup. (In my case it was a Seattle Expo 1985 chowder bowl.)
- 3 heaped tablespoons of Nestlé Instant Coffee.
- 3 heaped tablespoons of Milo.

(What is Milo? In 1934, Australian industrial chemist and inventor Thomas Mayne, who was working at Nestlé, developed Milo and launched it at the Sydney Royal Easter Show. Mayne came up with his formula for Milo combining malt extract (made from malted barley), full cream milk powder, cocoa, sugar, mineral salts, iron and vitamins A, D, and B1, in an attempt to develop a completely balanced food drink which contained all the necessary proteins and minerals.)

It was intended to help children to obtain enough nutrients in their diet. A child that needed nutrients was me.

The next part of the potion is:

- Half a can of Nestlé Sweetened Condensed Milk.

(Condensed milk is cow's milk from which water has been removed—roughly 60% of it. It is most often found with sugar added, in the form of sweetened condensed milk. Sweetened condensed milk is a very thick, sweet product, which when canned can last for years without refrigeration.)

The product is used in numerous dessert dishes in many countries.

This shit is amazing. The U.S. government ordered huge amounts of condensed milk as a field ration for Union soldiers during the Civil War.

I just realized that I was probably single-handedly keeping Nestlé afloat, and in turn this potion was keeping me alive.

Anyway… add boiling water to the above and stir, stir, stir.

Fuck man. When I got on the bus the lobes were humming. I was raving good. Singing Nirvana at the top of my voice and barking out excited yawps.

I had the juice and the fire. I was ready to Win School.

If you have those ingredients lying around, I implore you to try it.

ENERGY POTION... makes your hipster bulletproof coffee or dipshit energy drinks seem like ginger beer, man.

I digress... this story is about eels...

How is this about eels...?

Well, I started crashing from the ENERGY POTION high around lunchtime and my tiny lunch of maybe a yogurt and an apple was never enough.

In NZ and Australia, schools have these shops that sell food to the kids who have money. They were amazing.

They were called "Tuck Shops". Our school's tuck shop sold pies, mutton hocks, ice creams, sausage rolls, chicken and corn rolls, drinks and all sorts of amazing shit to the starved.

It was rare I could ever steal enough money to buy much... maybe a sausage roll and a 50c ice block, if I could heist a $2 coin out of the car's dash console....

One day on the bus, looking out the window (which is what miserable tired kids did before phones) I had a brainstorm.

I could hunt for food. I was a good hunter and had shot many a rabbit... but never saw them as a food source...

To me, they were just something to kill and be more powerful than.

I went hunting after school on the hilly farm paddocks down the road from our house. Shot a rabbit and carried it back home.

By the time I got home, the dank rabbity smell fuming off the floppy corpse was making me almost spew, so there was no way I would be eating that.

I sadly took it down to the waterhole on our property and threw it in. It bobbed about in the slow-moving pool leaking blood.

Long shapes emerged from the shadows... and started ripping at the rabbit. Eels.

The ancestors of modern New Zealand eels had been swimming up and down New Zealand waterways since at least the early Miocene (23 million years ago).

The longfin eel is one of the largest eels in the world and it is found only in the rivers and lakes of New Zealand.

I knew you could eat eels. I decided I was going to become a great eel catcher and grow strong on eel meat.

That night I made three hand lines out of my dad's fishing gear, and prepped the small smoker box, filling it with sawdust from the woodshed.

After school the next day I went up and shot another rabbit. This one I chopped into chunks with a hatchet and hooked the furry chunks onto the lines.

Just on dusk the eels came out and I caught one right away. I gutted it, skinned it as best I could and sliced it into rounds and smoked it.

As soon as it was cooked I tried it... It was amazing. The Japs know a thing or two I tell ya.

I pounded down probably about a kilo and almost spewed. I got the Eel Sweats.

An hour later I had dinner with the family, definitely not talking about the eel I had eaten and was hiding in the shed.

I felt a strange feeling. It was "Full." This was a new feeling.

I remember lying on my bed in a near-orgasmic state of bloated satiety.

Later I snuck down to the shed and put the rest of the smoked eel chunks into an ice cream container and stashed it down the back of the fridge.

I took it to school the next day and gorged on it.

A kid asked me what it was...

Shit... I couldn't say eel... that was fully gross... but we were a town that hosted many game fishing tournaments... and I knew what was good in the eyes of these kids and their fisherman fathers...

"Smoked Marlin."

I knew this went for about $40 a kg and was a delicacy.

Whoah! Can I have a chunk?

"Well this stuff is really expensive... but I could trade you for a pie or sausage roll from the tuck shop..."

Well... we have been here before, dear reader.

I was scamming kids for their lunches years earlier... as you have read... And so it was that over a period of months I traded a total of probably ten fat river eels for a tremendous amount of food and treats and even sometimes money or these kids' lunches.

My father caught me, as I had used up almost all the kerosene needed for the smoker... but when I told him how I was scamming the kids at school by trading slimy river eels that I was catching with rabbit chunks, he was so proud he bought me four bottles of kerosene.

I finally got snapped when a kid bought a whole container from me for $20.

He took it home and proudly served it to his game fishing father and his high-class family at dinner. He was not happy when he confronted me the next day.

"Bro, my dad says there's no way in hell that shit you sold me is smoked marlin. He says it's fucking eel. I know you live up in the bush on a river. It's fucking eel isn't it? You've been feeding us eel!"

Me: "True... but... in Japan, NZ eel is the highest delicacy... and you liked it... The Japs know a thing or two, I tell ya."

"Fuck the Japs, mate!"

I fled.

Eel was not a cool thing, but a gross slimy thing, and within hours my scam was exposed and I was once again shamefaced before my peers for duping others. It was not the first time that would happen nor would it be the last.

Here are Four other times I have properly duped people with food.

Found a candy gummy frog squashed on the sidewalk in Australia, I squeezed it back into shape and gave it to a fellow roofer to eat.

I Fed an Australian friend dog jerky when he came over to the USA to stay with us. I didn't tell him, ever. He ate the whole bag and loved it.

When I moved my new family to Australia in '09, I was hunting a lot and almost all the meat we ate was from these trips. I made stews of what I called "Wild Mountain Chicken."

One day my stepson found a weird hand-shaped bone... and said "What sort of chicken has bones like this?"

Rabbits of course. :) He never guessed what the Jumping Outback Beef burgers were.

When my wife was pregnant every morning I fed her sausages that I had made. She complained that they had a bit of a weird taste... I ate mine with gusto... showing her they were indeed great. What she didn't know was that there were two batches of sausages. Mine on one side of the freezer, and hers and the baby's on the other.

Mine were made with the best cuts of lamb and beef. Hers were made mostly of guts. Liver, heart and kidney.

Good organ meats for the growing baby.

There was no fucking way she would eat that foul offal without my trickery. And eat it she did. For the entire pregnancy.

Once I went away and she made herself some sausages from my side of the fridge, and went on about how they were so amazing...

When I returned from my trip she was shocked at how the sausages changed back to being kind of bitter... but I just gaslit her about how good they were and eventually our baby was born super strong and healthy.

I told her about the offal sausages when he was 2 and she was commenting on how unusually strong and healthy he was compared to other kids his age--kids who were mostly formula fed by sick drained mothers.

She was only mildly enraged.

Chapter 11
THE SKI TRIP (School trip at 14)

THIS WAS THE COVETED FOURTH FORM ski trip that the class spent half the year fundraising for.

Of course, it took place in August... Winter in New Zealand.

About 40 of us 14-year-olds were bussed down to the mountain from our country town 6 hours away and we stayed in some sort of huge lodge on the mountain. We all were outfitted with skis. Snowboarding was very new and openly mocked

"Gays on trays".

I didn't want to be a Gay on a Tray, so I did not push the idea of getting a snowboard.

It went as you can imagine. A few kids got so sunburned their skin peeled off. Ankles were broken. Skiing was done. Some of the weaker kids quit after finding it too hard on day one and spent the rest of the trip back at the Lodge playing cards. Those nerds were teased mercilessly. I found myself skiing alone most of the time... but I learned fast and spent day after day whizzing down the mountain.

On one of the nights back at the Lodge, I spotted a huge 1-kilo bag of instant coffee. I thought "I wonder what effect that would have if sprinkled on the snow?" So I stole it and the next morning stashed it in my jacket. In the morning on the ride up the chairlift and with no one in the few chairs behind me, I opened up the bag and wafted out the contents onto the ski field below me. A wind picked up the brown dust and blew it into the shape of a large cloud. As each tiny crystal of instant coffee hit the snow it bloomed into a vivid brown shit stain.

To my horror, it spread and spread and spread to the snow below. The shit stain was gigantic. Like 4 football fields worth. My eyes bugged out at what I had done.

I just carried on with my skiing.... feeling detached and ghost-like. I skied through the giant shit stain, observing people's stunned reactions to it. When I got to the bottom of the run, I looked back and saw that as people were skiing through it, they were tracking long brown skid marks down the mountain. I heard one of the lift guys say, in response to a question...

"Some fuckwit genius dumped a bunch of instant coffee on the mountain, it will look like shit for days, until the next big snow."

I was that fuckwit genius. It was there for the rest of the trip becoming sadder, dirtier, and more diffuse. I would see bits of brown snow tracked into shops, and down in the mud room of the lodge... poopy reminders of my crime.

Two years later at school, we were talking about how much of an amazing trip that was. Someone said "Yeah and remember that big shit stain that appeared on the mountain?"

I decided to confess...

"It was me. I emptied a big bag of instant coffee on the mountain that I stole from the lodge."

No one believed me. By that time at school, my reputation was firmly entrenched as a bullshit artist, as what I said was often so outlandish.

No one believed me. Wow. Maybe one of them will read this 33 years later... and believe me now. I read this to my son and asked,

"Would you do something this naughty?"

He said, "No, I would wait for someone else to do it". That makes me a bit sad.

I need to start being a worse parent.

Chapter 12
I WANT CAN DO!
(American exceptionalism meets Kiwi Apathy)

NEW ZEALAND IS A SOMEWHAT QUIET COUNTRY. WE DON'T have screaming birds like Australia, and our people—like the birds—don't generally scream at each other.

It is not culturally acceptable to yell or be pushy or demand good service or get in anyone's face or make a big deal of yourself.

And on that, I have a story to tell you.

I was 14 years old living in a small, sedate town in rural New Zealand, when onto this dignified stage walked a relative who had moved to the USA in his youth.

He was 6'4", weighed about 250 pounds, and had a huge red beard with a similar mop of hair.

He ran a fleet of crab boats out of Seattle and had a big, booming voice, a deafening laugh, and fists like Christmas hams.

He was alive in a way I had only seen in American movies!

He told loud crazy stories and spouted his own huge, definite opinions.

I would always lurk near, listening... as I was obsessed with the Promised Land (Merica), and it was my life's goal to live in America and have money and food.

If I couldn't be like the kids on Beverly Hills 90210, then maybe I could at least be like Al Bundy on "Married with Children".

No one in the family could tolerate him. They would be super nice to his face but behind his back, they would sarcastically mock him and his forceful, righteous, American ways.

His larger-than-life presence and thundering voice still echo in my mind to this day.

One moment I shared with him has stuck with me forever.

That moment changed me and put me on a path out of New Zealand's dark and rainy conservative clutches and into the healing, freedom-filled embrace of the Promised Land (Merica).

He, myself, and two other family members had gone into the hardware store to get some nails and wire to fix a fence on the farm.

We went up to the counter to get some help.

The clerk was reading the newspaper.

Big Red said, "Hey buddy, I'm looking for these particular nails (he described them) and this particular wire (described it)."

I should explain that customer service in New Zealand is almost nonexistent, especially in the service industry where there is no tipping. You just get what you get and like it. Or you just have to be sad.

The clerk, without even really looking up, limply gestured toward the aisles of hardware products and said, "I'm not sure if we have that, but you can look down there." And then he went back to reading his newspaper.

Big Red looked shocked, and I saw a terrifying transformation come over him.

He had just TOTALLY FUCKING HAD IT.

He was used to the good "Yes Sir" service he'd received in the USA.

Professional service and personal capability were important things to him, and he had ranted about this many times; never failing to point out to us how shit New Zealand was.

He liked to point out that McDonald's makes 100 times more than New Zealand, and it was all because we were poor, lazy, pathetic, and sad.

I agreed. Hoping he would one day hire me.

He ran a crab boat crew, and the guys on those boats had to be very capable and go into action right away. If you weren't professional, skilled, and swift, you could die.

Big Red had just had it with the can't-do, no-assistance attitude of the people in the New Zealand service industry. So he slammed his ham-sized fist down in full force on the countertop and yelled in his earth-shattering yelling-above-the-wind-and-waves voice, "I WANT CAN DO!!"

I swear everything on that countertop jumped a foot in the air, the clerk's eyes bugged out of his head, and his mouth gaped open like a hooked bass.

Big Red yelled again, "I WANT FUCKING CAAAAAN DO!!! CLOWN!!!! I WANT WIRE! I WANT NAILS!!!!"

The clerk jumped up and zoomed down the aisles like he was on wheels.

And guess what? We got our wire and nails in short order.

I watched the whole episode in awe.

The other two family members literally ran and hid in their cars after the first CAN DO!

They were so embarrassed.

Not me though! I marched along with him and carried the stuff out like a boss.

Yeah! I want CAN DO too! Get those fuckin' nails for us, dipshit! Us real men have a fence to build!

Afterward, Big Red and I fixed the fence and had a fantastic day together, where I had him tell me story after story of the Promised Land and how much better it was than New Zealand.

I think that incident kept me grinning for an entire week.

For years after that, I would yell, "I WANT CAN DO!" and slam my fist onto things whenever someone told me something could not be done. As I wasn't massive and had no huge, scary, red beard, my actions were met with varying levels of success.

We can always do with more CAN DO.

I'm writing this at 12:24 a.m.... FFS...

I do know that the idea of driving forward and getting things done propelled me to live a rad and adventurous life. I refused to be a victim that could not get shit done.

This came in very handy as detailed in my other stories about roofing and logging and demolition.

Over the next 20 years I pushed myself to become so CAN DO! that I would out-CAN-DO the toughest maniacs on the worksites. This was likely very unhealthy and damaging to my body and mind. But it makes for good stories...

People don't say "harden up!" to complainers enough anymore... but I used to do that.

Let's bring it back :)

Chapter 13
THE SAD TALE OF CANDY THE AMERICAN GIRL
(Bad Girls used to channel Courtney Love)

So there I was... a young man, a wandering rebellious grunge beatnik, pseudo-philosopher; hell-bent on "getting my end away" (NZ slang for sex). I was 16 in this instance... before the deep rot had set in... as detailed in the later stories... I had not yet left the safety of home and was still at school...

It was some Friday night in rural New Zealand at some time in late November '92 in the little town I lived in.

The place was the gun club. An actual barn-like club building for shooters... not a cool club-type club. The occasion was the senior prom after-party.

I had no date to that prom, of course, because according to the gals I surveyed... I was... WAY TOO FUCKING NUTS TO GO TO THE PROM WITH.

These parties were notoriously insane, as if all the pent-up frothing, screaming, boozed frustrations of the school year were culminating on this night. The parties usually started in the usual way, with people turning up calmly enough... rationally and shyly peeling back a few beers within moments of arrival, but then becoming more and more debased as the night went. Finally, descending into a debauched mess of weed blazing and hard liquor chugging, violence, and field or woods or car or truck fornication before midnight...

It was not the best place for me, as I was at that time. I was trying to be intelligent... and beat. Which, of course, meant "faggot".

If you spoke a line of poetry or sang out loud, or did a little dance, at my rural school in NZ back in '92, you may as well be wearing a dress.

It was awesome to be called a faggot when one piped up with a borderline sane non-arsehole opinion on something... but at least Kurt understood me.

Also, I liked to be happy and sing and talk to people. Classic Fag.

I stand as the guy who has been called faggot the most on planet Earth.

Easily 10 times a day for about 6 years straight. Maybe not so much on weekends...

Gays got nothing on me.

Also, "You fuck goats" was a common one.

When I left school, I kind of missed the continual verbal abuse in response to what I would say at school... Stockholm Syndromed to fuck, I guess.

But there were no other options for camaraderie in this town, and believe it or not, I chose being called a *faggot goat fucker* over staying home and watching *Married with Children* and *Red Dwarf*, every time.

I should have been sitting around a fire with a few friends, a bottle of red wine, and a book of beat poems to read aloud with wide-eyed and whispered gusto. However much that was my dream idea of a good time... I had to take what was on offer, as I had no friends like that, no fire, and no wine...

So there I was, bespectacled and resplendent in my grunge uniform —army pants carefully scissored off below the knee, army boots, a red plaid shirt, and a red beret carefully folded to the side.

Despite the NZ term "Nails that stick out get hammered in," I purposely stood out in the crowd of Swandri (a thick woolen coat popular with redneck Kiwis) and gumboot-wearing bush kids mixed with the casual surf-clothes-wearing townies.

I crept through the swaying crowd, carefully... as I wasn't particularly among friends here, being from the younger crowd, and any perceived slight bump or infraction could result in my boho form being booted about the place.

Latimer Redlance

I had a target... Her name was Candy. She was a severely mixed-up American girl from Portland, schooling in New Zealand. I think her parents sent her here to live with relatives, for going nuts in the USA. She had a loud demeanor and a penchant for sniffing things up her nose... sherbet... powdered drink mixture... baking soda... and she had many stories of the big cocaine binges that she used to go on back home to amuse and titillate us country kids.

"Cocaine? Like in the movies?"

"Yes, cocaine just like in the movies."

She was some sort of freewheeling, Courtney-Love type, and as we were in the eye of the grunge tornado, so she was a dream come true.

One day she wore black fishnet stockings and a miniskirt to school and got sent home immediately. BADASS AF, man.

She had made a comment that I was cute and funny. This comment had reached me, and over the previous two days, I had extrapolated and fantasized out many things from this statement. My mission now was to find her and push the whole newly formed romantic fantasy construct to some sort of conclusion.

After searching out the party for her wild blond tresses and meeting with failure, I headed to the dunny (NZ slang for toilet). With my head down, resigned and stumbling, I blundered into the dunny door and it swung open.

The sight before me hit like a tonne of moldy tangerines.

There was my grunge princess... on all fours, hugging the toilet bowl as if it were a buff porcelain lover, heartily barfing voluminous quantities of the beer/tequila/Baileys/rum/whiskey/wine cocktail she had been hooking back frenzied rockstar style all night.

Her blond tresses hung, slime-splattered around the pissy bowl, and an array of corn and peas decorated the floor and her cool grunge cardigan, like organic rhinestones.

Hunched over her like a rabid bull and pounding fiercely was one of my many nemesi. One of the many scoundrels who had bailed school at 16 and, for the past two years, had done nothing but sink beers, ride motorbikes, grow dope, surf, and hit every single party, making sure that with a wave of his magic "wand," every unspoiled happy gal was transformed into a sad, bitter, scathing witch with a hatred of all men.

Thus salting the soil of the green pastures of her heart so the shoots of real tender love could never sprout on the fields once so lush and green... fields that my friends and I wanted so dearly to munch upon ourselves.

He spun, red-faced at my intrusion, yelled "FUCK OFF CUNT!!" and punched me viciously in the side of the head as I turned to flee, all without missing a stroke, may I add.

I flew sideways out the door, tears bursting to my eyes as I crumpled, the combination of shame/loss/anger already growing into a nasty ball of hate within me... yet I steadied myself and pushed that ball of hate down deep inside to be released at an appropriate time in the future.

I bolted down the hall and back into the main party area, clutching my searing, fizzing head and ringing, swollen ear.

It was thronged with people screaming, bouncing, and swaying around a large table laden with bottles and cans and ciggie butts *in* bottles and cans.

Just get that smell for a sec.

What was playing? ...FUCK YOU, I WON'T DO WHAT YOU TELL ME!!... of course...

I reeled up against the wall to rest and recover... sure that my ear was the size of a Frisbee. I saw a guy called Bazza come charging into the room and power chuck at the table.

Bottles and cans went flying at the force of this event, and girls leaped about screaming as a river of vomit hit. A yellow waterfall cascaded onto the carpet.

This was just fucked and was too much for me, and I decided to call it a night.

Near was my friend's house... his mother was away, and he was back at the party somewhere. I couldn't find him, so I just went to his place and crashed in his room.

He had two single beds in his room on opposite sides...

I woke way later in the night... to some sound... and there was a FUCKING GLOWING GREEN UFO out there through the window... it was cigar-shaped and disappeared from one end to the other over and over and over... sometimes slow, sometimes fast!

I stared at it, transfixed in total fear for a few minutes, when suddenly it changed shape and flew up and around and down and then seemed to land IN THE ROOM on the floor... Now it was kind of squashed and small. I was terrified... I stared at it a while longer...

It was driving me nuts... I got out of bed and crept over... It was on the floor. I picked it up...

I heard my friend say, "What the fuck, bro?" He was there in his bed... I could just make him out... and a gal from a class above us — "Messy Tessey"...

I'm holding in my hand a full and tied, glow-in-the-dark condom. It was their doggy-style banging making it look like it was a floating UFO.

All I could say was... "WOW, I thought it was a UFO and I was staring at you guys rooting, thinking there was aliens and shitting myself."

They laughed, I laughed, we all laughed.

That kind of night is an experience 16-year-olds these days are missing out on... No phones in sight, just kids having a good time.

Chapter 14
THE CAREERS TRIP (The school trip to the big city—age 16 ½)

When 16, the kids from my school were taken from our country town in rural New Zealand to the big city of Auckland, where we would be bussed about to various businesses and factories.

The purpose of this trip was to give us an idea of what was waiting upon leaving school.

A nice introduction to the grim, meat-hook realities of working a job you hate to earn money so you can eat and live and buy things you don't need to impress people you don't like.

By this time, attrition had taken its toll on the class numbers.

50% of the kids from the last year's 15-year-old class had left school and were working on parents' farms or in a trade school of some kind.

Or some even optioned to live with an older hippie friend and grow weed for a living.

That left about 20 of us.

By the time our 16-year-old class was done, there were about 10 left to enter the 17-year-old class. "University Entrance," it was called.

I know some kids went on to get a lot out of this trip and went on to learn trades or become nurses and go directly into the "meat grinder of the MAN" as I had been led to believe it was called, by the counterculture books I favored.

Working and trying to get money and be part of society was not for me.

For someone like myself, homelessness, drugs, shivering desperation, and oft-times violent adventure was way more interesting than driving a forklift in the Coca-Cola plant, or trying to do construction tradespeople, or nurse school or whatever the kids who wanted to be humans were going to do.

One of my friends went to panel beater school, one went to nurse college, another into the air force.

I went to the streets to... be free and to learn how to survive on the streets... because I didn't want anyone telling me what to do... super smart move.

Kind of knowing that rough times were going to happen to me, I did not pay too much attention to where we went. But I do remember the Coca-Cola factory, Saatchi & Saatchi advertising offices... and an art school.

I just want to detail some crazy shit that went down on this six-day trip.

First thing, we were all put up in the Auckland YHA hostel.

I was in a room on the bottom floor. I chose that room because I had a plan.

The first crazy thing that happened was that we went to an art college, and while the other kids were being shown about, I took off and found the most twisted-looking students to talk to. I regaled them with my funny stories... asking questions about parties, counterculture books, and so on.

In my mind, I had it built up that this art college was going to be like something out of '60s Berkeley, San Francisco... but the guys I talked to didn't really know what I was talking about... It was 1993, and we were in New Zealand after all...

Then one guy said, "I know something you would like, you're crazy so you might get it," and took me to a small, totally dark AV room, where he put a VHS on for me.

It was *ERASERHEAD*.

YES. This is what I needed. The mental equivalent of an apple corer to the psyche.

A touchstone with which to resonate with the other freaks I would meet one day.

If you don't know what *ERASERHEAD* is, you can search it up...

Here's a small blurb:

David Lynch's masterful direction, impeccable cinematography, and experimental music and sound design all work together to create a surreal and unforgettable cinematic experience. While not for the faint of heart, *Eraserhead* is a film that rewards those willing to take the plunge into its dark and dreamlike world.

I took the plunge into its dark and dreamlike world... I came out forever changed.

I finished the movie just as the rest of the group finished the tour, and I quietly entered the bus last.

Mentally shifted.

There was a new world. Something I hadn't even seen before.

Surrealism!

This was HOW I FELT. Now it had a name.

As you can see from my other stories, I had had so many whack-doodle experiences in my life, that I was now just a thing. I resembled a '90s teenager in physical form only.

My personality was so fragmented, that I didn't exist to myself. I sought out two things: intense crazy experiences and sense gratification.

Like a reverse Buddhist. A hedonist sybarite hobo-freak?

Well, this movie did it. A portrayal of a world to match my mind.

I stared out the window.

Nothing was real. And little mattered. It was an illusion now.

A canvas for me to paint on.

What is truth?

That night I went to bed early, making a big deal about having a headache.

I needn't have bothered, no one cared. The bad kids were planning to meet up at midnight and sneak up to the hang-out spot on the roof with the foreign backpackers and drink the devastating gallon of cheap port one of them had stolen from their parents. That seemed dazzlingly lame to me.

My regular friends were distant from me, as I had been acting weirder than usual.

One of my other friends (He of the glowing condom) was also acting weird and hanging out with the new tall horsey-faced girl who wore floral print dresses.

I had a mastermind plan for this trip.

So I got to my room. I put on a set of what I thought were cool city-man clothes.

Stonewash grey jeans, a white shirt, my old boarding school tie. By rubbing a dark soft art pencil on paper till it made a large pool of black and, applying it to my face, I made a passable five o'clock shadow.

My only footwear was my black NZ army boots. But I had shined them up real good with KIWI polish and, by putting the jeans OVER them, they kind of just looked like big black shoes. Topped with a trilby.

A trilby is a narrow-brimmed type of British fedora hat. The trilby was once viewed as the rich man's favored hat in Britain and was frequently seen at the horse races.

I was now a dapper man about town!

I had saved up $200 ($430 in today's money) from mowing lawns over the last year, and now I was going to wax the fucking lot! Striding about this city like a latter-day dandy!

I squeezed out the room's window and, hanging onto the sill, dropped the last foot to the pavement and took off.

First off, I just wandered, sucking in the sights and sounds of vibrant but quiet Queen Street, Auckland. The tiny civilized core of New Zealand.

THE QUEEN OF STREETS!

After exploring, I stopped at TONY'S STEAKHOUSE for dinner. It was located down a thin street that ran parallel to Queen Street (Lorne Street).

I wanted a nice steak at a small table in the corner.

The real "man essence" of eating a big steak.

"How would I like it cooked?"

"Blackened—No blood."

Cue a frown from the waiter.

He goes to the kitchen.

Cue chef coming out and looking at me in the corner.

Cue other kitchen staff coming out and having a laugh at me.

I heard… "….some weird kid…"

The chef sent over a massive glass of wine on the house.

I raised it in thanks to the laughing staff.

This night was getting good.

Leaving satisfied, wine-buzzed, and happy and not having to tip because it's New Zealand, and thus I didn't even KNOW what tipping was… I popped into a shop and bought a pack of Camels.

Having never smoked before, it made total sense to start with something strong and cool.

This I could do legally. 16 was the smoking age. But it didn't matter, no shopkeeper gave a shit anyway.

Blazing up a harsh Camel, I cruised about watching the nightlife.

Now with my wine brain, steak guts, and Camel baccy high, I thought how nice it would be to find a bohemian café and have some dessert and a coffee and blaze more smokes… maybe have a whiskey, like a real-man sophisticate.

I found such a place on the High Street. The fashion store, and high-end café street.

The swankiest street in NZ. All 100 yards of it.

I sat at one of the tables outside and had four espressos. One after another, while blazing Camels and watching the world go by.

When I started to feel like I was having mini heart attacks, I tried ordering a whiskey…

The waiter was cool… probably about 25, but not fooled by my get-up… he looked back into the café, paused, and said in a low conspiratorial tone… "I can get you a Fernet… it will look like a Coke."

"YES!"

I didn't know what a Fernet was, but I was to find that it was a type of bitter, aromatic spirit, made from a number of herbs and spices including myrrh, rhubarb, chamomile, cardamom, aloe, and saffron, with a base of distilled grape spirits. Italian.

Wow.

And so my love of bitter herbal booze was born.

I sat there sipping on this massive glass of iced Fernet.

Latimer Redlance

Watching the high-class Aucklanders go by.

1993. A simpler time.

Smokes in hand instead of phones.

Steak, wine, Camel smokes, espressos, and now a big glass of Fernet.

Mashed but sophisticated. The lobes were HUMMING.

I was chilling at a boho café while the other kids were hiding from the teachers in the hostel drinking stolen wino port like a bunch of muddled babies.

Only one thing could make this better.

Something I had been planning all year: SEX.

Now, prostitution is legal and regulated in New Zealand. It was the first country to fully decriminalize sex work. I knew this. It was part of health class. We were very well educated on these things.

The history of sex work in NZ was taught to us right along with terrifying videos of abortions and condom use demonstrations.

I also knew where the bordellos were located. Jack Kerouac taught me that word: bordellos.

They were upscale places down off the bottom of Queen Street on a street called Fort Street. A long side street with upmarket strip clubs and high-end cat houses.

An older friend had told me all about how good it was.

Maybe seeking to justify his frequenting?

"The ladies are taken care of, they make about 20 times more money than they would if they were working in a supermarket, they are having a great time and doctors check them. It's all safe sex and it's very highbrow."

Is this true? Sometimes yes... and sometimes it's 10 Chinese students that were sent to NZ by their parents to study at our university, that no longer study, aren't going back to China, and now all live in a flat like rats, doing meth in between $20 Johns.

I headed down to Fort Street, which had a section that served as a high-end red light district back then. Down at the bottom to the right of Queen Street.

I went up the stairs of the nicest-looking one... let's call it the "Lords Club" and buzzed the brass buzzer. Someone looked through the peephole and then the door was opened by a good-looking blond older woman in a tiger print bodysuit and high-heeled boots.

Classy.

"Hello, darling. Aren't you a sweetheart. Come on in."

I was taken into the entry room of the bordello. I was now panicking. The room took on a fishbowl-like appearance.

"I have a really sweet girl, who will take great care of you and you're going to want an hour. That will be $100, dear."

I now realize this was a ploy to drive me off, as she knew I shouldn't have been there, and thought I was probably wasting her time.

But I counted out a handful of battered lawnmower-earned fives and tens and said, "Awesome."

Her eyebrows shot up and she took me through the door to a very nice lounge with a bar and a TV playing music videos.

There were two girls in the room. One freaky black-haired Eastern European-looking one, blazing a long thin smoke and sitting with her arms crossed and her crossed leg swinging like a metronome... wearing a small black dress...

And a plump smiling girl with short red hair, in jeans and a NIRVANA SHIRT!

The lady of the house took me to the red-haired gal and introduced us.

She led me off down the hall to an amazing room, wooden-paneled with mirrors and an ensuite shower/bathroom, and a fake fireplace heater.

It had a double bed covered in red velvet and heart-shaped pillows.

I'm a chatty one... and was pretty nervous.

She had me have a shower as I yammered away.

She was smiling and I think she genuinely liked me. I washed the pencil beard off and we sat on the bed and talked. I found out all about her, though at first she said, "I don't talk about my life with clients."

I said, "I'm not a client. I'm just a cool guy sitting on this bed with you."

This made her laugh. Also now thinking about it... cry a tiny bit.

She wasn't from a broken home. There was no history of abuse or drugs. Just this story.

Her dad had died naturally when she was 16, as he was a much older guy than her mum. Her mum knew what she did and was fine with it.

She had been going to beauty school from 17 but it was hard, and she said, "I'm not smart. I was always real shit at school." Then she saw some of her older friends graduate and only be able to get jobs for about ten dollars an hour working for mean-as-fuck stick-skinny bitches, doing the worst jobs like waxing old ladies' minges.

I think to us, old ladies meant 35...Her friends hated their lives in the beauty industry.

She was smart enough to know that that was a shit dead end. One of her friends, who was a "working girl" on the side of being at beauty school, introduced her to this.

So after flunking a class, she dropped out of beauty school... and that was a year ago.

She was now 19.

She now makes about 1000 dollars a week. That was BONKERS money back in NZ in '93. ($2200 today) She was saving up for a house and already had 35K.

She said that they only let good guys into the Lords. The Lords Club was high-class and priced to keep out the riff-raff. No drunks, no bogans (rednecks), and no dodgy old men.

Mostly young wealthy guys and older businessmen. And of course one sixteen year old adventurer!

We talked for ages, laughing and trading stories. Till there was one solitary knock on the door.

"That means only 5 minutes left," she said with a pouting frown. We had been talking the whole time!

I said, "Don't worry! That's all the time in need! ;) … … … …"

Before leaving I gave her the rest of my money, which was about another $40, and she gave me a big hug. I strode out of there like a demented rooster. The madame smiled at me and kind of laughed as I strutted out. I was smiling so wide my face almost broke.

I strutted up Queen Street feeling like a king. I was alive. I had lived more life in the last 4 hours than in many years prior. I got back to the hostel and leaped up, grabbed the sill, and pulled myself into the window.

I got changed into my regular grunge teen outfit and headed out into the hall to the bathrooms to take a piss.

Catching my friend (the guy hanging out with the new tall horsey-faced girl who wore floral print dresses) coming out of one of the gal's rooms.

He doesn't see me... he stops in the hallway and smells his hand.

I knew what that meant! I had been smelling MY hand for the last 30 minutes!

"Bro! You've been hiding in her room, banging Betsy Mae!" (Not her real name).

"Yip."

"What happened with the party?"

"Those spazes got so drunk; Dylan spewed in the hallway, and Jess fell down the stairs and they got busted and now they are all in deep shit."

"Idiots. Wow... I've been out on the town..."

"Nice. I'm crashing. Night."

"Night."

I realized I couldn't bring myself to tell him or anyone what I had done.

But now... now I have.

I ground out the last week of school and rolled out of my town. Thank you to that gal, that night meant a lot to me. You are out there somewhere... now 50 years old or older... Once it was just you and me together in that wooden-paneled room.

No phones in sight. Just kids having a good time.

This song, "Beauty School Dropout," from the musical *Grease*, messed me up when I heard it later in life.

Beauty school dropout
No graduation day for you
Beauty school dropout
Missed your mid-terms and flunked shampoo
Well, at least you could have taken time
To wash and clean your clothes up
After spending all that dough
To have the doctor fix your nose up

Latimer Redlance

Baby, get movin' (better get movin')
Why keep your feeble hopes alive?
What are you provin'? (What are you provin')
You've got the dream but not the drive
Beauty school dropout (beauty school dropout)
Hanging around the corner store
Beauty school dropout (beauty school dropout)
It's about time you knew the score
Well, they couldn't teach you anything
You think you're such a looker
But no customer would go to you
Unless you were a hooker...

Chapter 15
GUTTER BOSS (From the gutter to the stars)

Or... "How to turn a dream of becoming a cool grunge badass, into living on the streets of a rainy city, alone and numb, in three easy steps."

So there I was, a young man.

I had left home and moved to the big city of Auckland, from my rural New Zealand hometown to find fame and fortune.

I had just turned 17 and was full of hopes and dreams.

I had enrolled in a well-known drama school that was bonkers liberal in its attitude toward students.

I had heard stories of kids blazing weed on the field, an actual cigarette smoking area for kids who smoked, loose moraled girls, wild parties, and all sorts of other fun-sounding mischiefs.

Of course, most of the above was all going on at my rural high school, but I had grown up with all the kids at that school and they knew all my tricks.

At this new school, I would be able to reinvent myself as some kind of "Christian Slaterish" grunge badass.

My friend was going to help reinvent me and become part of the cool kids clique at this school. Something he had managed to already do.

I was going to be part of a clique called the "Munch Bunch".

This was done on day one by completely changing my clothes from the ragged grunge uniform I usually wore, to a kind of preppy CK 1-covered munch bunch uniform of baggy jeans and a nice polo shirt with the top button done up and gel styled hair.

The orders from my friend were simple. "Don't act weird, no crazy acrobatic shit, no stories, no jokes, don't sing any songs... just be cool."

So I rolled up to the school with him and was cool. Nodding to the cool kids. Standing back observing.

This lasted until about lunchtime.

My friend wasn't around... so I somehow said something funny... This got laughter and looks...and from there evolved into stories, jokes, and songs...

By the time my friend got back and saw me walking down the steps on my hands, to the laughter of the Munch Bunch... it was over. The court jester was in charge now....

He came over and informed me that I should be hanging out under that tree over there with the freaks. Looking over I saw a bunch of kids looking over at me...

An Asian goth chick in all black and also wearing a cloak, a tall weird-looking dude with a ginger afro, two Rasta-dressed guys playing hacky sack, and some kid in a suit with a briefcase.

They waved to me. The ginger Afro guy literally chanting "One of us, One of us."

I went over.

The next day I was back in my ragged orange cardigan with "I'm Grunge" painted on the back, plaid shirt, cut of army pants, and red beret and I was ranting with my people, the freaks.

My purpose in going to this school was to fulfill some kind of dream of being a famous actor and performer through the medium of hard work, showing up, and learning the craft.

Somehow... hanging with these freaks triggered something in me...

Even these freaks were conforming to what society felt they should be like as freaks. There were layers in this thing called cliques or groups... it was all a made-up act... I guess some people never realize this. For me, it was clear now…. my country school never had this… we were just a demented mass.

This was new…an ideological class system of sorts.

I had figured it out…

I'm not saying that I'm special or smart. It's obvious how special and smart I am by the series of incredibly bad choices I made. It is what it is.

By hanging with the beatnik freaks, and listening to their opinions on what is good and bad, right and wrong, I rapidly came to the conclusion that these partitioned off cliques were just another masturbatory exercise in human social conformity.

Maybe it was just layers of conformity to cliques all the way up to heaven and all the way down to hell?

If I was to really grow and know myself I would have to force it.

This is harder than it seems when you are so programmed to make correct choices.

It was going to take a bit of headbutting life and a certain amount of focused self-destruction.

My guides were Nirvana, Rage Against the Machine, The Doors, and every bit of beat literature stretching back to Lord Byron.

With this rubbish swimming around in my head I set to work on step 1.

I went directly to hang out with the baddest and most insane kid I could find, to blaze weed, drink stolen rum, and embrace a total lack of restraint in all things.

Terry the Munter became my guide.

Stank brutally. 17 going on 50. Bad teeth. Raised by a drug addict, alcoholic single mother. Personally a drug addict and alcoholic since 13. Wore a faded ripped Metallica shirt and leather pants covered in marks from stubbed-out cigarettes.

I was taking the crash course.

There's being *badass* and then there is a point where you become so badass that you get killed by actual badass gangsters. This is that story.

Terry and I crashed a Redneck party. It was a Wedding After-party at a church.

It was a ruralish area outside of West Auckland, which is a pretty feral place. Henderson... if you want to be specific.

We got the bus out there... it took an hour...

Churches in New Zealand are cheap to rent and often used for off-the-hook parties.

How he knew it was happening I don't know, but it had a band and, like everything out in feral Henderson, it was going to be nuts.

We rocked in—It was a small white church, cars parked haphazardly all over the lawn, people everywhere—totally wrecked... You don't see this kind of stumbling, screaming, spewing, swearing mess these days, outside of a few rare areas... It was a special time and place...

We sidled in and chilled out by the wall looking for any unattended booze or anything we could steal. The band played, and people moshed. We were just ignored.

The band played "Rage Against the Machine," FUCK YOU WON'T DO WHAT YOU TELL ME!!!" And people went nuts. It was awesome...

Then the craziest shit happened...

A weird-looking skinny dude fully dressed in white—white jeans, a white jacket, a white shirt, and white cowboy boots, and a big white cowboy hat—came out of nowhere and started dancing a weird sexy cowboy dance. Grooving up against any females he could. People were laughing, the girls were laughing and pushing him back... it was just funny to watch...

Then also out of nowhere two hardcore NZ gang members appeared.

This was bad news... they were fully patched members of the Mongrel Mob.

You should do a Google image search of the NZ Mongrel Mob now. So you can get an idea of what this brutalness actually was like.

The back of their leather jackets feature a British bulldog wearing a German Stahlhelm.

One was a massive Maori Guy and the other was a shaved-headed, short stocky white guy. Both with crude tattoos all over their faces.

The white shaved head guy went right up to the Cowboy guy and kicked him so hard in the arse with a big steel-capped boot he seemed to fly through the air. Then before he could get up he kept kicking, and kicking his butt as the poor screaming guy tried to scramble out of the way.

Kicking him all the way up the middle of the church... never letting him up... hat flying... begging... screaming.... utter brutality.

The Maori guy charged into the crowd, smashing people flying, and grabbed one of the church pews. Wielding it in both hands like a huge baton he just spun it about smashing it into people like a total maniac.

They were both obviously out of their minds on booze, weed and speed and this was entertainment to them... people were going down left and right and screaming...something wet hit my face... it was someone's blood... the band had stopped playing and I grabbed Terry and we fled.

This was too fucked for words.

We started walking down the dark road and decided to hitchhike back to his place in the city—the shitty concrete apartment he shared with his messed up mum... but his room was a cozy stinky sanctuary with Iron Maiden...and he did have a jug of cheap brandy.

A car was coming and we put out the thumb... it was coming pretty fast... but whatever... It slammed on the brakes and pulled to a stop almost hitting us...

It was a small Toyota Corolla two-door hatchback... The door flew open and the big Maori Mongrel Mob guy got out and clicked the seat forward. "Get in, you're coming to a party."

Instead of running, idiot Terry says "Sweet" and gets in.

Instead of running, idiot Me just gets in.

And they take off... as fast as it can go...

The radio is up full blast playing some rock radio station through the tiny speakers... It would have been funny if it wasn't so terrifying ... They both held big beer bottles and there was a crate of beer in the back between us with six left. This is how we drank back then. A crate of 12, 750ml bottles of beer. Lion Red... cheap generic.

Lion Red is a New Zealand beer brewed by Lion Breweries in Auckland. The beer is 4.0% alcohol. Because of its relatively low alcohol content it is widely regarded as an excellent 'session' beer, that is, a beer that can be consumed freely over a long session of time without all the adverse effects of a higher alcohol volume beer.

Kiwi Piss.

"Have a beer guys!" said the skinhead one.. so we each had a big warm beer...

We are roaring along now... all drinking and silent.

The driver seemed to be kind of blacking out ... and the car started dangerously swerving onto the edge of the road...

I decide to say "Bro... look out man... you don't want to cash your car."

He says "HAHAHAH, not my car bro I stole it!"

I'm sure we are going to die. So I just pound my warm beer hoping that when we all go through the windscreen I will be relaxed.

Terry is having a great time... he starts singing to the songs on the radio...

Spoiler alert... I didn't die... we drive for about 20 minutes at this insane speed through the dark and then they turn off the road onto a long gravel driveway and up to...

A big gang-headquarters shed house-party... with dogs everywhere and feral gang women and motorbikes and blasting music...

It seems like they were heading to this party and just stopped in at the church on the way to smash shit up...

They got out and rolled in... forgetting us.

We sat in the car.

Terry gets up and looks like he's entertaining the idea of going to the party....he said "Let's...and I cut him off with "FUCK NO."

"OK then but I'm stealing these beers."

And so we grabbed the last four beers and snuck out of the car. The only thing that watched us go was a mangy dog... The party was in full swing but no one saw us...

We snuck down the road and started jogging and then running. We got to the main road and the relief was like nothing I have ever experienced. We laughed and walked and drank our massive warm bottles of Lion Red.

Anytime a car came we rolled off into the ditch and lay down flat in case they were coming back to grab us. We walked for about an hour along that rural road. Finally, we were so tired and drunk that we just lay in the grass by a bus stop at the first point of civilization, and waited for the 5:30 am bus to the city.

That was my last foray with maniac Terry, bless his heart. No idea what happened to the guy. I have a fondness for total fucking maniacs. As you have read. There is a reason for this. No matter how bad shit got. No matter how insane I went. No matter how demented the scene... I still knew I wasn't as bad as them.

I could always hang onto that last rung and, while I might be in the gutter... they were in the drain under that metal grill thing where IT lives, looking up at me and telling me to come down into the drain and play.

And play I did:) As I have said... my mentor taught a rule to live by:

"Buy the ticket, take the ride...and if it occasionally gets a little heavier than what you had in mind, well...maybe chalk it up to forced consciousness expansion: Tune in, freak out, get beaten."

Chapter 16
GUTTER ARRIVAL
(Fleeing middle class pamperedness)

Within a week of hanging with my boy Terry, I was too twisted and baked to do any school work and after a period of class spent frozen and staring...reeking of the devil's lettuce, I burped and weed smoke came out of my mouth.

The teacher asked me "Do you really want to be here?"

So wise, was that teacher. The answer was *no* then and is still no, as I write this, now 30 years later.

I decided to leave and enter the workforce! Challenge! Freedom! Money.

The only thing holding me back now was the attachment of financial strings.

Due to well meaning parents paying to support me and keep me fed and housed, I could not be fully free to chart my own destiny. My parents were paying my way, further miring me in lame middle-class pamperedness.

I just couldn't handle the fact that these other kids I was hanging with, (Even Terry) could just go to the parents fridge and get food. Or come home and sleep in their bedroom after going out partying and pretending to be free and self directed.

It's a fucking scam. Unless you're totally punk and not dependent on mum and dad, you are just a trenchcoat wearing doofus from middle class suburbia.

Sticking feathers up your arse does not make you a chicken. Nothing will change that. I had to go it alone and cut them strings. I was going to get a job and go my own way!

The paper was the only medium of jobs back then, for a 17 year old who knew no one.

"SUPER ENTHUSIASTIC PEOPLE WANTED."

Your heart should be sinking right now.

That's right up there with "Must be able to handle pressure" and "We are like a Family" In a job posting. It means danger and abuse. People know that now, 30 years on. I of course thought "That's me!"

Turning up to an office that was just a partitioned-off part of an open top floor in a cheap and rundown, downtown building. I missed all the warning signs and signed on right away.

All I could gather from the harried and cheap-suited, 20-something running the place, was that it was some kind of sales outfit. They were sending me to a town on the other side of the country by train tomorrow, and that I was the greatest employee they had ever hired and that I would do great, and All I needed was a sleeping bag and a couple of nice shirts.

Zero red flags.

The anti-drug people were right, drug use can cause "Risk-taking behavior".

I was on that train early the next morning once again full of hopes and dreams. I was off the drugs and cutting free from twisted Terry the Munter whose hijinks had got a little less, "Blaze weed and go to parties and mosh and steal shit to eat", and more of the "cutting self while listening to Venom in your bedroom" variety.

Lame.

I was thinking about money and girls and freedom!

An eight-hour trip thinking about my amazing bright future ended with meeting my handler once I got off the train. A red-headed, leprechaun-looking Australian surfer guy in a green hoodie. Super over-the-top enthusiastic. "Greenie" welcomed me to the team.

We drove in the battered white van to the "Team House".

On arrival I see three miserable people sitting on the floor of a lounge in a cheap freezing rental. Wellington in winter. Wet, miserable... There is no furniture. Hmm, that's a bit odd.

Person one: Tall skinny guy in his 20s with long hair and black jeans. A heavy metal guy.

Person two: A short stout dwarf Afrikaner South African guy of about 30.

Person three: A really, really sad-looking overweight gal in her 20s with curly black hair.

And now Me! "Hi, I'm Super Enthusiastic Person wanted!"

Greenie showed me the room I was sharing with the Afrikaner guy and heavy metal guy. My section of carpet to lay my sleeping bag.

I stayed up late, talking to the Dwarf.

He had been kicked out of home when young due to drugs, and his father being super strict, and so he had wandered the world. Now he was here and he was trying to make a go of this. He had been here two weeks. He was so deranged he actually thought it was a real job.

In the morning we all assembled in the kitchen for breakfast which was oatmeal made in one pot and poured into four coffee mugs with no spoons.

"Where's Jess"

Greenie: "Oh she had to go."

Ok... so we got in the van and Greenie dropped the guys off and then worked with me in a park teaching me the job and the script.

Basically, it was a door-to-door sales company, selling $2500 children's learning programs. I would knock on the doors in the worst neighborhoods of this town, and give my pitch and try to set up appointments for Greenie to close them for a big package for their kid.

If he closed a deal I would get 250$.

It was easy and he even had a little rhyme that I should say if I started feeling like lying down flat on the sidewalk and not getting up again.

The rhyme went: "I've got the Juice, got the Fire, Got the Burning Desire!"

I was all set.

After a few hours of pitching to beer and baby holding, ciggie in the mouth single mums, old people with no kids telling me so, and people asking me "Why the fuck would you bang on my door and ask if I have any kids?", I had lost all hope and started to have out of body experiences brought on by a combo of terror and shame.

Looking at myself detachedly from above... 17, stonewashed jeans, short sleeve white dress shirt, sweaty, wretched, jonesing for a high. Withdrawing from booze and weed in a sour sweat.

The Grim meathook realities of life jabbing into me.

I was trying to be good! What the fuck! If you were good, wasn't the universe supposed to reward you? Nope... it seemed to me that it just lined you up for a harder kick in the nuts, for being so stupid and trusting. And this time you aren't numbed out from booze and drugs... so its gonna hurt.

Alone, broke, trapped.

I had told my parents to fully cut me off and had proudly told everyone I knew I was going it alone and I got an amazing job. On my way to success I was! I was off the Devils Lettuce, got a haircut, and I was going to really make something of myself.

Make 'em all proud...

I had the sad and scary realization that no one actually gave enough of a shit about me to talk to me about my life and try to explain what "Super enthusiastic people wanted" meant.

After watching myself bound up to about 10 doors, give my spiel, and be shut down I started to get a bit worried. I was doing the rhyme, and it didn't seem to be working! ... what the hell Greenie!

I started having panic attacks as I approached the doors now and would just veer off and walk down the street... I then fully bugged out to a nearby park. Within a few minutes, Greenie rolled up in the van. Probably was spying on me. You know it's a good job when you have to spy on your guys in case they try to make a break for it.

Super enthusiastic.

I explained that I couldn't do this anymore and he said I could, and tried to help me realize this by kicking a soccer ball back and forward with me while rambling on about harnessing the juice and the fire or something...I was too numb to really listen.

Dinner was a bucket of tepid KFC shared between us four in the cold house with no furniture. Had a lukewarm shower with no soap and used a T-shirt for a towel. Greenie had rolled out by himself...that night, likely to get himself a yummy dinner and a few beers with his own money.

I started chatting to the other lost boys, sitting dejectedly on the carpet of the bare living room. I can only remember one thing about that conversation. And it went like this...

Tall long hair Heavy metal guy: "I would literally rather live on the streets than do this job"

ME: "Same"

Him: "I'm going to bail tonight, it's easy to live on the streets. You just hang out at the library, eat leftovers from the food court, sneak into movies and there are lots of good places to hide around the city and sleep."

Me "Man let's go!"

We went to our room and packed, suddenly we heard Greenie pulling up the drive, so we hightailed it out the window. My last look at the place was the Afrikaner dwarf seriously saluting us from the window EXACTLY like he was some kind of left-behind wounded soldier, ready to hold the enemy back so we could escape.

And so we fled into the night.

Chapter 17
THE GUTTER BOSS RISES
(I live, I die, I live again)

FLEEING FROM THE OUTER SUBURB TWISTED GROUP HOUSE of Greenie the tricksy Leprechaun, me and the heavy metal guy trekked down the hill through the suburbs toward the city of Wellington.

The ground was wet from the perpetual rain that continually washed this part of New Zealand—but luckily it is not raining now.

We hiked into Wellington. Walking for miles, while I pumped the tall heavy metal guy for street survival tips.

These were:

You can go into supermarkets and eat food inside there from the shelves. Wandering the aisles like a shopper, but secretly eating chips and deli meat, quickly pounding down a yogurt or filling your pockets with nuts, and eating them one at a time. You stash the empty packets or tubs of anything you eat, in behind other products on the shelves and then you just roll out, free of any incriminating evidence.

You can spend all day in the warm library on a cushion educating yourself.

There are toilets there and you can kind of wash yourself in the sinks. There is a good drinking fountain in the library too, so you can stay hydrated.

You can watch all the new release movies. Once a movie has started the ticket takers leave... so you can sneak into the movies. Then stay in the inner movie theater area, hiding in the toilets between shows. This way you can watch movies all day.

You can get free cigarettes. Outside of expensive hotels, there are these small golden pillars with a little sandbox on top of them. This is a special rich people's ashtray.

The rich old ladies come outside to smoke but they only take a couple of puffs and then put the cigarette out, leaving 80% of it unsmoked. This is called an MB, or "Millionaire Butt". You get a cigarette packet and do the rounds of the high-end hotels and load up. Never again will you have to reach down shamefaced for a tiny GB, or "Gutter Butt" as it's called on the streets.

Of course, there is also food court leftover feasts and dumpster diving, fruit from people's trees if in season, or sneaking into people's backyard gardens at night, to silently dig up carrots and wash them even more silently with their garden hose, followed by shame-eating these vegetables behind their garden sheds.

Note that there is no begging in this street survival system.

Two reasons for this:

1) No New Zealander would give anyone any money, as they know full well that there is a rigid social welfare system. You could just hand yourself into the social welfare office and they would set you up in a halfway house, and within 24 hours you would be in a hi-viz vest, sweeping up gutter butts or scraping chewing gum off the sidewalks, for minimum wage with a nice cut taken out for your room and board.

2) No New Zealander would give anyone any money. It's just not done.

It wasn't even an idea that a person would think of doing even if they were on the streets because a huge percentage of NZers are descendants of the Scotts which genetically prevents giving anything at all away.

So yes, being on the streets was totally unneeded. I could have fallen on social welfare, or I could have just called a parent and explained that I didn't know what I was doing, the job was a total scam and now I'm broke, alone, and on the streets.

But Fuck that. I tend to push things as far as they will go... then a bit more...

Yo ho ho. It's the hobo life for me.

So we trekked on until we came to a freeway overpass near the city and went up the embankment and under where there was a space to put our sleeping bags on the hard concrete, in the dark.

Of course, it was freezing and there was no light as it was 1994 and we had no cellphones with lights on them. But we hunkered down.

Exhausted... on the damp hard cold ground.

Within about 5 minutes of lying down, I heard the tall heavy metal guy muttering in discomfort... and then he got up and started packing his sleeping bag.

"Fuck this shit! I have a friend here, I'm going to bang on his window and see If I can stay with him"

Me: "Do you think I could stay too?"

Him: "Nup".

And he just rolled on out like a fucking traitor. Leaving me to become a legit hobo.

The feeling of suddenly becoming a totally alone legit hobo made me actually shift mental gears. I felt an instant change blossom in my 17 year old newly-minted hobo brain.

I was better and tougher than the older heavy metal guy. This was obvious... as I was here, lying on the concrete being a legit hobo and he had folded up like a cheap plastic deck chair, and gone scurrying, like the lap dog he was.

One thing the world did not know, was that I had an edge because I had been training for this day for years.

When I was 15 I had started peeking behind the curtain of my possible future.

I was reading a lot of Beatnik books from the 50s and 60s and this, coupled with the beginnings of a number of bad life decisions I had started to make, culminated in a moment of clarity, while mid the out-window-stare, during science class.

The insight was that If I continued along this bad boy path, I was 100% going to wind up living on the streets. Instead of a course correct, I had a better idea.

What I did was take my bed apart and put it upstairs in the loft and practice sleeping on the floor of my bedroom with no pillow or duvet but in all my clothes and only my big blue trench coat for warmth.

It was cold in my room. There was only a thin worn layer of carpet between me and the concrete.

But I pushed on through. And soon I found that I could sleep on any flat surface.

This came in handy in the next few years when I was at parties and everyone was crashing and all the beds and couches were taken. I would just lie flat on the carpet and black out.

(Not but a few years back, in my early 40s I found myself stuck at Miami airport and the passengers were being shuttled to a hotel an hour away for about 3 hours of sleep – then a shuttle back in the morning to re-check in for the new flight.

I had never seen such a bunch of miserable pampered suburbanites...

I thought "That's not me... I'm a ragamuffin from the streets!"

I found a quiet space over in a corner of the airport, lay down flat on my back, pulled my hoodie over my eyes, and slept a straight six hours. Right till it was time to board.

I had not become soft. I still fuckin had it!

So the weak fake hobo had fled leaving me to my fate. It was time to survive on the streets.

For three weeks I put all his advice to use: The sneaking into movies, the millionaire butts, the straight-up shoplifting. And, in the library I found a bean bag to chill and read on.

I found an even better place to live than the overpass. In a fallen-down chimney up in an overgrown inner city section, which I lined with cardboard and slept in. My Chimney house.

I washed in bathroom basins, and I brushed my teeth... but without a place to wash clothes and scrub myself fully, I started to really stink.

I started to get frowns from the library people, for farting up that beanbag... so I moved it round a corner into a section where no one could see me or smell me.

While sitting on the street smoking MBs I would get concerned looks from the New Zealanders.

In the first week, I would strike up a few conversations with other teens on the streets...but these were teens that were going home to soft beds and warm meals...so there was always some kind of disconnect.

I failed to impress them with the MB system ... or advice on how you can get free food by eating food court leftovers.

"What if you ate some food with spit all over it and someone had some brutal disease?" One girl said, disgustedly....

I hadn't even thought of that... At this point I started to think there was diseased spit all over the food...which led me to shoplift food more... which started to cause me panic attacks at the sight of stores.

In the second week, I stopped talking to people.

On the third I felt like I was a ghost, walking through the streets, invisible.

Stinking and looking rough. Ignored... I had become the Gutter Boss.

It was cold and rainy in this town and it was time to flee north.

Still not willing to make a collect call to a parent and admit defeat and failure... I went to the train station and snuck on-board the early morning train—to Auckland 8 hours north.

And that my friends is how to turn a dream of becoming a cool hipster badass, into living on the streets of a rainy city, alone and numb, in three easy steps.

From a warm bed, hot meals, and good friends... to living in a fallen-down chimney, reeking of ass and 73% twisted, within 25 days.

And it gets worse of course.

Chapter 18
WORZEL WEZ (I become a living scarecrow man)

So there I was... a young man. It was heading toward a dark and dingy NZ Autumn.

I was 17, and certain wrong turns along the road of life had found me living in the central hollow of a large tree at the bottom of Albert Park in central Auckland.

I had a small backpack containing my worldly possessions, which were two pairs of pants, a woolen jersey, a few shirts, a pencil case, and a notebook filled with assorted musings and scribbles.

I wore a long dark-blue trench coat and black army boots. Both would keep me warm as I curled up in the hollow of the tree to sleep the darkened shivering sleep of the homeless.

I once had a good sleeping bag ... but I had sold the sleeping bag for forty dollars and was going with the super lightweight hobo option. One of many incorrect decisions I would make over the next few years.

I lived in that park for almost two months, most of the fall of 94.

I was a lost child of Nirvana.

One of the few who the nihilistic grunge tornado had left lying battered and confused in its torn, spiraling wake. A product of bongs, bags of wine and the album "Nevermind".

I would wake and peer about for passers-by before leaping out into the freezing dawn.

The only people who ever visited the hollow tree were drunk students coming from the nearby university and needing to piss, but I would gibber and yell like a lunatic when I heard someone climbing in, scaring them away.

I would wander around downtown talking to random people about random things, sneak into movies, scrounge smokes and feed pigeons small rolled-up bits of paper.

For food, I would wander into food courts and scarf down the remains of up to 10 meals in an hour.

HOBO LIFE HACK: following skinny middle-aged women about, is a good source of streetcarbs.

Staggering from the food court, with a bloated belly, all the goodies sloshing about in me from the dregs of 6 Cokes; I would lie on the pavement outside for an hour as I was so bursting it was too painful to walk.

For the rare shower (going with the warming and protective layer of filth option 9 days out of 10), I would sneak into the University gym where there was hot water and soap slivers aplenty.

I had started hanging out at the university more and more because of the facilities and game rooms. It did have its own little food court but the leavings of the starving students of New Zealand were slim.

I tried to make friends... it didn't go down well. They called me Worzel Gummidge after the Living Scarecrow man from "Worzel Gummidge" the BBC children's program. You-tube look up that demented shit. Worzel lived in a park, ate of the rubbish bins, and went on all sorts of Zany adventures.

The university students were mean to me, they were uncaring.

People are strange, When you're a stranger, Faces look ugly, When you're alone. Women seem wicked, When you're unwanted, Streets are uneven, When you're down. My boy Jim knew my plight.

It got so bad after a total of 55 days in that tree, and I had a freezing cold, late night meltdown and decided I would get a job! Back into the world of the living.

Being a FUCKING BUM had run its course. I decided that I had passed whatever demented legitimacy test I had set for myself and I felt the fire rise.

Taking time out of my busy schedule, I went to the gym showers.

There I scrounged many soap slivers off the floor, which I pressed together into a ball and used this ball to clean my spare shirt, my spare pants, and the scum from my manky greased-out skinny body.

I found a discarded razor and used it to skin the weeks of matted fuzz from my face.

Attempting to dry my clothes under the gray autumn sky met with limited success so I put them on damp and headed down the main street of town to get a job. I was sure I was in for a grueling and horrible ordeal where I would be seen for what I was, a Worzel Gummidge, and sent packing... but no!

I came to the door of Wendy's Hamburgers and the delicious smell of what I would later come to call "Wend" sucked me to the counter. I said, "I want a job!"

The Dude said, "I'll get the manager"

The Manager said, "Here's your mop, and here's your uniform"

I was in, and the proud owner of a clean dry Uniform! The warming goodness of 100% Rayon.

I soon got given the job of the upstairs dining room table-clearer-awayer and that meant all the half-eaten Wend I could scarf down when no one was watching. As I had nowhere to go and nothing to do, I worked from 8 am till 10 pm. Retiring to my tree after work, to sleep the sleep of the happy and Wend bloated.

Three days after I started, disaster struck, and I don't mean the mini-disaster of being caught stuffing down half-eaten taco salads (a valuable source of cheese) either.

I was emerging from my tree at 7 am to get ready to start, and the early morning Wendy's crew caught me as they headed through the park on their way to work.

After they questioned me and discovered that I actually was living in the tree and the laughter stopped, I begged them not to tell anyone at Wendy's. They promised they would not tell. When I arrived the laughter and mocking Ewok jokes gave away the fact that they had immediately told everyone. The manager called me in and asked if it was true.

I told him a tale of youth gone astray and how this job was my ticket out of the tree and into somewhere lovely, like a dank cellar or maybe even a moldy-smelling basement.

When he stopped laughing, he told me he would lock me in the restaurant overnight, and I could sleep in the upstairs dining room until morning, as long as I hid down from the windows and didn't let anyone see me. Then I could wake up and work until close. When he asked what I had been living on, I tried to convince him it was leaves, twigs, and grubs and not half-eaten burgers and scooped-out baked potato rinds, or leftover cold fries that I would hide in my pockets and then shame eat, in the bathroom.

Payday came and my hard work had seen me receive a whopping check of about 400 dollars for around 90 hours work. I was back in the game! A real human boy!

I secured myself a place to live for 40 dollars a week in the laundry of a student flat. I lived between the washer and the drier in a huge mounded nest of clothes I had bought for 5 dollars per garbage bag full from the Salvation Army. When it was cold I would burrow deep into the nest; when it got really cold, I would just layer up with the old man suits.

Life was good.

I continued to work at Wendy's for about six months. And due to my food foraging skills, I never had a food bill!

I still love Wendy's to this day... and strangely I formed a powerful attachment to red-headed women. seeking them out over all others... as a few future stories will detail.

Chapter 19
ESCAPING FROM BAD MEN THAT LOOK OUT FOR TEEN RUNAWAYS
(How I Escaped from a sex predator's rape dungeon)

Now, I know that in the last story I already detailed how I got OUT of the tree where I lived, and how I upgraded to working at Wendy's and living in the dank laundry of a student flat, down under the stairs between the washer and dryer... BUT... I was in that tree in the park for 55 days.

Many crazy things happened while I lived in that park... and this next is one of those crazy things...One of the many factual risks of trying to "keep it real" by living the legit street life, is that there are bad men who look out for lost teens living rough, and who try to lure them; using money, food and a place to stay; into a twisted and scary situation.

So there I was .... a young man...

I had not been warned of such bad men as I had no mentors in the street life, and it was not a subject in school. Put a condom on? Yes. How brutal abortions are? Yes.

How to survive a sex predator kidnapping you as a young man on the streets ... no.

I was living in a park as detailed in the story Worzel, and it was my penchant to chat with anyone who hung about in this park.

Well, this guy chilling on the park bench looked cool.

Within a few minutes he had discovered that I lived in the park and was a cool drifter, and I discovered that he was a hip guy who was really fun!

Let's call him Aldo. I have blocked out his real name. It might have actually even been Aldo...

Aldo was Foreign... a dark-skinned dutch guy... Moroccan or something...but from Holland...

He invited me on a cool trip! An hour north beyond Auckland to the hot pools!

I explained I have no money and live in the park, so I could not actually come as I can't pay for anything and have to be near the food courts and dumpsters so I can eat.

Oh, that wouldn't be a problem... he would pay for everything.

Wow! I couldn't believe my luck.

So I went with him to his car and off we went to his house to pick up some things.

He took me into his bedroom at his house and there was a double bed in there and a sofa. Sitting on the sofa was some red-headed guy, who looked about 19. Smoking. He was just sitting there looking a bit nuts.

I said Hi... the guy said nothing.

Aldo said "This is our bedroom"

OK – no red flags there... I didn't even register the gay rapey vibes. I was just thinking about the pools and the food.

So we piled into his car, chain-smoking redhead dude in the front and me in the back and we listened to Queen and chatted and drove north. Well me and Aldo chatted... there was just a sort of fearful abused silence from the red-headed dude.

Ok... I now thought this was slightly weird... maybe he's having a bad day...

We got to the Hot Pool place and Aldo bought me an awesome big fish and chips meal and both of them sat and watched me eat it. Also a bit weird...

Then we got into the big hot pools with all the other people.

This was great, there was a projector playing a movie, (Dick Tracy) there were pretty girls and I was fed and happy.

I kept going off to chat with girls and stare at bikini-covered boobs.

I do remember one particular girl with a saucy tiger-striped bikini top that caught my interest. She was happy to chat with me about TV shows and her favorite ice-creams.

Aldo was actually getting mad at me now for not hanging out with them, and any time I started chatting to a gal he would come over and scare them away being fucking weird and creepy!!

This was New Zealand in the early 90s... and if you were a foreigner and not a tourist you were viewed quite suspiciously. I remember back in my rural hometown, my Grandmother saying: "There's Japs downtown now! Your Grandfather fought them in the War you know!" I said "Yeah, he probably killed their grandparents. So we better watch out, but we have lots of guns so I'll take them out as they come down the driveway." This calmed her down.

I digress...

Aldo had managed to scare all the girls away out of the pool by being a total creeper and I was starting to see that he was not altogether nice.

When they were gone he excitedly said "We should get a private spa where we can take our pants off!"

Well, that sounded pretty gay, and about a million times less fun than chatting to good-looking gals in bikinis while in a hot pool with a movie playing, so I declined.

Aldo went off to sulk with the silent red-headed guy but before long they were both out and dressed and ready to leave. I guess because the pants-less spa pool dream was over and so there was no reason to be here.

We drove back to the city in what I hoped was going to be a weird silence. But Aldo was a chatty one. His topic of choice for the ride back was different kinds of sex toys. He kept this up with enthusiasm and kept looking at me in the rear view mirror and winking.

Now this was starting to slightly freak me out.

I was tough and had experienced a lot, but this was my first sex predator attempted kidnapping... I made a plan. It was: Don't go with him back to his house and get involved in dodgy stuff.

A good strong plan that was. We were at traffic lights close to the center of the city when he said: "Hey let's go back to my house, I've got some great Dutch porno movies to watch" NOOOOOOOPE!

That was my cue. My answer was to open the car door and run. Didn't even close it.

Just out and gone! Sprinting.

I told about 20 people in that park to watch out for him and maybe he got the message... I never saw him again. On telling a few other street kids the story they said they had also been approached by him for the dinner-and-swim-trip/trap combo. But they knew the game.

One runaway said he had a system that he used for these predators:

"Agree with them and pretend you are keen and go back to their houses with them, then hang out talking for a while in their house eating food and drinking their booze. When you feel ready, just absolutely beat the shit out of them and steal all their money and booze and any other expensive stuff you can. They don't go to the cops. Because what are they going to say?"

He had done this twice. I said "What if they are real tough like Aldo?

"Well then you just get raped and killed. Don't go with ones that you can't beat up dummy."

I decided to skip the whole bash sex predators system and just hide better and not talk to creeper guys who were too keen to chat

Chapter 20
THE GIRL FROM THE ISLAND (I become an ensorceled spaz because of witch tits)

As I have said I lived a block away in the downstairs laundry of a group of pseudo-intellectual university students.

I lived between the washer and the dryer in a huge mounded nest of moldy-smelling clothes I had bought from the Salvation Army. When it was cold I would burrow deep into the nest; when it got really cold, I would just put another old man suit on.

I lived in my Wendy's uniform most days, and was given the name Wendy Pretendy, by the young Christians that would eat in the upstairs dining room and try to convert me. "Wendy Pretendy" because I said I thought God was awesome and he understood and loved me but I was not into following rules made up by churches.

So I was like Jesus.

And that meant that I would not join their little bible group of sexually frustrated misery...I of course did not say that... but I didn't need to... as I inferred it with a facial expression.

I still liked to talk to them, and it annoyed them so much that one guy called me "Wendy Pretendy."

I told him that Jesus is now angry at him, because it says in the Bible, "And the King shall answer and say unto them, Verily I say unto you, Inasmuch as ye have done it unto one of the least of these my brethren, ye have done it unto me"... I then added "*So*, as I am just a recently homeless Wendy's guy, I'm definitely qualifying in the 'least category'... and thus you will be punished by his dad—God."

His jaw fell down in such shock and terror that I almost felt bad.

At boarding school I did six hours of Bible study a week for two years. My memory is good, as I have detailed in my three part Boarding School saga. We had to learn pages of poetry by rote, a few bible verses were nothing compared to Paul Revere's ride...

They stopped coming entirely after that.

That made me feel like God was mad with ME and the Devil had his eye on me... and oh how right I was about that...as you will now hear...

As I have said, I lived mostly on the left overs of the upstairs Wendy's dining room, as my job was Upstairs Dining Room Cleaner Guy. And clean I did. Pounding down all the scooped out baked potatoes and leftover taco salad bases I could eat.

Once someone actually left a fully uneaten and wrapped Junior Bacon Cheeseburger behind. They must have been foreigners... as no Kiwi would ever waste that much food. That made my day. I still clearly remember it now, 30 years later.

It was a bit cold but I savored every bite. The bacon had hardened slightly... the mayo congealed, but the sugaryness of the bun pushed it through.

I relished every cold bite and the saving of two dollars. I was literally eating money.

Ok that's the scene.

Onto this scene walked a girl. Straight, jet black hair, black, arty clothes.... a black lace choker...very white...well fed...big big tits... with that hunted nervous look of 90s parental abandonment and low self esteem.

I looked at her a few times and smiled.

She smiled back. Our damage beams crossed flows. There was an energy connection. Just two kids grinding through life on our leather asses.

We started chatting and I got her story...

She lived in some kind of big hippy share house on Waiheke island...

This island had always been a bougie sanctuary for the rich, a 40 minute ferry ride from Auckland... You should look it up online to really see what that place was like. It's really quite something.

She had gone to a Waldorf school her whole life. There were no warning bells at this point, but later in life, I was to decide that the kids who were products of these schools had a hard time fitting in with their fellow humans... not as bad as full blown bowl cut, sweater vest wearing homeschool kids... but in the same ballpark... and they should be avoided at all costs.

You would be in someone's kitchen at a party, looking for food to steal and suddenly, some dork in the corner would spout off about the Roman empire dying out because of lead in the pipes or the wine, or some shit that vikings didn't actually wear horned helmets, and it was just popularized because of a German opera or something. and you knew you were dealing with one of these Waldorf spazzes.

She was now at some art school.

I cannot remember what combination of bardic lathiro words or phrases I uttered... or if it was just a raw mix of sparkly eyes technique and smiling...but, after we chatted for a while, she invited me to stay with her at her house that night!

Madness. She was obviously insane. But then so was I, so bring it on!

She hung about till I wrapped up work and we went down the street and got on the Ferry to Waiheke Island. We stood at the front of the ferry and she spread out her arms with me holding her, way before it was a thing.

I was the king of the world.

She said she didn't really get on with her mum...who drove a taxi on the Island and was a lesbian, but her mum would be picking us up and giving us a lift to the place she lived.

Wow. This was NZ in the 90s. I had never met a real lesbian. But I had bought this ticket and was taking the ride...so I was ready to impress the lesbian mum of the strange girl who I was going to stay the night with...

The black taxi van pulled up and a tall good looking woman with short blond hair and a black leather biker hat and a black leather vest and black leather pants got out and shook my hand strongly...

She had me sit up with her at the front, where she asked me a million questions, finding each of my answers hilarious. This jazzed me up real good.

(As I write this it's freaky to think... looking at my memory of the mum... she was probably 38 or so... ten years YOUNGER than I am now!)

So she dropped us off at the hippie house that the gal lived in and it was a mansion! Decked out in native woods and massive windows, on a huge landscaped garden lot, tucked away in the bush with amazing trees and plants. It was filled with soft hippie fairy lights and three bathrooms, each with a giant bath next to a big window overlooking the bush.

This was so wondrous it was messing me up. It was like some kind of mushroom fairy fantasy... but of course, it was to get way more nuts as my adventures always seemed to do.

There was apparently no one else home! So she showed me around the hippie mansion and then her room, which was amazing.

The hippie boudoir extreme. It had its own hippie bathroom and a nice high balcony overlooking the forest and beach in the distance...

She drew us a massive bubble bath.. we got in and washed each other with nice hippie soaps. She told me to stay in there and soak because I reeked of Wendy's...(a very common complaint by those close to me at that time...) and she got out.

Then I heard her talking to someone in her room and lots of girlish laughing and shrieking... she had put on Depeche Mode... and now her and whoever it was were singing along.

I eventually got out. She introduced me to her friend. A tall big girl with massive boobs and tons of long red hair, wearing a flowing diaphanous purple fey gown... They were now drinking what they told me were "Tequila Sunrises".

Something I had never heard of. But it was brightly colored layers of red, yellow and orange, full of good booze and yummy...

So they give me a tequila sunrise and I'm sitting on the bed watching them dance and sing to me provocatively... we talk...smoke hand rolled drum ciggies inside, because it's the early 90s and we fucking rule... we laugh ... dance and drink ... on and on twirling into the dark night.

I felt like I was under a spell of some kind. I have never felt so ENSORCELLED in my life...

One does not become ENSORCELLED in regular human existence... but I was on the fringe.. and thus in constant danger of ENSORCELLMENT, as I tell of in many of my stories.

OK... so where is this going? This is not what I thought was going to happen... I thought there was going to be a romantic night with walks on the beach and then awesome all night repeated sex with my new girlfriend that I had just met in the Wendy's dining room that day. Because that's how we rolled back in the 90s.

We didd't just fuck our phones or sit about asking permission to be each others' simps.

We just got in there and ripped into each other. A simpler, more feral time...

Anyway they decide it's bedtime... they strip off to panties only ... bra off boobs out...and tell me that I can wear my boxers and sleep between them but no touching allowed.

Now this bed is a queen... but both girls are lanky and tall and bigger and way better fed than me... so I'm kind of squashed in the middle and they both turn to face me and say ...

"Put your face between our boobs." Yes we would say boobs back in early 90s NZ...

OK... so at this point I'm kind of stressing out... like what the fuck is this...?

But I think maybe it's like a crazy sex game thing and the rewards for my obedience will be unbelievable...

There were no prior signs that anything like this was going to happen so it was really confusing me... but anyway... I spent some time putting my face in between their boobs, with no other touching or anything... until I was half out of my mind.

Then the gal said "OK you can cuddle up to us but you aren't allowed to shake or move or try to have sex with us."

That was hard. Excuse the pun. But I managed.

I switched over from one to the other. Cuddling through the night.

It was an excruciating combination of erect restraint to not shake or move or try to have sex.

But it was also bliss. I knew in my heart that it's unlikely any 17 year old in the world would ever have had or would have this experience.

But all night I was praying something more would happen.

Nothing did.

Morning came, they were up and dressed and had made us an amazing breakfast of french toast, tea and fruit on the balcony overlooking the forest and beach.

So we ate that and I just sat there like a quiet ensorcelled spaz.

What now...? I was a good boy all night.. there must be a reward.

Maybe tonight!??! I thought... it's all a test...

The gal said "Well I have lots of art school stuff to do, so can you take him back to the Ferry?"

The other gal said "Sure" I was so confused... I just said "Thanks for the great night."... and shook her hand! Like the emasculated mong that I had somehow become.

Irreparably damaged from an entire night of Jizz backing up into my brain most likely... And we rolled out in her blue VW beetle to the ferry. In the car park before getting out I had regained some of my wits and I turned to the redhead and said...

"So what the fuck was last night all about really.... like what was going on... I don't get it?" She said "Kiss me and I'll tell you."

I leaped at that opportunity and when I drew back for breath she said.

"There is nothing to get...we are witches. Now get out of here or you will miss the ferry" My exact thoughts were:

"Fuck this!....Fucking WITCHES? What ... The ... FUUUUUCK!"

Horny and annoyed, I got out and got on the ferry.

I looked back to the island that now seemed to have a sinister cast... the leather clad mother... the strange brightly colored potions of the tequila sunrise... the frozen images of the massive boobs in my face, the feeling of big bodies with me trapped in the middle.

I had lived a rough life and experienced many mad things... but nothing could have prepared me for this. It was a true witchy spell.

Sorcery of the first order. I had some kind of mental episode on that ferry on the way back.

Fuses blowing in my brain... crying a bit... I went a bit nuts... a few "Who Am I?" and "Am I a man?" Moments...

An awesome mental fragmentation to pancake on top of the rest....

What saved me was one week later I was in the arms of another redhead witch, as will be detailed in the next story Witchy Chin.

That was healing of the first order, and from that point on in my life I sought out relationships with red-headed women (witches if possible) whenever I could.

Which of course must have been part of the witchy spell...

Chapter 21
WITCHY CHIN (I was surrounded by witches... They were coming in the goddam window)

So there I was a young man. Location Central Auckland New Zealand. Queen Street.

Age 17. In the prime of health. I was happily getting overweight and had greasy skin and pimples on my legs. For months I had been feeding myself on a festering diet of coke, shoplifted candy, Wendy's, and the occasional Chinese feed, foraged homeless-man style from nearby food courts.

But I was always walking everywhere in my heavy trench coat and army boots, and converting the sugars and fats into AWESOMENESS.

Having grown up in a household where there never seemed to be quite enough food, and always being in a skinny state of perpetual hunger as a youth, I was now overcompensating. Life was good.

I worked at Wendy's. I loved it. I ate all the leftovers in the upper dining room.

There were no cameras back then. No one could see anything going on.

I would stay in the upstairs storage room reading books. When I heard someone putting in the code for the door I would put the book away and start wiping down stacks of trays.

Every 30 min or so, I would do a round of the dining room. Clear tables away, do garbage runs if needed and eat any leftovers. A simple and good life in a simple and good time.

I lived up the road, in the downstairs laundry of a group of pseudo-intellectual university students. This was the progression from my pissy-smelling hole in the tree home. After the first payday, I had secured myself a place to live for 40 dollars a week in this laundry. I lived between the washer and the drier in a huge mounded nest of moldy-smelling clothes I had bought from the Salvation Army. When it was cold I would burrow deep into the nest; when it got really cold, I would just put another old man suit on.

I wasn't allowed in the house nor was I to speak to them unless spoken to. They called me "The Troll" or "The Wendy's Guy." I assured them I had a lot of cool things to say and they fobbed me off in an ultra-hip fashion with, "We know you do—That is why you are not to speak to us."

What did I know eh? To them, I was just a greasy trench coat-wearing maniac kid.

I didn't care! I had my own thing rolling, cool stuff that nobody knew about.

One thing they didn't know about was that I put the drier on and loaded it with some of my clothes pile in the middle of the cold nights, receiving the double whammy of warmth from the hot strange smelling air that blew out the back of the drier and then the hot clothes that I pulled steaming from the machine. I would mound these super-heated clothes over me for a few minutes of life-saving warmth, then when it got too cold I would repeat this procedure.

If you ever do this, be very careful of metal buttons. Those bastards tend to heat up quite a bit!

The other awesome "cool stuff that they didn't know about" was my Friday and Saturday nights.

Weekdays were spent working from 7 till 4 and after that, I spent most of my time annoying people and hanging out in the games rooms of the university where I would also occasionally shower in the gym changing rooms.

When Friday came I would finish work and start off my night of fun by actually *buying* two bacon cheese burgers and a biggie fries for carb and fat-filled staying power, and then I would drink a "Big Slam" of Mountain Dew. I did not know it was caffeinated.

NZ sold what was called THE BIG SLAM. One-litre bottle of Mountain Dew for $2, and this was good.

I would buy another Big Slam, to stash in one of the many inner and hidden pockets of my heavy trench coat. Into the pockets would go my superhero/vigilante kit.

A six-inch army knife, a heavy steel knuckle duster, a 10-inch long lead cosh, taped around and around with duct tape, a butterfly knife, and a small red vegetable knife that I had sharpened both sides of the blade of to turn it into an instrument of secret stabbing power. I also had a small glass bottle full of petrol in case I felt something needed to be torched... but more often than not I left that one at home.

Surprisingly at this point in my life, I wasn't doing any drugs... which is just as well probably. My drugs were Mountain Dew and wandering about in my trench coat, furtively peering about like a lunatic. I would also wear a brown cardigan, army pants, and large, black army boots that were two sizes too big for me, but I stuffed the ends with socks from my clothes pile.

I was a hero in my own mind called The Super Drifter!

Up Queen Street I would stride! Past cafes and night lifers and moviegoers and people driving by in cars. I was a kid from a small country town. The very whiff of traffic lights or someone hollering out obscenities as they whizzed past in a car was energizing and intoxicating to me. I would scream back at them and then buzzed from the whole rebelliousness of it would scream out long screams of "FREEEEEEE-DOOOOM!!!!!!", into the night.

Try it. If you can't do big long freedom screams into the night... there's no hope for you.

I was blazing my own trail man! Making my own way. While other 17 year olds were at home with mummy and daddy making sure they were in bed by 10, I was carving out my own little piss-ant section of existence. No one could tell me what to do. No one would know if I wound up face-down in a dumpster.

I could yell out and shriek into the night all I wanted, and if you had a problem with that I was armed and ready to fight you to the death.

. . .

I would arrive at the Ponsonby Community Center. This was the underground hardcore/punk scene of New Zealand. One small hall... 50 people. 5 bands for 5 bucks. I was there in that special time and place. I was one of the chosen. How did I find out about this place? Flyers on Telephone poles...

Often I would see a friend of mine "RA" sprawled out in the bushes or half on the pavement and half on the road. He would be absolutely munted and it always seemed like some girl would be taking care of him. One time he had all sorts of strange waxy green stuff in his spiky punk hair. I later found out it was melted crayon.

Even at such a young age, he had decided to embark on the wastrel life. He was a young punk, only 14 years old—I was 17 and on a mission so I only nodded coolly at his shouted drunk greeting, before striding inside.

He was doing his school of hard knocks young punk training. I could respect that by not interfering.

The inside was a sweaty, crowded room of exploding punk noise. I would mosh to the frenzied melodies. With my arms held around my head to protect against blows and smacks, I would keep my eyes on the ground- occasionally diving down to grab a stray dollar coin, condom, or bus pass that had flown from a partier's open pocket. I could gather from five to ten dollars throughout the night this way. I would occasionally find small bags of weed and many lighters which could be given away to older kids for a momentary and fleeting feeling of being appreciated. This feeling was like a little warm 40-watt bulb flickering on in my heart for a few seconds.

One night upon staggering exhilarated, bruised and gasping from the hall I saw a tall thin red-headed woman eyeing me like a calculating shark...

She was in her mid-20s, wearing a black leather jacket and rainbow-striped tights ending in black Dr Marten Boots.

She had a slightly witchy chin...

Not incredibly pretty, nor wholly terrifying. Definitely a woman.

Her long black painted nails drummed upon the wooden railing as she looked me up and down.

I tried to put on an air of experience and cool. I might have even tried my new "Sparkly eyes technique on her...

This may have worked... she suddenly smiled and I began to talk rapidly and hopefully convincingly.

I don't know what the hell I was going on about but before long she was leading me down the road to a park. She threw me down on the grass and in seconds I was kissing and fumbling. At one point someone yelled "Get into it mate!!!"from across the dark and shadowy park.

"SHUT THE FUCK UP AND FUCK OFF PRICK!!" She screamed at him before returning to me. Exciting.

In the middle of the hot and heavy excitement, she leaped from me and said mournfully "I can't do this! You're just going to leave me like all the rest!"

What followed was an unbelievably pitiful display of promising, pleading, and cajoling on my part. I was not suitably conversant with my own hideous and savage male teen beast nature and did not know that my own lust, when properly slaked, would seek to destroy any sort of sane relationship, not based wholly on sex or food, in the search for more and greater amounts of sex and food.

After listening to my shameful beggar-worthy appeal she grinned a witchy grin and said "OK I'll take you home."

This meant a high probability of sex and thus I was accordingly hypnotized and helpless as I was driven to her place, stripped of clothes, thrown down on the mattress and demanded to "Do this and do that now. No! That's too much!" and, "Yes! Good, but it's not enough! Faster! More! etc etc etc. etc etc etc.

It is not the purpose of the story to provide the reader with a pornographic panorama.

The final freaky twist is far too funny to bother with detailing the ability of a completely sex starved 17-year old to get another erection within a minute of spending himself; or with how it may be possible for said 17 year old to carry on through the night in this fashion, until finally after the 14th time, no amount of goading by the red-headed succubus could produce anything but a small drip, which felt like equal parts knee cartilage and blood, and caused the young man to scream out in agony, crawl to the edge of the mattress, and desperately attempt to unhunch the twitching ball of cramps his body had become.

All to The HOLE album Miss World, which played loudly and looped ALL NIGHT LONG.

To this day I cannot hear Courtney Love's voice without shivering.

Awakening from a depletion-induced unconsciousness, I saw the Witchy Chin sprawled naked on the stained mattress on the floor that was her bed.

After getting up, silently removing the (still playing) Hole CD from the player and hiding it under a book on Wicca, I took stock of my surroundings.

I had no idea that the squalid, ciggie butt, bong water, incense, ash, and spilled booze-soaked flat style of living was a sure sign of financial, and moral destitution. Coming from living on a concrete floor in a pile of clothes, with rats running across my face in the middle of the night, I thought she had it made.

The abundance of candles, crystals, sharp knives, and animal skulls gave the room a nice pagan look.

The huge hand-painted mural on the wall, depicted a gigantic bat-winged, naked, red-headed woman, holding a bloody knife and one foot raised up on a human skull, surrounded by kneeling black-robed figures and headed in Ye olde timey script with "SATANIC BLOOD ANGEL" should have made me think twice about staying in the room a moment longer... but it thought it FUCKIN RULED!

I was the boyfriend of THE SATANIC BLOOD ANGEL!

I put on undies and crept down the hallway to the kitchen. I may have done a little dance...

A skinny half-naked man on the couch said "Prancing about in your just got laid underpants eh..?" He had burns in the shape of pentagrams on his arms, a huge tattoo of a goat's head on his back, and was rolling a cigarette from the butts of the dead cigarettes in the ashtray.

I tried to smile and crept back to the room.

Witchy Chin was awake and all smiles and hellos.

I put my clothes on and she drove me to work at Wendy's.

We chatted in the car like regular humans.

She was waiting for me when I finished. I was refueled and keen. She took me back to her house and threw me in the shower, complaining that I smelled like fries and burgers...then back to the mattress.

Nature – She's a Savage Beast.

That night, there were noises coming from the ceiling and I had the horrid feeling I was being watched. It was just too creepy. Too many candles going- too much light and too much actress-like screaming (on her part of course).

This was getting a bit nuts... even by my drifter wastrel standards... and I usually LOVED things that were nuts...but this madness was just too crazy.

I felt like I was being literally drained of my soul's essence...

The next morning waking once again as a hunched and depleted husk, I realized that a normal sort of breakup would not cut it... I would have to move to another town... possibly even go into hiding...this was the end of my life in this city of course. I would have to flee Auckland.

I dressed and made sure I had everything.

I braced myself and said...

"I'm leaving, I'm off down-county to go fruit picking. I've got a new job."

Something I decided to make true that week.

She leapt off the bed fast and witchy, like a big scary jumping spider!

"THEY ALWAYS DO THIS!" She screamed!

She was a perfectly terrifying naked ginger demon. She started hurling hard sharp things from the dresser at me. I was trying hard not to laugh at the spectacle but when I was hit full in the neck by the pointy part of a goat horn, I snapped out of it. I took off toward the door.

She caught me by the hair and swung a long sharp Satan knife up towards my chin.

I saw her plan was to hold this knife against my throat and make me some kind of love hostage? But I was fast and punched her brutally hard in the left tit with all I had.

POW!

She went down with a crone-like shriek and I ran out the door and up the street and straight to Wendy's to quit and flee the city.

Star wipe to seven years later, I was back in that city at a party (actually on the roof of a party) when the evil of those nights came full circle.

I got there because I had overheard two people talking in a café and they happened to be talking about a party. They mentioned a name I recognized... The name of a slender black-clad Goth temptress that I had had a tryst with in the graveyard a short walk from the Ponsonby community center, a few weeks before the Witchey Chin episode...not worth writing a story about... It was sane PG 13 and vanilla.

Healing even. Well as healing as a graveyard hookups could be...

I never saw her again after that night. But hey it was her birthday—what better present than ME?

When the two girls left the café I followed them, calmly tailing them into the party.

I saw her in the kitchen eating a large piece of cake. She had more than quadrupled in size since I saw her last... so because I was a shallow bastard, I just kept rocking right through the party and out the other side.

There was a ladder leaning up against the roof so I climbed it and got up on the roof where I was safe.

I laughed and joked, smoked, and drank with the humans on the roof. After a while, I discovered that a freaky, wet-wool-smelling, dreadlocked, punk, feral-type girl was really, really interested in me.... This was interesting....

We talked and joked for some time...and she eventually revealed the source of her fascination...

She told me of two 2-hour VHS videos of a 17-year-old me, above, astride and under some skinny Redhead. All filmed from a secret room above Witchy Chin's room.

. . .

How had she come to watch these videos?... About a year ago she had a short and twisted relationship with a tattooed and burned satanic guy. He had a "home video" collection featuring many young men and Witchy Chin. It was obvious to me from Witchy Chin's theatrics that she was in on this.

It's scary to think that those videos of me, and likely other guys, are out there in the world somewhere... but life is funny and crazy and you just have to live it and own it.

We must experience everything, not just the good, but all of it: The pain, the degradation, the horror, the sadness, it makes us whole. It makes us People of Substance, not flighty untouched children.

Then we can know the world and when we know the world... The world is ours.

No Ragrets. Know what I'm saying?

Not even a single letter.

Chapter 22
POISON APPLE (Is this rock bottom? No, but it's a start)

So there I was a young man.. 17... alone... hungry... guts cramping with acidic knives.

Under a bridge on the outskirts of Napier, a sizable farming town in eastern New Zealand.

I was in an old sleeping bag stuffed with my clothes and scrunched-up balls of newspaper for extra warmth. I was staring into the flames of a small smoky fire, which seemed to be my only friend, the only thing that offered me comfort.

For some time I had cut myself off from my friends and family... This didn't take much doing: family gave zero shits, and old school friends were all happily living their middle class lives...I was living the lonesome hobo life again.

I had fled Auckland, and hitchhiked south east. because of Witchy Chin, as detailed in the last story...

I had a desire to live rough. This desire would take me over now and then through life, and I would just bail whatever I was doing and go and be a hobo.

I had lasted about 5 months at Wendy's. Getting some Witch sex. Surviving. Winning, Dancing.

So here I was down-country as we say... at the start of the fruit picking season.

There are feelings of aloneness in this world... and then there is under a bridge in 1993, with no money, just a few tattered books, ("THE STAND," "BRAVE NEW WORLD," "THE POTATO FACTORY") a small fire and your psychosis for company, feelings of aloneness.

Hunger would send me out in the evening into apple orchards to steal sour, pesticide-tasting apples which in a short while would turn into a briskly ejected stinging foam.

I had hitched hiked down to Napier way too early and had a week to go till I could start work in the apple orchard so I just slept and read, only venturing out from under my warm bridge and bag shelter combo to forage for food or freshly tossed roadside cigarette butts.

I KNEW I would be OK, and at some point in the future, I would be in a nice warm bed with a good meal in my belly and bag deep in the cooch of a horny woman.

My self confidence has always bordered on the level of supernaturally insane.

But for now, sleep, dreams, cramps.

The first day of the picking season came, so I packed up my smoky belongings and rode my stolen women's mountain bike (pink) to the orchard.

The kindly boss took one look at me (a hunched shivering weasel with matted, dreading, greasy hair; a month of fuzz about my face, unwashed, wearing grimy army pants, boots, six t-shirts and an unraveling, brown cardigan; teeth green and gray with mank...) and asked Do you need somewhere to stay?

So now I was sleeping on the floor of the orchard office and, during the day I worked from dawn to dusk picking as many apples as I could.

I made a friend. A fellow fruit picker who had a heavy British accent. After a day of hanging out and talking I said "Man... every single person from England I've met has been a rude, stuck up cunt, who just continually complains. But somehow... you're different. You're friendly and happy. You're the only person from England I've ever liked and gotten along with... why is that?

He said, "It's probably because I'm Irish."

. . .

I managed to beg an advance of 40 dollars from him, and rode into town at night to purchase a 5-dollar KFC meal deal (savoring every maggoty, greasy bite).

This special meal I had seen advertised outside KFC and had been dreaming of it. It was one piece of chicken. Two rolls, potato and gravy, coleslaw, chips, and a drink for $5. Carbs and fats, super gut blast.

I now was on a special extreme hobo diet of one meal of the above a day and apples.

8 KFC meals and 75 apples later was PAYDAY.

$450 dollars went into my bank account, which for the last three months had negative $4.25 in it.

Joy, pure joy, threatened to engulf me. This meant I could start my climb to success and out of the little dip I had done, into homelessness again!

I loved the success climb almost as much as I loved being a fucking bum.

Now I had money, it was mandatory that I spend a percentage of it on getting blasted in celebration to reward myself! The most important things were attended to first: Booze and food.

Roaring into town on my bike I bought a nine-dollar, 16% percent alcohol, three-liter bag of white wine.

In the liquor stores of NZ there was almost always a cut-in-half wooden wine barrel filled with what we called "baggie o' wine". Almost always bought by teenagers... the amount of poisoning and vomiting these caused was later proven to have almost single-handedly destroyed the NZ wine industry, as it created an entire generation that gagged at the smell of wine.

I stopped right outside K.F.C to spigot drain almost a liter of it down and, with the vile bittersweet fluid burning in my guts, I strode into K.F.C like a king and ordered the $9.95 Super Special, Got Bucks—Big Man Now—Going all the way to the TOP, meal deal.

The rest of the night gets a bit hazy but I do remember wandering about Napier with the diminishing bag clutched in a dirty fist and kneeling on the grass in the park purging my body of vile winey poison (my last ever drink of wine) while raising my fist in a devils salute to passing cheering teenagers and saying, "It's OK, I'm a professional."

Awaking the next morning to the sound of children playing, I scurried away from the reeking piles of greasy vomit that surrounded me and cured myself of my blindness and pain by stripping off to the waist and immersing my upper body for extended periods of time in the freezing duck pond.

Finding my bike where it lay nearby, I rode blearily back to the orchard where I lived and went about organizing my life with the new money I had!

Two days later I was sitting on the doorstep of my rented caravan, a big mug of earl grey tea in hand; belly full of tofu, avocado, and peanut butter on toast; looking out across the land, the sky purple and orange with a beautiful sunset and, within every fiber of my body, hummed the powerful thrum of possible hope, for a probable future.

I had made it back into society!

I was a real person again.

Now it was time to initiate sinister phase two of the operation... to see how high I could climb so that I could bring it all smashing down!

Chapter 23
DARK MASTER (The wooening)

THIS TOOK PLACE WHEN I HAD RECOVERED SOME OF MY sparkly eyes' strength and was living in a trailer as a fruit picker in East New Zealand, as detailed in the prior story.

Well, there I was... a young drifter, 17 years old. Eyes wide to the darkened brilliance the world can offer one, if one looks.

I would ride my bike about the town, after work, looking for people to talk to. High school kids were good. 16–17-year olds together strong! They lived in warm houses, went to school, ate good food and did what their parents said...

And I lived in a freezing caravan on an orchard and did whatever the fuck I liked because I was free. I was Kurt Cobain's beatnik disciple.

I had started referring to myself in third person as, "The Dark Master". Mental Fragmentation had begun. The Dark Master was now back on the Devils Lettuce (bought, by the joint, for $5 each, from a Maori fruit-picker guy called Rawiri. That means: one who is loved by everyone).

And I played it fast and loose sir.

After a few conversations with me these kids either took off in terror or stayed about for the Dark Master's stories such as you have been reading...

I had started dating a gal who was not only a reluctant virgin, but whose parents were also severely Christian. Many weeks of cask wine and pot fueled schmoozing in the park after school, had jazzed her up to the point where she truly wanted to have real sex with me.

Now, that weekend her parents happened to be going on a small trip away, and I had convinced her that it would be a great idea if I came round on Friday night and hung out.

There was no "Netflix and chill" back in 1994.

You just had to bang.

Well I arrive and the young vixen greets me at the door in tight, black jeans and some sort of even tighter, black half–t-shirt thing, with enough makeup to look like she had already consecrated herself as a sacrifice to the Dark Master.

So, as any drifter\wastrel would, I carry on polite conversation with her as I satiate myself with goodies from her parent's larder and hook into her father's whiskey.

My God it was good.

No phones in sight, just kids having a good time.

You gotta get this.

I'm 17, in a nice house. Johnny Walker Blue label, super-hot, keen girl who really liked me and loved my stories.

I could have died right then and there on that couch happy.

A little while later, I was irresponsibly and barebackedly taking my enthusiastic new girlfriend from behind—on her parents king-sized bed —candles burning; Iron Maiden blasting from the stereo; among her mother's religious icons; while a figurine of Jesus, nailed to his little tree, watched over us from the wall.

This had gone on maybe a minute and a half and I was deep in the vinegar strokes, grimacing and uttering silent and happy prayers as I prepared to fill her up.

Then there was this ear splitting shriek! The lights flashed on, and something fragile and shattering stabbed me in the back (parts of which I would have Rawiri help me remove the next day with a pocket knife— It was the trunk of a crystal elephant).

I slipped out, cursing... spraying goo onto her bloody thighs and generous dollops onto the cream duvet. I turned to see the screaming mother, purple with rage, charging at me and flailing slaps and claws.

Tumbling off the bed I grabbed my Iron Maiden tape (Powerslave) and my pants and shoes and dove to the door, leaving some of my hair in the fist of the poor girl's mum.

Bolting to the hall I sought to flee. To do so I had to get by her old man, who I met in the corridor.

The sight of me naked, bleeding from claw marks on my face; red, flaccid willy waving; was adequate to stun him enough that I made it past, by fending him off at full charge, and made my escape on the pink mountain bike.

Never before (and never again) will I ever ride so fast, naked on a bicycle through a middle class suburb.

Suffice to say she wasn't at the park the next day when I did a careful roll by...

I wonder what happened to that young lady, she would be 47 now... and hopefully living a happy life somewhere...

Chapter 24
WHACKY STICK (Bad kids should be beaten with sticks)

So there I was, a young man... Far away from parents, teachers, well-meaning friends with good advice, or any other civilizing influences.

I had decided I wasn't going down fast enough and so I made a phone call to a friend who was totally insane. I told him I was living in an old caravan on an apple orchard and needed a friend to go crazy with. He got off the couch at his mum's house in Wellington and drove 6 hours straight, to where I was.

As you may have surmised from reading my stories, I always felt akin to the truly demented. It was as if I needed someone crazier than I to hang with... A mutual friend in debauchery...

Pairs such as these happen now and then...
Withnail and I
Hunter S. Thompson and Oscar
Cornelius and Tyler
Thus it was with us

We had gone fully feral. Had been living in the old caravan in the back of the orchard where we worked picking apples... when we could be bothered... which wasn't often... but were now kicking back in a house... which wasn't ours.

Life was a haze of dope smoke and huge mouthfuls of "Mississippi

Blues," which was labeled as a "general-purpose alcoholic beverage." It had a trio of dank-looking Black jazz musicians and a riverboat on it...

It was a thick and syrupy dark yellow mixture that tasted like cough medicine mixed with kerosene. At 30%, and 10 dollars a liter, it was only the numbers that mattered to us... And after we had drained the filthy brew (always wincing and letting out a rebel yell followed by our catchphrase "Nature, she's a savage beast!") little mattered.

A wacky team must have a catchphrase...

We were filled with an ever-present dread. We always felt as if we were running up an ever-collapsing stairway. The type of dread that fills anyone who knows they should be being good, and yet is not heeding the voice that tells them to get this train back on the rails.

I had been not heeding that voice for so long now that I was trapped.

Trapped because I was addicted. Addicted to many things, one of them being the whacked-out, zany hi-jinks and tomfoolery-filled adventures, that *not* heeding the voice took me on.

What really got me going was DANGEROUS ADVENTURES!

I had a comrade in debauchery now. A crazed scalawag that within a few years would wind up pushing his zany hi-jinks too far, and be arrested and incarcerated in a mental hospital.

Not before I got off the crazy train though, blessed be.

People like that make great friends if you are terrified of boredom and don't want a calm-filled life. Your dear author was on this rickety mine cart... and down we go...

The stories get rougher from here... but... my motto was....

"Buy the ticket, take the ride... and if it occasionally gets a little heavier than what you had in mind, well... maybe chalk it up to forced consciousness expansion: Tune in, freak out, get beaten."

My comrade in debauchery and I were at that moment watching a raunchy Eddie Murphy comedy video, eating food taken from the fridge, drinking tequila, and smoking weed with our feet up on the glass coffee table. Nothing seems overly wrong with that scene outside of it not being very healthy.

Yet it was horribly wrong. We were jittery, Goldilocks-esque, interloping naughty fellows.

The house belonged to a Māori family who were on holiday in Fiji. Their long-awaited, hard-worked-for family holiday. Happy photos of them beamed accusingly down at us from the walls, their dark eyes following me at all times.

We were there because once again my silver tongue had won over the weak of will.

We had picked up a young hitchhiker who was on his way to feed a cat belonging to some friends of his—a Māori family who were having their first family holiday together in Fiji.

Plying him with camaraderie and stories, he let us into the house, on the promise that we would feed the cat for the next two days and then leave the place as we found it. Promises were swiftly made and we had a free hotel—complete with food, booze, and as many long-distance calls as one wanted to make.

We stayed the night in unfamiliar-smelling beds and the next day were helping ourselves to everything there (*Why not? It will probably just go rotten anyway...*) not forgetting to feed the cat, as was the arrangement.

We were men of our twisted word. So while in a peacefully paranoid state, we watched the video.

Until...

Suddenly the sliding door burst open! Screeching, in flew a skinny, wiry old Māori woman, brandishing a long, thick, dangerous-looking Whacky Stick!

She pointed at our stunned and terrified faces and proclaimed in a high shriek, "How dare you come into someone else's home and watch their TV!!"

She was red-faced and livid with rage.

I scrambled up, the silver tongue kicking in on impulse, immediately firing all the blame at the young man who had let us in, and orating a story that was being made up as rapidly as it was being told: that the young man had told us it was his uncle's house, and he had asked said uncle if we could stay a few nights, and that aforementioned uncle had said it was fine, and we were but unwitting dupes tricked into feeding a cat!

The whole time I was gathering up the weed and the booze and ramming it into my bag while edging towards the door.

My friend was not so wise and tried to make a break for the bedroom where his stuff was, not being possessed of the kind of future sight that the perpetually paranoid are darkly gifted with.

Rule number one of living in the HEAT:

"Don't let yourself get attached to anything you are not willing to walk out on in 30 seconds flat if you feel the heat around the corner."

Channeling the mana of her ancestors, she cut him off with a vicious swing of the Whacky Stick which caught him crackingly across the side of the head. He caught another one across the back as he ran into the master bedroom.

I was outside by then, cowering in the shotgun seat of the car, praying that my friend would prevail and beginning to formulate a plan if he did not and was killed.

About 30 seconds and a whole lot of swearing and crashing and repeated hard stick beatings later, my bloody-faced companion leaped out of the house and into the car, roaring it into life.

The lady was directly after him, dentingly smacking the Whacky Stick once across the bonnet. She then went to work on the left headlight, destroying it utterly with two well-placed blows.

It was to remain unfixed for over a year, a cyclopean reminder of that crazy day.

We roared backward out of the narrow, fenced-in driveway so fast and loose that the right wing mirror was ripped away and exploded into fragments.

Spinning the car about, we whizzed off into the day.

One more substantial sector of that town—a no-go zone....

Chapter 25
OUT OF TREE (Feeling the heat in an Art Deco Danger Zone)

MYSELF AND MY FRIEND IN MUTUAL DEBAUCHERY HAD GONE fully feral, in the town of Napier New Zealand... bless its Art Deco Heart...

Most of our evenings, as the sun went down, were spent driving really slowly through the huge fields of long green grass, next to the orchard, while baked on the Devil's Lettuce.

The grass reached the door handles of our beat-up blue Mazda. I would trail my hand out the window and gently touch the grass in a blissful dream world while Pink Floyd droned at us from out of the car's tinny stereo. We would drive in huge looping slow circles, listening to music, and the susurrus of the grass until the driver would fall asleep and the car would gently roll to a stop. I would reach over and turn the key off and we would sleep in the car in the field.

It's the simple pleasures, right?

Some evenings the isolation would drive us into a claustrophobic frenzy and the only solution to the feeling was to "Hit the town!"

So we would meander in, sure that we were going far too fast, and pull up by the park in the center of town where we would creep like ninjas up our "hidey tree".

We were obsessed with hiding from the world and looking down on it from above. We didn't feel right unless we were perched far up and looking way down on the world below.

Having such a remote viewpoint was the only thing that stopped the fear.

Well, it didn't really stop it. It was just that when we were hiding like that, the feeling that the whole world was after us, and that everyone was judging us and snickering, was put on hold because we had found a place to hide for a while.

We would go through periods of severe paranoia where we would have to "go to ground" and hide on the orchid for a few weeks. And then to moments where we would brazenly walk along the main street smiling at everyone and boldly involving ourselves in loopy conversations with worried looking strangers.

Now, as an older wise man... I see the mental fragmentation that was beginning...

This particular night we had decided to go to a party.

This involved driving around the suburbs until we heard one going on, then parking the car outside and psyching ourselves up to get the guts to go in.

We crept in just as the party was starting and walked through the house. We were greeted by a barking Alsatian and two smiling grown-ups who were sitting on the couch, in the lounge, having a glass of wine and listening to something from the mid-eighties.

The kindly-looking father smiled and said "The Party's upstairs boys".

So upstairs we clambered, sighing with relief that he hadn't asked us a question. We barreled into the upstairs bedroom.

A group of about ten 15 or 16-year-old girls turned to look at us.

We were stunned ... I looked about the room ... wine bottles, casks of wine, and bags of wine. My paranoid and shy friend could do nothing but shake, yet I remained calm and got to happily chatting!

No reason for our presence was given until I had them under my charming spell. By then the story of two wandering drifters who live in a caravan and cruise the streets at night looking for cool people to hang out with, seemed like a perfectly rational explanation.

The party slowly started to fill up with young men and women carrying bottles and bags, and a few of the girls left the bedroom and went downstairs to entertain.

My friend and I continued to party in the upstairs bedroom and had finished off a bottle of Mississippi blues, which was our chosen tipple....and we were leaping and prancing about the room to the music, much to the disgust of the few young rednecks who had been pushed up into the room by the growing party downstairs.

A young man came up to us and kindly asked if we would join him and his friends downstairs for a large weed-smoking session funded by them.

Yes Sir! So down the stairs, we pranced...

I did dress flamboyantly... if you wore too many bright colors in rural New Zealand you would be labeled gay immediately. I was currently wearing a gold disco jacket, a black mesh T-shirt, and fluorescent green tracksuit pants, with army boots and a red beret...

I was not gay in the 90s definition at all, I was actually wearing this peacock uniform in an effort to woo women. I was of course SUPER gay, but in the 1920s definition.

The whole party seemed to follow us out and within seconds we were standing on the lawn being called faggots by a large crowd of rednecks and Māori gang prospects.

Tricked. We were just happy rascals wanting to have a good time. This was dark...

Some poor kid pushed my friend from behind.

My friend was not only an aggressive PSYCHO, whose normal hostile tendencies were greatly exacerbated by drugs and booze... but also, he was 6 foot four, and not only very solid, but an incredible fan of superstars of wrestling

So the guy was pushed back, through two rows of surprised and sprawling people, and went upside down into the garden.

Another stupid guy tried to punch my friend in the back of the head, but wound up only delivering a glancing blow, and making my friend spin around and grab him by the neck, then flinging him to the ground with a splat, where the guy lay gasping.

An intoxicated young lady yelled at us "You better go, you're going to get beaten up!" To which my friend said "Bullshit!" and punched a random guy (whose only crime was trying to look tough and menacing) in the forehead, so hard I didn't see where he flew. The sound was so horrific it made people gasp in shock

This was strange... there seemed to be a lot of yelling yet no one actually seemed to have the balls to do anything to us anymore.

Then I saw him coming at me, a big Māori warrior gang-prospect kid who was far more than a match for little ole coughing drug addict me. I couldn't jog 50 steps without stopping for a smoke and a lie-down, let alone fight someone.

Yet my utter paranoia had prepared me for situations like this. As you may remember from previous stories I never went anywhere without a large arsenal of weapons.

As he approached I ripped the equalizer from where I had it, in its sheath strapped to my back with duct tape.

A 10 inch long army combat knife, just the thing from my collection for such a situation.

I stood in what I hoped was a professional knife fighter's stance and declared in a loud and authoritative voice. "We are now going to leave and if anyone tries to stop us I will kill them!"

My adversity looked suddenly uncertain of his future and the crowd went kind of white and cleared a path for us to escape to the car.

My friend led the way and we made it to the car but not without a bit of trouble, the Māori warrior kid was trying to get me to put the knife away and fight him, man to man, while battering me with a tirade of insults to my manliness.

Fuck that. If I was going down, I was going down stabbing.

As my friend opened the door of the car to get in, a guy attempted to punch him and my friend had to turn, grab and lift the guy up over his head, and throw him down hard onto the road where, despite all laws of physics, he bounced once and then quietly thrashed around on his back, suppressing what I'm sure was the loudest pain-scream he never uttered.

I was impressed by the staunchness of it. He didn't want to seem weak in front of the 40 or so onlookers. I was amused by how he suppressed this, so that he would not further embarrass himself in front of his friends.

We had got into the car now and I was yelling "GO GO GO!" As the revelers banged on the car and made a huge racket. Bottles smashed against the back window.

The car flared into life!... And stalled.

A triumphant cheer and laughter went up from those surrounding us but then we got going! We thought we were free.

We stopped at the lights fifty meters up the road thinking the whole show was over...but then there came a terrible whacking on my window! It was my gang prospect assaillant! He was trying to break the window so I wound it down hoping to stab him with the knife which I was firmly gripping (and would continue to firmly grip for some time to come).

Once the window was down a little bit, his pudgy hand shot through and grabbed my shirt. The car was starting to take off and I had only a small amount of time to inflict as much damage as possible.

So, in one fluid motion (like the matrix only cooler) I wound the window up on his arm, grabbed his little finger and bent it back until it lay flat against the back of his hand and, at the same time, I savagely bit into his hand with all my strength, trying as hard as I could to make my teeth connect with bone. This caused him to scream and rip his hand back so fast, that it wrench-slammed my head up against the door, almost knocking me out.

We sped away and I was left with a mouthful of foul-tasting hot blood, and large chunks of ragged flesh which I spat out the window.

Two cars were now chasing us, and so we blasted through the streets of this town as fast as we could handle. We evaded them after a few minutes with the old "indicate-right, then turn left at high-speed trick," and roared back to our caravan, where we sat shaking and ranting, replaying every exciting moment.

I then for some insane reason decided to call the police from the phone in the orchard office and tell them what happened.

The sergeant who I talked with, politely listened to the story and then told me that we should immediately come into the police station to "sort all this out" as people from the party had called them saying that some guy had pulled a knife and threatened to kill everyone.

I assured him that that was not the case and promised to come to the station immediately to "sort it all out".

Fuck that shit. We did what we did best—we fled.

Minutes later we were packed (Remember rule number 1? "Don't let yourself get attached to anything you are not willing to walk out on in 30 seconds flat if you feel the heat around the corner.") and in the car roaring south toward Wellington—safely driving at a few Ks under the speed limit and heading onward, toward new realms of adventure and confusion, which the next few stories will detail.

Chapter 26
ON THE COUCH OFF THE COUCH (The decision to pretend to get our shit together came suddenly)

WE HAD FLED NAPIER AFTER THE SHIT THAT WENT DOWN AS detailed in the last story, and drove 6 straight hours to Wellington.

We rolled up to his place and we moved in and started living there with his mum.

Harried, 47. (Wow... my age now...) had a 7-year-old kid to some random. Worked as a bank teller. Miserable as fuck. Good bottle and a half of mid-range red a night. Real class act.

Me and my mate were 18... and he had a 5-gallon metal bucket packed full of stolen weed that he had hidden under the shed out the back.

So we started living there, and by living, I mean spending all day on the couch blazing weed and watching TV while my mate screamed at his mum to bring us food...

Which she would, bless her. We fell into a good solid routine.

Wake up 2:00 p.m.

Lie on the couch, starve till his mum got home, then eat the food that was brought to us, smoke bowl after bowl of spirit-crushing, mind-numbing old dope and watch "SKY TV" (the eight cable channels you could get in NZ for 20 dollars a month).

6:00 p.m. Go for a walk down to the beach and breathe in the healing salt air.

Lyall Bay it was.

It's important to get out of the house and get exercise and some small bit of light.

7:00 p.m. Back to the couch.

Midnight. Crawl to our respective rooms and black out.

Sleep 14 hours a day.

On Friday we would get the bus downtown and wander about seeking hidey places to look out at the world from, and smoke dope in.

Commenting on people while refusing to interact with anyone but shopkeepers.

That was the rules.

Sometimes we would get baked and then go to Pizza Hut then to a movie.

At Pizza Hut we would buy a 1-litre carafe of white wine each, and pound it while each eating a large Hawaiian pizza. Life was simple.

Working our way through the big cookie tin of weed. Full TV world plus hiding. Pizza Hut feasts... and the movies. We had had enough adventure and excitement out there in the big bad world. It was not to last forever though.

We refused to listen to the well-meaning, shrill and ranty advice of his mother, about how we should do some higher education (excuse the pun) or perish the thought, get a job!

We ignored her, mostly replying in grunts, and if she was interrupting a show my friend would get up from the couch in a rage and force her out the door of the lounge, while I stared mullet-like at the Box trying to hear the show over her loud screams of protest.

After about two months of this she told on us to her huge and angry bricklayer brother who took it upon himself to burst through the door one night.

In the middle of *The A-Team* too, the cheek of it.

"STAND THE FUCK UP!" he yelled at our degenerate zombie-like forms.

We burst up off the couch like there were snakes on it, and were standing at attention in seconds, while he battered us with an angry verbal tirade that tore tattered holes in our fragile stoner-life belief system.

He gave us a simple choice—a 180-degree life change, forsaking our warm, cozy, numb lives of 8 hours of being "awake" per day and straightening the fuck up, or being beaten like the insolent children we were and then dragged out onto the street, not necessarily in that order.

Within 3 minutes we had promised to go to the city's polytechnic and learn ourselves up on some sort of skill that would facilitate our smooth transition off the couches and into the real world of people living gainful, productive lives.

Even for us in our degenerate dream state it was not a hard decision...

1994. Tough love at its finest.

So we went to the polytechnic and did the easiest course they had. Tourism and Hospitality. Sadly, this just got us into contact with harder drugs and contact with more losers like us who had been kicked off couches by screaming parents.

A polytechnic is often like a government-funded community college for fucking losers... Sometimes it's not... there did seem to be some people paying attention there... but I didn't talk to them... We didn't last long there, just a few months. The whole getting-up-in-the-morning thing wasn't really for us.

So we fled back to the North... to our friend's oasis of ill repute.

The Purangi Winery, located on the east coast of Coromandel Peninsula, which was our original home.

Our friend's hippie dad owned it.

It was a haven where a young man could while away the hours of the day, drinking before staggering through the undergrowth looking for good places to fall unconscious in the recovery position.

We spent a few weeks there living in a rotted-out caravan.

Back when we were 15 and 16... School kids, full of hope, we would head out and stay over at this friend's place on weekends, at the winery. I remember an interesting conversation with my father at the dinner table, having just turned 17, once the school year ended.

Me: "I'm not going back to school next year."

Him: "OK! So you're going to come up into the bush and work for me?" (He owned a large logging company.)

Me: "No. I'm going to have a wee rest."

Him: "Like fuck you are! Not on my fucking dime you're not!"
Me: "Well then I'll go work at the winery."
Him: "You'll fuckin' die."
Me: "Yes... I may die... But at least I'll die free."
(I did basically die three times.

1. Alcohol poisoning.
2. Going over a cliff in a car, while all of us drunk.
3. Swimming in big waves at Hot Water Beach while stoned and drunk after spending hours in the sun. But you cannot kill that which does not live. So I rallied to keep partying.;)

My dad knew what "working at the winery" meant for a young skallywag of 17. A summer of doing about 2–3 hours of faking work about the winery during the day, then spending the rest of the day blazing weed and pounding liqueurs.

Then an afternoon of cruising the beach looking for tourist girls to bring back to the winery half-barrel jury-rig spa pool we had made.

"Hey come to our winery!"

Swedes and Norwegian girls YES.

Germans and French NO!

Brits if you were desperate or an animal. So maybe...

Weed and wine and a floating salami and cheese board in the tub and if the stars aligned and your date didn't barf or black out and half-drown, you were in for a good night.

No phones in sight... just lots of looking into each other's faces and telling stories to each other till you were so horny you ripped each other's clothes off and spent the rest of the night rolling about on top of a stinking and stained sleeping bag giggling and panting.

If you're over 40 you know what I mean.

Forgive me... I digress... into Gen X nostalgia...

Now, I was not the person at 18 who had arrived at that winery a year earlier at 17, all free from school and full of vim and hope for the future. The happy-go-lucky extrovert I used to be had become a crazed Gollum-like creature...

The Engollumfication is detailed in the previous 13 stories. All taking place in my *Annus Horribilis*: 1993. We showed up... insane... and on the run from the weasels...

We stayed a week but we were too nuts even for the standards of our winery mates... and so we drank our fill of the place, but I knew we had to move on...

"Jesus! Bad waves of paranoia, madness, fear and loathing, intolerable vibrations in this place. Get out! The weasels were closing in. I could smell the ugly brutes."

I decided we had to "go to ground" and hide until the storm blew over.

We had to find a good place to lie low which was comfortable and secure from the ravages of all and any semblance of responsibilities, dirty looks, worried glances, concerned conversations about facing life, or any chance of running into school friends from a year before and having them ask "Bro, are you ok? Cause you look well munted."

The compatriot had a place in mind.

Great Barrier Island – The promised land.

Chapter 27
STOOLS—I live, I die, I live again

THIS STORY TAKES PLACE WHILE WE WERE AT THE POLYTECH before we fled to the winery...

Disclaimer: I am now drug free 28 years, and have worked in the Chemical Dependency field for over 25 years. These tales are meant as a warning and education with an entertainment quality. There is more fun to be had in life than half killing yourself with poison toadstools. I hope that this story gives my readers some understanding of why people with pain in their lives turn to drugs. I hope this story gives more than that and gives you understanding enough, to help people in this situation. I like to think that my bad times can set a good example.

So there I was, a young man, certain that I was about to perish, although never had this certainty prevented me from doing anything in any of my many adventures.

How did I arrive at the poisoned state I am about to write of, one may ask?

I shall tell.

For a young man of no means, drugs were quite hard to find in Wellington. And being one who was desperately seeking the inky embrace of the void or the scintillating colors of the womb of the infinite, I had to bend my shattered wits to improvisation.

After many treks to the library for research, and many sessions of sampling strange and exotic plants, torn from the gardens of the denizens of Wellington and many hours spent clutching my crawling skin/cramping stomach/burning eyes or fizzing lips, chance gave to me a twisted experience that nearly finished me.

A German friend of mine had happened (while strolling in the forest one day) to chance upon a large patch of Fly Agaric Amanita Muscaria, which is of course the red with white spots fairy story toadstool your parents told you to never go near.

He had a whole jar of the dried caps of these, and had bravely tried one, the result being a "strange out of body feeling" and a sore tummy.

So when I expressed my interest he gladly handed over the jar to my trembling self.

I hurried back to my den where my brother in debauchery waited, anticipating my arrival with some new potion to poison ourselves, as was my job, being the smarter and more daring of us. My prize being the lion's share of whatever I brought back.

So I burst into the lounge and said to the form sprawled on the couch "Are you ready for an adventure?" Showing him the jar and its malignant contents.

"Aren't they poisonous?" he said.

"I think so," I replied.

We hurried to the kitchen where we divided the booty, 6 caps for him, 10 for me, which we cut into small pieces and washed down with lots of Earl Grey tea as the earthy and acidic taste was horrid.

The next step on any adventure was to go into town and roam about, while gauging the exact effects of the drug on our toxin-laden forms.

We were just arriving at the top of the main street when we felt a growing desire to run.

And so we ran, charging down along the street, our booted feet pounding the pavement!

We then felt a desire to jump! So we jumped, leaping over sandwich boards, hydrants and the occasional small child.

So great was our strength that we felt nothing could stop us, I literally felt 7 or eight feet tall and the power coursing through my body was bordering on supernatural. At one point I leapt from the cement edge of a garden over a parked mini, blasting into the air with my powerful legs and tucking my knees up to my chin I watched the roof of the mini drift under me in ultra slow motion, seeing every speck of grime and chip of paint sparkle beneath me in garish detail, then back to the ground I flew! Pounding along the pavement.

We charged down a side street where a concrete barrier would prevent us from further travel. It was not a barrier to me and I, using my newfound strength, quickly cleared it.

I heard a noise behind me that sounded horribly like a person trying to leap a large concrete barrier, hitting the top, slipping and falling down from the top onto one knee.

I turned to see the sprawled form of my friend to whose side I rushed.

His face a mask of pain, he gripped his knee and stuttered "The whole world is rushing into my knee! Whoosh, whoosh!"

There was only one cure for such an ailment and that was to quietly sit in the café in the library and drink Earl Grey.

So to the library we struggled, yet on the way we decided to get tickets to see a movie and we purchased these from strange looking people with elongated heads at the ticket box in the theater before hobbling and striding to the café.

When I entered the library I was amazed to see the towering walls of volumes, stretching in all directions and the thick luxury of the carpet, which I felt myself sinking into.

I alerted my friend to the fact that there were things here I must investigate and that I would meet him at a table in the café presently.

Into the halls of towering bookcases I ventured, the bright-multicolored books leering out at me. The tops of the shelves must have been towering 20 feet above me, and I myself was at least 15 feet tall and the whole room was round like a huge fish tank, curving up and over my head threatening to topple at any moment.

I had figured it out! I was in wonderland! The most logical thing to do would be to find the book Alice in Wonderland for a clue on what to do next!

I ran down the halls searching for that book but, from the corner of my fishbowl vision, I spied my friend fleeing the café into the street so I charged after him as he was in great need of my help, because only the strong and canny can survive in the nightmare world, which we currently inhabited.

I was watching him hobble to the bus stop when I slid in something very soft.

I looked down and saw that I had just immersed my foot in a pile of dog shit the size of a basketball!

My friend was lost. There was nothing I could do but contemplate this situation.

My world became dog shit.

The very essence and true nature of canine feces I alone knew.

I tore off my gloves and used them to wipe the mess from my brand new Airwalks. The stench was brutal, it permeated my very existence.

Hurling my gloves into the gutter I hobbled down the crooked heaving street and into McDonalds where I locked myself in the bathroom and using masses of toilet paper cleaned my shoe to the best of my impaired ability.

Yet the stench was not to leave my hands as I was compelled to regularly smell my fingers in the same way a child with a loose tooth has to wiggle it to see if it's still sore (which of course it is). Dejected, I tumbled back into the street and went in search of a beautiful woman who would accompany me to the movie.

The tall buildings lent over me, colors threatened to engulf me and people with elongated faces passed me making strange hissing noises.

The footpath was like a steep wall, which I climbed into a restaurant and with my swirling vision located a princess sitting at a table with some dark-shrouded, leering people.

I pulled up a chair and made myself space at her table.

I heard someone behind me say "Do you want to come with me to the movies? I've got a ticket right here you can come if you want, it's in half an hour. It's supposed to be really good".

Then one of the people turned to me and said in a slow voice " Are you ok man you look kinda hot?

I said," sure I'm fine, nothing wrong with me, I'm fine."

But then I started to feel hot, a slow red heat starting from my face and burning its way down into my chest, the walls were also closing in, and the people and objects in the room started to squelch and slowly spin, their colors coming off their edges.

This was not a good sign. I fled.

Out on the street, I decided to get my money back for my friend's ticket.

I appeared at the ticket box, I was looking at a young man with a halo of blue fire, tinged with red sparks, which I couldn't help staring at while I explained that my friend had been hit by a car and wouldn't be able to make it to the movie. "Oh yes he's fine... well he's in hospital but he will be ok, but he wants his money back."

Arriving back into the street, a dark border had appeared around my vision and it seemed to be threatening to engulf the edges of my swirling world.

I realized that my kaleidoscopic wonder land was under attack and I marched forward in a positive manner focusing on the deep lush colors of the gray stones of the sidewalk, keeping the darkness at bay with deep breaths and a single focus.

My body was trying to shut down all auxiliary and non-vital functions (like consciousness) and focus on staying alive.

But I'd be damned if I were going to miss this!

All of a sudden I was aware of a huge pounding in my chest like a hundred dogs were jumping inside me and trying desperately to escape!

With every third pound of the dogs, the black border was getting nearer until after 9 pounds I was winking out of existence and appearing some distance up the street.

POUND! I'm by a phone box.

POUND! I'm holding on to a street lamp.

POUND! I'm standing in the middle of the street, and there's a guy who's going by in a car looking at me and he says, "Are you ok mate?"

I stare at him with my mouth open and wonder why he's asking that.

POUND! I'm sitting on a bus bench and feeling like millions of fish hooks are hooked into every part of me and are pulling in all directions.

POUND! I struggle to the bathroom of the food court I've found myself in and look at myself in the mirror.

A frightened ghost stares back at me.

Drenched in sweat. Skin white and waxen. Eyes yellow, rimmed and shot with red.

Pupils going huge, tiny, huge, tiny, huge, tiny...

And when they would go tiny all sight would gray over.

Hmmm... this is probably bad.

I went to the toilet and pissed a long stream of reddish brown piss that smelt like the forest just after the rain, when the sun has come out, and is shining down hot on everything.

Hmmm... this is also probably bad.

I then fell to the floor feeling so strange... It was like being encased in pine needles and a huge evil poisonous cow pat which was killing me, while my entire body had been filled with some sort of boiling, witchy brew, made of poisonous toadstools and Earl Grey tea.

This is definitely bad.

I vomited huge amounts of lumpy witch brew, and pooped my pants a bit as I did so... My last thought, before surrendering myself to the inky embrace of the void, was a future conversation my mother was having with someone who asked, "where's your son?" her answer being "Oh, he died on the floor of a bathroom from an overdose of poisonous toadstools."

I had no dreams, only the dark Nothing... where there was nothing except dark. Well, if I *was* conscious of anything, it would have been *that*. Although, thinking about it as it happened, I'm just sort of saying that there was a dark Nothing because I probably had my eyes closed—but I'm not even too sure about that.

I suddenly awoke! Struggled to my feet, and had a big tap drink and washed my face.

I felt remarkably better. Just a lingering inner sickness remained.

It seemed my body wasn't doing exactly what I wanted, and it was kind of twitching and shaking. My head would twist to the side and I would attempt to walk forward, while looking out of the corner of my eye.

I made it to the movie theatre, driving my body like the harshest puppet master ever drove an evil puppet down a Wellington street.

I handed over my ticket and, not unlike a robotic Frankenstein, lurched down the aisle and into a seat.

My central nervous system was lit up like a Christmas tree with faulty wiring and was firing off at random intervals, twitching and contorting my body into strange positions, much to the amusement of those in the rows behind me.

I was able to face the screen for most of the movie, so all together I thought the whole venture was quite successful.

I finally arrived home and burst into my friend's room to see if he was still alive.

He was! And he excitedly told me a tale of hallucinating the wrong bus, winding up far from home, and having to journey in an exact straight line across peoples' back yards, and along the edges of the Wellington zoo, at one point slipping down a bank and hurting his knee even more. All the while having the feeling that the world was collapsing behind him, and to stop for even a moment was to be sucked into oblivion.

He felt the need to spew for most of the way, yet he courageously managed to save it until he got home, where he spewed through a sieve into the toilet—salvaging the pieces of toadstool, which he then ate again.

I looked down at his white sweating form and saw a frenzy going on inside him.

I left him to the dark fairies and went to bed.

I awoke from an earthy-tasting slumber and urinated into an ice cream container I kept under the bed for such purposes. The urine was a light red color and smelt like a grave.

I had learned in my studies that the Romans fed their slaves these toadstools and then supped on the Hallucinogenic urine. Using the slaves' bodies to filter out the toxic part of the brew.

I thought I was smart...

I would do this too, but instead, take the role of both slave and Roman. Twice the adventure!

Swigging from the container and my bottle of water, I managed to get all of the horrid pissy red brew down without throwing up and I slowly felt the familiar and unwelcome feeling of thousands of needles poking at my innards.

I headed off to polytech.

Things get kind of hazy from there... I do remember laughing manically in class for no reason and then bursting out of my chair and up onto the table to put my hands around the neck of an Indian guy, knocking him from his seat and onto the floor, where I continued to choke him until pulled off by my classmates.

I then started laughing again and they (although confused) laughed with me.

I also remember climbing a tall tree in the yard, yelling out and waving to people.

It took me weeks to mentally and physically recover and for my eyes to lose the yellow tint, and for the blood to stop showing up in my piss.

Six years later, while doing some work with a spiritual healer, she sensed some kind of heavy scarring on my liver. I looked at her in faked confusion and exclaimed I had NO idea what she was talking about...I told her I don't even drink more than one beer a month!

She said Sorry.. "I guess I'm having an off day."

Every so often I worry that the liver damage I did to myself has knocked 20 years off my life.

Will I one day soon rip open like a rotten pumpkin and spill moldy guts onto the floor?

Or did all the detoxes I've done and organic food I've been eating catch it in time...?

And that's the story of me being an idiot but very luckily cheating death and going on to be a good example and deciding to dedicate myself to helping others NOT do stuff like that!

Chapter 28
THE BAZ (The promised land)

He had grown up there...

A haven for people like us seeking respite from the ravages of reality.

An island off the coast of New Zealand, it had been a pirate-like hideout for hippies and burnouts for years. People there would understand us. They would not judge us and they would leave us alone if we just wanted to hole up and gibber.

The hut he had grown up in was in a very secluded place, an oasis in that utopia-like land, where marijuana plants grow wild and so large they had to be harvested with chainsaws.

We could stay there. *There* we would be safe.

The hut now belonged to his scary yelling uncle but he was in the faraway city and thus the hut would be ours for the entire summer or more!

We readied for our journey.

Scrounging together the funds for the journey, we purchased two large boxes of food: sardines, crackers, apples, porridge, raisins, powdered milk, cans of beans, rice, and 400 bags of Earl Grey tea. Which we called EARL.

The drinking of "The EARL" made us feel as if we were somehow connected to the royalty of England and thus upper-class drifters. The royal seal, and the words "By appointment to Her Majesty Queen Elizabeth II" in one-millimeter high caps under it, completing the delusion.

We made the 14-hour journey to the island on the weekly ferry. We arrived at the wharf and hitchhiked across the island carrying our meager swag, and the two boxes of provisions, to a friend of his familys', who would put us up in his backpacker hostel for free if we played the poor, lost teenage wastrel-looking-for-a-disaffected-wastrel-father-figure role well enough.

We arrived at this place and when I saw the guy I saw a glimpse of a possible future for myself. Fifty-seven going on seventy, bitter, divorced, unhealthy, and so thoroughly damaged by drugs that it was all he could do to speak in a harsh rasping whisper and gaze about in a perplexed fashion.

I immediately blocked out this portent and encouraged my friend to harass the old guy for drugs. We had been without for a day, and the dark fairies were starting to pull at my insides, as reality threatened to come creeping back in on me like some sort of swift spreading fungus.

He told us in his wheezy voice that he was trying to give up—yet he would not give us any from his dried store of poor-quality leaves in the cupboard (so I had to steal it, creeping like a shaking sock-clad ninja into his kitchen at 1:00 a.m.).

The next day, suddenly feeling unwelcome (it probably had to do with the nourishing muesli breakfast he kindly brought us), we started the 8-hour hike over the island to the hut with the intention of beginning our experimental isolation which I had subconsciously named:

"Operation – Hide from the World."

We were nearly there after the grueling eight-hour hike carrying boxes and our packs... when we met with quite a surprise.

Exhausted, dirty, stumbling and numb, we rounded a forest bend where we saw HIS UNCLE AND FAMILY GOING ALONG THE PATH TOWARD THE HUT WITH A FOUR-WHEELER MOTORBIKE LOADED WITH FOOD AND OTHER HOLIDAY STUFF.

SURFBOARDS AND PLASTIC BUCKET AND SPADE SETS SPARKLED IN THE SUN AT US IN AN ACCUSING MANNER.

We dropped to the ground and hid, ninja-style. Of course we hadn't

Latimer Redlance

ASKED if we could stay at the cabin... why risk that? The last time we had seen this uncle he had screamed at us and told us that if we didn't get our shit together, he would beat us to death with our own shoes.

Spoiler alert... we didn't get our shit together.

We stashed the boxes and groveled forward in the dust peering.

Yes, it looked like they had just arrived and were gearing up for quite a fun couple of days/weeks/months...? We shuffled back into the wilds and hid, stunned and mullet-like, pondering what to do. It was decided that we establish some sort of base from which to spy. Then, as soon as they moved away, we could move in.

Actually going and seeing the uncle and asking him if we could stay was not an option. We were the types who were heavily biased in favor of subterfuge, and thought that if you could trick someone into giving you something, or steal it, then there was no need to ask.

This is because we thought nobody really owns anything anyway as it's all just made of energy, and perceived by us because we believe it's there and thus it's not really real, and so nothing exists!

So stealing is ok. Obviously this mindset was helping us live a rich fulfilling life... as you will see...

We found an old abandoned boatshed, roofless and empty except for a few old polystyrene buoys and leaves. You could crawl underneath it, into a sandy hollow where there was a bit of space and this became our new home. We constructed crude beds from our packs and clothes and hollowed out spaces in the sand and lay back to plot.

We would hole up here and explore the wilderness, spying on the houses, maybe doing a bit of Viking-style "raiding." And gathering shellfish to live on, while searching out people's marijuana crops to rip out of the ground and smoke.

We plotted into the night. The companion remembered some friends from his childhood who may be into drugs now, and we would call on them as soon as he remembered the way there.

We slept in sandy, lower-level abandoned boatshed darkness.

We woke at the usual time of around three and hiked into the wilderness across the island, looking for small trails that would lead us to a huge dope plantation—yet wary of traps that growers use against "Rippers"... Traps like fishhooks dangling at eye level from tree branches and hidden boards with rusty six-inch nails—coated with infectious fish guts—and sticking out of the ground. Also, razor blades embedded in the plant stems to rip eager ripper hands...

We were the lowest SCUM of the NZ 90s druggie world. Right in there with Narcs.

We were rippers. That big tin of weed my friend and I had burned through... all someone's crop... stolen.

We had only gone for a few hours along the trail when we were confronted by a wild and angry-looking beardy man who burst out of the bush and growled at us, "What are you doing here!"

My compatriot said, "Hi! You're Paul, right? I remember you from when I was little. I used to live not far from you... I used to play with your kids Jess and Danny... you live over the hill there... your wife's name is Sam?"

The Wild Hill Man's eyes narrowed, yet he seemed between deep worry (that he had suddenly been hit with so much information about himself—something that only a true surfer of the waves of paranoia can know the terror of) and slight recognition, of the boy he once knew, who had grown into the grizzled hobo he saw before him.

He demanded to know what we were doing. The compatriot told him we were just missioning through the bush on the way to some guy's house.

He said, "THAT'S HOW YOU SEARCH FOR PEOPLE'S CROPS!"

We shrugged, pretending to look confused. His eyes narrowed again, almost disappearing into his beard. He told us to follow him and he would lead us there.

He led us there along the trail, not allowing any deviation, stops or meanderings, and then told us that if he found us in the bush again, there would be trouble. I wasn't scared. I was too dumb to be scared. Lamentably, my myriad addictions had long overridden all sanity in their quest for satiety.

We found the long-lost friend in the nice big house and, after introductions were made and the required amount of childhood reminiscing attended to, the question was asked.

The childhood friend, who had grown into a large and healthy candidate for acceptance into middle-class New Zealand, was still keeping the BAZ dream alive. And when he had been given a huge 20-litre paint container of dope a year ago, he had diligently stashed it up in the woods behind his house.

It was there he led us. It was there we received... the PAIL.

It was full and heavy—there was at least 3 pounds of dope in there, crammed in and solidified.

We fled with it before he could change his mind. We dashed into the bush and along the path—then down a bank to survey the prize.

Tearing the lid off, we were met with a huge cloud of whitish-yellow spores. Waving away the spore cloud, The Pail seemed to be filled with large yellowish lumps of mold... Questing fingers discovered that the dope was hidden INSIDE the mold!

What a score! A huge pail of marijuana with bonus—maybe toxic—mold.

We raced back to our boatshed palace to blaze up a storm.

A storm of fungasaurial proportions was blazed and we sat in the shed looking up at the stars, rolling fungus joint after fungus joint.

This weed was indeed "different." As one took a big pull of the filthy, stiff, stale sock-and-spore-filled dank bonfire taste, an equally strong pull occasioned from the back of one's head. Pulling it back with a whip snap and a teeth grit... followed by a pained silence, then a bout of serious hacking, (dry at first—but later to be a cough of grey, sooty phlegm and later still, a greeny-black sooty mold-smelling festaspaste).

The drugged feeling was like one was encased in a stiff hay-smelling marshmallow—with all feeling of the body dropping away but for a slight tingling of the extremities. Time and speech seemed to slow down drastically and it took a long time to perform the simplest tasks.

This was to cause problems later on when we attempted to communicate with the world outside our shed, where time seemed to move more rapidly.

But for now—no worries.

We settled into a good solid routine as we always did when we had a large pail of dope.

We would wake—smoke—eat—do lots of poos in the forest (another unfortunate side effect of the moldy dope was that it caused a condition of *bowelus uncontrolus*)—smoke—yabber to each other—sleep—wake—smoke and yabber about old times—eat—do lots of poos in the forest—smoke—talk and laugh about days and adventures gone by, while lying on the floor of the boatshed all wrapped up warm in sleeping bags, and staring upwards at fuzzy stars that slide about the sky—go off to try to do more poos but discover you can't—smoke—eat—smoke while telling mystical bedtime stories—fall down into oblivion.

I think that we dazedly wandered about the beach a little—in those six days of complete inactivity—but I cannot be sure. I do remember throwing a soiled pair of underwear into the sea when a moldy marijuana potty emergency got away on me, and spending a lot of time underneath the shed in the cool sandy shade, like some sort of subterranean lizard trying to escape the searing daylight.

We did not explore the wilderness. We did no spying on the houses. We forgot all about our plan of Viking-style "raiding." And gathering shellfish to live on was just not an option—it was all we could do to push dry cabin bread and sardines into our mouths without being killed by the sharp edges of the sardine tin.

Using a plastic grocery bag as a container, we mixed up milk powder and an Earl Grey tea bags with the funny-tasting water that dripped from the tap on the side of the boatshed.

To Quote Silverchair:
There's no bathroom and there is no sink
The water out of the tap is very
Hard to drink
Very hard to drink

All thoughts of searching out marijuana crops to rip and smoke were gone, as we were "sorted," and the days blurred into each other with a moldy wet pile of leaves-smelling numbness.

We were a few days in, planning the big mission-hike, up to spy on the uncle and the cabin. But, as the possibility of our sighting and capture was too much for us to confront, we decided it would be best to creep through the woods and across the island to the house of the Wheezer and ask him if he knew of the uncle's arrival—first smoking up a storm of our moldy stash with him to damper down any possibility of reproach from the stealing of his cabbage.

Preparations were made which included the hiding and burying of the pail under 2 feet of sand—with our food and belongings lying about enticingly as distractions from the real treasure to any would-be thieves.

We trekked.

We barreled into his cottage with a moldy joint blazed and found him in a secretive discussion with a black-coated, dark-skinned Italian-looking man. He nodded to us and introduced the man as **Jaz** (*THE* Genius/Legend Jaz Coleman, ladies and gentlemen—yes, Google search that now). The stars aligned on that fateful day and Jaz Coleman did indeed stand before the demented hobo greatness that was I.

Hands were shaken and furtive greetings given. We interrupted their talk and pushed the joint at Wheezy, asking him if he had any news of the uncle. He wheezed that he knew not of the uncle's arrival and took a shallow tentative hit on the huge yellowing joint. He then looked at it and us suspiciously. We quickly told him it was pretty rotten stuff and had been buried for a long time—deflecting any thought that we were feeding him back his own stash.

He offered the reeking joint—which was now burning like a torch, sending up plumes of superheated greasy brown smoke—to Jaz, who swiftly declined the toxic thing, commenting offhandedly that smoking moldy dope will make you go mad and then kill you.

When it was handed back to me it was mostly on fire and I took it outside to extinguish on a stone and save for later.

When I reentered the room, I saw Jaz was rolling a big joint from a bag of dope that glowed with magical green light. A scent of thick, strong, heady, demon-cleansing perfume filled the air as he shredded the weed, rolled a joint to perfection, and then blazed up.

We hovered around like parasitic moths, but when the Friend expectantly put his hand out to receive the benediction of the good stuff... Jaz shook his head sadly.

It was not for us.

We cowered back and literally scurried off shamefaced into the gathering darkness.

We crawled into the forest in silence and made our way back to the shed in the dark.

We finally staggered, scratched, twisted and bleeding, to our seaside shed kingdom, to blaze up and black out after unearthing the pail, so it could be placed in its rightful and protected place between us.

The next afternoon dawned bright and full of hope. After a breakfast of raisins and milky coppery water, we buried the pail and in the heat, headed up the hills into the forest along the path, making for the uncle's hut for spying and information-gathering purposes.

Chapter 29
The Mold Gods' Reckoning

So, when we left our heroes they, or should I say "we", were heading up to spy on the uncle and the family at their cabin...

We arrived at a suitably camouflaged lookout place and saw his uncle and family playing merrily down below. There was a tree and presents and food.

It was Christmas. We had no idea, lacking watches or a sense of time...

We both felt the tendrils of Christmases past seeking our sooty hearts... he suddenly announced, "I'm going down."

This proclamation that he was going to initiate contact caused me to reflexively scuttle back into the forest.

I made him swear an oath that he would not tell them of my existence on the island, or remind anyone of my existence PERIOD! Nor that we intended to stay there after they had gone until starvation or fire drove us out—on the chance that the uncle said, "NO you cannot stay in, stink up and possibly destroy my cabin that I have worked very hard to make nice."

The oath was taken and he headed off while I crouched in a bearded, ninja-like fashion in the woods.

The day wore on, punctuated by high and happy laughter from the hut. I maneuvered into a better position from which to spy.

I could see the family and the friend out on the porch, smiling with his uncle and cousins. There was happiness and beers and said friend was eating what looked like a whole meal of food.

I shrank back into the shadows and cowered in the undergrowth into a lonely sorrow, wishing death down upon them. I consoled myself with a large stale mold joint and forced the misery deep within.

I spied on him leaving, all happy, and followed him along the path from in the woods, as he called out, "Yooo... Yooo... come out I stole some sausages for you..."

Well, the lure of stolen sausages was too much and cheered me up enough to cause me to burst from my hiding place. I received a full briefing. They were leaving in a few days and we would be able to move in and get some seriously real sloth cranking.

He had told them that it was him alone here, and he was staying on the other side of the island with some friends from the Polytechnic that the uncle had encouraged us to go to! It made him happy to hear that!

They left in a few days.

We found out through our daily ninja recon missions.

We packed, scurried up the mountain, got to the hut, burst in, threw our swag down and blazed up to banish any conservative spirits that may be inhabiting the place.

I got the kettle going to brew up a big pot of EARL, while he put Iron Maiden on the stereo which was hooked to solar panels on the roof. These panels provided power for lights and the stereo. There was one gas element and we found a good iron kettle for boiling potions in.

The PAIL took its place in the center of the breakfast bench where it was to stay for the duration.

Bliss! A shower and toilet! Beds!

We were there for a while—how long I cannot recall exactly... more than six weeks but no more than ten... every time I set myself to penetrate the green smoky darkness of that part of my memory I am set upon with coughing, the shakes and small fits of delirium.

Uncontrollably, these spells send me forward in time to the nicer meadows of my mind.

Latimer Redlance

Yet some incidents stand out like mist-cloaked, garbage-strewn islands in the fog. And I will tell of these.

The day we arrived, we searched out anything edible and were pleasantly surprised to find that they had stocked the hut with lots of food. We did not know that it was for the brother of the uncle, and thus my friend's *other* (and less terrifying) uncle and *his* friends, who were going to arrive at the end of summer—not that it would have stopped us eating all of the food anyway.

I did not know that the provisions were "boobytrapped", in the form of a large quarter-full container of orange juice that had been sitting in the hot sun for days. All I did was pick it up and it exploded with an insane amount of concussive force and a loud sonic boom, showering me with incredibly hot orange and acidic-smelling, napalm-like liquid and glass shards The metal lid hit me in the forehead like a bullet and sent me flying backwards, shrieking into the rack of pots and pans, where I lay screaming and blind for several moments. My face and hands were bleeding from numerous tiny cuts.

The friend helped me up, after he had recovered from his terror and had ceased cowering behind the breakfast bar. He told me later that the orange juice looked like fire in the afternoon sun, and his immediate thought was that the gas bottle had exploded and I had been incinerated!

We pushed all the glass to one side of the kitchen. I washed myself as best as I could with a wet tea towel then attended to the glass splinters with a sharp kitchen knife, while healing the shakes and terror with a large dose of moldy dope.

Comfort and blissful numbness returned, and we ate an entire rummy Christmas fruitcake we had found in a tin.

It rained and so we stayed inside, listening to our three Iron Maiden tapes, drinking tea, talking of fun times past and crazy things; singing, eating, and I read occasionally while he slept.

It was nice and sunny and so we stayed inside listening to our three Iron Maiden tapes, drinking tea, talking of fun times past and crazy possibilities of the now; singing, eating and I read occasionally while he slept.

All the while we sailed further and further onto a sea of madness.

The spore-covered tendrils of moldy dope were taking their toll on our already fragile grip on "reality."

Our ability to really come to some sort of agreement with anyone but each other, as to "the way things were on Earth" had been left in a glasshouse at the Purangi Winery along with a large portion of our minds. This was caused by snorting crushed lines of LSD in tablet form.

Just don't do it.

Don't do drugs at all. Start a garden, and take up healthy hobbies.

Drugs are a dead end. Even Tim Leary learned that.

You will go mad and wind up in a hut trying to escape imaginary demons. And the realization that demons are the monkeys on your back, and that you carried them with you to your sanctuary, will send you shrieking into the void.

The Greenhouse Incident at the Winery was the nadir.

That was the moment we had a dual experience of mental fragmentation.

soo..... in the cabin in the woods...

I would wake up from a deep vacancy of consciousness, sitting on the bed with my eyes open, staring and dry to see my friend crawling on all fours about the house like a little baby.

I would find myself in the garden with no memory of how I had got there.

I would sometimes catch myself in the middle of a conversation with the friend and, as the words were leaving my lips, the memory of what I was saying was leaving my wits. Consuming me with a feeling like I was running up a stairway suspended in a starry space, the stairway falling away behind me into the gloom; nowhere to run but upward... but soon nowhere to run and nothing to say... so I would simply stop and say "I'm going to make some FUCKING EARL."

We held great faith in the healing properties of the EARL, and the flavonoid antioxidants, which according to the box, may help protect the body from damage caused by harmful free radicals. I read the box at least three times a day and repeated the words **"may help protect the body from damage caused by harmful free radicals"** like a magic spell that would weave a shield of light around me keeping the festering tendrils at bay, even as I took their long green fingers deep into my blackened lungs. To this day I think it may have been the only thing that saved me.

My cough had got so bad by this time that I could scarcely breathe at all. Sunlight hurt my eyes and I felt weak and feverish.

In sleep I was beset with sweats and fever, as well as the feeling that some demon was sitting on my chest. I would wake coughing and would have to go outside and cough and hack to purge my lungs of sooty tasting gunge.

My throat was swollen and sore and I felt as weak as a kitten that had been born dead.

I lost the full powers of speech within a day of the mold tendrils embracing me in their silage scented coils, and was forced to communicate by mouthing words and hand signals.

My gasps came in long thin whistles, in and out, followed by deep chuffing coughs and intense hacking splutters, then a wheeze in-out, and a harsh bout of deep KA- KA-KA-KA sounds. The final result was a greeny black, sooty mold-smelling festaspaste, filled with specs of blood, hacked up and spat into a manky old dishrag, kept for the purpose of holding the festapaste for inspection.

Inspection and analysis of the festapaste by me, in the searing light of day, enabled me to diagnose myself.

I was pretty much fucked.

My friend's mold cough was starting to evolve as well and he had reached the second stage of the mold sickness.

He could not complete a sentence without having to take a little breath to carry him through to the end.

It was decided. We could smoke no more, lest we die and our twisted, poisoned and bloated corpses would be found at some time in the future rotting in the hut.

We would have to eat the dope from now on.

Tentative experimentation discovered that directly eating the mold chunks "straight up" was impossible as it tasted like incredibly rank, flaky and dry, moldy dogshit.

I got the iron kettle and put in three cups of brown sugar and five cups of water. When this was simmering away nicely, I added about two huge double handfuls of finely chopped up mold-dope. I let this boil and bubble for about three hours adding water when needed. It was a simmering sickly sweet-smelling black mass.

I could see a tormented soul within the seething brew and occasional heard snatches of demonic song wisping up to me as the skuz bubbled and boiled.

Eventually, when it was but a one inch thick blackish green paste on the bottom of the kettle, I added rolled oats and more water. Soon it became a dark neon green porridge and I deemed it fit for consumption.

I scooped the steaming creation into two bowls and we sat down in front of it and dug in.

As soon as the first portion hit my tongue I knew to the depths of my black soul that I would not be able to take another spoonful lest I fall dead.

I had created the defecation of the toadstool god.

I swallowed the mouthful and washed it down with tea. As soon as it hit my tummy I could feel it radiating out like a black spore-filled explosion.

I was terrified. I could already feel the death spores growing within me.

I looked over. My friend was almost finished with his bowl.

I said nothing but pushed my bowl in his direction.

Inwardly I shook my head in horror and watched, ready for him to explode or at the least say something truly profound: a phrase that would unlock all the secrets I had been searching for and explain the meaning and purpose of my existence.

(At this point I had the meaning of my existence figured out as "Don't Die". However, even on that I was not entirely sure.)

He said "This is yum."

He was half way through my bowl when I actually saw his pupils shrink to pin points. He sat there stupefied. The spoon dropped from his numb twitching fingers and he made motion to indicate I should assist him to consume the rest. And so I did.

I was a good friend. He would have done the same for me.

When the last of the bowl was scraped I helped him to his bed, where he lay, mouthing words I could not hear and seeing visions I could not see.

I went out onto the balcony and into the darkness to quietly reflect on what I had done.

This would not be the first time I had seriously incapacitated someone with a magic potion of my creation. This would be the fourth time; I was getting quite good at it actually.

I looked over to him. Green spittle adorned his beard and he was curled into a rigid ball.

I went to bed as I was rapidly falling unconscious also, overpowered as I was by my one spoon's worth of monster porridge child.

I awoke late the next afternoon to a loud roaring noise. He was sitting bolt upright—eyes open and blindly staring ahead. He was making loud burping roars like a dying lion from the depths of his belly. His beard was blackish green with dried drool. He was gunna spew.

I was a creator of potions, a shaman and a wizard of sorts. I knew the signs.

I felt like I was in a nightmare, the hallucinatory effects of the demon porridge were still with me but I got off the bed and willed myself to the kitchen where I grabbed up a big bowl.

The spew came in little burps and tiny torrents, in a base of almost neon green foam.

I reeled from the stench of the partially digested, moldy marijuana porridge that my companion in experimentational debauchery burped from his foaming green lips.

Had I been of sound mind I would have thought "What series of decisions led me to this point where I now stand? Holding a pink Tupperware container to catch the barf of my compatriot. The main constituent of the barf being a concoction so vile, that even my useless bastard self, a scalawag so debased that I had once supped on my own hallucinogenic urine, could not stomach?" Yet I did not think such thoughts.

Such thoughts I did not think....

Chapter 30
DODGY DEEVO (The Decision to Flee the BAZ Came Suddenly...)

IT WAS TIME TO CHILL THE FUCK OUT OR DIE. A RECURRING theme of my life, ages 17–21.

Chill the fuck out or die means I better reintegrate myself with normals who have jobs and party hard on Friday and Saturday... recover Sunday and then go back to work on Monday.

This non-stop debauchery was a fool's game. I needed to take at least a year off so I could regrow my damaged organs and shattered psyche.

No drugs, no booze, no smokes, no nothing. And get a job where I work hard!

I was such a wise 18-year-old.

I would build my body back to life with Chinese food, burgers and protein shakes! Tuna and bananas and being tough like my dad raised me to be!

We had eaten all the food in the cabin, drank all the booze and trashed the place by farting it up and blazing moldy weed in it for weeks on end.

I left my friend still in his moldy weed porridge-induced coma. No note, no nothing.

I'm starting a new life. First step: was to get out of his zone of "bad Ju Ju".

In my mind I actually blamed him for starting me on the road to despair.

After I had left Wendy's and was Drug Free and winning, I met up with him, for a weekend in my hometown, and he convinced me, after hours of persuasion and refusal, to blaze weed with him ... just as a "Once'er".

Well I guess you now know what this Once'er turned into.

I was going to take my power back.

I hiked out of there, and fled to the ferry, camped in the bush for a day and as soon as it arrived I got off The Rock and back to Auckland.

I crawled back into society using the time-honored method of begging and the friend's couch, and from there to getting a job out of the newspaper...*Labourers Section*—that means you're a meat sack with no skills. I was a meat sack with no skills.

Within a week I was gainfully employed by Best Demolition, a confused Christian demolition company full of goodwill and bad management. Bad enough that the boss would lend all the company's money away to crooks he barely knew, so he couldn't pay the crooks he employed. Which caused the crooks he employed to be angry with him because they didn't have any money to spend on alcohol, gambling, and prostitutes. So they would steal equipment and stock and sell it to a rival company.

The first job I did with them sent the company near to bankruptcy.

We were given our orders, which was the usual: "Go to this address and demolish this house and put all the good timber, doors, and windows on the truck and bring it back here."

Which we did with all the exuberance of dudes who are getting paid to smash things.

We had the whole site cleared to a bare dirt square in five days.

There were some things left by the last owner in the house too, but a quick call to "base" handled that. "Can we keep any of the stuff the last owner left behind?... sweet."

So we divided up the stuff. I got a big box of books, clothes, a good alarm clock and a few pots and pans, and the others got the TV, the video player, and the rest.

Unfortunately... for the company (not me, as I was but a lowly worker) we had demolished **the wrong house!**

We were supposed to demolish the house across the road! And when the tenant came back from a holiday down south, the owner found out that his house had been removed and he filed charges, claims, lawsuits and other litigation that signaled the end of Best Demolition.

Well, we did a good thorough job—we couldn't be faulted on that.

We also had to give the stuff back too, which was quite sad as I did like that alarm clock and had already painted it black and glued small toys to it in fondness of it becoming one of my most treasured possessions.

But all this really meant to me though, was that I kept away from the office because the boss looked pretty sad, and my new job became to work around the yard.

This entailed sitting on an old couch by a 40-gallon drum and keeping it topped up and blazing with all the worm-eaten wood I could get from racks in the yard, and thus "clear out some of this stuff we can't sell."

Funny thing was, a good check of the yard revealed that most of the wood ranged in quality from "worm-eaten" to "on its way to becoming soil." Hmm. Never mind. It was winter, the dry, dusty wood burned well, *and* I was being paid $350 a week to read a huge cache of 60s beatnik books that I had recently acquired while sitting on a comfy couch by a warm fire.

So merrily, merrily, I burned and read my way through the winter.

Now, not 20 meters away from my couch was a huge tower that was used (in times gone past) for making shotgun pellets by dropping hot lead down a huge tube from a high height where it would form into pellets on arrival to a pool of cold water on ground below.

It was a huge steel framework, supporting a high and wide chimney-like tube which went up to a covered steel room, towering about 25 meters above the land. The bottom of the chimney-like tube entered the roof of a shabby shack which was almost obscured by piles and piles of ratty, shitty things, which may have been slightly useful to someone who was trying to build a huge sculpture out of ratty, shitty, useless junk—like old plastic pipes and soggy pissy-smelling foam rubber.

The inhabitant of this shack was a guy we called Dodgy Deevo. And from my observation he *was* a dodgy deviant.

Dodgy Deevo looked like a ratty fifty-year-old burnout with ratty yellow teeth and equally ratty yellow/gray hair. He always wore clothes that the young grunge teens of the time wore, except for the addition of dodgy mirror glasses from the 80s—always worn to hide his dodgy ratty yellow burnout eyes, I suspected.

He would be occasionally seen ushering thin, worried-looking trench coat-wearing teenagers into his shack and, after a few hours, they would emerge by themselves, more furtive and worried-looking and also slightly slower moving.

Through enquiring about Dodgy Deevo's "occupation and demeanor" by the diligent questioning of "Rizz the Bogan" (the ute-driving, mullet-sporting, violent redneck psycho who lived in the dive next door), I discovered that Dodgy Deevo was a "Kiddy-fiddling, dodgy junkie maggot. And if I see him again I'm gunna kick his fuckin' head in! Called the fire brigade on me the bastard—I'll fuckin' kill the cunt!"

OK.

So I had taken to spying on Dodgy Deevo, my interest being fueled by his dodgy activities. He did indeed seem heavily medicated as he sometimes stumbled into things and only emerged from his shack in the late afternoon, coughing and glancing surreptitiously about, his fumbling hands all a-quiver.

He did not like me waving over from my couch and yelling, "Morning man!"

The stream of possibly abused teens did not abate. The puzzlement I endured trying to speculate as to what exactly was going on in there, had me in a spin. And so I decided to up my espionage operation.

I waited for him to leave as he usually did for an hour or so around 2. Then I snuck over to the shack and climbed onto the roof. From here it was an easy thing to scale the ladder that ran up the side of the huge steel pipe, and climb up and up into the little house at the top of the tower.

It was empty except for a few beer cans and a moldy-looking mattress. The tube exited out the floor of this room and the room was filled with a horrid burning-socks smell.

I went to the window and looked over the city as the tower afforded a great view.

So, I stayed up there watching my little barrelled fire down in the yard burn merrily away.

Things started to look fuzzy... I was feeling strange and kind of poisoned. I realized that the burning-socks smell must be a bad thing!

Looking down the tube I could see—far below—little saucepans, glass tubing and burners. Deevo had a mini homebake (homemade NZ heroin) factory going on down there and was using the tube as a chimney to carry the smells of the acids and poisons from his drug lab up and away.

I then heard voices from down there and saw a hand, muck with some of the gear in the fireplace... He was back with some sorry simperer.

I had to get out of here... I also had to spy... so I spied for a while, but the combination of the fumes, and the fact that I had to take a massive dump and a big long piss, drove me to the ladder and I quietly started down.

But then I had a great idea! Dodgy Deevo was a weasel and I could easily beat his head in if it came to it... so why not...

With my stomach rumbling and my bowels full to bursting with the most rancid and festering mixture of ineptly digested fish burgers, bananas, tinned tuna and onions, plus Mega Mass 5000 protein shake, I squatted over the chimney.

I started with a good long wee, just to get the train moving until the goods car arrived. Then I let loose a torrent of poisonous foamy and fizzing slush, down down down it dropped, forming a huge cluster of small hot wet pellets (just as the lead that had dropped down this pipe sixty years before did).

It went directly into all the baking gear with an indescribable spattering sound and probably splattered about the room in a most disturbing manner.

I was finished, wiped, and on the ladder in one bound. Climbing down as fast as I could (feeling really uncomfortable actually, as the last thing you want to do after you have gone to the bathroom is move about swiftly)

I leapt from the bottom of the ladder over the edge of the shed and to the ground in one swift movement, skidding and rolling on the gravel and diving onto my couch.

About three seconds later, Dodgy Deevo came bursting out of his shack to spin and gaze intently up at the tower. He then slowly and dodgily turned to look at me.

Before he opened his mouth, I said in a moment of extreme cowardice, "I just saw Rizz rush down from the tower, is that who you are looking for... why? What happened?" and tried to look as though I had been sitting here innocently all along.

I thought maybe he would try to attack Rizz and be killed... I realized to my gladness that I was not above arranging the deaths of truly evil men.

Dodgy "maybe dangerous" Deevo slowly turned back to me, looking furious.

Regaining some of my composure and reminding myself that I was a hard-hitting demolition dude with a fist of steel and a will of iron, I picked up the strongest-looking bat-shaped bit of wood that was near and said in a more forthright and sinister tone, "What happened? You look like you wanna take a swing at someone?"

Deevo said, "Nothing," and slunk back inside his ramshackle hut.

I spent the rest of the day shaking and amassing weapons, like bats made of steel pipe and huge broken Frisbee-shaped pieces of glass that could cut an enraged junkie's head off if thrown with strength and accuracy.

The next morning I went about my business, putting wood into the drum and reading on my couch. I occasionally tested myself as to how fast I could get to my throwing glass and bats.

Around midday a rough, hard-looking demo boss from another company, who was looking for some stuff in our yard, saw me sitting on the couch trying to read, but being hampered by the constant compulsion to check in the direction of the shack, for the appearance of a screaming cold-turkeyed-out junk monster running at me with some sort of weapon.

The appearance of such an apparition would, of course, be dealt with by some sort of commando roll/glass-hurling/bat-smackdown combo.

Thus, I made the mistake of complaining to the hard demo boss, that I was sick of sitting around in front of the fire with nothing to do, and made up a story of the good old days, where we would demolish a whole house in 5 days like productive and diligent hard workers.

The hard demo boss said, "How much these guys paying you to sit around on your ass?"

I told him.

He said, "Shit! I've got heaps of work for you to do! I'll work your fuckin' bag off and pay ya 400 bucks a week. Go sit in the truck, I'll sort it out with your old boss."

DOH!

I had blown it and got an actual hard job.

The rain started in, and I felt a horrid and unfamiliar feeling. Cold.

I looked to the work site—grey-faced, exhausted workers stumbled over gigantic piles of bricks chipping mortar away, while other sullen-looking dudes stumbled through the rubble carrying bulging armloads of cleaned, recycled bricks.

My new boss turned to me and said, **"Well? What are you fuckin' waiting for!? Get into it ya bastard!"**

Chapter 31
APEY (Chimping out in rural New Zealand)

SO THERE I WAS, A YOUNG MAN... A YOUNG DEMOLITION MAN as you have read.

The healing power of months of demolition work had hardened me, and I was now able to control my intense hedonism and just ease back to the pounding of booze and blazing of weed; only on weekends... with recovery—fetal position in the shower—Sunday morning, followed by a full-day-house-laze-bong-pund with nourishing and healing meals, lots of water, and an early night. After this, back to work on Monday just like my other mates who had their shit together, and who were glad to have me back after hearing I had spent months living like a manky dog in a caravan, or living like a mangy kiwi up in the deep bush, going insane with a friend who was a known psychopath.

I was living with friends and paying rent: fifty dollars a week to live under their house, in a cave I had made out of carpet and mattresses. I was turning the corner!

Anyway, this story is set at a party that my companions and I had spent 3 hours, in a little ute (The term "ute" is a common Australian and New Zealand abbreviation for "utility" and broadly refers to vehicles with an open cargo area behind the passenger compartment, aka a "pick-up") driving to.

The party was at a bush retreat, a palatial house far up in the forest of The Coromandel where I grew up.

The party rocked, it was packed with all types, mostly school kids and kids who had left school to pursue a life of drinking, surfing and not having their shit together...

The music pumped. I wandered about, gibbering almost coherently to people I had known for years, trying to show them that I had grown up big and strong and was no longer the nerdy glasses-wearing weirdo I was at school, but was now a hard-working, hard-drinking, pipe-hittin', soot-coughing wastrel worthy of their respect, as well as a place within their ranks.

They were a group of hard-looking dreadlocked dope growers who surfed, rode motorbikes and hooked into any of the school girls who were unwise enough to leave the safety of the town and adventure into the wild parties of the wilderness.

The house was built on a big cliff, and a tiny path ran underneath the house alongside a three-story drop into a huge firewood pile.

Scaffolding had been erected with a long and frightening jump across from the path, and it was a challenge for the brave and intoxicated to run across the path, leap this gap, and continue to party on the rickety scaffolding.

I wandered through the crowd to the tiny path and started across...

Coming across from the other side was "Ape Man." He was a wiry logger with features like an ape, he was rumored to be insane and to have once, in the local pub, flattened 4 assailants with a flurry of frenzied blows, hitting one of them so hard the guy's face caved in and his eye came partially out.

Ape Man glowered at me with his beady black eyes and I was afraid...

I tried to squeeze past him as we met in the middle of the tiny cliff-side path and he would not move, he just stared at me. I tried to go back the way I came and he hit me with a large group of slurred insults...

I said words to the effect that I was sorry that he felt that way, but this did not secure my escape. I was trapped trying to explain to this angry lunatic that I meant no disrespect in anything I said to him, which in turn was taken as an insult from me.

Half an hour I stood on the edge of the crevasse while he stared at me, occasionally coming up with new reasons as to why I had slighted him and thwarting my attempts each time I tried to leave, ignoring my pleas for sane conduct from him.

Fucking insane situation. Why was he acting so crazy?

The entire party stood at both ends of the path watching silently while a few of my enemies called out "Bash him, Apey!"

My friends seemingly stood by to rush in and try to take him down but they were hesitant not only because of his reputation, but because of the spine-shattering drop that awaited any who would be hurled over the edge.

Suddenly I sensed something... maybe my recent line of pleas had offended him terribly. In a heartbeat I saw his eyes narrow and fingers start to clench.

It was time to die.

From standing on the path I leapt sideways from a standing jump, with supernatural strength.

Everything moved in slow motion as I flew through the air, tucking my feet up as I flew to the scaffold.

He flew after me, his grubby gorilla hands clutching, yet in his rage he did not have what it takes, because anger clouds and stiffens, while fear lends flight and speed.

I landed on the platform. His chest hit the side of it and I saw his face for a second—no pain or anger on it, just a kind of wonderful astonishment.

I could have reached out and grabbed him, maybe... yet I did not, being content to use that precious nanosecond to create an evil smile for him to gaze upon as he bounced back and plummeted.

As I looked over the edge, I saw him falling, arms and legs to the sky, down, down, down he went until with a SMASH, he landed on the woodpile. Firewood flew out in bits all around him.

Nobody yelled, "Call an ambulance!" These were not that kind of people, they just crowded around the edge and looked down to see if he was still alive... he did not disappoint them...

He got up and started charge-climbing up the scaffolding!

I felt as though I was being chased by something that cannot be killed, it was a nightmare gone solid!

As I stepped back for my run-up for the jump back on to the path, which was my road to freedom, I saw my enemies closing in, thinking they would hold me until he got up to deal with me in his own special way. But my friends were ready, and swiftly moved, blocking them off and threatening punishment to those who would not allow my escape.

And, escape I did, tearing up through the empty house and up the hill into the bush, running up and away as fast as I could. Never had I run so fast uphill through scrub in the dark before.

I kept going until I collapsed and the house was a distant light far below me.

I could hear him coming, crashing through the bush below, far away now and not so scary, yet single-mindedly focused on my destruction nonetheless.

I crept down silently and passed his noisy charging a few hundred meters to the side.

My arrival back at the house was met with cheers, which I quickly tried to hush.

My friends wanted to keep partying on, so I went and hid under the ute till they decided to leave.

He apparently came back to the party an hour later, scratched and bleeding from brambles and falls. He stomped about the house attempting to search me out and furiously questioning my friends as to my whereabouts, before plunging back into the bush to "FUCKIN KILL THAT CUNT!"

My friends took that as a signal to flee before he focused his rage on them.

So off we fled, into the night.

FOOTNOTE:

Years later I was told that Apey's behavior that night was caused by being given LSD without his knowledge.

Watch your drinks and don't take candy from strangers.

Better yet... maybe don't be around drug users that might think it's funny to drug you without your knowledge...

Chapter 32
BABBY SATAN (A story of 90s NZ pub life)

WHAT THE WORLD HAS A DEARTH OF THESE DAYS, IS demented old bastards in pubs that basically live in the pub and annoy people with their twisted old stories about rationing during the war and how they ingeniously got around it. People forget the WW2 rationing of goods such as sugar, cloth, tires, petrol and meat.

If you want to educate yourself on rationing in New Zealand during WW2, to make this story make more sense, you should do so.

Well these old guys were there in the pub to make sure no one forgot. You can't smoke in pubs now and many pubs are not so much the social gathering places anymore due the phone bullshit. Those times are gone.

But they were alive and well in NZ in the late 90s. Where if you were 18 or so you would be a very small fish in a pub-bowl of tough working men, twisted alcoholics and crazed floozie lush hags.

You had to politely get your beer and hide in the corner, because fighting was a thing.

I'm not saying that pockets of pubs like this don't exist around the world, but with the advent of smartphones, and the testosterone destroying prevalence of internet pornography, soy, roundup and plastics in the food, most pubs I've been into in the last twenty years are "Gayer than Aids" to use a phrase from back in the day. Filled with fat bellied fake men with thin arms, high pitchedly screaming at sports they never played, eating troughs of sugary fatty food and drinking weak roundup GMO poison beers.

They look like tubby fat children, faces red and bloated with inflammation...

It seems to me that men's voices are higher than they were in the 90s..for some reason...no balls maybe...I feel safer now, than in the 90s where the bars were filled with singlet and boots wearing macho gorillas spoiling for a fight... but that safety does not make me happier.

I digress into GenX nostalgia and bitter social commentary...please forgive me...So anyway it was in one of these pubs of rural NZ that this story occurred. It had that perfect smell of spilt rotten beer, stale cigarettes and body odor. That smell will never be forgotten by one who has inhaled it. It's almost extinct.

It's only created by decades of spilt rotten beer, stale cigarettes and body odor, seeping into industrial carpet. If you know you know. Once you're inside and have got a few ales and smokes down your black guts, you can't smell it anymore, but on entering the pub, its welcoming "Abandon Hope and enter Oblivion" smell always hit you.

Ok so it was onto this scene that my friends and I would slink after a hard day at work in rural New Zealand 1993. I was almost 17 and that was old enough to be in the bar. I could grow sideburns and act serious, and thus could buy booze. No one IDed anyone that had sideburns, a job and money.

For a month one summer I had a job trimming the lower branches off mono crop planted pine trees, with little saws, and for this we got 1$ a tree. If you went all out you could make about 200 dollars a day.

If you got up and ten and smoked weed all day you could make 100.

Anyway we would go to the Pub every night for a meal and a few jugs of the cheapest beer in New Zealand. It was called "Coromandel Bitter" and for some reason you would always have to run to the toilet with the most brutal shits after about two glasses... but after that you were ok...

It was utter swill with every corner of the brewing process cut. But it was only 5$ a jug. It was discontinued after a year probably due to the bars losing money on toilet paper and cleaning supplies and people buying it over other beer which was twice the price...

OK! I hope I have set the scene.

This story is about twisted old dude rabbiting on about rationing and how he got around it with true Kiwi ingenuity. So this particular super old demented alcoholic was called Bobby Saton.

But everyone called him "Babbie Satan". Because he was twisted and evil. And his Kiwi accent was so thick and he had so few teeth that when he introduced himself it sounded like "Babbie Satan".

He wore an old black trench coat, brown polyester pants, rubber boots, and had thin black dyed hair in a comb over. He was short with a pot belly. He was missing teeth, his breath was foul, his eyes yellow, his nails hooked, longish and nicotine stained. He smelt just slightly of piss.

He was probably about 80. He would wander from person to person starting loud blurting conversations with "Back during the war... When asked why he didn't fight "Oh I had a gammy leg back then and they wouldn't let me sign up." Like most of the rubbish he would spout it was continuously changing lies.

Everyone hated him but tolerated him. People said he killed his wife and had a kid that ran away... Ok you get the scene... where are people like this now? Modern society just creates bums that then die early I think...

On entry to the bar people would yell "BABBIE SATAN MY MAN!!" and laugh. And he would smirk and raise his glass.

One day he brought himself and the warm beer he was nursing over to our little corner booth where we would hide, and said...

"Move in you little cunts, I see you hiding over here. Buy me a drink. I've got a story you're gonna wanna hear."

We didn't want to do any of those things... but we also didn't want to draw attention to ourselves... So I got up to buy him a beer...

Quick as a flash Babby Satan held up two fingers and yelled out to the Publican...

"Two whiskeys in the Barrel for me Jim!".

Jim nodded and marked something down on something.

So now he had a "Credit" of two whiskeys at 10$ each on us ... on account.

Wow. Just Wow. Such scammer skill I wasn't even mad. I was impressed.

He launched into his story. Foul breath gagging us...heres the gist.

Back in the war petrol was rationed and he and his mates never had enough to get around. They worked the shearing sheds on the sheep farms in the top ranges of the mountains (which had since been converted to pine mono crops and co-incidentally was where we were now working doing the pine trees).

To save money he and his mates would push the car from the top of the mountain along the road to the first hill and then by utter skill as ONLY possessed by those in the old days, carom and coast the unstarted car the entire 20 kilometer drive down the mountain to this very pub.

You had to build up a lot of speed and be so skilled to get round the corners without breaking and be going fast enough to get up the hills that were there, but they would do this every day and thus save enough gas to be kept in beer money for the entire war.

He repeatedly emphasized that:

"No modern truck or person is this bullshit day and age could do it... as the trucks are jap shit and too light and no one these days has the skill because you kids these days are all pissweak faggots, present company very much included."

And that's an exact quote.

And with that, he saw someone else come in that he wanted to fleece and departed our booth leaving nothing but a slight pissy odor... and our incredulous loathing.

. . .

After work that day as the three of us piled into the truck at the top of the mountain, I said...

"Hey what if we could do it...that would fucking show that Babbie Satan eh?"

So we tried... We failed miserably... running out of steam on the first hill.

But we kept trying. Coasting faster and faster, taking turns more and more dangerously... getting up to 110 kph on the big dip and with a straight shot down the mountain to barely roll up over the lip at 10 kph, cars honking madly behind us.

Almost going over the cliff multiple times due to taking the corners too fast as we didn't want to lose any speed... The best we got was running out of speed on a long flat after a curve, 500 yards before the final 3 k downhill to the pub. We couldn't get past it...

Then I remembered what Babbie Satan had said about the WEIGHT of the trucks back then. Of course! Our piece of shit tinfoil thin Toyota Jap ute was too light! The next day we overloaded the truck bed with heavy, wet logs. We could barely push it to the starting point.

But holy shit did it fly. With that extra weight we skidded round the cliffside corners twice and almost went up on two wheels but we got to 120K down the long shot mountain drop. We coasted along the flat for its entire length, cruised down the final hill and triumphantly skidded into the pub parking lot!

Running into the pub in a high exhilaration we saw Babbie Satan at the bar, but as always facing the door to see who was coming in. We ran up to him cheering wildly and startling people in the pub...

"We fucking did it! We went all the way from the Top of the range to the pub with no gas! It took us two weeks but we fucking did it, just like you did back in the day! What do you have to say about that! You crabby old cunt!"

Babbie Satan looked shocked... he could believe what he was hearing. This could not be! His mouth opened and closed like a goldfish and then his face closed up and he squinted and smirked at us...

"You're a pack of lying cunts. It can't be done!"

We protested that we had done it and the only thing he would say was

"*Can't be done." "You're lying cunts*"

When we kept insisting, he got up and walked off to the other side of the bar. We just stared... and laughed...got our beers and went to our booth hiding spot. He somehow cursed us with his evil nay saying and we never did it or mentioned it again.

* * *

But dear reader, you now know that we did it.

And we showed Babbie Satan that young forestry workers in the 90s still fucking had what it took to drive dangerously and almost kill themselves to prove an old man wrong. I look forward with all my heart to being the Babbie Satan of my generation.

Chapter 33
BUTCH FLABBACINNI AND RATSO HAGGISI (Handmaidens of Pestilence)

SO THERE I WAS, A YOUNG MAN... BODY GLUED TO A SAD, sagging, ragged couch, eyes glued to the glass garbage chute, which was currently feeding me my daily Simpson-shaped dose.

I was 18 and had settled into a good NZ demolition worker's routine.

I was in my numb survival rut.

Get up early, work all day, often in the rain. Come home in agony and covered in filth. Shower. Sit on couch, and kill all the pain with a TV and weed combo.

By my side was my mate joining me in numb solidarity after a hard day of working in a plant warehouse. All my friends had bullshit jobs. It seems most 18-year-olds don't have bullshit jobs anymore, but back in my day; if you teamed up with a few of your mates and all got bullshit jobs—like warehouse mong, landscaping spaz, or gas station dork—you could all live in a rundown flat and earn enough to party yourself half to death on the weekends, as long as you lived very cheaply and never bought anything besides food, booze, drugs, and bus tickets.

There was a knock on the door. Curiosity and laziness getting the better of my paranoia I yelled, "Come in."

In—snuffling and snorting—shuffled a mountain of what I decided was a girl.

She was made huger by the gigantic gangster-type puff jacket she wore—the type of jacket that makes the person look as if they should be inflated, branded with some kind of beer commercial, and floated above a football stadium.

She had a huge moon-like, yellowy waxen face. Somewhere in the center of which hid two piggy little eyes (glistening with malice of course), a snout, and a sour piggy mouth. She possessed a sort of hunchedness and an air of inbreeding. Stubby little sausage fingers protruded from the arms of the blimp jacket, and dirty little trotters poked out of what could have been baggy gangster pants to someone without barrel legs.

My friends, always seeking to give new and exciting names to people, later dubbed her Butch Flabbacini.

Shuffling in behind her was a specter... a wraith... a wisp... another thing that I decided was a girl also.

This one wore a holey *Metallica* t-shirt, that would have once been a cool black, but had now faded to a dismal, dishcloth gray. The picture and lettering on the shirt had come away, and now could only be discerned with the use of the most diligent connect-the-dots type imagination.

It hung upon her skinny, gray frame like a funeral shroud. She was so skeletal that she seemed to be made up of coat hanger wire. Tiny and pointy braless tits, like minute, sharpened witches' hats, poked from her shirt. She wore a pair of rancid, black jeans that she probably stole from a Barbie, and on her head she had a black beanie that was (I am sure) disguising that her hair was coming away in patches.

Her face was so narrow and skull-like, that you had to look at it from side-on to get a good view. It was pocked with craters and newly forming pustules and cankers. A moldering cold sore started at the corner of her mouth and seemed to be threatening to engulf her entire head.

Her whole demeanor was permeated with rattyness; from her yellow, ratty teeth, to her twisted ratty claws. A festa-face whose only future prospects were either: *emaciated druggie* or *hideous witchy scarer of innocent folk,* who are just trying to get along in life and don't need such shocks.

Latimer Redlance

I later came to find that she was well on her way in both these careers.

All you would need to do would be to put a couple of bolts on her neck and the villagers would be after her with torches and pitchforks.

She was dubbed Ratso Haggisi.

They shubbled over to me and in the pained conversation that followed, I deduced these facts:

1. They wanted drugs.
2. They had no money.
3. They were friends of Timo, the psychotic Samoan alcoholic baker and professional boxer, from next door, and he had sent them over here to get drugs from me.
4. The huge one was 18.
5. The waif was 16.
6. The waif claimed to drink a forty-ounce of Jack Daniels a night (which, looking at her condition, was the only nutrition she got).
7. The huge one wouldn't stop seeping out disgusting farts and trying to secretly wave them away with her hand. The farts were so deeply from the graveyard of the long-gone, and were so festering, that I was sure I was going to spew and indeed, actually felt the rise of bile, the eyes water, and the strange pre-spew saliva being produced at the back of my throat. Their personalities were so vile, and the perverted statements they made were so profound, that all of my friends had fled to their rooms on hearing a few sentences from these handmaidens of pestilence. To this day I have blocked much of that evil and pained conversation from my conscious recall; pushing it back and away into a dark, dungeon-like corner of my mind, where even my other bad memories fear to go. So anyway, in a short time, they had somehow fit the topics of rape, incest, and serious personal crimes into each topic of conversation. Never had I ever encountered such a gross scene, and I was a pretty rough individual.

8. They wanted drugs.
9. They had no money.

Pure survival instinct kicked in, and I suddenly said that I was very tired, and had to go to bed because I usually go to bed at 7 p.m. because I work so hard and must get up at 4 a.m.

I pushed them out the door, and fled downstairs to my room which was a large hollowed-out, carpet-lined cave under the house. I slammed the door, and jumped into my damp, moldy-smelling but always-warm bed, to cower under the covers.

The whole experience of being subjected to those two, had left me a husk. A drained, shivering, sick-feeling ruin. Such creatures are where the legends of human vampires come from.

My sense of light and love in the world, a feeling that I tenderly and tentatively fostered over time, (because the soil of a man's heart is stony, but he grows what he can... and he tends it) had been cruelly snuffed, and my mind had experienced such terror—due to being long enough in the presence of these malicious beings—that my sanity was broken down into shards, so tiny that the bits would have easily passed through the eye of a needle.

Well maybe not *that* bad... but I knew I didn't want to ever see them again.

I hid in the darkness for a while, then I heard it... the approach of cloven hooves followed by the clacking of bony reaper feet.

There was a knock on my door.

In reply, I snored a loud fake snore in terror..

They opened the door and came in anyway.

I felt their approach like a wave of poisonous swill.

Some kind of evil auric field?

A stubby hand pudged me "awake."

"Hey, we were thinking..." a skinny voice cackled.

What followed was indescribable, and I will not bring the conversation to memory lest I run shrieking from this world. Yet I *will* tell you, dear reader, that the goal of the negotiations they embarked on, was for them to establish some sort of "sex for dope deal" with me. At the start they were offering very little sex for lots of dope and at the end they were offering lots of free sex if we shared a thin joint.

My racing heart, my bile-rising terror, and my freezing sweat got the better of my miserliness... I gave them a small handful of weed for them to promise to "Never *ever,* under any circumstances, come back to me *ever* again *forever...* that's *ever...* I said *ever...* I mean *ever.*"

They left... I was only to see Butch Flabbacini one more time a few weeks later when I possibly saved her life. A story to be told next.

Chapter 34
SAVING LIVES AND BURYING BODIES (Nun-chucks to the dome)

SO THERE I WAS, A YOUNG MURDERER.

This is a tale that is hard to tell… as it's the most harm I have ever caused another human being.

It was to be the beginning of a slow transformation in me from a hard-hitting, tough, macho dick, obsessed with survival and martial arts, with long black warrior, heavy metal hair into a two-year stint as a vegetarian.

A super peaceful, deadlocked, near-impotent tofu muppet of love and calm.

Never judging, never blaming.

Allowing others to just BE.

Desperately trying to be the calm center of the world.

Reading pacifistic Eastern religious books… and basically being a deeply miserable, tired wimp.

Ok… that's the preface…

But cut back to the scene of "friend and I on the couch watching TV and blazing weed after work"… it's dark, as it's New Zealand, and so it's basically dark after 4 p.m. six months of the year.

SUDDENLY…

Screaming! SUPER DYING, HELP-ME SCREAMS!! Like a woman-being-raped screaming.

It freaked us badly. We leaped up and grabbed weapons.

We always had weapons nearby because we were CRAZY NINJA WARRIORS!

I grabbed the nun-chucks and Buzzy grabbed a bo staff.

We ran outside... running towards the screaming.

That was my rule then, and to this day it's my rule now.

Always run TOWARD the screaming. If you want stories and adventure. Which I do.

If you want to live a quiet life, involving zero combat and nice quiet correctness and no pain... run AWAY from screaming.

Living with three guys in an old flat, with a garage that decked out as a fight gym, and with the 19-year-old toughest of you being a psycho ring fighter—groomed by his crazy martial arts teacher; which he is passing on to us, in all its batshit glory—is a recipe for madness.

It's hard to get a grip on... only those who have purposely trained in being beaten, and beating others, get it... but its end result is usually injury and brain damage, as well as seeing the world as a way more dangerous place than it really is...

So, the screaming... We ran out of the house towards the screaming, which was coming from the lawn of the house next door. It was Butch Flabbacini being held on the ground and having her clothes ripped off by Temu the psycho Samoan Alcoholic Boxer. An actual rape in progress.

Well... Temu was our neighbor, and we knew he fought in the ring often, and often while very drunk. Which made him numb to the blows.

He was very dangerous, as you can imagine all Samoan boxers would be.

We were terrified of him. But he was our friend, and we would chat with him now and then and give him weed to make sure he stayed as our friend.

But there we were and a decision had to be made. And that decision was to hit him as hard as possible in the back of the head with the nun-chucks.

BAP!

It made a sound like wood hitting a 200-year-old oak. I was hoping it would knock him out... and he would go down... Butch Flabbacini would run off and he would never know what happened.

That did not happen at all. He just stopped the clothes-ripping and got up off the ground and turned around with a confused look on his face.

This was one of those dream-nightmare times, where the monster can't die, no matter what you do, and it's coming for you.

Well, I had decided many years ago in my early youth, that it would be better to actually die fighting than dishonorably run away or lose a fight and beg for mercy.

Why? Because I thought I was a Samurai. Yes, a druggy, Simpsons-watching, demolition-site-working, nun chucks-wielding Samurai.

So here we go: We are fighting to the death, right here on this lawn at around midnight in 1994. I was, however, well-trained in the nun-chucks and they are quite deadly. These were real hard hickory ones that cost $80. So as Temu advanced to kill me, he got a series of massive smashes to the hands and head. With all my fear-terror strength.

Where was Buzzy with the bo staff? Hiding inside like a terrified maggot. The moment he saw it was Temu he just bailed, thinking that I would bail as well and leave Butch Flabbacini to die.

Well, I couldn't let her die.

Why? Because I was also a chivalrous medieval Knight as well as a Samurai.

So I backed up across the lawn, raining down hickory blows as he reached out blindly through rapidly closing eyes. Finally, a super hard blow to the temple took him down. I must have hit him 20 times as hard as I could.

I stood there feeling numb. Butch Flabbacini had run off.

What to do... call the police... and be charged with assault with a deadly weapon?

Wait till he wakes up and then threaten him? Reason with him? I would have to carry the nunchucks everywhere.

So I sat and waited... thinking he would wake up. He didn't wake up. I checked the pulse. I couldn't find it. He was dead.

Well, here we go.

I had sort of predicted this. I kind of knew that if I continued on the dangerous path that I had been on, I would probably wind up killing someone or being killed.

And now it had happened.

It was scary how fast the answers came to me. And in retrospect, it was 100% the drug use that made me choose that path.

Get a spade and bury him in the small swampy lot next door, so I can get a few days' head start on hightailing it into the bush wilderness of New Zealand to live like a weed-growing hermit, on the run for the rest of my life. Straight-up wilderness hobo boss.

I went down to the garden shed to get the spade. It took a while, as it was dark, and remember we had no phones with lights. I got the spade and headed back to the corpse.

It was gone!

I went over onto his lawn and could see the light on in Temu's kitchen... He was making toast. His whole face was a massive red puffy mass of smashed-up, bleeding welts, and his hands were all smashed, bleeding, and puffy where I had whacked them to prevent him from punching me.

But he was indeed putting thick slices of white toast into the toaster. I heaved a huge sigh of relief... but then fear of his revenge kicked in.

I crept back to the house and locked all the doors and windows. I told Buzzy what had happened and then called him a fucking cunt bitch coward and told him to get ready because when Temu comes knocking, I'm going to tell him that it was HIM who did the smashing with the nun-chucks.

I fortified the house, got weapons ready, and watched through a crack in the curtains.

Nothing... so I went to bed with a chair holding the door shut and everything in the house locked up.

In the morning I woke to knocking on the door.

Here we fucking go.

Holding the still blood-covered and dented nun-chucks behind me, I went to the door to see Temu. Fully smashed... trying to smile and see through swollen slit eyes.

"Whoh Temu! What happened bro?"

"Got in a fight with bikers at the pub bro! Fucking smashed them all though!"

Oh wow... blackout drunk, and probably brain damaged.

"Wow bro, well here's some weed man, you don't even need to ask. Good one on smashing those bikers."

"Yeah bro, chur."

(*Chur* is a Kiwi slang word that can be used in many situations. It's widely considered to be a shortening of the word *cheers*. It can be used as a greeting, or as a goodbye and to say thanks. It's also used when something is cool, sweet, or all good: "Fish & Chips for dinner?...... Chur!")

And he rolled out.

Chapter 35
GALAXY OF DELIGHTS (Glowing Condoms feature again!)

It's amusing to me that in my middle years, I'm no longer boastfully proud of my youth's sexual exploits. I do take some pride in the fact that it was the 90s, so you had to actually WORK at it.

Anyway...

These women of my youth are now in their late 40s ... two are now 60!... as I dated women in their mid thirties while I was in my early 20s because I'm a goddamn maniac.

... All of the wonderful women I loved are very, very possibly no longer the crazed vixens they once were, just as I am no longer some kind of pompous, self aggrandizing, heavy-metal Lothario.

I was working in demolition as I have said. Off the hard drugs and insane hi-jinks.. Yet Weekends were spent on the Devils Lettuce and *The Pixies* on loop...

This story finds me in a spa pool with 4 others, swimming round and round, stopping only to take a lung-bursting hit from the bong, and then disappearing under the water to take long, chlorine-laced hits of the stale air that came out the bubble holes.

We were truly lost in a world of mind-destroying bliss.

There was a lovely blond gal with a rounded, lithe body and unbelievably perky tits in the spa with me, and as she ran her feet up and down my legs the others bailed out of the pool and left us alone to engage in intelligent conversation. The conversation went like this.

Me: Man I'm out of it... I'm fuckin bombed, I can't even feel my face.
Her: Yeah same.
Me: ... uhhmmbbzz.
Her: Yeah.
Me: ....
Her: ....
Me: Whaddid I just say? Did I just say something?
Her: Ummm I don't think so.
Me: ....
Her: ....
Me: Whaddid I just say then? Whaddid I say?
Her: You just said whaddid you just say.
Me: No, before that.
Her: I dunno.
Me: Man I think I'm blacking out as I go.
Then kissing!

I suggested to her that we grab a blanket and head up to the inner city volcanic mountain—which was located a 15-minute walk from where we were—and continue this mutual exploration. Mt Eden Auckland it was

The moon was shining full and romantic-like as I tried to get some sort of sexual feeling from my numb body. Both our eyes were closed for quite a while as we tried to make our drug fucked bodies feel what sex was like.

Something huge and wet had covered my bare foot. Blasting my eyes open I saw... that cows surrounded our little blanket oasis! One of their number had just licked my foot and now they were staring at us! There must have been 20 of them!

I knelt there glaring at them, the upper part of me upright and waving. They looked back boredly. I knew I wouldn't be able to perform with so many onlookers so I shooed them away and they stampeded off before I resumed.

So, the upshot was that we fell into some kind of "relationship" that consisted of her coming around to my place after she finished school, smoking a few joints, and then going down to my room for a while to "chill" before going home.

I had become that guy that every father would like to Kill.

I once went round to her place to meet the parents for dinner. It didn't go too well, as I was far too stoned to behave rationally, and spent most of the meal staring at the tablecloth trying to not piss myself laughing at the spectacle of obedient respectability my young lady presented to her mum and stepdad.

I put forward no such pretense and happily told jokes and sang songs until dessert, which I consumed in a munchies-induced frenzy.

I was a recently rehabilitated ragamuffin from the streets and had nothing but contempt for anyone not as "Free" as me. I had zero censor, at all times.

However, the whole romance was to come to a crashing conclusion about 3 weeks after it began.

It was party time in my room. My room was the space underneath the house, which I had made habitable by nailing four layers of carpet to the floor, walls, and ceiling to give a fuzzy bouncy castle furry cave wall effect.

My bed was two double mattresses laid side by side on a huge raised platform at the end of the room.

My room was packed with a small number of refugees from the upstairs, beer and popular music party, who had filtered down to the sanctuary of "the furry cave" because all the people upstairs were really, really weird and were freaking them out.

My room was a fun house for the insane. We rolled around on the floor, flicked the black rave light off and on to the tune of 90s rave music, made magical inscriptions with glowing incense, and then forayed out to the lawn to spin around on the clothesline.

We had the great idea of taking the mattresses off my bed and putting them on the floor to bounce on, so we hauled them off. What was revealed underneath would shock us into speechlessness. A cosmos of bright multicolored stars! Small galaxies in green, yellow, orange, and white, great big clumps of stars lay everywhere in the portal to another universe we had revealed.

All of it glowed amazingly in the glare of the black disco light.

"Wow!" we said, and stared into the stargate as the stars within pulsed and glowed.

A young lady dared to reach into the void, and what's this? She picked up a star, which grew long, and jiggled in her hand... she examined it closely and screamed, then threw it. It landed on another girl's head and tangled in her hair. She stood stunned... then pulled it out, looked at it and also screamed, joining the first girl bolting for the door. We all leaned forward to examine the glowing thing closely... then there was a huge and frightened exodus for the door.

Except me who was left to remove a huge double handful of condoms (which over the past six months I had carelessly tied and hurled under the mattress, like an 18 year old grot who cares nothing for post-sex decorum, before blacking out into the arms of my unsatisfied partner), the contents of which were in varying stages of decomposition, changing color depending on which state of fermentation the product was at.

I deposited 72 civilizations worth of latex-encased goo into a nearby McDonalds bag, and went outside to tell everyone the coast was clear! And we can do the cool thing with the bouncy mattresses on the floor now.

Most of the people had already fled, preferring to brave the upstairs party than stay and be subjected to any further mind-unraveling surprises like what they had just witnessed.

The brave few that had reconvened on the lawn met me with frightened stares and backed away shaking their heads.

I sort of realized that my underhouse dog-like living and gutter-rough lifestyle was just too much for regular folks... but the ability to live like an animal has actually been revealed to me as a superpower later in life.

And of course when civilization collapses, and everyone is still trying to figure out how to get a generator to charge their cell phones to hook up to a grid that doesn't exist, I will already be leading my tribe wearing assless chaps and a metal mask.

I digress...

My young lady stayed over the whole night for the first (and last) time that night. We were woken from our hungover hibernation, in the afternoon by banging on the door and the screeching sound of her mother calling her name in an angry-worried-mother fashion.

The first thing to hit me as I woke was the horrid stench of wet rotten carpet combined with cigarette butts, bong water, beer and the smell of the ghosts of joints long smoked. I looked down to see the floor flooded with water, bobbing in it was the festering trash of last night's party. It had rained heavily in the night and flooded the room, as it was prone to do when it rained. I had not thought of this when I had stapled all the carpet up around the room. In the past, the water just pooled on the concrete floor and exited through the door when I opened it in the morning.

The poor girl's mother opened the door, and a wash of brown water and party refuse exited onto her shoes and past her, to soak into the lawn where it belonged.

She shrieked to her daughter that she would be in the car, and to get her butt to said car immediately.

We cowered terrified under the blankets. All of her clothes had been passionately thrown off her and flung to the floor last night, and were now grimy and soaked. So, dressing up in some of my moldy-smelling but dry gear, and promising to call, she crept out to face her fate.

She arrived around at my house that night, and I knew the dream was over when I saw her long beautiful Barbie blond locks had been shorn into some bullshit pennance haircut, which was short and dyed red. I knew what this meant.

My good-time gal was now a beaten-down-by-mum-and-dad slave with her shit together.

The raw facts of teenage rebellion only last as long as the phrase "While you're living in my house..." and basically no teen is willing to say... "Well fuck you then, I'm just going to go live on the streets so I can be free!". You know why? Because 99% of the time "Free" loses to being fed and warm.

An entire societal philosophy could be built out of this, but I'm not in that business. I'm in the business of writing out my demented Gen X hobo capers.

Ok so back to the gal...

. . .

She gave me a chocolate bar, and from the door told me that she wouldn't be able to see me again as she really must concentrate on her schoolwork from now on.

I said, "Yeah, whatever, I get it." I shut the door on her and cried like an abandoned baby, down in my floody misery room.

Deeply alone super sobs, at the unfairness of it all.

Did this experience help me... Yes.

I eventually moved up into the garage, where it was dry, and decided to stop acting like such a pig. I got a few new shirts and a silver necklace and overall, started lifting my game.

Did it work?

Fuck yes, it did! I'm a fast learner and pushed ahead to a better blond, whose father was a hip book publisher... *He* was learned enough to kind of dig me.

And so we beat on ... boats against the blah blah...

Chapter 36
PEACHES (I was a courier of a mummified cat to the other side as I began another deep downward slide)

So there I was ... a young man and shit had gone bad.

As you read in the last story, I had lost the sweet blond gal. Additionally, I had started smoking the devil's lettuce *at work*, with some of the other guys.

This was allowed by the boss but always a bad idea. The Boss, his name was Robbo, was a mad blazer. A huge Maori guy. Deadly, but funny... he had grabbed me off another job as detailed in the story *Dodgy Deevo*. He was a very fair guy but also violent when needed...

No one in the fucking WORLD fucked with this guy.

Within a week of being on the job I did a naughty thing by selling $100 worth of bricks off the site when no one was around. Thinking to give Robbo the $100 the next day at work... but I was very forgetful... And I just blew the money on weed and pies.

A month later...

Robbo rolls over to me as I'm stacking wood and says, "A guy just called wanting more bricks... I didn't know what he was talking about until he told me he gave the money to some guy with long hair..." Shit...!!!!! I am suddenly covered in freezing sweat...

I told him I just forgot! But he can take it out of my pay! I had never been so terrified, and ashamed. Robbo: "I don't care about the money. It's just the cheek of it. If you want to keep your job, we can go a few rounds... if you get a few good hits in, you can keep your job, but if I put you on your arse, you're out."

ME: "Nah I'm good."

I almost RAN out of there, like a loser coward weasel.

This act began my *Annus Horribilis*... as you will see from the next batch of stories that come down the pipe...

So I fled back home shamefaced... sat on the beanbag and blazed weed at midday on a Monday. I lied to my friends and told them I had been laid off as there was no more work with Robbo.

I farted about for about a week... mentally circling the drain... and grinding down to my last $20.

I needed work for sanity and survival... and a friend told me of another demolition job a few hours north in a town called Whangarei.

I hitchhiked up there and within 24 hours was living in the "BAT CAVE" with the "LOST BOYS."

Yes, the place was called the BAT CAVE. And yes, they literally called themselves the LOST BOYS. I had hit the ground and bounced up into this loft where the crew lived.

Was it to be a full upward trajectory, or just the apex of another arc downward? Well there is a lot more to this book...so you can guess the answer to that...

The "Bat Cave" was the name of the fire-hazard-loft living arrangement above a shady operation called Bat Demolition. The Lost Boys were tweaked out, weed and speed smoking criminal druggies to a man; who lived in the cave and slept on stinking mattresses that lay about up there like mini turds in the toilet bowl of our loft home...

There was also a woman.

She was a skinny, brown and callous-handed 45-year-old pseudo-Wendy mother to this crew of misfits, and she bunked with us all in that festering cave at the top of the stairs.

She was trying to have a baby — no strings attached — anyone who wanted to mount her and shoot her full of life-creating goo was welcome. I don't think this was ever successful; as the combination of her hard life, her advancing age, and the amount of drugs being done by the studs, all amounted to firing blanks into barren soil.

I almost got up the courage to plant a seed myself—but the room never seemed dark enough, nor the drugs I was on strong enough to enable me to climb onto that double bed in the corner and deliver the goods.

In the mornings she would get up first and make porridge in a big black pot and then bang the ladle on the side to wake us for breakfast.

It was nourishing enough, as she threw in a few handfuls of peanuts and raisins, and after downing a few cups of strong instant coffee, the Lost Boys and I climbed into or onto the various trucks and headed off to the job site.

On one such day, I was on the way to a jobsite in the cab of a long flatbed truck. The driver's name was Dave the Cranker, and he, with his constant twitching and black wrap-around shades, was the poster boy of paranoia. We were stopped at the lights and I noticed him sunk low in the seat and looking in the side mirror at a police car behind us.

To me, and from the corner of his mouth he whispered, "If that pig gets out of his car I'm bolting and you're gonna have to drive the truck to the site... 'cause I'm wanted."

I just stared at him blankly and both my eyebrows went up a tiny bit...

The light went green and we rolled on.

I was assigned to pull nails out of the wood that the other guys were removing from the walls and ceiling of a dilapidated house. I was partnered up with the woman from the Bat Cave, who was the lead nail puller. And, in between her whining about not being pregnant yet, and pulling nails, she would see ghosts coming out of the house and describe them to me. One of them I found particularly disturbing; an apparition of a middle-aged man in a grey suit. He was just standing in the corner of the yard staring at the house being taken down. She told me he was an old music teacher who drank himself to death.

All the rope that I was smoking in the shed with the other workers, every time we took a break, was not helping to shield me from the ghost's evil gaze at my back. And so, I took off into the undemolished lower part of the house to search for treasure.

I wound up working in demolition for a few years off and on, and hidden treasure in the walls and floorboards is not a myth.

Every worker has a tale or six.

One I recall, tells about how a guy was supposed to break a wall down, but was too lazy, and was avoiding the work. The boss then, had taken it upon himself to sledge the wall in, and out from the first hole made, tumbled a fat gangsta roll of sweet hundys in a plastic baggie.

I found treasure myself once, when tearing a wall off. It was two-sixty dusty dollars in a brown paper envelope—obviously some builder's paycheck from the late '70s when the wall was built. The guy must have put it on the ledge and then walled it over. I made it disappear into my pocket.

Anyway... The purpose of the above paragraph was to engage your interest in the subject of pirate-style treasure hunting, while you follow me into the musty old house.

I searched out a few loose floorboards before turning my attention to the chimney. Taking my pry bar I levered out the boards around its base. A hollow-eyed feline face stared up at me and shocked me back a step. I pulled more boards away and liberated the remains of a cat.

Somehow this cat, in decades past, had crawled under the fireplace to die. Once dead, the radiant heat of the fireplace being lit each night for half the year—for who knows how many years—had completely mummified the poor creature.

Its fur was long gone, and it had smooth and hard, yellow, leathery skin—the texture and hardness of a dog-chew leather thing. It was curled into a letter "C" position, but its head was twisted upwards; every whisker intact and splayed, its mouth and fangs wide and yowling, and all claws out and hooky. Most amazing of all was the dried leather collar from which a silver disc hung. Inscribed on the disc, and causing tears to spill from my bloodshot eyes, was the word... "PEACHES."

The main reason I was saddened was that my treasure hunt had revealed nothing but a mummified feline; yet I was gladdened by the fact that my hunt's treasure was found to exceed, by an astonishing difference, the wildest expectations of the most imaginative.

That weekend...

That weekend, I was in the Van Damme Mobile being driven by a young man who was equally driven.

The car was a small and old Mazda 232, two-door hatchback, called the Van Damme Mobile, due to the martial arts prowess of my friend the driver, as well as the fact that the words *"JEAN CLAUDE VAN DAMME" were* emblazoned across the trunk in four-inch letters of black, magic marker.

A typical means of transport for the dispossessed. It could get you to the party on two dollars gas, and get you to the gas station on white light if, by using your magic powers, you could focus enough of it into the engine.

The pilot of the car drove it with the precision of a short-range, high-powered Star Fighter. Storms, wind, headlights turned off—it did not matter. It was always piled high with garbage and scurvy lunatics. We lived out of the thing. It was our pirate ship—we plundered gas stations and *parties* were our pirate coves. There was not much rum, but there were plenty of wenches and shouting. The captain was sailing us to a pirate cove at this very moment, far to the southeast.

We had to stop and get something though.

I had them stop at the demolition site. Went ashore and dug up my treasure. Wrapping it in a long purple curtain I secured "Peaches" in a large plastic paint pail. I put the mummified feline into the hold of the ship, telling everyone that it was not to be opened until we reached our destination.

Through mountains and forests we sailed and, on dark, we arrived at the party in the bush. It was full, drunken and pumping, and I staggered in swaying, sea-dog style.

I soon met a young wench who handcuffed herself to me! Had I been in a less bewildered state, I may have been able to take advantage of the situation and gotten down to some serious wenching—yet, as the Egyptian errand boy and courier of Peaches to its final resting place, I had responsibilities.

I got the coffin out of the car and, leading a group of interested partygoers who begged me to tell them what was in the pail, I headed through the bush to the river.

Someone had a flashlight, and this prevented the coffin from being too seriously bashed against the trees as we blazed a trail to the river— where Peaches would be interred with enough ceremony to appease the gods.

We were nearing the river when I tripped, dragging the handcuffed wench down into a ditch with me. The coffin spilled open, and the wrapped package tumbled out.

The wench got up and, in stepping backwards, stood on Peaches with the sickening crack of a mummified cat bursting asunder. I was shocked at the violation of the sacred relic and gently opened the shroud. The scene was illuminated by the torch bearer, and it showed my beloved Peaches in many pieces. The head was still good though— and staring up at us accusingly with its dark, empty sockets, mouth and fangs wide and yowling in protest.

That's when the screaming started.

I tried to grab the silver medallion on the collar, to show everyone that it was a good, happy cat once, and would not curse us with its wicked Egyptian magic. By reaching for Peaches with the handcuffed hand, I dragged the handcuffed girl close to the broken feline body and only succeeded in grabbing a small handful of dried Peaches.

Her frenzied and desperate attempts to get away, caused the *handful* to catapult out of my grip and to hit her in the face, letting loose a small cloud of yucky-tasting, yellow powder from the main pieces of the dried Peaches. The main "bones," I guess you could call them, somehow tangled in her hair and we both went down in a shaking, shrieking mess.

She managed to find the key, unlock herself, and flee to safety. But not before she stood on my crotch...

I made a mental note to have the Pharaoh execute her later on. The fickle party people left me there in the woods. I lay there for a bit, and when I could crawl, I picked up Peaches, wrapped it in the shroud, and staggered to the banks of the Nile.

I commenced the ceremony to the gentle, protective goddess Bastet —to ferry sweet Peaches to the other side of the Styx, and to soothe my aching balls.

When I had finished with the sacred prayers and chants, I flung the shroud into the waters and watched it drift off into the darkness.

Chapter 37
ACTUALLY CRAWLING WITH BUGS (Festa Infestation)

So there I was, a young man...

Well, not really a man—more like a deranged freak who was living such a debased lifestyle that I got scabies. This is an infestation of the skin with a microscopic mite. It itches like hell, and makes your skin smell strange and sourish, as well as giving you tiny pimple-like blisters that, when you pop them, oily stuff comes out of—which is actually full of the eggs of the little bastards.

When you get warm, like in bed or in the shower, the little scabies wake up and start going crazy—which itches like fuck and you can get no sleep.

When you are in the shower, the site of the infestation shows up as a red rash. What you thought was just a few on your chest, is actually a fully harsh PLAGUE of them, up and down most of your body—making you feel like a degenerate dog, a social outcast, and a festering leper. Which is pretty much what you have to be, for these little mongrels to get hold of you in the first place.

Often in the past, when taking drugs, I would have bad trips. These gibbering nightmares were frequently characterized by the feeling of bugs crawling all over my skin.

It was one such time, when I felt that my skin was crawling with bugs; which did not cause me undue duress, as it was, of course, hallucinogenic drugs as per usual. But...

I REALIZED THAT I WAS ACTUALLY CRAWLING WITH BUGS!!

I experienced a freak-out of Jurassic proportions. I went into itching-my-skin-off overdrive. Then I went into the shower to scrub with every liquid in the stall *and* the harsher ones under the sink.

Soon, my cock and eyes started burning, and all the cuts from my harsh scratching started fizzing from the brutal cleaners. I started thrashing about, weeping and screaming quietly, as there was a party going on in the lounge.

Regardless of the "treatment", I could still feel them—they were going to crawl into my organs and kill me!

I turned the shower on cold in a desperate effort to drive them into hibernation. I lay on the shower floor—a tripping, shivering, hyperventilating, wigging mess.

With my eyes closed, I began my guided meditation. I went to my cave. I found my power animal. It had scabies too, and I had to kill it.

The cold killed the itching and I somehow got out, dressed, and dried. I made it back to the party, chain-smoked marijuana cigarettes, put on a happy face, and just rode it out like the trooper I had trained myself to be...

Later that week, I was staying at my girlfriend's house and she couldn't sleep. And she felt very itchy.

I calmly told her that she was now a festering, scabies-hosting dog like myself, and there was no hope for us.

She got up to have a shower, but I dispassionately informed her that a shower would just make the little cunts come alive and start chewing —and that her best hope was to try to block it all out with gin.

As gin was from the olden days... my twisted logic was that it would somehow help?

She crawled into a little ball on the edge of the bed and cried for a bit, whimpering out, "I'm crawling..." to herself for a while.

Then she left me there in the scabid darkness, and went to cry to her friend in the next room about it.

By morning, I was a TOTAL outcast.

My festering little parasitic secret was out. And I was banished from the house.

I holed up at my friend's winery, spending most of the next five days in a numb dreamworld I had created, by nibbling poisonous toadstools and washing them down with a strong, white spirit made from kiwifruit.

I got a call to come back, as the girlfriend had the cure, and the entire flat was gonna knock the bastard scabies on their heads—as they all had the infestation now.

Apparently, one girl had got it from sleeping in our bed while we were away.

Why? Because she liked my smell... fair enough...

She had given it to a guy in the house through sleeping with him, and the grot transient, who lived on the couch in the lounge, got it from using everyone's towels.

They had all put in money and bought a big tube of horrid-smelling grey cream.

So I went back to the house and that night, I smeared it all over me and lay back to enjoy the final death throes of my microscopic chums.

It burned me like napalm. It burned my eyes and willy worse than the Draino I had rubbed on myself to try to kill the bugs in the shower.

I thrashed about and screamed a little—but you weren't allowed to wash it off. The shit reeked like petrol, and I was dying a poisoned death. It made me feel really sick and washed out.

The girlfriend was sleeping in her friend's room by now, and I could hear muffled crying and thrashing about from both girls.

And I don't think it was because of some crazy lesbo sex romp—because I heard them both puking out the window around midnight.

The next morning, we got rid of all our bedding, and washed all our clothes in hot, hot water, then dried them on a hot, hot cycle—which, explained the doctor who prescribed the cure—kills them.

I could have got the scabies from any of a number of places, as I lived like a dog, just sleeping wherever, a lot of the time.

Now, I think back almost fondly to my little time as the owner of a festering scabies infestation. I was a good host, and probably would have let them stay until I peeled the flesh from my bones.

I still haven't paid for my $12 share of the poison goo that was used to kill them. But if they ask me for it, I'll just charge them for renting my scabies.

Chapter 38
CHIMNEY HOUSE (I was a psychic witch for one day)

So there I was... a young man.

Shit had gone bad... It's two fucked years. I'm 20 going on Keith Richards.

Lost the last real job at 18, when I gave being a tough Demolition worker a shot... gave everyone scabies... descended into non-stop partying and mind bending drugs...

Mysticism, Aliens, crystals, dream catchers. The *Celestine Prophecy*... If you know, you know.

At this point it was 1997. I was 20.

Sleeping away Monday through Thursday... partying Friday through Sunday.

Crimes. Living rough, with a girlfriend who had followed me out of her upper-middle-class world into the grodie hell I lived in.

You know how parents say, "She was doing great at university and then all of a sudden she quit and now she's with this guy, and she's doing badly and is acting crazy."

I was that guy.

My mind was made of black stone. A thick dark haze everywhere I looked. Cough up a little more black soot and keep brushing my teeth. That's the way.

A voice from the left of me, sort of low and whimpering:

"Babe, if you don't love me anymore just say so and I'll go back to Mum and Dad's in Auckland, 'cause there's no use me staying here if you're going to be like this."

I looked down to see her, white and shivering, wearing my pants, my hat, and my jersey, sitting on the floor... dejectedly looking up at me.

"Be like what?" I said.

"You haven't said anything in weeks, you're like a robot! All you do is grunt and smoke dope!" she yelled.

It didn't even startle me. A robot? The truth was much worse. I was Iron Man. I had been turned to steel. What had done this?

An ounce or two of grass a week, hundreds of doses of LSD, magic mushrooms, poison toadstools, speed, opium, amyl nitrate, nutmeg, morning glory seeds, datura, mescaline, assorted pills, bags of wine and hard booze.

I was a wooden doll staring out from the eyes of a wooden doll. A drug-fucked mess.

A disappointment to all. I had done the right thing and not contacted my parents in two years, except by phone every few months to give them a rambled bullshit update that I was still alive and working somewhere.

I looked at her...

I said, "Nah, I'll go to Wellington, gimme a lift to the highway, I'll hitch to the ferry."

I decided to go back to living on the streets. The man with no name.

The poor girl drove me down the road in tears and said she would meet me in Wellington in a week or so, to give the relationship another shot. I mumbled some sort of reply... *how will you find me...?* I thought...

With my backpack on, my ferry ticket in my pocket, forty dollars in my wallet, and skateboard in hand, I headed down the highway into new realms of adventure.

Free from the nagging.

An aged gray and slightly shaking hippie in a battered Volvo picked me up a short time later.

I hitchhiked to Picton. I crashed in the plastic bubble at the top of the slide in a playground, which doubled as a drifter's bedroom.

Inside the playground bubble, I slept until woken by the words "There's someone in here!" coming from a worried-looking child who was peering at me from the top of the slide.

I slid down the slide and headed to the ferry.

I arrived in Wellington with my backpack, my skateboard, and my new life. I headed down the street into new realms of adventure.

The first people I met were a crowd of young teens, kids of well-off parents, running wild in the center of town. They gave me handfuls of cash to purchase them alcohol from the liquor store.

I came out of the store loaded up to head height with boxes of beer and casks of wine (and a huge tax on the mountains of change nicely stashed away in the top of my sock).

One of the kids gave me a ticket to see a popular NZ band called *Shihad*, who were playing up in the university at the top of Wellington —a distance and altitude which, in his state, was impossible to cover. So up the hill I fled, fueled by hearty swigs from their beverages, which I freely taxed.

I got to the concert and just walked in! Not needing my ticket at all! Being the powerful entrepreneur that I am, I grabbed a ticket stub and headed outside, past the doormen who had suddenly appeared.

Scalping my ticket outside to some happy punter for $20, I headed back in on my floor stub to buy a big frosty mug of ale and sit up on the balcony (thinking to myself that I was far too old and wise to be leaping about downstairs, and was more suited to watching the show from up on high).

Now I had money, a show, and a glowing warm numb feeling. I was the king of the world.

After the show, I headed into the graveyard to reflect on my part in the grand scheme of things while I looked over the lights of Wellington below me.

The realization of my life path came to me: I would forever be a drifter. Wandering from town to town, relying on my wits and my luck to get me through... having crazy adventures, and perfecting the art of being a rip-off artist.

It was time for bed, so I headed to my old house.

My old house was half of a huge fallen-down chimney which was located to the side of a long flight of stairs in a patch of over head-high weeds that only seem to grow in the center of cities.

Three years previously I had lined the chimney with cardboard so I wouldn't get all sooty, and I had stashed a candle stub and some matches in there.

All was in order — still totally untouched. I read my book (*The Stand*) for a while then slept.

Something was smashing into my feet! I awoke!

"Who's that!?" I said.

"Ohhhh... sorry man, I locked myself out of my apartment," came a drunken voice. "I sometimes stay in here but I'll sleep outside."

"Right... goodnight," I said.

In the morning I looked over and saw a young man in a business suit blacked out on my doorstep.

I said, "Wake up bro, it's morning."

He blearily looked at me and went, "Oh... yeah... see ya." And staggered off.

The view from my chimney was usually pretty dull—the back of an empty building, with windows looking into an empty building. But not today, dear readers, oh no... not today.

That building had been renovated into nice apartments. Today the windows looked in on the kitchen and lounge room of some kind of student flat. *And* the bedroom of a young couple who were at that moment performing some rather vigorous morning exercises.

I was transfixed, half hiding, half staring, all in the name of knowledge and learning, of course... Oh, and in the name of purely perverted voyeuristic spying too.

Anyway, I was at home in my chimney. I roamed the town, falling back on my old street survival skills: smoking, browsing, shoplifting, meeting and talking to people I didn't know; acting like a crazy man and then having them go weird on me, and then having the whole scene go weird, and then weirdly slinking off, to quietly hide somewhere, while looking out into the city and smoking dope, while convincing myself that I've got it made because I'm not living by the rules of society, and I alone have unraveled the innermost mysteries of this sector of the universe by means of heroic doses of hallucinogenic drugs.

Latimer Redlance

If someone had just yelled in my face, "You're a bad-smelling sweaty, feral loser with a slippery hold on reality who lives in a fallen-down chimney, wake up to yourself!" I might have snapped out of it.

But in all seriousness, I probably wouldn't have, and would have dismissed the yeller as just another victim of "The Man" in a severe state of denial, and what I would later call "Matrix Pod Person Lockdown."

Over the next few days, I learned more about the couple who lived in the house next to mine. They enjoyed each other's bedroom company very much, and would sometimes use objects on each other they would get from a box beneath the bed. After each episode they would write something on the wall under the calendar, before retiring to the kitchen for a few cones from the bong before blacking out.

People do funny things when they think no one is watching them. Things like farting on a pillow and then smelling it, picking their nose and eating it, sitting and staring at nothing, staring at themselves in the mirror for ages, standing and staring at nothing while twitching their fingers, or having a pretend argument with invisible people.

From this social experiment, I deduced that most people do worse things in private than they pretend to be shocked at in public.

A whole world of "not thinking that anyone was better than me" opened up before my eyes.

I always must suppress a little smile when something bizarre I say is responded to with "That's terrible!" or "That's just fucked, you should be put away."

Yes... suppress a smile, and imagine the person who is berating me farting into their own cupped hand and smiling happily while smelling it.

Anyway, I was climbing a flagpole located in a small park when I saw two people laughing below and swigging from a bottle of wine.

I climbed down and regaled them with stories of my adventures while taxing their wine.

They found me so witty and interesting they invited me back to their place for some coffee, chatting, and dope smoking.

We chatted away as we strode through the city and eventually arrived at their house.

It was in front of my little chimney! This was the couple!

Woooooooo.

We proceeded to the lounge and she got some coffee on.

She said, "Where's the bong."

I said, "In the gumboot."

They froze and stared at me. The pregnant silence that followed gave birth to my sudden outrageous claim...

"I'm psychic and sometimes receive pictures from people's minds."

I explained that I came from a line of witches from Denmark and these talents had plagued me for many years, the visions I received sometimes being so much that I would have to leave town and live in the bush for a few weeks where there were no people, just to get my head straight and convince myself I wasn't going insane.

The lies flowed from me smoother than shit from a waxed arsehole.

They sat on either side of me and tried not to stare at my trench-coated form. I must have made quite a picture there, sitting on their couch, my grubby black hands clutching the bong like it was a sacred idol, and taking huge pulls from it like I was born with a third lung. Long, dreaded hair, ratty beard, green teeth, long filthy nails, and piercing ice-blue eyes furtively glancing about.

"What else do you see?" she asked.

I began a story of looking into the souls of men and gauging the darkness or light thereof, peppered with spice about people's minds being filled with worry about what people thought of them and stress about wondering if they have been caught doing what they think they shouldn't.

They both looked concerned.

"What do you see about us?"

I knew this was coming and I was ready for it.

"Ohhhh, you don't want me prying into your head. I have found it just makes people angry and scared, so I don't do it anymore."

Now I had them. They pleaded, they pretended they thought I was a fake, and they offered me more weed (which I accepted as I said that dope has magical properties which help expand psychic power and awareness. The more weed the deeper the reading).

A burning fire rose up in me, a huge golden lion roared like a pillar of white-hot light. My head felt as if it had been filled with hot, soft sand. All exterior surroundings took on a hazy sheen, sounds were muted, and I felt as if I were encased in a huge soft velvet cushion.

I put the bong down and something inside told me that any more of that would precipitate unconsciousness.

I lay back on the couch and they stared at me while I sank into it and pretended to be concentrating on conjuring up images from their minds, adding just the correct amount of twitching and gibbering to give it a dangerous, mystical quality.

I let my eyes half close as if I were in a trance and made some strange yet convincing noises, suggesting I was in a deep, hypnotic state.

"Ohhhh... I can see a blue bedroom with a red duvet... I can see a calendar... now this calendar hides something... there is something behind the calendar."

I stopped and opened my eyes. "You're getting worried, I cannot possibly continue!" I exclaimed suddenly.

For five minutes I let them convince me that they were definitely not scared and really wanted me to continue.

More cones were needed to penetrate the shield of fear they had put up, and we had to go into the bedroom for a clearer reading.

So bong in hand I marched into their boudoir.

Now this was freaky, seeing their room from the inside. I kept my mind on the task at hand, and resisted the temptation to look up at my chimney house.

Closing my eyes to draw more pseudo-psychic power I said, "Yes...

Yes... a lot of sex goes on here, you really do enjoy each other's company..."

I opened my eyes to see their smug proud looks, and I asked what was behind the calendar. They pulled the calendar back to reveal a chart with lines depicting who was the first to orgasm, being some sort of sexual contest between them to see if they could outlast each other.

I decided it was time to start firebombing.

Why? ... because I was a WHACKO!!

I painted a picture from my mind's eye of various acts and particular instances, complete with times and descriptions. The look of worry and fear on their faces was delicious as I described the conjugal acrobatics they had been performing.

Then I dropped the bomb.

"Wait!" I said. "There's something under the bed." And reached down as if to look.

He was on me in a trice! "This has got far too personal," he stuttered, red-faced.

I hung my head in mock shame and said, "I understand all too well, never again shall I use my powers for such a purpose, I see now that it is a secret I must harbor within no matter how much pain it brings me."

"Nice meeting you," they lied as I left.

I headed around the side of the building up the stairs and over into the bush to my chimney where I crouched and watched the frightened conversation going on between them in the room below.

They took the box from under the bed and hid it under a whole lot of clothes in the wardrobe.

I never saw them again in my existence... but out there in the world are two people who believe in psychic witches because of me. I think that's a good thing.

A few days later I rang the friend I had left for dead in a weed coma on THE BAZ—he was yet to be incarcerated in the mental institution but was furiously working towards it. He was living at home with his mother like all great psychotics do...

His mother answered and happily told me that the cops were looking for me, and had called their house, and I should go and see them at the police station. Well, that was terrifying...

But I went to see what the hell they wanted... there was no chance of arrest as I'm way too smart for that shit... or was I...? I would see—maybe one of my many crimes had caught up with me...

When I told them my name the female cop smiled warmly and said, "Ohhhh your girlfriend has been worried sick about you and she has been calling us to see if we had located you. You can call her on this phone here if you like."

I called, and we met up.

When she learned I had been living on the streets like a hobo for the last two weeks, she was not impressed at all. She was to learn a lot more about me to be not impressed with as the next few months went by...

We took up rent-free residence in her psychotic aunt's house, whose husband had just yesterday dropped to the ground on the path in front of the house, almost dead.

She discovered that he had been cheating on her for two years with a lady from his office they called "The Rottweiler," and he had taken to downing whole bottles of gin after breakfast, and throughout the day, then hiding the bottles under the bed.

We crashed there eating all her food and stinking up the place until deciding to move on.

Chapter 39
THE CHANGE OVER (This is Major Tom to Ground Control)

I AM NOW GOING TO DOCUMENT A CRAZY AND BRUTAL THREE months of my existence in one multi-part story.

It's the tale of when I decided to leave behind the free-wheeling life of hedonism, drugs, sloth and mysticism. And get off the drugs, get a haircut, get a job, and re-enter Earth's orbit.

Since that decision there have been many days where I wistfully wished for my former bean bag and bong life... but I never went back... I went from strength to strength... From strength to strength I went from and to...

This is that story.

I will set the scene on how bad shit had gotten... you may have a bit of an idea by now...

I'm 20. It's Dec 1997 and I'm in a damp and ramshackle hut-like house up in the cloudy ranges of East Coromandel, New Zealand.

I'm chain blazing bush-grown weed on a sagging couch with the old (45) weed-growing mystic who was my mentor.

I had fully gone to rot. My hair was just one dreaded beaver tail, my memory was shot, my lungs black, and my grip on reality was gone. I wore no shoes and just had black hobbit feet. As I have mentioned, the cause of the mental shattering being an ounce or two of grass a week, hundreds of doses of LSD, magic mushrooms, poison toadstools, speed, opium, amyl nitrate, nutmeg, morning glory seeds, datura, mescaline, wine, and hard booze.

Never beer! Beer was the drink of "The Man"!

My survival system was that the energy from the earth flowed up through my bare feet, into my body, through the chakras and out through the crown chakra, then back through my beaver-tail dreadlock and down to the earth, then up and around me in a cycle, forming a powerful energy shield around me that kept all the evil out.

A great system. The best system.

My mentor was a wise old (45) hippie and he was currently listening to me lamenting the crossroads I was at.

For the last two years, I had a girlfriend whose parents were rich and had houses about the country. Our survival system: live in these houses rent-free while leaving them only to travel about the country going to raves. Income was created by selling this old hippie's weed, supplemented with the odd scam. I had the rave network for the product.

It was a life, but not one that wound up in sanity or health... as you can imagine.

My mental state was: vegan, druggie yoga psycho with a twist of grunge.

My crossroads was that the girlfriend's parents had put their foot down and were pushing her to get a job and re-enter society.

They were becoming more concerned for us as we became more deranged and incoherent... but they were super liberal permissive types... so we pushed it as far as we could... which was two years, culminating in an episode of giggling insanity at an important family dinner, followed by loud, baked and drunk sex in the lounge, which the little sister walked in on and watched for some time before bursting into loud screaming hysterics.

So... the girlfriend had a serious meeting with the parents the next day, which I was not part of.

This harsh parental meeting precipitated in her, a mental crisis, and she started talking nonsense like going back to art school, and living in the city. She gave me a rehearsed dream-sell speech. I was encouraged to get a haircut and a job and clean up. Ease the throttle off the drugs back to very occasional, and stay in the city where we would live with her parents until moving out and getting a place together...

I knew where that leads: wearing shoes, a job, wine bars, bank accounts, taxes, going to dinner parties, eating meat, and getting on the hamster wheel.

Just a rat in a cage. A brick in the wall. A patsy of The Man.

Death would have been preferable.

Crisis point for me. What to do? I didn't want to change my lifestyle, but it looked like the end of the line for her and me.

The old hippie commiserated with me and my plight.

I was not at all a "wearing shoes, job, wine bars, bank accounts, taxes, going to dinner parties, eating meat, and getting on the hamster wheel" type of guy. I was a: "meditate amongst the weed crops in the woods, on mescaline, while covered in mud, crystals, and dream catchers and wait for the Aliens to land" type of guy.

He offered an alternative to selling out and cleaning up...

"DON'T DO IT MAN!"

Instead, he offered: Can the girl, move into a teepee on his property, take on his daughter as a partner, buy a motorbike, and do midnight weed runs to the city, while living with them in the off-grid survival base helping him tend the farm.

His back had started to give in, and he couldn't bring the weed down from the high hills anymore... he couldn't grow as much food as he wanted and I was young and strong.

We hole up here, put on parties, blaze, do yoga, and rock back and forth in our rocking chairs at night... waiting for the end, as predicted by the Mayans (2012).

Living our life according to the teachings of our dog-eared *Celestine Prophecy* paperbacks, and supplemented by what the mushroom elves told us.

And so it was that I put together a pound of weed into a backpack with my minimalist gear, and headed back to the big city to drop the bomb on the girlfriend.

I was going to move up into the bush; live in the teepee with the old hippie's daughter, and have a good 14 years before the end of the world.

Latimer Redlance

It was a calm sunny November Saturday in Ponsonby, Auckland when I announced my plan to the girlfriend.

She was fragile at the best of times.

The bomb was dropped in her mother's brand new, million-dollar mansion.

Pure white and glass, huge fridge full of the stinky cheeses, olives, and the best salamis... the house had a catwalk over the lounge for fuck's sake.

I don't know if you have ever been in one of these mansions... but they are very rare in New Zealand. The top 1%...

White Range Rover in the driveway... you get the idea. Over-intellectualized outrage at everything... after two glasses of wine.

I was the bottom 1% as you have read... a cunning ragamuffin from the streets. On an off day I was Jack from *The Titanic*.

I needed to be back with my people. I had stunk up the lives of the upper class long enough... It was time for me to roll out and embrace my earthy family.

So I told her the plan.

I didn't quite think it through.

One moment she's happily talking about how we should go to the beach tomorrow... The next she's hysterically screaming and crying and going on about how she's just wasted two years, while trying to rip my face off.

Her mother came in, concerned but so permissive she didn't say or do anything. There really was nothing more to say... but...

"It's been good."

And I rolled out after being together for two years, every day since our first night.

You're as cold as ice
   You're willing to sacrifice our love
   You never take advice
   Someday you'll pay the price, I know

. . .

I shouldered my bag and sauntered out and up Ponsonby Road.

I then realized I had no money, and no friends that weren't connected to her—*and* who also all saw me as a super sus, purple polar fleece wearing, deranged druggie mystic... *especially* the guys, who all loved her and would POUNCE... before the bed was cold.

BUT—I had my wits, my charm, and my pound of weed...

I stopped at a kids' park and got talking to some forty-year-old single mum. We seemed to get on as we sat on the swings and chatted, but she was not keen on the idea of putting me up for a few days in exchange for "help in any way she could come up with" ;)...

She suggested I call upon family in such a situation as I had lamented to her.

I remembered my sister who I had not seen in more than a year. I had heard she was living in the empty house of a deceased relative of ours.

Perfect. I rolled across the city and presented myself.

I told her of the breakup.

She took one look at me and said, "You're not on drugs are you? You don't have any drugs with you do you?"

"No!" I said. "I'm off the drugs, I live a clean hippy life."

She allowed me in, and through our catching up I guess she ascertained that I was certainly on all the drugs.

At this time, my wonderful sister was living a clean, productive life, working at a Spiritual Life Improvement Center. A place where they helped people clean up and get educated and improve their lives.

She told on me to the people at the Life Improvement Center the next day.

I can imagine it now: "My brother showed up, I'm worried about him. He wears tie-dyed clothes and no shoes. He laughs at nothing... his front teeth are green, his fingers are black and he smells like burning leaves... he keeps talking about aliens and magical energy... what should I do?"

She convinced me to go in and meet her workmates.

I was highly sus of any kind of Spiritual Life Improvement Squares, but I thought, "Nothing is real anyway so it doesn't matter."

I went in with her the next day and they were so nice. So friendly. It was scary. No one can be that kind and nice to an insane dude with a beaver-tail dread matt, and a belt bag full of drugs and money.

After chatting for a bit, one happy, bright and clean-looking guy started calmly showing me some info on drugs and the damage they do to the mind, body, and spirit... "Just for your own interest," he said...

It was such spooky information, that I suddenly realized I didn't want to know anything about it. But like seeing a car crash... I could not look away... I had read some of the words... It was too late! I learned that: drugs are toxic to the mind and store in the body. Certain drugs can become reactivated in the body's system long after taking the drug, and you can get flashbacks or the drug-like feeling of numbness or stonedness later on.

Also that learning ability becomes damaged, the endocrine system gets disrupted, and with that the hormones and the emotions... the organs can atrophy and the body's functions become worse and worse... insanity and serious mental issues can result...

I had heard from a few drug-free hippies that drugs blew holes in one's Aura and I apparently looked like a black hole to them... but here was similar information in a fancy book...

I was living with daily flashbacks... all I had to do was look at the wall or floor and it would shift and melt. My brain at this point was composed of about 45% LSD crystals, my blood was 77% THC, and my cock was a big green mescaline cactus...A number of my friends had killed themselves after a few hard months on drugs, and some had been incarcerated in mental asylums...

Hmm...still not sure if there is anything to this dangerous drugs malarkey.

The guy gave me a tour of their drug detox facility and claimed that they had great success in helping people detoxify and become drug-free and all cleansed, healthy, and aware. It was affordable and safe. The happy clean-looking guy asked me if that's something I would be into?

"Nope. No need! I'm perfectly fine, sirs! I'm heading up into the bush to put on parties, blaze, do yoga, and rock back and forward in our rocking chairs at night... waiting for the end as predicted by the Mayans (2012)."

I peeled some smelly money off my gangsta roll and bought two books from them: one about the mind, and one about past lives, and then I rolled on out into the street.

Suddenly the world swam and twisted about me. Like a bolt from the blue, I realized that on my current hard-partying trajectory I would be dead way before 2012. I then had a thunderous panic attack, from the depths of which emerged a cunning plan. I went on back in, and to their surprise I said yes! I would quit drugs and do the month-long medical detox!

My plan was to get the five solid years of drugs out of my system and be reborn.

I would *then* be able to get high off *one* toke! Instead of having to smoke ten joints a day just to function. Genius! The horrendous flashbacks would go away, and I could live my dream of using the drugs for more spiritual reasons, like the smarter hippies advised. I had started to suspect that there was possibly nothing spiritual about taking acid on a Wednesday morning and watching a box set of *Dr. Who* VHSs.

I was going to be able to be one of those weed growers that MADE MONEY because they weren't blazing their entire crop, and blowing all their money on munchies-enforced purchases of takeout five times a day.

I made a beeline to the girlfriend's mum's mansion to inform her of my new plan. I was going to do a Health Program and get fully clean and become a proud member of society! This was a bare-arsed lie. The truth was simple.

I missed her and the big house with the huge shower, expensive soaps, and the fridges full of food. Clean sheets, her mum's awesome vinyl collection, and the delight of a warm tall blond female. Man, I was a cunning bastard. I'm not proud, I just write it out—what happened.

I rolled up to the door having been gone only 48 hours. One tearful conversation outside with the girl, detailing out my new plan…

"I'm going to do a Health Program and get fully clean and become a proud member of society. Get a good job, maybe start a landscaping company, and only smoke a bit of weed on weekends, but mostly stick to beer. Might even start wearing jeans…"

The mother's pained and disappointed look when I rolled back into the house was a sight to see.

We had loud, victory make-up sex and I mentally prepared myself for the cleansing...

What of the rocking chair teepee plan? Well... I thought... I would just switch back to that plan when I was cleaned up a bit... That plan was the safety net... which I would probably do in a few months... because fuck the city.

However...

The best-laid schemes o' mice an' men
    Gang aft agley,
And bring us nought but grief an' pain,
For promis'd joy!
The phrase *'gang aft agley'* means *'often goes wrong.'*
As usual, shit was about to go down...

Chapter 40
THE DECISION TO FLEE CAME SUDDENLY
(Ripping bongs to prove I'm not brainwashed)

So... I endured the disappointed and slightly terrified look on the girlfriend's mum's face as I rolled back into the mansion... went to the fridge and made myself a charcuterie platter and then listen to her vinyl collection. I ate food, watched TV, farted up the mansion and carried on as if nothing had happened, hiding my pound of weed up in the closet.

I was scheduled to go into the Life Improvement Center and start the detox the next day, but what I really needed to do right now was boast to our friends about my new life plan, particularly how it was going to make me so much better than them.

And... a big weekend of partying was coming up. *Dancing in the Streets* was on—a summer thing in Auckland where they block off a street, music blares and people dance and get fucked up... I didn't want to miss that... but I was going to start with being drug free for the weekend...just to show those saps how strong I was, then head in on Monday...

Just dancing and a natural high. I would show everyone!

Logical.

So I strode into the dirty, smoky, lava-lamp-lit flat of my friends like a king, and master of my domain. I looked down at them ripping bongs with a sly elitist smile. They were shocked to see me. They had all heard of the breakup and my plan. With word of me abandoning the city, two of them had already made tentative plays for my girl... as is the way in NZ.

I took my place on the stinking, sagging, burn-hole-covered couch and waited till I was offered the bong.

"Nope! Not for me! I'm off the drugs! I'm going clean. Sorting myself out."

My girlfriend beamed over at me proudly. Like she had won a contest for "most shit-together boyfriend." I was tamed. I was not going to disappear into the bush, live in a teepee and pound kids into a hippie chick.

I explained my plan.

"I'm going to do a Health Program and get fully clean and become a proud member of society. Get a good job, maybe start a landscaping company, and only smoke a bit of weed on weekends, but mostly stick to beer. Might even start wearing jeans..."

Their eyes bulged in terror. Mouths opened and closed like hungry goldfish.

They realized their cheap weed supply was about to be cut off. I was their guy. The weed prices in the city were insane.

I was the hippie Santa Claus with the good deals.

I was their shaman that knew all the twisted mystic wisdoms.

I had all the crazy stories...

I took them on crazy adventures in both the inner and outer worlds...

I was just going to do a 180 and get on the fucking wheel?

Like fuck I was.

I was the guy who always gave them no end of shit about having jobs and paying taxes. Over the years they had endured hours of my elitist hippie berating and shrill denouncements of them being "Patsy's of The Man!"

They questioned me at length about the nature of the Life Improvement Center and the program, becoming very concerned that I was going to become a square.

One said:

"You sound brainwashed, man. Those guys really did a number on you. You have already started changing."

Me: "Have not..."

Another said: "The YOU we know would never fall for shit like that. You must have been in shock from the breakup."

Me: "What a load of shit! I'm fine. This is what I want."

Them: "Are you sure... you don't sound sure... you sound panicked and nuts."

"Yeah bro... look, if you have three big bong rips, then we will know you aren't brainwashed... otherwise you are."

Man... I DID feel panicked and nuts... I hadn't smoked any weed in 48 hours, which was the longest without it in about three years. My loving friends were right... I needed the three big bong rips to show I wasn't brainwashed and help get me seeing things straight. So they packed me big cones and I blasted them as if born with a third lung. The girlfriend resignedly joined in... and all was numb and well in the world...

As we monged, baked on the couch, the friends indulged me with the current gossip. Yesterday Bozza had been robbed while taking the money from his workplace to the bank. He was taking a piss in a public toilet, and some balaclava-wearing rogue had come up behind him and put a knife to his neck, grabbing the satchel he had, containing just over $10,000 dollars.

He was currently at the police station. The police had come to the door this morning and had more questions for him. Wow. Crazy stuff.

Soon the door burst open and Bozza burst into the flat... he looked as white as a ghost.

He had a bandage on his neck. He stood there and saw me.

"Yooo... I have something to ask you."

We went off to his room.

"Do you still have that pound?"

Yeah...

"How 'bout 5 grand for it." *(Adjusted for inflation, that's $9,000 today.)*

Ok...Nothing dodgy about this.

I pulled the girlfriend off the couch and explained that we had to go back to her house and pick something up. In the car I told her about the deal. She was happy that we were going to have money, and no more stress about hiding a bale of weed at her mum's place. The deal was done. Now I had 5 grand... and a haunted and hunted feeling...We fled back to the mansion...

A call came in the morning... a good friend from my hometown, not a city folk—let's call him Jazza—asking me if I wanted to drive with him down the east coast of New Zealand for about three weeks, sleeping on the beaches, surfing, chilling, blazing... and culminating in riding our bikes from Picton to Nelson, to a giant three-day rave on New Year's called *The Gathering*, where we would meet up with all our other friends, but we would be the legends arriving in style after a three-day bike ride, which we would do while fasting like total health beasts.

Then rave dancing and drugs and carnage...

THE GATHERING was like a late '90s *Burning Man* in all the best ways, and none of the lame ways. The decision to flee the city and go on the road trip with my pal came suddenly.

I explained my new plan for the male-bondiing road trip to *The Gathering*, to the girlfriend and her mum. I gave $1,000 of hot cash to the girlfriend to shut her up and told her to meet me there. *(Adjusted for inflation, that's $1,900 today.)*

The mum made conflicted faces. I packed my shit, and my mate came and picked me up in his big old Holden station wagon and we burned out of town to beachy freedom.

Chapter 41
BEACHY FREEDOM
(Freedom once more screams out into the night)

So, my friend and I burned out of Auckland into a world of 20-year-old young man adventure towards beachy freedom.

He was a good friend from my hometown and he was a "Worker." This meant that he worked. In this case, on random building sites about the city.

I had not worked in two years, since the incident with the stolen bricks as detailed in the story *PEACHES*.

Of course, my friend did not work in December or January though — that's summer in NZ, and working in those months is a fool's game. He had saved up his money for what we call the "Silly Season. And; with me riding shotgun, two surfboards in the back, two mountain bikes on the roof, a box of sweet potatoes, rice noodles and eggs, a frying pan, sleeping bags, and a large stash of weed; we zoomed off...

We were cruising to the crackly cassette-blasted tunes of *Soundgarden's Superunknown*, new guy *Marilyn Manson*, *Tool*, and of course a glove box full of *RHCP*, *Nirvana*, and *Led Zep*.

Our guide was a tattered book called *Surf Spots of New Zealand*.

The next three weeks were amazing. It rained once. We slept on the beaches. We found beaches that were mostly deserted. We surfed, we blazed, we laughed. We bought lots of fish and chips and burgers.

However... my recent experience with the info about drugs and the damage they do, had impinged on me something fierce... I stopped chain blazing weed, morning to night... and followed my friend's example, allowing him to have a good influence on me.

My friend was not a drug fiend... he was a Worker Guy... fair enough, he was on holiday and 20 years old in New Zealand, so daily blazing was normal... but just one shared joint in the morning and one at night...that was hard for me, but I managed.

I was really getting into the surfing now... And now that I wasn't continually baked, I was not totally useless...

I was reading the spiritual books from the Life Improvement Center, and sharing far-out stories about past lives from one of them, with my companion as we sat around the beach fire at night.

The trip took on a healing quality... fresh... wise... cleansing... It was so peaceful, surfing all day, cruising about the small towns of the east coast...

We were away from all the stress and the haters.

I had a bunch of money and so we were living large. Almost daily I would buy us the best and hugest T-bone steaks and we would cook them in the cast iron pan on an empty beach at sunset after a full day of amazing surf.

To paraphrase one of my mentors...

"The beaches of East Coast New Zealand in the late 90s was a special time and place to be a part of. Maybe it meant something. Maybe not, in the long run... But, no explanation, no mix of words or music or memories, can touch that sense of knowing that I was there, and alive, in that corner of time, and the world. Whatever it meant... I felt that I was going to win life. My energy would simply PREVAIL. There was no point in fighting or pushing or worrying. I had all the momentum; I was riding the crest of a high and beautiful wave..."

I had my 21st birthday on that beach with that friend. We had a beer each. The beer was a nod to my vague idea of quitting the batshit hippy life, and getting on the wheel with the rest of the humans.

This worker friend was all about balance.

"It feels good to come home to my parents and have them be happy to see me, because they know I'm working and learning skills," he would say wisely.

Parents... wow... I was firmly in the "Fuck my bullshit parents!" camp...

I had rolled out of home at a late 16 and never gone back. Four years... sometimes I would be in their area and show that I was alive, then leave. They didn't exist to me. He must have had a normal upbringing... with like Christmas and shit.

The beer we had was called *Tui*, in 745 ml bottles, which is what real men drink in NZ. It was an *East India Pale Ale,* and we had no idea what the fuck that meant because it was 1997.But it was good. And all was good in the world as we sat by the fire, belly full of steak and watched the sun go down, drinking our beers.

We drove through Napier, a beautiful town that was rebuilt in the '30s in a full and amazing Art Deco style after a massive earthquake.

It was good to see. I had been here and had done some seriously bad shit when I was 17, as detailed in the stories: *Poison Apple, Dark Master, Whacky Stick*, and *Out of Tree*...

But I was with a good friend now... and I was not being super crazy and bad anymore... I was in a car and had money. The last time I was here I had been living under a bridge, homeless, starving, and up to super-dooper mischief. I paid for things now. I told my friend as much.

"When I was in this town last, I was literally stealing carrots from people's gardens to eat, and living under that bridge we just went over. Now I'm doing great. I'm buying things with my own money..."

He said, "Well not really... I mean, you know how you sold that pound to Bozza for 5 grand... well, he robbed it from that place he used to work at before he suddenly quit, because of the stress of the 'robbery.' His other mate cut his neck to make the story about being robbed seem real, and they stole the ten grand he was supposed to take to the bank... then he panicked and got rid his share of money to you, because the cops kept asking him questions... everyone knows they did it..."

Wow... this made me think deeply... and then I said...

"Well you gotta say that me having this money is better than not having it... right? And I'm going straight soon so... I guess it's all good..."

He wholeheartedly agreed and we drove on to Wellington.

Now, if you recall from my earlier stories, you will remember a friend I had... a deranged companion in debauchery who went on many adventures with me, as featured in *Out of Tree*, *Stools*, and *The BAZ*. and who, in the end, was too insane for me to be around anymore... lest I drop off into the void with him... I had abandoned him in a hut on an island off the coast of NZ at the last bit of the story *The BAZ*.

We heard he had been incarcerated in a mental institution, due to LSD-caused psychosis, but had been let out after a few months, and had gotten a job with the post office... We found where he lived by calling his mum, as you did back then. He lived with his girlfriend in a small flat that backed up to a scrubby cliff... in a dodgy area.

We rolled up...The house stank. There was no furniture but a mattress in his room, which they slept on in a bundle of scratchy-looking wool blankets—no sheets or anything. There was no TV or couch, just three mismatched chairs they had found on the side of the road. They were on the bag wine, and Glade Air Freshener in a bag to huff (lemon). It was madness.

Only the most debased of us drank the bag wine. I was a man of class. I had not drunk bag wine for three years, since my story *Poison Apple*.

In the liquor stores of NZ, there was almost always a cut-in-half wooden wine barrel filled with what we called "baggie o' wine." Almost always bought by teenagers... The amount of poisoning and vomiting these caused, was later proven to have almost single-handedly destroyed the NZ wine industry, as it created an entire generation that gagged at the smell of wine.

The hag-looking girlfriend was 19 and yet somehow looked like a scary old hag. She was... shapes.

Teeth pointing inward, greasy black hair... terrifying.

She was making dinner for them when we arrived.

Here's the recipe as far as I can remember. I'm gunna call it the **WITCH CHUNK.**

- Get a big roll of hamburger meat and put it on an oven tray.
- Chop up an onion without peeling it, and sprinkle it on the meat in big hunks.
- Cook at the highest temperature.

- Get it out when the outside is black, but the inside is raw, and all the onions are black coal-like chunks.
- Put it on a dirty plate from the sink and bring it into the lounge.
- Sit on a mismatched chair, and eat the whole thing, chewing with your mouth open with your witchy nicotine-stained hands and pointy rat teeth.

For best results, wear a very dirty and stained rayon NZ supermarket uniform while eating.

My old friend was raving, and happy to see us. He ranted hard, filling us in on what he had been up to for the last few years...

The long and the short of it was that he had been taking so much acid since seeing me last, that he had had a psychotic break in the middle of a massive thunderstorm.

He thought this girl from work (not the rat-witch) was at the top of a very, very tall telecommunications tower near his mum's house, which he had to climb to "save" her.

He climbed up to the very top, and she wasn't there, so he sat on the top and tried to meditate, but a wind almost blew him off. He hung on, "tripping balls" and screaming into the storm for some time.

Cue police, ambulance, and incarceration.... But now he's all good, and works at the post office. Cue my friend's and my sideways eyes to each other... I mean... if you are tracking with me, dear reader, I was into being totally fucking nuts, but this was some next-level shit. We shared stories and laughed about the old days...

But there was no doubting it... my friend was gone. He was mostly jammed in a bizarrely constructed reality composed of the psych ward, our high school, and the year spent with me when we were 18.

Mid-sentence, he would interrupt us to ask us to list out who in our high school class would be best in *Superstars of Wrestling*, with the main goal of getting us to say that *he* was the most like *Macho Man Randy Savage*...

His strange-shapes girlfriend had fallen asleep on the floor in a food coma from eating the WITCH CHUNK.

Face down, mouth pressed against the manky carpet. It gets better...

My good friend came out of the bathroom and said, "Bro, help me get something out of the car..." That was a signal...

We made an excuse to get something out of the car... Once out of earshot, my good friend proposed the argument that we should flee... He had gone to the bathroom and the toilet was full of poos—to the top! Like the toilet was broken and they had just been pooping in it over and *over*.

"If I took a dump in that toilet, bro, my balls would be sitting in the poos!

"So he climbed out the window to take a bush dump, as there were trees behind the house..."

He walked round the back of the house and saw something that just fucked his brain. There was a small piney shrub outside the window of our old friend's bedroom. It was covered in used condoms. Like 200 or more.

Our old friend had been rooting this witch-shapes gal and throwing the condoms right out the window, where they wound up making the most scary and unsanitary Christmas tree of *all* time.

It was almost Christmas too.

"That's Christmas trees fucked for me now," my good friend said.

I sighed. The decision to flee came suddenly. I came up with a plan.

"Bro... we lock the car up and leave it here. We pack our stuff for The Gathering and ride on out of here right away. We fast, and cleanse ourselves in the rivers on the way. We sleep in the bush.

No drugs till we get there. Doing this will get the stink off us for sure!"

And so we did.

We said goodbye to our old friend, and rolled out on our bikes to the ferry terminal, catching the evening ferry—we'd get in around midnight, sleep in a park I knew—and from there start the mega ride-quest. Over 300K (190 miles).

Smashing out 100K a day over the mountains like the beasts we were.

Chapter 42
THE GATHERING (The Mothership)

The scenery between Picton and Nelson is magnificent. The Marlborough Sounds, curve out into broad expanses of blue and green water, studded with islands, and maintain brilliant views to your right most of the way. Once you pass the Rai Valley and start climbing the saddles, you can look back down steeply sided valleys of bush and pine forests. Breathe the air... welcome to the South Island.

My good friend and I were biking from Picton, to Nelson, to THE GATHERING.

This was like a late '90s Burning Man in all the best ways, and none of the lame ways. Set at the top of a mountain, with only one tiny access road.

It was total carnage...

Our ride through the mountains was beyond punishing. We had cheap mountain bikes, and carried all our gear on our backs in backpacks. We tried to do it while fasting and drinking river water. Blackouts and uncontrollable shaking were the result. Luckily we did bring some food and rationed it out—Cabin bread and sardines...

And so, we did the three-day ride on about 500 calories a day. We slept off the side of the road in the bush, in our sleeping bags and hammocks.

We made it to Nelson and went to some hippy cafe where we hung out; annoying people until we got a lift to The Gathering in the back of a guy's truck.

The people arriving were a freak show. Few had any frame of reference for how to be or behave at one of these giant festivals. New Zealand didn't have a culture of this type of thing. This was its beginning.

There were people in robes, girls in bikinis and glitter, old hippies, lost teens, and people having meltdowns before it even started. The stages were set up, the music pumping, and the food stalls expensive. No booze though, so no one was getting bottles broken over their faces, which is always a plus.

We stashed our stuff in the forest near the tent city and wandered about until we found our friends (you couldn't text "Where R U?"). I was reunited with my girl! The month away from each other had chilled out all the craziness, and there I was looking fine and sane!

So you can imagine how it all went. Dancing, raving, swimming in the river, and a grubby bush sex session to take the backlogged pressure off...

In the dancing, and music, and excitement, I totally forgot all about my decision to chill the fuck out and get my life back on track. So I got back on the powerful mind bending hallucinogens and had a monumental wig out...

The wig out came on, like an old-timey unstoppable iron train. All aboard. Next Stop: Spaz Station, Crazy-town..

It was late at night, with the pounding "Goa Trance" and the lasers... I was with my friends, dancing, and watching people dancing, and I started seeing glowing grid-like energy lattices form around people... spherical in shape... people were moving close to each other, holding hands, sometimes dancing together...

I saw an ambulance volunteer walking calmly through the crowd; he had some kind of cleaning bucket with him...I then realized, with deep clarity, exactly what was happening...

The grid energy lattice was an energy field that merged two or more people into a ball of pure bliss... your whole essence would merge with another and you would hang in the middle of the air in a vortex of ecstasy. This would be too much for the body and brain to handle, and your whole system would short-circuit... causing you to simultaneously orgasm, piss, spew, and shit yourself. Everyone was doing this, and the ambulance volunteers were cleaning people up after this had happened. Wiping your bum and washing you down, so you could do it again and again. That's pretty normal for a rave like this... right?

I wanted in on this ecstasy vortex game, so I grabbed my girlfriend and started holding her close... kissing her and dancing with her to activate the vortex. I stared deep into her eyes and her face started shifting... her eyes became large and black; her pupils were like dinner plates already, so that didn't help...

I then realized, with deep clarity, exactly what was happening...

She was an alien!And she had been sent to test me to see if I was worthy to come back to the home planet. She had been watching me for these last two years... and it it had all been a test! It all made sense—how easily we hooked up, the total lack of stress over my continual insane behavior, her willingness to roam about with me doing whatever for two whole years...

I said, "OH MY GOD! I love you! I'm ready! I'm ready to leave this planet now!"

She looked concerned and said, "Let's get away from here and talk."

We went off to a quieter area by some trees and sat down and talked.

I explained how I had figured it out. That she was an alien and had been sent to test me. And that now I am ready to board the ship and go back to the home-world.

She listened concernedly and said, "What the fuck are you talking about!? You have totally lost the fucking plot, you're fully wigging out. I'm just your girlfriend, remember... we have lives back in Auckland, I have parents... I'm not an alien!!"

I looked back at her... the alien eyes were gone... and there was just a scared girlfriend...

"Oh wow... I'm so sorry... yeah I was losing it there..."

She smiled with relief...but then...the alien eyes were back...SHE WAS an ALIEN. This was part of the test!!She saw the look on my face.

"Do you still think I'm an alien?"

Yes...This went back and forth for some time...

She would convince me that I was just having a monumental wig out... I would realize this and come right for a bit. Then she would give me a funny look and I would see the eyes, elongated and black, and round we would go... I would try to explain that I had truly passed the test and was ready to get into the spaceship, that she didn't need to lie about "not being an alien" *and* that I was worthy and ready to leave the planet.

She would try to convince me that there was no spaceship. This was, of course all part of the test.

Finally, I realized I had to trick her into thinking I didn't know what was going on, while we still both secretly "knew" what was going on.

"OH WOW I see it now! I totally realize you are "not" an alien! Well that's that. Let's get back to the party..."

So we strolled back towards the dance area.

A group of people ran past us screaming, "THE ALIENS ARE LANDING!!"

Hearing a roaring noise, and looking over the field, I could see a bright, white light and the blinking lights of an alien ship. Suddenly a number of my friends found us and they were grinning at us saying, "Let's check it out."

I then realized, with deep clarity, exactly what was happening... It was a TRAP. My friends were ALL ALIENS and they were EVIL, and they were trying to get me onto a ship so they could sell me into some kind of space slavery!

I sprinted off...

I ran. I ran until my muscles burned and my veins pumped battery acid. Then I ran some more. I ran into a deep patch of bush and hid, down in a dark, mossy gully about a kilometer away from the party. I assumed my meditation posture and focused on generating a spiritual shield of invisibility around me. I stayed in that position in a trance of zero thought, constantly projecting the shield around me, to hide me from the alien search parties.

It worked.

Dawn came and with it a sense that maybe it was all the drugs... But... I would have to check it out.

I walked back to the rave and found my distraught friends. They had been looking for me all night, after watching me have a monumental wig-out and screaming, "IT'S A TRAP!!" and running off into the bush. The alien ship had actually been a rescue helicopter picking up someone who had broken their back falling out of a tree. My wig-out, and total disappearance, precipitated a bad trip in all of them and totally ruined their night, as they had to console my panicking girlfriend.

I almost explained that they would not have been able to find me, due to the invisibility field I was generating to hide from the aliens... but didn't...

I started mentally collapsing under the pure truth of my situation.

Suddenly all the words in the Drug Education brochures, which I had read at the Life Improvement Center, started rolling across my retinas like bright red ticker tape:

Hallucinogens are drugs that cause hallucinations. Users see images, hear sounds, and feel sensations that seem very real but do not exist. Some hallucinogens also produce sudden and unpredictable changes in the mood of those who use them. This leads the user to a serious disconnection from reality.

FUCK.

I'm disconnected from reality... I just came from seeing my old friend who had totally lost his mind ... that would be *me* soon—a totally disassociated animal, overflowing toilets with my poops and throwing full condoms out the window without any regard for right or wrong.

I'm freshly 21 years old, completely twisted. I'm standing in a field with no shoes, a beaver tail dread and no future.

A switch flipped inside me.

We call this THE CHANGEOVER.

"What it lies in our power to do, it lies in our power not to do."

I immediately apologized to my friends and got a healthy breakfast and a bunch of water. I went for a cleansing wash in the river. I stopped all drugs and booze and sugar and caffeine. I started talking to the Hari Krishnas. I walked about smiling at people and trying to act sane. I bent my mind towards trying to do the work to recreate myself into something good.

And...

This worried the fuck out of everyone even more.

I talked about how I was going to clean myself up "for super reals"; They wanted me to find balance.

YIP.

Let's go the other way, full throttle. That will balance things. I had come down from the high and smashed, face first into the hard-packed, danced-on dust. We rolled out of there and I went back to Auckland with my girlfriend and friends. Refusing all drugs and alcohol. Being quiet. Looking out the window and commenting on the beauty of the world.

Scaring them.

Try to see it once my way
Everything zen, everything zen
I don't think so.

So...

On arrival back to Auckland, I essentially crawled back to the Life Improvement Center on my lips, my brain the consistency of fried chicken, with a side of mashed potatoes. I told them I was ready to start my detoxification journey into a healthy, drug-free life.

POW!

Well, the first thing I did was an interview and a medical check, to see the level of toxins in my system. The results would decide if I could start right away or not.

Alas, it was too much...

There was a near deadly amount of drug toxins stored in my tissues... cycling up through my brain and giving me drug-induced psychosis on a bad day and, on a good one, flashbacks and a mystical dream-like feeling towards life where all was unreal...

Oh and to top it all off I had that ONE beer on my 21st birthday.

I was not allowed to start the program right away lest I drop dead. I had to "Dry Out" for two weeks. This entailed thrice daily vitamin and mineral hits, liquid calcium and magnesium, calming walks, three good meals, good rest, and doing some basic Life Skills and Communication training. I was staying with the girlfriend's mother and they were ostensibly supporting me on my detox journey.

I was sleeping 10–12 hours a day, reading the *Bhagavad Gita* that I had got from my Hari Krishna pals, eating at a lot of vegan restaurants, and being calm.

It was very scary. Raw-dogging life. No filter. Just the grim meat-hook realities that were lying in wait for me. Was I now a **"permanent cripple? A failed seeker? One who never understood the essential old-mystic fallacy of the Acid Culture: the desperate assumption that somebody... or at least some force—is tending the light at the end of the tunnel?"**. I was so munted mentally I rarely spoke; I just tried to smile and be the calm center of the world. But sadly no amount of Zen quotes or hippie catchphrases seemed to help me at this point.

I just kept pushing forward. One day at a time. I started the detox and it was intense. Supplements, saunas, exercise, good food, rest and liquid body-rebuilding potions. The drugs started coming out on day one.

I tripped balls every day, as the procedure broke up and unleashed the drugs in my body and sent them back into my bloodstream. I had body-stoned mini comas similar to those I experienced from eating weed cakes black with resin. My skin and piss actually took on a green tinge at one point. I coughed up black sooty shunt from the depths of my lungs.

Every morning when I woke up, I felt like I had come down from a quadruple-tab rave weekend during which I drank nothing but bong water.

But bit by bit, I began to feel better. On day ten, I realized I could smell the mold in my matted beaver-tail dread. I shaved my head to the skin.

My sense of smell and taste went through the roof. I could smell a cigarette on the wind from 300 yards, detect if a woman was in heat, instantly notice anyone's sneaky farts, and other preternatural abilities. My eyesight improved markedly. The world became crisp and sharp.

On day 15, I threw away all my old clothes, which reeked of death to me now, and the many burn holes from all the joint ashings were visible to my sharp eyes. I bought myself a space monkey uniform of sorts so my outer world would match my inner world: Grey cotton tracksuit pants, a light grey hoodie, and white sneakers.

The drugs and the evil continued to pour out of me daily. On around day 30, my sex drive exploded. I realized I had been neutering myself with the amount of drugs I had been doing. The girl and I were having sex about once every ten days. For a healthy 21-year-old in the '90s, this is the sexual equivalent of being castrated.

Now I wanted it the normal amount. Which apparently was: once in the morning on waking rock-hard, once in the middle of the day, and once more in the shared shower before bed... And then maybe once more, in bed.

My sick girl, filled to the eyeballs with soy-milk, tofu, drugs, and wine—her occasional period and sex drive were of no consequence to her. I was starting to drive her crazy. I didn't want to keep hounding the poor lass... So I decided to just lock up the sex drive and focus on my new life.

I had also dropped off the map from all my old druggie friends, but she, of course, was relaying to them the crazy shit I was saying about drugs being bad, what I looked like now, and the scary fact that my eyes seemed to glow. Buried under the drugs, my eyes were a piercing light blue, and now, as my organs were cleared up, they took on an incredible brightness.

On day 40, I completed the program and felt reborn.

I was calm, healthy, drug-free, educated in the ways of how to function in the human realm, and I had fashioned myself a new personality: a calm, friendly, loving, caring man of peace and happiness who sets a good example and is a productive member of New Zealand society.

I would look at people with my magic sparkly eyes, smile, and say things like:

"I understand."

"I'm not judging you for what you're doing. I'm just choosing to live in a way I feel is better for me."

"Everyone is more or less right from their viewpoint."

"What is truth?"

I had spent over a month daily with good, happy people who were not half-nuts druggies...

This world was very new to me. I, of course, swung SO HARD the other way that it even concerned the people at the Life Improvement Center, though they didn't say anything. My new perceptions could sense it...

But the world was gonna have to get used to the new me... cause this is how I'm rollin'...

I was no longer drinking, smoking, having sex or whacking it, doing any drugs, watching TV or movies, reading fiction, listening to music, swearing, eating meat, ranting about mysticism or conspiracies, judging people, being mean or having unkind thoughts, objectifying women, engaging in pride, greed, wrath, envy, lust, gluttony, sloth, or idle chatter.

You get the idea. I was now the MONK, on the path of the RIGHTEOUS MAN!

In the first week after wrapping up the program, some shit went down. My gal was now drinking and doing drugs daily to "cope with the fucking stress of you changing so much!"

Driven mental by the lack of fights and being laid off from her main job of stopping me from doing really stupid shit, and slammed by my sudden absolute change — and now my refusal to fuck her — she had started to lose it.

As a man, it's not kind to repeatedly refuse offers of sex from a gal. Guys are used to it... Being knocked back has a deleterious effect on a woman's psyche. She had made a few desperate attempts to get me going again after the third knock-back. A mouth on my cock while I was asleep, and a naked leap at me that ended in a distressingly tearful begging session.

Some other super racy things were tried to get me going... I'm not going to describe them in detail, but they involved her creating sexy shows for me to suddenly walk in on in the bedroom.

I told her we wouldn't be having sex again until I felt I was ready, and no more showers together, because I only had cold showers now... This pushed her over the edge.

On Tuesday: a tongue ring — for amazing blowjobs, she explained.

On Wednesday: nipple rings — to enhance sexual pleasure...

On Friday: a sexy dragon tattoo on her shoulder.

Now, this was some intense shit for someone to do back in '97, and all in one week no less...None of these things worked on me, so on Sunday morning she shaved her beautiful long blonde hair off, then razored it to the skin like an absolute boss. That's always a good sign. A woman fully shaving her head means she's on a good run, knows the boyfriend loves her so much he is about to propose... or she got the great job...

Now my poor gal was a ringed-up, tatted skinhead whose two dark raccoon eyes looked out from a face that looked like a swollen red pumpkin from all the crying. The black rings around her eyes from her hard-partying life and bad food choices were usually concealed with thick makeup... now she didn't give a shit.

She was 6 foot 1. But now she walked hunched over, when she wasn't bed-rotting. Spiraling down into a black abyss of depression that my cheery Life Improvement slogans made zero impact on. She was not willing to give up drugs, get a job, or go back to university. She was just going to rot in bed and cry, blaze weed, and drink her mum's wine.

Her mother just let her rot — she had failed to help her for the last 20 years and was such a miserable divorced husk herself she knew there was no hope for either of them. I was the light of that house, kept happy, being super nice and eating the yummy food. I refused to let any of that get me down, because as my gal Sarah Connor taught me... *No fate but what we make.*

She did not have the strength to kick me to the curb. I truly thought my positivity would eventually penetrate and she would do the detox, get off the drugs, and be reborn like a hot, sexy, healthy, and ethical angel.

I thought wrong.

I had not seen my friends since The Gathering, and so it was that I went to visit them. I would show them the new me and they would rejoice.

I had some pamphlets that talked about the detox program... maybe I could get everyone off drugs...

What hit me first was the smell. B.O., stale weed, spilt bong water... mold... rot... dog piss and the awesome smell of ciggies put out in beer bottles. The lounge looked like it smelled of sick. I never had noticed this before. On the stinking, sagging couch were Buzzy and John.

Buzzy was a long-time stoner mate, who worked at a plant store, and John was a 17-year-old hanger-on and Buzzy's apprentice in debauchery.

Moldering pizza boxes stacked to the ceiling. Beer bottles everywhere, the coffee table covered in ash and fast food wrappers...

They were hitting Buzzy's pride and joy "Mr Wong." A large white porcelain bong in the shape of a huge cock. Buzzy loved to make gay insinuendos when someone smoked it. It was on that evil couch that I had the three fateful bong rips that precipitated me not starting the detox months earlier and sent me off on a month-long surf trip culminating in a bender in which I went batshit crazy.

Over two months prior, I had announced my plan... "I'm going to do a health program and get fully clean and become a proud member of society. Get a good job, maybe start a landscaping company, and only smoke a bit of weed on weekends, but mostly stick to beer. Might even start wearing jeans..."

If you recall, the following conversation went like this:

Buzzy: "You sound brainwashed, man. Those guys really did a number on you. You have already started changing."

Me: "Have not..."

John: "The YOU we know would never fall for shit like that. You must have been in shock from the break-up."

Me: "What a load of shit! I'm fine. This is what I want."

John: "Are you sure...? You don't sound sure... you sound panicked and nuts."

Buzzy: "Yeah bro... look, if you have three big bong rips, then we will know you aren't brainwashed... otherwise, you are."

Well, now there they were on that stinking, sagging couch again... and I was standing before them, drug-free and resplendent... trying not to judge.

They were reading *High Times*, pulling cones, and talking about how they were going to save up and go to Amsterdam.

I used to sit on that same couch with Buzzy reading *High Times*, pulling cones, and talking about how we were going to save up and go to Amsterdam...

Spoiler alert: no one ever went to Amsterdam.

In the room with us, barking at the rats that lived behind the pizza boxes, were Tripod and Cyclops. They were Buzzy's small, mangy dogs. Tripod was called such due to having three legs. Buzzy had backed over

Tripod with his car and the leg had been amputated. Tripod's name, until that incident, had been Max. Cyclops had been called Rocky before he had been bitten in the face by a rat, causing an infection in his eye, which had to be surgically removed.

So it was quite a scene as you can imagine — two little mangy dogs, one one-eyed and one three-legged, barking at rats behind moldy pizza boxes, in a house that reeked of ass; my friends sucking on a big white bong cock and making mean wisecracks about how I'm now just a "tool of the man", and that I had become everything I had once hated... and honestly, they felt just a bit of pity that I could have let this happen to myself, because once I was so cool.

I remained calm and looked at them with my magic sparkly eyes and said:

"I understand."

"I'm not judging you for what you're doing. I'm just choosing to live in a way I feel is better for me."

"Everyone is more or less right from their viewpoint."

"What is truth?"

The detox brochures sat forgotten in my bag... my dream of helping them crushed...

The bedroom door opened and Buzzy's girl came into the lounge to pound Mr Wong. Wearing only a worn and faded Cure shirt and panties. She was a malnourished stick of a girl, hard on the booze and drugs, and a city vegan.

"City vegan" means she just ate things like chips and tofu burgers and candy bars. She was sick as fuck and explained she had recovered from a hard, bad couple of days caused by some very moldy opium tea that her and a friend had brewed up.

I used to be prideful of people pounding concoctions like this. Now I just looked at her and said, "I understand."

She put her whole mouth around Mr Wong and tried to give me a sexy look. The weed sent her into a coughing fit, which she tried to restrain while holding in the smoke so as not to waste it. A wet farting sound came from the back of her panties as a shit spray was precipitated.

She yelled "FUCK!" — and went beet red — coughing and wetly farting.

I turned and left them to it.

A week later, I decided I needed to:

TAKE A STAND FOR WHAT I BELIEVED IN NOW.

People love it when their newly drug-free righteous friend takes a stand, right? With all their new energy and sparkly eyes and hope!?

Swallowed, borrowed
Heavy about everything
But my love
Swallowed, hollowed
Sharp about everyone
But yourself...

Chapter 43
THE TWIST (Taking a stand)

I was driving the girlfriend and her mother batshit. I got a job as a house painter. This enabled me to listen to Life Improvement tapes eight hours a day. Voices of wisdom and reason directly into the brain. Forty hours a week.

A month of this went by and the girlfriend, now with the nipple rings, tongue ring, tattoo, and shaved head, was leaving me home on the weekends to go to parties, and come back smashed and puking. That'll show me.

I understood.

I used the weekends to jog and walk around Herne Bay, Auckland, do hours of yoga and even MORE self-improvement studies. This also gave me the time to read her own personal documentation of her mental fragmentation via her diary. She had started being hit on heavily by friends of mine, as is the Kiwi way.

In one recent entry, she wrote: "Nothing like a good flirt to recharge my batteries."

Bless her. *I understood.*

Now here's something I haven't talked about...I had a large weed crop secretly growing in the bush-covered hills above my hometown. Ten plants. Each monster plant would yield about a pound; each pound was worth about 5 grand.

The strain was from seeds brought over from India in the 80s. Purple, before it was a thing. This was my backup plan. No one knew about my weed crop because if you are a grower with your shit together you never tell anyone.

It was harvest time. The girlfriend was having a big party down at her mother's beach house... and I shocked everyone by saying I was coming down for the weekend.

We drove down, and I was in high spirits. She had hopes that I had come to my senses and would become more of my old self and enjoy the party with our friends. I had different reasons for being in high spirits.

First thing in the morning, I took off, and taking with me a backpack with water and lunch, I hiked up to my secret weed-growing spots. Each plant was a monster beyond what I could have wished for. The sight of them was so bizarre to me. What would have, in the past, brought me to my knees in rapture and joy, now just seemed like... big smelly plants... The marijuana had no physical or emotional connotations to me anymore. The spell was utterly broken. The idea of selling this crop was a spiritually criminal act to my fellow man, to say the least. I could not even dream of it. But I could still use this crop for good.

I harvested all of it and loaded it into the backpack — I harvested the lot and packed it into my backpack and then hiked out of there to a secluded clearing, where a slip had exposed a large area of raw soil. I built a crisscross of dry sticks and stacked all the weed on top of it. I pulled out the girlfriend's father's video camera, which I had borrowed from the beach house, and filmed the massive pile, giving an excited and enthralled speech on the quality and quantity while zooming in on it.

"As you can see here, I have harvested my crop, and it's a good ten pounds of Barry Crump, Skunk Clone. Sativa-Indica cross, purple calyx super suprandis."

I stopped filming and put the camera aside. Pulling forth a can of petrol that was for the beach home's mower, I doused the weed and wood. Making sure I was downwind so as to not breathe in any weed smoke, I turned the camera on myself, and lighting a dry branch, I threw it at the petrol-covered pyre.

WHOOF!

It went up and started roaring. While the weed blazed in the background, I unloaded a very heartfelt, demented, righteous, serious, staring-eyed diatribe of: *Why I have quit all the drugs and why they are all super bad. Why everyone on Earth needs to be drug-free and live a healthy, clean life. How I'm dedicating myself to being the best example of honesty and purity possible. How anyone who is doing drugs will just get worse and worse and wind up upside down in the dumpster of life. How by burning all this weed I am severing all ties to my old life, its crazy ideals, and becoming reborn like a phoenix from the ashes of my weed crop.*

When I was done, I proudly signed off and set to ensuring that all the weed was burned down to ashes. This took a couple of hours, and I had to continually move around to ensure I never breathed in any of the plumes of stoning smoke.

By the time I got back to the beach house, the party was in full swing. Pulsing trance hummed from the sound system. It was a glorious beast of a music tower that could play multiple CDs.

My old beach house daily ritual was to wake up around 1 p.m, make a huge black coffee for breakfast, take my bong to the Lazy Boy I had parked in front of that exact stereo, and put on either Bush's song "Swallowed" or Soundgarden's "Black Hole Sun"... and pound cones until I could face existence.

Anyway... by the time I got back to the beach house, the party was in full swing. Pulsing trance hummed from the above sound system.

I roll in smiling peacefully. My good old friends from my hometown were there... all the boys and girls that I had adventured and partied with over the last two years... They said "Hi," politely but of course worriedly. The grey tracksuit, and my shaved head, bright eyes, and perpetual blissful half-smile weirded them right out. I had dropped off the map for months since they saw me at New Year's, and according to all reports, gone nuts then gone square as fuck.

I was so calm and focused it was not human. The girlfriend staggered up to me, a hammered mess, and asked me where the fuck had I disappeared to all day?

"I'll show you."

I smiled beneficent smiles to all and turned the music off.

"I have something to show you all. Please watch the following educational video."

I popped it in and turned it up.

The first part was met with sighs of relief! I was back on the weed! I had harvested my crop! Many thought that I had come to my senses and now was back in the fold! I would be blazing huge 4-skin trumpets with them once again! I was smiling, the gal was smiling, my friends were smiling...

"As you can see here, I have harvested my crop, and it's a good ten pounds of Barry Crump, Skunk Clone. Sativa-Indica cross, purple calyx super suprandis."

But it was a ruse. I was setting them up for the crash.

The scene changed to the fiery WHOOF!

The weed blazed, and I unloaded my cringing BE DRUG FREE LIKE ME SPEECH OF THE RIGHTEOUS MAN.

I don't know what I expected really. I didn't care. I thought I was making a penitent stand for all the drugs I had done and encouraged others to do. Everyone started screaming insults at me. CLOWN was the main one. The girlfriend was in my face screaming: "You FUCKING CUNT! We could have bought a house with that money! FUCK OFF! I never want to see you again!"

And that was it. I popped the VHS and rolled out. Smiling and nodding like a bobble-headed spaz. I drove back to the city, went to her place, and packed my meager possessions. Her mother was happy to see me go, and I was happy to start my new life.

I had made one good friend at the Life Improvement Center. He was a musician and once-druggie, now gone clean and creative. I moved into his music room, on a little monk-like mat in the corner. All ties with my past were now cut.

I continued my monk-like life for a number of months, but thankfully I made good friends who slowly brought me to reason and real balance. I started to pursue my dream of acting and comedy, putting together a new personality for myself... and wound up with a powerful and loving clean-living witch for a girlfriend. It took a while but I learned how to at least pass as a functioning earthling.

And that is the tale of when I decided to leave behind the freewheeling life of hedonism, drugs, sloth, and mysticism and get off the drugs, get a haircut, get a job, and re-enter Earth's orbit.

Epilogue

I WENT ON TO BECOME A HIGHLY SKILLED CHEMICAL dependency counselor, getting hundreds off drugs—musicians, artists, vice cops, mothers, fathers, sons, and daughters... To this day I still help the organization that salvaged me.

Www.narconon.org

I must say the way I went about it as detailed in the story above was incredibly stupid and the wrong way to go about it. I have used my bad example to coach many addicts to not ruin relationships with others with crazy righteousness, like I did. All I did was put people off, turn friends away, and give the rehab world a bad name. Because of what I did, I could never set enough of a good example to those from my past to show that there was another way. It is one of the worst mistakes I have made — but luckily one I learned from and used to help others.

Black hole sun
Won't you come
And wash away the rain
Black hole sun
Won't you come
Won't you com

Chapter 44
YOU'RE MY BOY RG (My life and times with Ryan Gosling)

THIS IS A STORY THAT MUST BE TOLD.

I was once sort of friends with Movie Star Ryan Gosling.

Back in New Zealand in early 1998 when I had cleaned up my life, I started on the road to becoming a world-famous superstar actor. This led me to work on a show called *Young Hercules* as one of about 10 extras.

We had many different roles, one moment you were a cadet... next you're a blacksmith—we were constantly recycled. The whole thing was low-budget, but the food and the pay was good.

There was a clear division between the "Stars" of the show and us, the peasant extras, and we were mostly ignored by the guys playing the main characters. They were actually kind of dicks a lot of the time. Our opinion of them was not helped by our jealousy. However, I made it a point to talk to RG who was 18 or 19 at the time. Not Famous yet... Humble, nice and friendly, and an all-around nice guy.

He would actually talk to me, and (to the disgust of his co-stars) we kind of became off-set friends, chatting now and then about Canada and a few of the movies he did before, and how he had an apartment and played Sega and mostly rested after work.

I was 4 years older than him and tried to give him good, healthy, older-brother type advice. I had lived harder and more badass-legit-hobo gangsta than any of these bullshit TV actor mopes. So I felt I did have something to contribute.

I remember the vibe and it was good. It always felt like he granted me my own importance and was encouraging to me. He politely listened to, and agreed with my advice about hard work and clean living. I don't know if he really needed the advice... but you never know...

The other actors would go out partying, take drugs, and come back to the show with no sleep, cranky as fuck and keep ignoring us. Except Dean O'Gorman (who played Fili in The Hobbit). He was pretty dedicated and he actually did stoop to chat with us now and then. From that show, no one made it to the big time except RG and Dean and they were the ones serious about their craft. They also were the ones who were nice to me... sooo.... my blessing was probably what did it...

So, Spoiler alert: I did not become a big-time actor; RG didn't hook me up with Stardom, and I actually just moved to Australia to get away from the misery of New Zealand and pursue Auzzie gals and money to buy food with, as you know.

STARWIPE TO 2006. Eight years later.

I'm in Hollywood. I am doing intensive training to become a counselor, and some fellow students take me to some super popular hipster cafe.

I'm eating my 23$ something or other and I hear.

"Wez! What are you doing here!"
It's my boy ... RG!
"Oh wow! Ryan. Good to see you man! Yeah, I'm here studying to be a counselor! I married an American and now I live here!"

RG: "Oh. So you didn't keep up the acting"

Me: "Nah.... did you?"
(My friends are at this point just staring and fucked)
RG "Ah... yeah, I was in this movie called The Notebook"
Me "Oh I didn't catch it... I don't really watch TV anymore."

RG: Just starts laughing. "Ok man, well it's great to see you! Have a good one!"

Fist bump and he rolls out like a boss, back to his mates over at a booth in the corner.

He... HAD fucking made it and I had been living under a rock for the last 8 years.

After that, I made a point to catch up on all his movies and they always had an intense effect on me—a pride in him for making it, and a personal sadness for a career not pursued.

But, I have high hopes that some badass director will read my stories and make a movie out of my life, and then me and my boy RG will be reunited on some red carpet thing somewhere.

Chapter 45
HOW I BEAT STARBUCKS (Fighting the system like a true modern-day Robin Hood)

As you know, dear reader, I had wrapped up my badass drifter wastrel years and gone clean.

It was 1998, and I helped build and paint the first Starbucks in New Zealand. I thought it was some super boutique thing. I was too dumb and hick to realize that my actions were allowing this disgusting corporate giant its first foothold into the grea t Green Land of NZ.

I was pretty amazed by the machines and the fact that there were actually DIFFERENT TYPES of coffees! Coffee was not just a high-powered dust from a tin or a plunger full of blackness??!!

This was '98 NZ and Coffee Culture wasn't fully a thing yet. We were still mostly on the tea and the instant, and I think it would have been better if we just stayed there. Instant coffee is for beasts of legend...

My relationship with coffee goes back to when I was 14, as a key ingredient of the ENERGY Potion, I basically lived on.

The Starbucks I was painting was in Auckland... I was 22 years old... There was a good-looking blonde gal running the place who had been sent over to SEATTLE to the original Pike Place store to learn all about coffee! A NZ gal... sent over to AMERICA. The AMERICA FROM THE TV!

This blew my mind too... and I convinced her to meet me for an outing.;) Yet alas, the powerful coffee fumes shielded her from my amorous advances, and after our one "PG rated date, she explained that I was just "too intense for her"...

My rebuttal was that she should be able to handle it as she was SELLING COFFEE!! The actual distilled ESSENCE of intense.

To which she replied: "These sort of conversations is exactly what I mean—and now that you are starting to get really into Starbucks you're just going to become more nuts, and I saw you going through the bin outside the shop... what the fuck are you doing?"

FUCK! Caught.

Well, why was I going through bins...? Well, I had thought: "Man, it'd be cool to have hundreds of paper coffee cups so I could always drink from a paper coffee cup and never have to drink from heavy, cold, and uncomfortably wide-mouthed porcelain cups again."

Then the very NEXT DAY... I happened into possession of two plastic-wrapped towers of 100 Starbucks cups. The cups were in the Starbucks dumpster as the outer plastic bags they were in were slightly damaged. I live and die by the dumpster, as you know...

Yet I needed lids. The cups really aren't any good without lids. The lid seals the cylindrical structure that is the coffee cup and keeps the heat of the fluid within its protective paper shielding. On leaving a painting job, which was near the Starbucks I had built and painted, I spied many, many lids (on their single-use cups) in a trash can outside the Starbucks...

A strange, almost inexplicable superhero-like transformation took place, and almost instantaneously I was *The Post Grunge Drifter* once more. I became focused on the bounty of the much-needed lids within the garbage receptacle. I hunched my shoulders, put my hoody up, and reactivated The SHIELD! "The Shield" is a powerful force screen that deflects all and every degrading comment or horrified look from anyone who sees you rummaging in a dumpster for food—or in this case a garbage bin for lids outside the window of a Starbucks.

The Shield was a bit dusty, having not been used (to the credit of increased attention to my own financial planning) since the great Dumpster Feeds Summer of 1997, but to my joy was still fully operational. Not unlike a bear fishing for salmon on the rocky shore of a river in the wilderness of British Columbia, my hand shot into the bin liberating ten good lids within seconds. I stashed them in my hoody pocket and jogged off, deactivating the Shield as I went.

(This gal must have seen me just after I deactivated the Shield!)

So I had lids and cups. To my good fortune Starbucks packed up the used grounds and put them in big bags in a barrel by the door for COMPOST! I had grabbed 4 big sacks of this. Taking it home, I would put about two cups of this black gold into a saucepan and boil it up good.

Straining it through a T-shirt I would pour the filthy black brew into a thermos. I would take it to work and secretly fill my Starbucks cup with it. So it looked like I was drinking Starbucks from the cool new place all damn day long. And technically, I was.

I had it all: cups, lids, and the Starbucks coffee.

Mates would say: "You're gonna go fucking broke drinking that pricey Starbucks shit all day, mate!"

HA! I had them all fooled.

I started to really like the feel of the smooth and warm, lidded cardboard cylinder in my hand. I really liked drinking through the tiny hole in the top of the lid, which seemed to me to be created by some sort of super genius to deliver the exact amount of liquid at the exact speed needed to imbibe the hot and healing fluid in a safe and efficient fashion.

Also, the healing power of 25,000 leached microplastics per cup. Due to the fact that I was re-using it over and over, I was literally drinking the plastic waterproofing as they degraded...

This is the source of my magic powers...

It was a good life. It was the best life! Fully putting it to the man and getting free coffee!

TAKE THAT STARBUCKS! I BEAT YOU. Fighting the system like a true modern-day Robin Hood, right?

Decades later I went to the Pike Place store in Seattle.

I strode in like a commanding god and told them all about how I built that first Starbucks in NZ. This was mid-hipster times, and they did not seem interested at all in crazy-looking Kiwis excitedly telling stories... I got an eyebrow raise and a half nod...

So be it...

Latimer Redlance

So I just rolled out... but now you have heard my tale and know that in all the broad universe there is one guy that beat Starbucks.

Chapter 46
THE DOME (Birth of the Coppersmith Cowboy)

I SAVED UP, AND FLED NEW ZEALAND. I ENTERED THE BLUE-collar Aussie workspace.

Back in New Zealand, I had burned my whole weed crop (about 50K worth), made a video of it, and shown all my old crew, in an affirmation of drug-free freedom so reckless and unqualified that it amounted to a denial of any kind of restraint and limitation. This did not have the effect I thought it was going to... and I was not seen as strong or cool. My rep was so bad from that day on, I basically hid, working as a painter in Auckland until I saved up enough to flee NZ.

So I moved away from New Zealand and found my way into the harsh, dry land of the Aussie bloke jobsite. My twistedness was not even noticed. The crazed experiences of my insane life were just funny smoko stories now...

What is "smoko"? It's Aussie slang for a work break in the morning or of the afternoon, originally to allow time for workers to smoke tobacco, or consume food or drink. If you look it up online you will go down the rabbit hole of the Aussie smoko world—songs, articles, and smoko culture.

My "crazy past" was just relegated to insane stories to make workmates laugh... Everyone I worked with was a battered, twisted freak—I was in Australia. The top-level New Zealand twisted hobo is about an entry-level Aussie job site apprentice. So I fit right in.

Through the time-honored medium of physical toil, the long road of true healing had begun. It is around this time I started writing. And in bouts of late-night stream-of-consciousness catharsis, I found that I could spin a yarn... this is one of my first attempts...

Here is a raw document of a young man's life as he claws his way up the ladder to respectability. Still clawing to this day, of course, respectability always just out of reach.

THE BEGINNING.

It is the year 2000 and the place is Goulburn, New South Wales, Australia. Me and my team are building a huge copper dome—the New South Wales Courthouse Dome. I am 23 years old at this writing...

Some maggots broke into the worksite of the big copper dome we are making, and ate all our chocolate biscuits. They threw our tea bags everywhere and stole our crowbar. Then they came back and smashed our jam jar, spatting jam everywhere, and did the same with the chili sauce.

They threw the vice off the roof into the field.

So we rigged up this pressure plate alarm system, so if anyone stands on the boards of the second landing, a huge hidden car horn goes off at face level!! This alerts us in the hotel across the road.

It went off by accident in the middle of the night, and I got there with a hand-carved wooden sword in hand in 55 seconds. That's about enough time for them to wonder what all the noise is before they find themselves at the wrong end of my whacking stick.

Just for extra harshness, I devised a trap that tips a bucket of freezing water on them if they try to climb a ladder—it's so effective I have caught myself with it twice. A bucket of freezing water and a huge horn blaring into your face is not what they might want at 3 a.m., followed by 4 angry guys appearing a minute later and arguing over who gets to bring the punishment down first.

My day:

- 6:30 – Wake up and eat protein bar then go across to dome. Make coffee. Work on dome... hammer... bend, fold, pin work, shape, and mold.
- 11:00 – Go to deli for a massive 10-dollar breakfast of eggs, bacon, toast, mushrooms, spaghetti, onions, and a double-shot mochaccino.
- 11:45 – Hammer, hammer, bend, fold, etc.
- 6:00 – Go to hotel, shower.
- 6:30 – Go to the workers club for yummy dinner.
- 7:30 – Back to the hotel. Watch television, read, write letters to music on internet radio. Listen to progressive melodic power metal and worry about where I have gone wrong and why the choices I have made in my life have led me here instead of into the arms of the voluptuous Tarja Turunen— power metal opera singer of Finland's progressive power metal giants Nightwish.
- 12:00 or 1:00 – Blackout and wait in trepidation for the horn which will cause me to spring into action, snatch up my wooden sword, and go and seriously prod some buttock.

Harsh dome traps on the maggots update...

The maggots broke in again and they threw our kettle off the roof, causing us to lose three smoko-times of tea's nourishing goodness—and that is a harsh thing when you are a hard dome worker. They also ate the rest of our fruit cake.

Anyway, what we think happened was that they set off the car horn alarm, but we did not hear it as we were so tired. And they jumped off the pressure plate fast before it gave a long scream. I'm pretty sure they got doused by the freezing water, as the bucket was smashed to bits— probably in some sort of cold-induced frenzy.

We had to initiate sinister phase two of our trap-setting operation. The dome is now fully locked up and we have the horn alarm and the water trap (in a different location), as well as 36 pieces of specially wrapped (and kind of hidden but not quite) laxative chocolate, placed in a regular high-end chocolate bar wrapper.

Extra strength!

Latimer Redlance

. . .

A constipated adult should have a max of 3 pieces. I had two as a trial and I'm not even going to talk about what happened. So if the kids munch it all down—which they did with the last normal chocolate we left up there—we should be able to just follow the brown trail to where they lie in a shit-induced paralysis.

The coup de grâce of our citadel of pain was a powerful electric fence unit hooked up to heaps of wire hanging around the head, hand, and groin level. The shock is enough to make you cry and be all fucked up and shaky and worried about touching anything for about 3 days.

(I had decided to test the wire out as well, as I didn't believe it would hurt, so I know.)

So now we wait.

I also bought a big black velvet cape from some goth chick at the market. The dome was nearing completion with no sign of the maggots. And the scaffold crew arrived to start the dismantling process.

When I went to pack up the traps, I found half of the "chocolate" missing. Someone from the scaffolding crew thought he would sneak some! Woe betide the naughty scaffold guy as he heads home in the truck and thinks to sneak out a little fart—and winds up POOPING HIMSELF!!!

Chapter 47
TRADING MAGIC CARDS FOR A NEW LIFE (With Roo Stew Recipe)

MAGIC: THE GATHERING, WAS CREATED IN 1993 BY A North-American mathematician named Richard Garfield as the first trading card game. It was a new genre that combined the collectible aspect of trading cards, popular in the US, with a game itself, in which players could build their own decks and duel between each other.

I was really into this game back in the day, when I lived in the hollow tree in Albert Park Auckland, (as detailed in the story *Worzel Wez*). It was the desire for these expensive cards that drove me to get off the streets and get a job. So they saved me from the streets…

So, in this tale I'm working on the roofs of Sydney, lugging roofing materials up ladders in the harsh unforgiving Aussie Sun.

I was earning about 360 AUD ($360 Aussie) a week. I think a pack of magic cards was about 5 AUD and a good indian curry about 8$, a bottle of cider 5$ and movie tickets $12—to give you a reference. The cost of living is high in Sydney, so a friend and I shared a tiny studio apartment in a hipster suburb called Glebe. I slept on the floor on a thin old air bed that would stay inflated MOST of the night, under a blanket I had found on the beach one day.

To save money I would forage from dumpsters out the back of supermarkets and buy loaves of three day old bread for 50c a loaf from this old Chinese bakery. I would make a nourishing stew of ground kangaroo meat (see end of article for recipe) that you could buy in the supermarket for $3 for 1.25kg. It was many months before I saw the tiny PET FOOD—NOT FOR HUMAN CONSUMPTION label. I still kept eating it. With these money saving techniques I got my living costs down to about $80 a week.

All money that I didn't spend was spent on Magic Cards. Quite often I would spend ALL my money on cards and then have to sell cards for enough to eat (if there were no dumpsters or food courts to eat leftovers from nearby...

My schedule was: wake – work – then after work play magic cards at the game store and trade them till it closed – head to a cafe to play magic till it closed – head home to make card decks till past midnight – sleep – work. Weekends were wake up – play magic – with rapid breaks for bathroom and food – sleep. I did this for about 2 years, interspersed with dating and the Goth life.

It was called CARDBOARD CRACK by some... no idea why...

One day I went up into the back room of a Sydney game store and there was a guy with a box of cards and a sign that said "Rares 1$ Uncommons 20c Commons 5c". He was looking a bit tired and rough, and on enquiring why he was selling cards, he told me that he really needed the money for food because he couldn't buy dinner or a bus fare back to his home, which his mother was about to kick him out of. I really wanted some of the cards he had, and told him I had sandwiches in my bag that I would trade for 10 rares right now! And at home I had delicious kangaroo stew and *lots* of bread! I would put on a feast for him in exchange for more rare cards! And then he could stay at my place over the weekend and play magic and eat feasts! We headed back to my place on the bus (which I paid for at the price of another three rares).

By the time we got back to my tiny place he had eaten the sandwiches and was hungry again and so we started negotiating the cost of each feast and the cost of staying in my friend's nice bed (friend was on holiday in New Zealand for two weeks).

He didn't have enough rares left in the box to pay for the weekend BUT opening his backpack he pulled out a binder! Full of Old School high end card goodness.

I said "Why didn't you just sell this stuff."

He said "I would rather starve than sell this stuff to someone who isn't a friend."

I thought.... *I would rather starve to death and be buried with that stuff in my coffin than sell them*!

We negotiated a bunch of high-end cards for a full weekend of feasts and board. The games began. He was good. I lost every game. We became best friends.

I got his story. He was one of the TOP players in Australia at one point and had even played at the Pro Tour Qualifiers in the mid 90s. His secret of magic success…70 % skill 30 % cheating… and he told me the sad tale of how it all came crashing down—his magic career, his friends, his company, his health and part of his sanity.

The story of how it all came crashing down is a harsh and dark tale of disco biscuits, trance tokens, loose women, fast cars and power poles. Leading him to the point of painful, hungry aloneness, selling rares for food and a bus fare, and living back in his old bedroom at his mum's, surrounded by boxes of Cards. Painful rectangular reminders of his glory days.

He had a court date coming up for a jailable offense, and needed to stall for time while his mum got lawyers and money together. He needed a sanctuary. I decided that I would save him. I was actually hiding in Australia myself, from my redeemed gangsta life in NZ. I told him he could hide here with me and rest in a healing stress free zone. I would feed him and let him stay, in exchange for cards! He loved the idea.

Over the next few weeks I had him eating well, taking vitamins, doing weights, running and taking saunas plus healing swims in the sea . When my friend arrived back from New Zealand and started freaking out about this strange guy who had been sleeping in his bed and wearing his clothes for two weeks, we just shut him up with some high end cards from the shrinking folder.

However, he did want his bed back, so we put together what we called the Cocoon. A bed made out of my winter coats. He would lie on the ground and I would wrap him up with coats so he would be nice and warm. (It wasn't too cold in Sydney anyway and *moreover*, with three guys in a room about the size of a large car, the air was composed of 25% warming kangaroo methane...

He got better and better, and eventually underwent a full physical and mental resurrection. Through the healing power of non stop magic playing and friendship, he rose from the ashes of his old collapsed life like the phoenix, undergoing a glorious transformation and, with his parents money and some smart lawyers all the charges against him were dropped!

I got him a good job and he went from strength to strength. He was fully healed and rocking! I moved to the US; he started playing professionally again, and then went on to Copenhagen for a Grand Prix in 2005.

On the way to Denmark, he stayed with me in the US. He was the best man at my wedding and told the story of how we met in his best man speech. He now lives in Sydney and has a massive and flourishing company and 15 employees, a beautiful wife and two amazing children.

So sometimes... just sometimes when the stars align... you can trade magic cards for an entirely new life.

RECIPE: ROO STEW

- 2 lbs of ground roo meat
- Chopped onions
- Bottle of tomato sauce
- Any vegetables you can find
- Anything else you can find
- Salt
- Boil it up in a big pot till it's cooked
- Serve on Toast
- Spoon it down while playing magic cards on the floor of your reeking studio apartment.

Chapter 48
BETTING GONE CRAZY IN AUSSIE (You've gotta be in it to win it!)

People in NZ and Aussie are batshit gamblers. They have been forever. The Aussies even bet on coin flips as a general practice. Look it up if you don't believe me. Google search "*Two Up Australian game.*"

There are what we call "Lotto" shops everywhere. We are mostly an un-proud, poor people desperate for a peanut of financial happiness or a quick way out of the poverty trap.

It is onto this stage I strode as a young man.

My first introduction to gambling, besides a costly night experiencing the spiraling insanity of roulette at the Auckland Casino, was working on the roofs of Sydney, roofing in the unforgiving and blazing Aussie sun.

THE DREAM

We called it "*THE DREAM*".

I first encountered *THE DREAM* by overhearing other workers talking.

"I'm gunna get myself one of them Ninja motorbikes."

"I'm gunna live in Bali for a year, mate."

"I'm not gunna tell any cunt, just gunna disappear! Fuck 'em."

"If I don't show up to work tomorrow, you know what's happened." (laugh)

"I'm gunna invest half right away, that's what I'm gunna do."

"I'll give you 20% if you give me 20%."

"I'm gunna get three hookers at once, mate."

"I'm just gunna buy a boat and live on it and hide from all the cunts. Fuck my family—they are a bunch of shit cunts."

It just went round and round like this all day, every day—going on about a bunch of trips or things they were going to buy and what percentage they would give each other—'cause mates.

Always at the end of the rant, they would detail how they would just disappear and who exactly could completely and utterly get fucked now that they were rich.

Inquiring as to what they were talking about, I learned about *THE DREAM*—which was, of course, the weekly lottery. Or "Lotto."

They would all buy about $20 worth of tickets, and then dream out all week long on the roof about how they would be free of the pain and heat and shitness that was the life of a broke-ass Sydney roofer. I got in quick. And *THE DREAM* was awesome.

Occasionally someone would have what Alcoholics refer to as "a moment of clarity" and would say, "I'm not doing *THE DREAM* anymore! It's just a waste of money and you never fucking win!" The entire roof would then turn on this person like a pack of rabid weasels; explaining in detail how he was "never going to win now!" They would repeat the Lotto slogan like a magic chant: "You have to be in it to win it."

Thus, if you were not in it... you could not win it. And they would detail how, when they win, they will ESPECIALLY not be hooking the doubter up with any bucks. The offender would usually last till about Wednesday before caving, and getting back on the "*Dream* train!"

Did anyone win big? Nope. I won $90 once, and bought a nice lunch and even more tickets.

I spent about $3000 in all probably. But *THE DREAM* was good.

Special friends. Special times.

THE HOW SURE ARE YOU BET?

Every now and then someone would stupidly announce that they were:
"Off the smokes."
or
"Off the piss." (Booze)
Sometimes causing gasps of shock about the roof:
"I'm off the piss and the smokes!"
"Buy the girl a dress!" would come the call.
Or even the classic:
"Come over here so I can check to see if your balls are still on, mate!"

Following this would be a punishing amount of derision—that they were a weak maggot with no willpower at all—after which they would be back on the smokes or the piss by the end of the day.. This would escalate to betting, because...Australia.

Most of these job sites started drinking at lunch. A happier and simpler time.

The accuser would ask:
"How sure are you that you are off the smokes and piss?"
The ex-smoker/drinker would say:
"Real sure."
"50 bucks sure? 100 bucks sure? 200 bucks sure? I want an exact amount of sure..."

The fool would take the bet... and the grueling withdrawal and smoke-blow mockery would begin. Everyone caved eventually. Sometimes they paid, sometimes they started secretly smoking or drinking, sometimes they just lit up and told the bet holder to "get fucked and come try take the money".

I won this game. It was with a guy who was a daily two-packs-of-Marlboro-Reds maniac. One morning he woke coughing blood. He said he realized that if he smoked one more smoke, he was going to die. I had an idea.

"You give me 1000. If you start smoking again, I keep it. If you last a year, I'll give it back. Your lungs should have healed by then, and you can go back to blazing up a storm."

Logical.

He took the bet. I took his $1000 in crisp plastic Aussie hundys. He was off the smokes a full month. In that month, he started drinking three bottles of wine a night to take his mind off the smokes. Then he got so drunk he didn't care about dying anymore and started smoking again.

On the weekend I found out from a guy at work this had happened —and that he said he was gunna get the $1000 off me anyway, and fight me for it if I didn't give it to him.

I bought a flight to New Zealand with the money and spent the summer there living it up with my $1000. ($1000 Aussie in 1999 was basically about $99,000 NZ back then...)

Got a different job when I got back and never saw him again. I'm one crazier. You will not win. I'm a cockney trickster raggamuffin from the streets.

"LET'S MAKE A BET TO HELP YOU"

The different job I got when I got back was working down-country from Sydney as detailed in the story *THE DOME*.

So I was working the dome and sharing a motel room with a pal and fellow roofer...we were in this motel and we would play cards and watch movies after work.

My pal, overwhelmed by the fact that he had money now, starts buying all kinds of treats and sugary snacks—cakes, biscuits, chocolate —and would then down cans of energy drink in a desperate effort to stop the sugar crash. It didn't stop the sugar crash.

He would pound down all that sugar right after dinner, and then totally black out, go into a sugar coma, and sleep all night in his clothes. He would wake up only when I woke him for work, feeling like total shit.

This was pissing me off! I wanted him to stay up and play cards with me and watch movies or—even better—listen to me rant. I was not one for sleep. 5-6 hours has always been enough for me. People warn me that it all gets taken off at the end of your life...

Well, Dennis Leary learned me all about that:

"It's the ten worst years, isn't it, folks? It's the ones at the end! It's the wheelchair, kidney dialysis, adult diaper fucking years."

Now I'm 48, Leary is 67... we don't have long...

Anyway...

This blacking-out malarkey was not OK with me—and he really didn't like it either. After calculating that he was spending about $20 a day on sugary shit, I enacted the **LET'S MAKE A BET TO HELP YOUR SYSTEM**.

I would give him $200, if he did not eat any more sugar until the end of the job. If he caved, I kept the $200. Hands shook and it was on. The withdrawals were bad. The other guys on the site could not help but tease. No sugar in the coffee or tea—I had to remind him of that. No dessert for dinner at the pub was a bit rough... He made it through the night. The next day in the grocery store he found this expensive French jam that was nothing but fruit. You may know it... He bought a jar and ate the whole thing on bread in about 10 minutes...

This continued for a few days... This was bad. He might make it through the job on jam and then get the money, despite the fact that he was blowing his margins out with this jam... so I started buying Tim Tams and ice creams and chocolate and eating them in front of him... I came up with a plan...

"See this Tim Tam? This Tim Tam exists outside of the bet! And you can buy it for the low, low price of just one dollar."

He bought 5.

This continued each night—he would buy about $20 worth of treats off me and started blacking out again. I was fine with that. I even started putting prices on the treats and made a little store for him in the small motel fridge. I was now making money on the front end of the bet.

About a week into this, I bought a full-blown chocolate cake from the flash bakery and was happily labeling it at $5 a slice. He stared at it hungrily... and it finally dawned on him that he had now spent almost $200 on my treats—and that expensive jam.

"I've spent so much money on these treats, I think you should give me a piece of that cake for free."

Me: "Fuck no, bro. This is an expensive cake. It's not for you. I'm just putting prices on the slices in case you really want a bit. You really should stop eating all this sugary shit. I'm not the boss of your lack of self-control."

In a rage he grabbed a slice. I grabbed his wrist and his throat to stop him getting it into his mouth, and a struggle ensued. At full-force pull of the cake, I assisted his pull and rammed it into his face and eyes, spattering it everywhere.

A fistfight eventuated, which he rapidly lost, and he fled out the door of the motel, face covered in cake and blood.

I locked the door. It was a cold night... this was going to be funny.

He went to the gas station, loaded up on treats, and ate so much he spewed. Dejectedly arriving back at the door, he explained how much he regretted the situation getting so out of hand and how in the morning he was going to quit the job and get the bus back to the city. Fuck. This would get me in a world of shit with the boss.

So I said: "Bro... let's just do a 100-dollar payoff of the whole bet and you can have your life back."

It was agreed, and he went back to pounding treats every night and blacking out. I had made about $300 and all was well in the world.

I took these **"How sure are you?"** and **"Let's Make a Bet to Help You"** systems with me to America and made good money off weak-willed yanks—who always pay up because I make them pay first, with the promise to give the money back plus ten percent in one year. This really dings in the stress.

Bet Total Made:

- "I'm quitting sugar."—$500
- "I'm quitting smokes/vaping." — $700
- "I'm quitting all fast food." — $400
- "I'm quitting all social media." — $350
- "I'm quitting all video games." — $400
- "I'm not getting back with her/him." — $500
- "I'm going full Paleo, Vegan, Carnivore, Atkins — whatever the fuck fad diet." — $600

- "I'm never going to miss a gym/yoga session." — $100
- "No more poker nights." — $200
- "Never going to Vegas again." — $400

I have never had to pay up.

Chapter 49
THROWING LUNCHES OFF ROOFS (The archetypal struggle between the young and careless and the older and cautious)

AS A YOUNGER, STRONGER MAN I WORKED UP ON THE roofs of Sydney in the scorching sun, as a roofer. Hard as a coffin nail. Like all proper construction jobs, we gave each other no end of harassment. Things sometimes got deadly as I will later detail. I was 23 and just a shitbird slate "lugger." It was my job to haul stacks of slate on my shoulder up long ladders and carefully walk it along the roof to be laid by the real "slaters." I would lug about 5 tons of slate up a roof and then go back to my apartment and do weights, pound this cheap protein powder called Mega Mass 5000, and take huge dumps. I was strong and powerful. Rock-solid... virile as fuck and had hair. A big proud black mane like a beastly gothic lion.

Glory days, well they'll pass you by
Glory days, in the wink of a young girl's eye
Glory days, glory days...

I digress...

So up there on the roof working away in the sun, we would hustle till lunchtime... which was around midday... no set time... just when the shakes of starvation hit.

I really looked forward to these lunches; there was a whole world of shops and bakeries in Sydney that catered to the working man. Many just went with the classic Aussie meat pie and a Coke, or a burger, fries, and maybe a Powerade...

If you were a tight penny-pinching fuckwit, you would make your lunch and bring it and not leave the worksite... sadly stuffing it down quickly before getting back to work... Not me!

I churned through about 30% of my pay on extravagant lunches because I was living my best life before that was a thing. Huge Greek salads, large flat white coffees, big bits of battered snapper, crab sticks, sweet potato fries, slices of cheesecake, lobster bisque with French bread, steak sandwiches... maybe a delicious Thai duck curry with a side of sushi! Or... the crowning glory... a fisherman's basket served with a salad, not fries, consisting of mussels, fish, crab sticks, scallops, prawns, and calamari. The lunch equivalent of kicking your wallet right in the nuts.

One guy always harassed me about spending my money on these bountiful lunches. I'll call him Shitbrick. He was a real person, had a truck, had money, didn't live on a floor in a one room apartment with two other guys, and didn't skateboard to work... He also had misery, a hostile attitude, no woman, few friends, and his lunches were tea in a thermos. Brown rice. Carrot sticks. Tuna. An apple.

I was too happy, had a positive attitude, many great relationships with healthy Aussie gals, many good friends, and as you have read, my lunches were the food of the Gods.

The conversations went like this:

Shitbrick: How much money are you wasting on these big lunches a week?

Me: Dunno... I love these lunches, they make my day.

Shitbrick: Probably like 100 dollars.

Me: More like 200.

Shitbrick: You should be saving that money.

Me: I could die falling off the roof tomorrow... I want to die with my belly full of scallops, not carrot sticks.

Shitbrick: You could be saving 1000 dollars a month. You're being stupid wasting all your money.

Me: Oh my GOD! This fish is SO GOOD. Each bite is better than the previous bite!

Shitbrick: You're a fucking idiot.

Me: OH WOW. This is likely the best latte I have ever tasted... each sip is actually making me stronger.

Shitbrick: You're wasting your money. You will never get ahead.

Me: I'm already ahead, just from eating this amazing food. I'm super happy and tonight my hot girlfriend is gunna wash this slate dust off me in the shower at her rich parents' place and then get pounded for fucking hours while I drink her dad's expensive scotch. You will be at home, chopping up carrot sticks and boiling rice all alone, thinking about me fucking ruling it and then you'll have a miserable crywank before getting a sensible early night.

And so on... I would keep escalating it to see if Shitbrick wanted to have a fight on a three-story roof.

He always broke off the conversation before that point, with a sigh and a shaking head eye-roll.

Then one day something amazing happened. I wore him down with my enthusiasm and description of how amazing each bite was. He opened his lunch box and the gross fishy reek of tuna wafted up to him... the carrot sticks looked particularly dry today... and the rice was grey and unappealing...

He looked over at my lunch—a full fisherman's basket and a tall, quad-shot mocha to die for.

I saw intense mental turmoil roiling inside him.

Shitbrick: Fuck this! I'm going to get a good lunch!

And in a rage brought on by years of groveling self-denial, he threw his entire lunch off the roof! Dry orange sticks spun end over end and rice flew everywhere like lame tan confetti. Without looking back, he hustled off the roof and down the road. He came back grinning ear to ear. He still cheaped out and only got fish and chips and a small salad. No drink.

We sat there eating without him trying to smash me down and without me retaliating to the point of a roof fight. He seemed kind of happy with it... it was hard to tell... When he was done I asked:

Me: How was it?

Shitbrick: It was 15 dollars.

He spent the rest of the day stressing over his lost 15 dollars.

Spaz.

I went on in life. Partying and blowing my money, loving every moment of it. Later in life, I was to become a financial advisor with a wife and kids and started going nuts when they left the lights on, saying: "I'm not made of electricity."

But I still sit here in my office and wistfully remember my crowning achievement: The time I worked my ass off for six months up in Toronto as I will detail in the *Cowboy Coppersmith* stories.

I saved up over 30 grand Canadian in 2003. ($30,000 in 2003 is worth $46,364.96 today. And I waxed the fucking LOT in six months partying about Toronto and Vancouver Island, like some kind of latter-day dandy.

I regret nothing.

Chapter 50
I DIDN'T CHOOSE THE GOTH LIFE (The Goth life Chose me. With a note on Freaks)

I WAS GRINDING IT OUT ON THE ROOFS OF AUSTRALIA. Lugging slate and folding copper. Sometimes working on old castle-like houses, whose ancient owners could afford to repair.

My life had become a twisted grind of roof work, overlooking the city. I shared a studio apartment with two friends in the last Beatnik suburb in Sydney. It was called Glebe; we were there for its last days. It was a classic NZ immigrant apartment. Three mattresses on the floor. Weights bench, surfboards, blender for protein shakes. Bodybuilder magazines everywhere and a system for when one of us had a girl over.

This system was for the other two guys to ashamedly go out and stay out till midnight watching movies and drinking tea in a cafe because I was the only one of us that seemed to have any romance in my rad life. Great system.

Work was: roofs of different houses, different mansions, amazing lunches, smoko after smoko, cigarette and coffee after cigarette and coffee. I either smoked Ganesh Beedies, a bizarre Indian cig, that were $2 a pack or Drum rolling tobacco mixed 50/50 with Gudang Garam clove cigarette tobacco. That's important for you to know.

The Australian social scene of the late '90s was so incredibly redneck, if you weren't at the pub pounding booze, bashing people, and screaming, you may as well be wearing a dress. Now, I was a hard partier and good fighter and could pound booze and scream and fight like the best of them. I had my time in demolition work and logging to draw from.

I had forsaken vegetarianism, pacifism, soy, and drugs and now that my balls were growing back, I found that I could yell and get angry at things. A few late-night street fights and punch-ups at the pubs had brought me right back to fitting in with the Auzzie Munters.

But I actually didn't like hurting people and being hurt. I liked "intellectual stuff." I was still learning more about what this stuff was... and I was on a mission to get some.

I had fallen into the blue-collar scene at 22, first with the calm gradient of being a painter... which I found was the bottom of the blue-collar toughness ladder...

This is not a complete list but I'm writing it out as:
BOTTOM.

- Painter/Interior decorator
- Landscape gardener
- Warehouse guy
- Electrician
- Plumber
- Builder
- Truck driver
- Roofer
- Demolition
- Logging

I had started with logging, in my father's company... at 17. I only lasted a few months, then moved to demolition. From there, fruit picking, and from there beatnik destitution. I came back on the ladder at painter... and due to my past in demo and logging, I was able to bluff my way into roofing... third from the top.

Because I had spent all the years—years in which I could have been getting trained and educated into the upper class of the high-brow intelligentsia—doing the crazy shit I talk about in my other stories, by the time I had finally got my shit together, my job options were basically worksite guy or warehouse guy or leaf blower guy.

What am I going to put on my resume? From 17–21, I was trying to be some kind of cross between Jim Morrison (without the band) and Neal Cassady (without the bus).

I'll pause here for you to look up Neal Cassady. If you have to look up Jim Morrison, just please stop reading, and go and watch the movie The Doors. ;)

I bulked up and got good at working in the sun.

So... GOTH.

I was introduced to the Goth scene by a super vampire-looking Goth who was a DJ, Goth scene leader type, who I happened to get chatting with one day in a comic store.

He was happy enough to talk to me even though I was wearing a hard hat, reeked, and was covered in slate dust. I explained that I was actually kind of a Goth inside and was super into heavy metal and Scandinavian Power Metal.

He didn't even laugh. He just said: "You're coming out with me tonight to the Electric Hellfire Club."

He dressed me up in entry-level Goth gear and took me to this club where people were having pegs put on painful parts of them, getting whipped and spanked on stage and... well, you get the idea. Fucking madness.

I maintained my cool... I was the Post-Grunge Drifter... but I was really trying to clean up and get away from crazy shit... because I know where it leads. Every time it's the same... Midgets, marmalade, and a lubed-up and lit road flare up your ass... every time... without fail.

After a few shows, he saw I was unphased and said: "What do you think?"

I said coolly: "It's cool... but I'm not really interested in watching people dressed as nuns hurt each other with mousetraps... I was hoping for more like a cool Goth club with people talking about poetry and shit... and maybe dancing..."

He laughed and said:

"AHHHH, I was just fucking with you, man. This club is for fucking losers. I was just testing you."

The good old Auzzie jokers. No matter the social scene, they will play merciless and painful tricks on each other. It means they like you. If they call you a cunt, you're their mate. If they call you a mate, they think you're a cunt. I was still pretty fresh from New Zealand... and not yet a pranked-out husk, desperate to flee the insane island of Australia. That came later. So with the help of... let's call him *Goth Scene Leader (GSL)*, I invented a new persona for myself. It was the **Heavy Metal Warrior Protector of the Goths.**

They didn't need protecting from shit really, as the scene was closed and policed itself... and they were all basically nihilists and didn't give a shit about being harassed or beaten up... But anyway, I had to make myself make sense.

I loved the Goth scene but the whole thing was just a little too effeminate for me, being a blue-collar roofer guy now... Yet I found that with my long hair and my *Marlon Brando Wild One* leather jacket, rings, boots, black nail polish, eyeliner, Thor's hammer on a silver necklace, and a big copper wallet chain, the Goth girls sometimes preferred me over the thin wispy guys of the scene.

So that was my life. Roofer during the day and Gothic scene guy during the night. Like some kind of tradesman vampire. The Goth cynicism and dissatisfaction with absolutely everything matched my attitude at the time, so we all got on great.

There were three clubs that were not really clubs but just "nights" set up on a Wednesday, Friday, and Sunday at a dive bar. They would spend hours decorating the place into a Gothic Halloween wonderland. The club nights were called *VORTEX, CONTROL,* and *RITUAL*. In a glory of Goth scene self-mockery, the attendees called these *SHITUAL, WHORETEX,* and *CUNTTROLL*.

Everyone made out that the whole scene was lame and sucked and that they were about to quit the scene and put on a pair of shorts or a dress and go to the beach. But no one ever did. We loved it. We sat at our black plastic-covered candle-lit tables singing along to *Blue Monday* and drank $2 red wines. I loved everything about it. I felt truly loved and accepted by a group of humans for the first time in my life. I felt safe and I felt at home.

Anyway... I loved the candles, the makeup, the music, the gossip, and *Depeche Mode* on repeat... But most of all... I loved the freaks.

THE FREAKS.

I've always loved freaks. I've watched every freak movie ever made and in my youth would fantasize about running away and becoming a Carnie.

I of course did a lot of running away... but there were no real carnies in New Zealand or Australia. Being a Carnie was a dream I did fulfill in my late 20s. Living the carnie life up the West Coast of the USA.

I'm a wannabe freak... but sadly my innate charm and rugged good looks always prevented me from achieving true twisted freakdom. I had a few runs at it... I gave it a shot... But even in my most insane, dreadlocked, tripping balls with no shirt or shoes, tie-dyed pants and howling-at-the-moon phase... there would always be a bunch of guys and gals... looking at me... thinking... wow... he's actually pretty cool.

Well, here it worked in reverse. If you were a Freak, you were actually really cool. With *real*, super legit freaks—only now do I realize this—the Goth scene was a sanctuary for them. There was nowhere else in Australia where they would be accepted. Even the gay scene in Australia was super judgmental and cliquey, a wealthy, fashiony scene based around some of the most expensive suburbs in central Sydney.

Let me tell you about three of the best freaks.

Zilla.

I think he just wandered into the club one day by accident, as he probably went to it when it was a regular bar. Most people who went to the bar on other days, and forgot which nights were the Goth nights, would see the Goths at the door and just nope on down the road.

Not Zilla. He must have just paid his five bucks and rolled in. 50+ years old. Old brown woolen suit covered in animal hair. Very short. Tight brown curls in a hairstyle like a helmet. Somehow his name was Zilla because no matter what, he would always talk about a dog he once had called Godzilla.

When you asked, "Oh, did you like that movie?"

He would say, "I haven't seen it."

When he entered the club people would cheer:

"ZILLLAAA!"

And he would sit down randomly with anyone and nod along to the music.

No one knew anything about him. Every single new person after a few nights (including me) would say:"Sooooooo what's with the old weird dude in the brown suit?"

To which the reply would be: "Oh that's Zilla, he's cool, man, he's old school. Go ask him about his dog."

Bonkers. Raging Goth club, and no one over 27. Old Zilla is in the middle, in a brown suit.

One-armed Jess.

Literally would introduce herself as One-armed Jess. Good-looking Goth gal, with a nubbin arm — her arm nubbin actually looked a bit scarred and chewed. Ripped off at about 5 inches before the elbow. Hung her little black purse off the nubbin. How did she lose her arm? A shark bit it off when she was 10. No shit. For actual reals, a shark bit it right off. So Auzzie.

The Ball.

Literally would introduce herself as The Ball. Why was she called The Ball? Because she was about 5 feet high and about 4 feet wide. Looked like a ball. Wore homemade dresses of either black or red and princess tiaras—also homemade. No neck. Short black hair. Seemed friendly enough but I wouldn't really know as I totally couldn't handle even being near her, because I was as shallow as fuck. So I made sure I kept my distance.

There were other mid-level freaks... A huge Goth bodybuilder guy... A 27-year-old gal that looked and dressed like a little girl from a horror film... And general tattoos and face piercings before they were mainstream.

These were my freaks... and I dated in the scene and rocked out and felt like I belonged.

Ten years later, meeting up with some people from "the scene"—older, less serious, and more able to communicate—I described to them how those times seemed to me now, and how the scene was actually a mental refuge from the brutality of roofing work and the harshness of Auzzie blokes.

Back in the day, it was forbidden to say *Goth* or talk about the scene;

no one was to break the illusion. But in our mid-thirties, we didn't give a shit anymore...

They told me that my nickname back then was *Roofer Guy*. Someone had seen me in the daytime without my Goth uniform on, working in my hard hat and lugging stuff around in the sun, and had stared at me till they figured out that I was a crazy double-life living motherfucker.

The only jobs you were allowed, in order to class to be a legit Goth back then were:

- Bookstore
- Liquor store
- Student
- Musician

...Or similar

So they all thought I was a freak because I worked in the sun all day on a job site.

Now I'm middle-aged and still **SO Goth** I fart dead bats, even though I lost the battle to comfortable clothes around 32 and traded in the leather and chains for hemp hippy shirts and camouflage-patterned baggy sweatpants.

Because as we say in the scene... *If you were Goth, you never really were Goth.*

Chapter 51
LOVE QUEST (On a Quest for the Real Love)

As a young man full of hopes and dreams, I wanted an amazing life partner. Me and Her against the world! I thought romantically. I was obsessed with the 80s and early 90s romantic movies and they had of course warped me badly. *Sixteen Candles, Some Kind of Wonderful, True Romance, Heathers*, and others....

Me and Her against the world!

I had tried to find this partner in New Zealand...

Now the following is what I found in NZ... and I consider myself quite the social scientist...

NZ DATING SCENE of the 90s: a totally uneducated social scientist's look.

I did a lot of research. Intense personal quests to gather empirical evidence and of course the best test—romantic beat downs. My first good beating was at a late 15 where I finally asked a girl out in my class.

She was a wonder. Well above my league, looking back now. A Blond beauty with boobs and ass and friendliness and intelligence. I always thought I could do anything and was the greatest so I made a romantic play!

Fail.

She informed me she had a boyfriend.

"Who? I know everyone in school!"

"Oh, he's not at school. He works..."

I just reeled back...Works... what the fuck? Like a grownup? I thought. Standing with my slack mouth open... she sadly smiled at me and walked away.

I secretly spied on her. She was being picked up by some motorbike-riding leather jacket-wearing dude... probably 18 years old or so, with a mullet, who literally slapped her on the ass in greeting. She seemed very happy about this and got on with him and they roared off in helmet-less freedom. To probably have sex in a field somewhere!

This destroyed me. But it burned into me what might be successful, and I made a mental note to grow my hair long and buy a leather jacket... I decided I would skip the ass slapping though, because I hopefully fancied myself as an intellectual ladies' man.

OK so moving forward in life I learned that in order to find a partner in New Zealand, you must have something to offer that helps the woman SURVIVE!

The reason **"something good to offer"** is such a thing in New Zealand is because it's cold and there is a resource scarcity. It's a thin island way off on the edge of the map. Financially it's a bit rough. I would say poor. People think NZ is a great country and it is of course, from all the pictures, but it is actually quite poverty-stricken compared to many places.

Any country sucks if you're poor. Being 16-17 and having no money in a poor country trying to find a good woman sucked assssss.

We will never say NZ sucks, because we need your tourist money. There is an actual branch of New Zealand that is dedicated to getting people to come and give us their money. It's called The New Zealand Tourism Board, and one weekly class at school was called "Tourism", where we learned about other countries and cultures, and basically how to treat tourists from these areas in order to maximize dolla dolla billz.

-

I was obsessed with American shows and movies.

Shows like Beverly Hills 90210 and movies where kids' rooms were full of toys, and they would go and open full fridges and just grab out armfuls of food and cans of pop! These kids' parents didn't scream at them or do drunken insane shit either.

The kids had phones in the shape of footballs in their rooms and also TVs and video game systems. I mean just fuck right off. It killed me to see it but I couldn't stop watching.

So the shows showed me that NZ was pretty poor, (like one phone and one shitty TV and one shitty small car). Two of our NZ fridges could fit into one of these big Yank fridges... and all ours ever contained was a quarter loaf of stale bread, a jar of vegemite, and the lower half was all dads beer. So that's the scene... feel the cold rain and hunger...So back to the story of survival and getting ahead with a good woman.

The mindset was that if you hook up with a serious gal, you can both join forces with another three couples and rent a rundown freezing-cold, four-bedroom house in the city.

You do the bills and food sharing, the roster wheel on the fridge and the wine nights and the pot plants and the cats. You grind your job for years and you save save save so you can get out of New Zealand, get overseas and get the Auzzie or British or American real money and actually make enough to come back and buy a real place and eat real food and be a real person.

Well, I saw people pairing off and doing this major grind, ladder-climb undertaking, or even just giving it a go and coming apart like soft bread under the stress of it.

I saw the interview dates... where the guy had to show that he had a vehicle and a job and could buy dinner and maybe a gift and had his own place that she could move into... like some sort of nest-building, pea-cocking bird thing.

"LOOK! I've made a nest for us to drink cheap booze and bang in, while we grind out the 50-hour weeks at our bank and landscaping jobs, to afford to go to Fiji for a week and bang and drink cheap booze where there is no freezing ice-filled sideways rain 7 months of the year.

The girl would subtly ask about income, and prospects for the future, and the guy would play big daddy with gifts and bought dinners and small shopping trips.

There would be parent dinners and nods of approval and it would **lock in.**

Sometimes the gal would leave a guy for a better survival prospect... I'm sure this has been going on since caveman days.

I truly witnessed the following one night in 1998:

I was out at a party with a bunch of friends. There was a couple there that was having a rough time. The guy had lost his job and had become angry and depressed. Depression was a new thing back then which I think had come over from America in magazines.

It was a luxury. I daily wished for a time that I could be doing so well in life that I could get depressed. When you are fighting for survival you don't get depressed... you're just trying to survive.

But obviously he was doing well enough at some point to become depressed, and had stopped wanting to go out to parties or find a good job, and his car was in the mechanics, and he had quit mountain biking and was going to sell his record collection and other depressed crybaby rubbish.

He complained about how rough his life was to us. We were floored. He had this great-looking gal that he could bang, he had a place to live and money and food. He was trained in something that paid good money, I think he was an accountant... and wasn't just a monkey-grunt laborer meat axe like us. He went to the bathroom and both my friends made a frenzied play for his girlfriend.

This was totally within their rights per our twisted New Zealand survival code.

"Girl, Billys fucked! He's gonna cap himself soon. You don't wanna deal with that—let me tell you what I can offer. I have a big room in a nice bush rental with good mates, I have a good job at the plant nursery, and I'm going to be managing soon ..." Said one.

"My parents have money and land and a batch (holiday house) and a boat that I can sail and I can take you out on it... I'm working in my dad's fencing company that I will own one day." Said the other.

She listened attentively... thinking hard... weighing the options. Her eyes flicked to me.

"Im funny, intelligent, and great in bed. I have spent many years as a wandering wastrel. I have a deep hatred of the establishment, and anything resembling the middle class or the rich. I'm a beatnik but no one here knows what that is, because no one reads.

I have an encyclopedic knowledge and a deep understanding of all boho literature from the 50s through to the 90s. I think I'm quite possibly Jim Morrison reincarnated, having a wee rest down in rainy New Zealand.

My brain is damaged from mind-altering drugs. I'm not sure if anything is real and If you wind up with me you will certainly come to ruin. My motto is "Buy the ticket, take the ride...and if it occasionally gets a little heavier than what you had in mind, well... maybe chalk it up to forced consciousness expansion. Tune in, freak out, get beaten."

Well, I didn't really *say* those things... but I of course didn't need to... she could feel its essence humming out from my 1.21 Gigawatt auric field.

She broke up with Billy that night. The next weekend she was on the boat with Jimmy, eating KFC. Winner winner chicken dinner.

So that's the NZ gal scene... but there is a dark outlier... that floats across to NZ on dark shrieking wings... to taunt and tempt... to break apart the system of control and kiwi sexual matriarchy...

The Auzzie gal!

Lookout!

She's a man eater (Oh here she comes) **Watch out** boy she'll chew you up!

She's a man eater.

Chapter 52
THE AUZZIE GAL (Out of the Cold Darkness and into the Light)

Now, I had only two run-ins with Australian Women while living in New Zealand. Both were madness. The first was the Australian daughter of my father's twisted redneck fisherman friend, she lived up the road from us in the bush of rural NZ. I was 14. She was 16. We started hanging out and madness ensued. I'm not going to write about it in detail, but I will say, I wasn't really ready for what went down.

Our fooling around didn't damage me permanently. But to give you an idea of the madness, when she strongly started suggesting we bang without a condom, I asked "But what if you got pregnant?" She calmly said, "I would just get really pissed and kill it."

Smooth.

At 14 the idea of being a baby killer was a bit much for me so I bailed her off and went back to listening to Iron Maiden and whacking it to a Kelly and Peggy Bundy Threesome.

The next day at school she got caught with a bottle of Jack Daniels in her bag, got chased by a teacher, ran, fell over – bottle smashed, booze everywhere... and that was the last I saw of her.

The next Australian girl I met was what we called a "Blow in". It's not a rude term, chill out. A "Blow In" was the slang term for a new kid that suddenly appears at our small country school in the middle of the year. At the school that all of us had been attending since the age of 5. It was always a shock and big news.

Some of the meaner kids would say to me " Hey there's a new kid that you can be friends with like you always try to do because they don't know how weird you are, and everyone at this school thinks you're crazy, but the new kid doesn't know that yet. So go on, go try to be friends with them."

I would always try to be friends with the new kids and welcome them in. And try not to be too weird. And usually fail.

Well, the Auzzie Gal who showed up was 17, kind of Goth (before I even knew what that was). She had big boobs and low-cut tops and lots of jewelry. Sometimes she wore a red velvet dress. Madness. Alive, full of spark and attitude, flirting and electrifying the guys, cooly dismissive of the gals.

Imagine the women of New Zealand are like the birds of New Zealand: Quiet, conservative, drab-colored nest builders, on the lookout for weasels, ferrets, and rats.

The women of Australia are like the birds of Australia: Loud, brightly colored, crazy, squawking, sporty and fit, and looking for mates on the go as they fly about in big screaming groups.

The two countries couldn't be more different. I'm speaking from my experience in these two countries in the randy as-hell 90s here…

I'm now happily married to a woman who is just as stuck in the 90s as I am.

Teenagers just have sex with their phones now or not at all because their diet is 90% soy and microplastics and all the dudes are chicks and all the chicks are dudes or something.

I'm exaggerating slightly for effect here, but that don't mean it ain't true.

Now the gals in NZ work TOGETHER to keep the guys in line. If a gal started to get out of control and got a little promiscuous, thus disrupting their control through a scarcity system, the other woman would work together using the well-honed and ancient NZ social control tools to put her back in line. This will range from gentle reminders, or small whispering campaigns to full-blown public shaming, throwing liquids, or anything else imaginative to run them off or smash them down.

They will turn on one of their own fast. And that "Good Time Girl" *(Good Time Girl: A young woman who engages regularly in partying and romantic or sexual liaisons)* will not be having a good time for very long. So when Auzzie Gal... let's call her NIGHTSHADE... rolled up and started flirting, the first thing the gals at my school did was talk to her about how she should get a good boyfriend and lock him down. Just one. And they would help out.

She wasn't having any of this. She was a crazy Auzzie bird. Loud, crazy, squawking, sporty and fit, and looking for mates on the go. She told them to "Rack Off" and she would do whatever the fuck she wanted. How did I know this? Well because of my "become friends with the new kids" system. I hung out with her a ton. Sitting and chatting in the middle of the school field. The most private place in the school.

She told me everything that was going on between her and the mean girls at my school, while not flirting with me at all—by being a good friend, I had "friend-zoned myself" before even knowing it was a thing.

Ok, she had been warned.

That weekend there was a party on Friday and then another on Saturday, and she rolled up at the first one with *one* guy, and then at the next with *another* guy. That was it! That was not allowed.

By Monday the rumor mill was grinding hard:

- She was a lesbian (Contradictory I thought)
- She pisses on tea bags, dries the leaves, and then smokes it (Just bizarre)
- She's a total slut with aids. (chance of AIDS, unlikely to be a total slut after two dates)
- She banged both guys; one on Friday, one on Saturday (Normal behavior for the average Auzzie gal back then)

By Tuesday after that weekend, she was a crying mess with yogurt tipped into her bag and white out flicked into her beautiful long black hair. No one would dare talk to her, except spaz, friend-zoned me. She told me she was going to be ok because she had met a guy and was leaving school.

"You met a guy?! Who? I know everyone in school!"

"Oh, he's not at school. He works..."

Works... *What the fuck? Like a grownup?* I thought. I had been here before.

By Wednesday she was gone. I never saw her again.

Time went by and I left school, moved to the big city, and had other adventures as detailed in other stories.

At a party one day I saw a group of guys quietly talking, over in one part of the back garden. One of the guys in the group looked about, around and behind him furtively... like he was making sure someone was not about. I went over and joined the group. One of their number had just come back from six months in Australia. He was now tanned, rugged, and worldly... and he even seemed slightly drained.

The topic of conversation was "Auzzie Gals". Well the way he told it, a Kiwi guy could take his pick and many times be swarmed! We were tame, smart, calm, hard-working, polite, and attentive, due to years of training and kiwi girl beat-downs. And Kiwi guys had a really good name over there for the above.

The average Auzzie guy was wild, dumb, manic, lazy, impolite, and inattentive, due to years of getting his way in a super chauvinist country that is wild and crazy.

They are all of course descended from wild and crazy convicts.

Our friend painted a picture of a half-naked beach-going paradise of cheap beers, high wages, good food, and wild healthy eager women. And no freezing rain.

Actual sunshine! 300 days of sun, compared to our Gollum cave level of 75. My head swam and my eyes hurt at the thought. I added my two stories about the Aussie gals I had run into. This raised eyebrows. The speaker said "See! This guy gets it!"

I felt good! I was a guy that got things!

At this point, one of the Kiwi gals at the party had snuck over and scared the shit out of us.

"What are you guys hiding over here talking about!?"

"Rugby!" We all said in unison.

"**Hmmm**" She stood there frowning at us until we dispersed... but the damage was already done.

Someone had gone to the sunshiney, and promised land, and come back with the golden hope.

A better healthier way? Very probably not.

A more exciting way with more fun, wild-beach times and less behaving yourself due to the terror of getting a bad name as a creep, while running from party to party in the freezing rain trying to be good enough to interest someone? "Fair dinkum!" (see below definition)

I left that party with one goal. And I worked my bag off over the next six months to save up enough to make that goal a reality.

Find the love of my life... Is she over in Australia? We will see....

* * *

Fair Dinkum. slang, Australia: unquestionably good or genuine: **Affirmative.**

—often used as a general expression of approval.

These cigars are *fair dinkum.*

Will you be at the party? *Fair Dinkum!*

Chapter 53
Into the Meat Market (Ground up into love patties)

I MADE MY WAY TO AUSTRALIA AND RAPIDLY FOUND THE stories were true.

I went to blinding bright Bondi Beach and it was just a total invasion of naked tits and asses out on the sand. It was almost too much for my tame Kiwi eyes.

And It was Hot!

I had never felt *hot* in my life, except for on the front half of me when standing next to a bonfire at a bush party in NZ. It never got hot in NZ. While I was in Auzzie it seemed that every day was just a "scorcher". It felt so hot to me that I would often think of going up to cops on the street and begging them to shoot me dead.

But I was locked, cocked and ready to rock.

I'm a Kiwi, a friendly guy and I will say, I was good-looking and healthy. I was a strong young working-class worker lad, lugging slates up ladders or mixing concrete like a blue-collar boss. Let the adventures begin!

Now, of the adventures, I am not going to go into raunchy detail because I am not that kind of writer... and I feel sex is a sacred bond between two people—even if one of them is a completely feral Australian hippie rave gal, with ribbon-wrapped dreadlocks—and the sex takes place in the fine red dust of an outback rave chill out area.

But the results were in...

Ultimately, within a few months, I was an ashamed and drained husk and so I switched over from physical gratification, and making up for lost time, to actually trying to find a soul mate. Goal: to build a sane, stable relationship based on love and trust.

Well, I discovered that I was not going to find a partner who wanted to settle down from any of the following:

1. A crazy redhead heavy metal gal, who had been kicked out of home for being too nuts and lived in her friend's lounge.
2. A sly secretive Goth gal who was in a total state of hate against her parents, and the world, who I could only meet at the clubs or after midnight by climbing through her bedroom window.
3. A 36-year-old very rich Afrikaner gal who, at least once a day cried over the fact that her tits were starting to droop.
4. A possessed witch gal who was 33 and lived with her strict religious parents.
5. A good-looking blond super healthy gym gal, whom my friends started calling Man-hands. She was great ... but the callused hands... and the muscles... and the super thick Auzzie accent, and the intensity of doing too much sports... and the muscled cooch... These I just couldn't handle., And so I had to fake a sick relative and fake fleeing to New Zealand. I even had her drive me to the airport with all my shit, fake packed in a backpack, then I got the bus back to the city and hid. I could write a story just on this.

I'm not going to go on... as it's just too sad, but I loved them all deeply.

I would try to create a sane stable relationship based on love and trust with these girls,. and it would often start out pretty good but soon they would realize I was obsessed with self-improvement and the improvement of others.

My energy and my enthusiasm for things were never-ending... and as I type this late at night... may still just be so...

Apparently my "Rules" were too harsh for the Auzzie Gals. The rules were.

1. Eat food.
2. Don't do drugs and don't drink so much that you spew.
3. Don't cheat or flirt with other guys.
4. Don't be crazy and get super sad or super angry for no reason.

I felt that I had to put guidelines in this game... gotta be strict! The relationships would almost always end the same way. Usually, we would be walking along and I would say something like...

"**I punched him out because he was fake fucking you on the dance floor!**"

Or

"**Why haven't you eaten all day?**"

Or

"**You're grumpy and feel sick because you drank three bottles of wine last night.**"

There would be a pained silence then she would literally sit down on the footpath and say ...

"**I can't do this.**"

Me: "Do what?"

"**This!**"

Me: "What's This?"

"**The always-trying-to-be-better. I think you need someone who, you know, wants to be better. Someone that wants to take vitamins and stuff**". Then she would burst into tears of loss and relief.

Analyzing it now... *Loss,* because I was fucking amazing and the best boyfriend they would probably ever have. And I *can* say that as truth, because almost every one of them reached out to me through Facebook as they hit 40 or so, to thank me for the special time we'd had, and to "See what I was up to now?" Which was being happily married and living in America... much to their disappointment.

And *relief* because I was relentless, driven, testosteroned out, and obsessed with self-improvement. Even I find myself a bit much to handle... and I'm me.

And so they would end, but that would NOT be THAT. Because I was Goth as fuck. I could get more out of this breakup, than sadly walking away from a gal crying her eyes out on a Sydney sidewalk... I would go back to my place and put my purple beanbag right by the stereo, turn all the lights out and light one solitary candle and put on something super sad.

Bands such as:

- *London after Midnight*
- *Girls under Glass*
- *VNV Nation*
- *Wolfshiem*

Or others of that ilk. Some pretty super-sad goth, darkwave super sadness.

OK. So on that beanbag, with that candle going, listening to such songs (I've given you a starter list of sad goth songs... but you have to supply your own candle, dark room, and bean bag)I would just focus, with everything I had, on the pain and the total dark essence of abandoned aloneness. I would just let it consume me. Every part of my being focused on the loss, the gothness, the words, and the beautiful sadness.Till I was a crying shaking wreck.

At this point, the friends I lived with would usually come home and say

"What the Fuck dude! Is this sad enough for you?"

And I would say

"No... can you put it on track 7?"

I would do about 4 hours of that. And it would cleanse me. I would cry it all out and emerge reborn!

Because I had a way of confronting and processing the pain with my candle-beanbag system, I could be right back in the game the very next fucking day, and would not have to write any sort of teary, embarrassingly heartfelt, and slightly beggy Facebook message, 3 kids, 20 shitbird boyfriends and 20 years later.

I'm a very slow learner and love emotional pain, so it was a full two years of hope that *THIS* gal was the one... followed by the crying and my bean bag system before I realized something had to give...

Chapter 54
OPERATION FINNISH PRINCESS (Locking it up)

THE BEAN BAG SYSTEM WAS GOOD BUT I COULDN'T JUST KEEP throwing my love away like cheap wine. I had so much to give. I was listening to a lot of Finland's greatest melodic power metal band, Nightwish, at night and working doing heritage restorations of copperwork and slate roofing in Sydney, by day.

One night while watching a music video on DVD of Nightwish featuring all the Nordic glory of the snowy trees, the dim winter sun, and the mystical goodness of the fantasy-like world being portrayed in the video.... I had a revelation.

I would move to Finland and marry a Finnish Princess. Can you guess what I called this operation?

Why Finland? Well, I knew they were Nordic... so must be healthy and intelligent. The compulsory military service would make them way less likely to crack up under the stress of being my lover. From what I could research, they were family-oriented and damn good-looking. I needed someone mentally strong. Becoming personally weaker, or maybe more tolerant of bad behavior so a gal would stay with me longer, was not an option.

I used a pretty new thing called THE INTERNET and MSN Messenger!

There was a Search function on MSN so I typed in FINLAND FEMALE AGES 19-36.

BOOM, over 300 emails were listed! So I wrote out a letter. It went like this:

Hi! I'm a Canadian-born New Zealander currently living in Sydney.

I am a coppersmith. I am into surfing and snowboarding and living a great life.

I'm all about the health of the mind and body. I'm interested in learning more about Finland and I'm looking at coming over soon. Who are you? I'm interested in you and would love to talk. Here are some photos of me.

AAAAAAND you can imagine the badass sort of well-muscled and sparkly eyes, Auzzie sun-lit and tanned young man bullshit photos I sent. I got about 30 replies!

I soon progressed from emails to MSN Messenger chats, sometimes having so many windows open that the laptop froze. There was a lot of cut and pasting and keeping track of which name went with which hobby or interests. Once I had a good week's worth of communication going, I started getting photos and even requested them when I did not get them. This enabled me to cut the number down to a final six. It's hard to imagine the Brave New World of the internet back then. How exciting and slow.

I would get one in an email and start downloading it... and go get a cup of tea... come back and see the face and neck... oh... is it topless? Whoah... this looks like its topless! Still downloading line by line... Go make some toast... come back aaaaand no... just a low-cut top. Sadness.

OK, so that was my life now. Talking to Finnish Princesses on my laptop whenever I could. I became celibate, worked out, ate really healthy, and started having cold showers. I think I even went jogging once. This was pure stuff guys. No sex chats or dick pics or anything, I didn't even think that was a thing back then. I guess the gal would see the pubes as the photo started to download and just stop the transfer in horror. Now it's just sprung on people.

These were classy dames and I was purging myself of the Auzzie minge invasion that had put me on the wrong path and drained me of all my vital chi.

THE PRINCESSES

1. 21. Tank and truck mechanic in the army. Really really good-looking. Like Elven Princess level.. Fantasy live-action Roleplayer and very smart. Looked like an actual blond elf. And the photos of her in uniform... and lots of nice long emails...were just almost too much.
2. 21 Goth, very pretty. liked the same music as me, smart.
3. 19 Lived at home with her dad. Bit chubby but very upbeat.
4. 22 Went to Veterinary College. Bit horsey-faced.
5. 22 Went to university. Into horse riding. Also a bit horsey-faced.
6. 36 Two young kids. Rich. Very good looking and blonde. Healthy, and really, really keen on me. Husband had died in a car crash. Owned a ski resort. Wanted to pay for me to come over **right now**. The fact that I insisted on paying my own way just proved that I was the right man for her and that I needed to get on the plane right away. When she started with the sexy talk, and a classy bubble bath nude pic, pert boobs ABOVE bubbles, I almost packed my shit and went. But I was still only 24. My thinking was that there would be plenty of time for a very good-looking healthy rich 36-year-old blond with two kids when I'm 50.
7. No need to rush into things. I knew all about 36-year-old gals and the stress and creeping doom they deal with as they begin the slide to 40 and over its peri-menopausal edge...I had dated a few and the mind blowing sex wasn't worth dealing with the late night full body shake-crying over tits starting to lose their battle with gravity.

My friends all knew I was totally nuts, so when I told them about Operation Finnish Princess they just nodded, and kept living their normal lives. I of course didn't tell anyone in my family about it, because fuck them, this is how I roll. I play it fast and loose. I do shit like suddenly decide to move to Finland and get married.

THE STAGES OF OPERATION FINNISH PRINCESS:

1. Keep the Princesses on high boil with continual Emails and MSN chats. DONE
2. Get ticket to Finland. Got one via an air-hostess friend. Business class to San Francisco. Open ticket. On to London. Train to France and from there up to Helsinki via train and ferry. DONE
3. Arrive in Finland and email PRINCESS NUMBER 1 that I have just flown in from Auzzie and I'm here!!
4. Meet up and push it through to a relationship and true love and marriage, before the Visa runs out.
5. If within a few weeks, it doesn't look like it's going to be a taker, email PRINCESS NUMBER 2. **"I have just flown in from Auzzie and I'm here!!"**

Repeat until 6 if needed.

Well... spoiler alert... I didn't make it to Finland. I had a wild adventure in America and was rapidly engaged to a Finnish LOOKING American gal. But I DID keep the princesses on the go as a backup... right up till the day before my wedding. I gently let them down, with a heartfelt tale about meeting the love of my life...

But... I also kept princess number one on... and we are still friends to this day on Facebook. She's 46 now of course... and I'm 48. I won't be marrying her. I'll be staying married to the mother of my child... unless when I'm 50 some very good-looking healthy rich blond 36 year old Finn with two kids rolls up.

Chapter 55
THE LIFE AND TIMES OF THE COWBOY COPPER SMITH (I am the Cowboy Coppersmith and this is my story)

I HAD MET THE LOVE OF MY LIFE IN THE USA AND HAD gotten engaged. My brother moved to the USA from NZ in 91 and married a coked up nurse in West Palm FL.

My Sister moved over and Married a guy who wore a gold chain—in Ft Lauderdale in 95. It was easy for her. Just pick a guy 10 years older and shake ass.

Me... after the events in Operation Finnish Princess, I got over in 2004 and stayed with my sister and her husband where they lived in Sacramento, capital of California. Lame by LA and San Francisco Standards... but I was just visiting my sister on the way to Finland, to marry a hot Fin... as detailed prior... so its lameness was not an issue.

But having been raised on American Shows and blond Californian 90210 fantasies... I felt I would be super remiss if I didn't at least have a romance or two.... before locking it down in marriage... So I rode my sister's bike out to the mall, trying to find someone who wanted me to become their latest bad decision.

The following occurred all in one day.

1. Big Goth Gal who worked at Starbucks... way too eager. Called her mum within an hour and had her come round to the store to meet me... what the fuck. NOPE.

2. Waitress at a TGI Fridays. I came from NZ, we don't have tipping. I TOTALLY misconstrued her tip grinding super friendliness and chattiness as hot blooded romantic interest. I proceeded to leave NO TIP as I didn't even know what that was, and then asked her out. She looked at the check and then at me, like I was a fuckin alien...turned and walked off scowling....I left TGI Fridays with a belly full of fatty Merica meats, but a brain full of confusion. NOPE.
3. That night my sister took me to a Halloween Party and I met a Single mum, 5 years older than me whose Ex was in jail. YES!

I stayed at her place, fixing things around the house, being a super cool pseudo-father to her son and going to the Mall, Blockbuster, and the newly opened and amazing place called Whole Foods, in a loop. I filled the big American Fridge with food and took a photo of it to send to friends back in NZ.

EMAIL SUBJECT LINE: TAKE THAT! I'VE FUCKING MADE IT!

I could hear them now.

"Did you hear that he is shacked up with some blond bird over in California?"

"NO!"

"Yeah... and he has a whole fridge full of food!"

"I always knew he would make it"

After 5 nights with her I proposed.

Me: "You know... the only way I will be able to stay in the US is if we get married...."

Her: Three second pause... "OK"

Me: "Sweet."

My big plan was to head to Canada, as I was born there as you know.

I would work hard and make a ton of money and bring it back to the USA for a great wedding and to start my amazing new Merica life.

I googled "Copperwork Companies Canada" and found one!

I sent them an email and told them I was a professional copper-smith, and I sent them photos of the dome. Yes the dome as detailed in the story THE DOME.

I was not a pro. I was a talker. I was a Cowboy in the full sense of the Australian slang term.

Cowboy: *noun*

The word "cowboy" is used to describe somebody who is not good at their job, usually unreliable types. Ads for carpenters will often have "no cowboys".

This term is used in a derogatory sense in the world of work to describe someone who cuts corners, ignores proper procedures, and takes unacceptable risks to get a job done.

How did I know that I was a talker and not a pro at anything? My Dad told me :)

Once when I was a hard-partying 23-year-old concrete mixer guy, I had gone back to NZ from Australia with my big gangsta roll of brightly colored plastic Auzzie money to play "**breakfast buying big daddy**" to my old friends.... and I was visiting my childhood home and my Father.

I had left the house, but had forgotten something... I went back in and from the kitchen, I overheard one of my Dad's rough-as-fuck biker friends say kind of carefully...

"So that was your son? ... What does he do...?"

My Father: " **Yeah....**" Sounding like a blend of 70% uncertainty and 30% disappointment....

"He's..... a .... he's ... a ... he's a talker..."

Then my Dad perked up a bit and his voice went to 97% Pride 3% confusion...

"**You should see the women he brings here... wheeeee doggie... he has them standing over there at the counter in a mini skirt making him breakfast...**"

A product of the 70s my old man was, and the fact that I had a woman in a mini skirt in the kitchen making me breakfast at 23 was a prideful moment for him as a father.

I was a bit short on providing my Dad with prideful moments... as you can guess from my lifestyle detailed in my other stories...

These mini-skirted women were not making me breakfast out of any sort of subservient gender role rubbish. It was 1999 and they were probably just hungry and were in the kitchen making breakfast without me as I was still asleep because I'm as lazy as fuck.

But that's not how my dad saw it and that was fine by me.

Sadly I think this may have been one of the only proud things he ever said about me and it wasn't to me directly. I never forgot it. I hung onto that moment... and thought, **"I'm gonna make you proud Dad! That's what I am! I'm a TALKER!"**

So.... back to the talking...

I flew to Toronto, rolled up to the company, and started work with them.

Like a true legend Cowboy I had boots, a leather jacket...very little money, and nowhere to live so I asked the boss if I could live in the workshed.

As you hopefully know from my previous story **Gutter Boss**, I am trained to sleep on any flat surface, so the carpet-covered bench used to fold the copper was perfect.

It was very very cold. Winter as fuck. Canada. You can die. But I slept under the heater vent and in all my snowboarding clothes so I was warm.

I also stank pretty bad but only under the clothes.

On my first day of work, I had not expected it to be so cold in the winter of Canada...

It got to −15° C up on the roof and my hands and face were numb in minutes, a great incentive to work hard ... You find yourself arguing with people over who will race up the ladder to get the forgotten hammer.

They put me on a 12-foot-long plywood dormer and said, "You know what to do eh?"

"OH yeah. Sure." I said.

So I had to copper-clad the whole thing including soldering.

There I was... a cowboy posing as a professional (far better at convincing others of my ability than convincing myself), yet real cowboys surrounded me. They didn't give a shit about their job. I was rolled out as a highly trained bigshot. I immediately went into a state of total confusion. I survived by taking measurements and getting started with what I knew, and then calling my old *actually* professional friends in Australia, at night, and asking what the fuck to do. Taking detailed notes. I learned fast.

AUTHOR'S NOTE: I wrote the guts of the following stories at the time of their unfolding... but I have edited them up a bit.

If it slips into present tense it's because that's how it was as I wrote it...

It's gunna probably jump back and forward between tenses... parts of the following stories were sent as emails to my friends back home... friends who never replied because most people are fucking useless cunts.

Cowboy 1: Bruce, Chain smoker, brown teeth, balding, has a big handlebar mustache, wears a trucker hat. I have never seen him eat food. Only drinks coffee.

He is grim as fuck. He has a cd with 100 farting, spewing, and pooing noises on it and he likes to play it as we eat lunch. That is when he laughs. Always ready with a snide remark or a put-down.

He is evil and must be watched.

Cow Boy 2: Jim. Former stripper and playgirl model. Got a model girlfriend pregnant and quit his life of partying for one of pretending to be a hard hard-working dad. He got a job at the company and had never done anything like it before. He makes his way by whacking things with his hammer, asking Bruce how to do things, and keeping busy by cleaning up the site and going and getting coffee.

He has heaps of nice tools that I always borrow as I have the hand-me-downs of the hand-me-downs: A ripped pouch sewn up with dental floss, an old cracked wooden handled hammer fixed with glue and tape, the rustiest and most grease-coated pair of snips ever, a cutter with half an inch of blade left, and a tape measure with a broken spring (and of course, it's in inches, which I had never encountered).

Jim's car is always broken so Bruce picks him up in the work truck.

I'm working with them but they are not too friendly. Jim is nice enough but he goes sour quickly due to Bruce's EVIL and corrupting influence.

Anyway, I managed to copper-clad the dormer by using a synthesis of what I knew, the phone calls I made, and a duplication of the completed one over the other side of the building. I had to sneak over and have a look on the pretense of seeing if Jeff needed a hand chipping inch-thick ice off the roof.

So yeah I was mostly hanging off the side of a 70-degree roof, which was coated in thick ice, with howling freezing wind ripping around me as I struggled to put this stuff called ice/water (it was like a tar paper stuff) and copper panels on the bloody dormer. I roped myself on for my own personal safety. It was not suggested by anyone.

The company has a policy "Safety ropes are optional but if you slip, then you were fired as you were going off the roof, at the precise moment you passed the gutter edge.

It was a terrifying, mind and nerve-wracking day that taxed me to the end and prompted me to write this story as a tribute to how a Cowboy who arrives via an email can flourish in such harsh conditions. Carving out a little igloo of a home for himself among the rough and ready wild men of Ontario.

I sleep on a bench in a work shed all alone in Canada.

I work outside in the super-freezing weather all day long.

I eat lunch from a weird food truck and chili for dinner at a place called Tim Hortons.

I am the Cowboy Coppersmith and this is my story.

THE FIRST BIG JOB

Well, I have returned from my insane week up in Ottawa where I built a big lead-coated copper dormer at a private residence for a surgeon and his wife. They had a huge house in the forest and were very nice people fussing about the place and picking up each little piece of copper that dropped from the roof into the garden.

The dormer took me six days. The whole time Jim and Bruce worked on something over the other side of the house. Twice a day they took off to town in the truck to "get things". I later discovered that it was all a **ruse**. A FUCKIN RUSE!!

It was actually their job to do the dormer together, and my job to fix up the broken guttering at the back of the house. They put me on the dormer to do by myself and then pissed about for a week on the other side between visits to the strip club.

Jim the retired stripper, Bruce the Dodgy Deevo, and I shared a room in a hotel. On the first night we arrived we played a game of pool to see who would have to sleep on the little fold out bed on the floor.

I was winning and I was on the black ball. I was playing Bruce and he was supposed to be a big-shot pool player. He was even wearing his Las Vegas 2002 pool player's tournament qualifier T-shirt. He had only one ball on the table and he was getting angrier and angrier as I calmly sunk ball after ball. I had been playing quite a bit of pool out at the Goth clubs and fancied myself as a bit of a COMPLETE POOL PLAYING LEGEND...

So I was in top form ... but then I kind of realized that if I beat Bruce and forced him to sleep on the little bed, he would be so demoralized he may not recover and I would have to work with his sad sulking ass the rest of the week, and surely he would plot to get me back somehow, as was his evil penchant. So in the interests of a calm peaceful stress-free week, I flunked the last very easy shot, and grinning and happy Bruce took me down. The little fold-out bed was a million times more comfortable than my bench anyway.

So work went sanely enough as I was by myself 90 % of the time.

The nights consisted of me quickly having a shower and bolting down to hide in the restaurant, while they stayed in the room, watched hockey, and sunk beer after beer. Jim smoked fat joints of potent weed which he would whiz up in a coffee grinder.

Another reason it was good I got the little bed... there was no ventilation or operable windows in the room and I could sleep down the far end, as far away as possible from the stench of manky socks, stale farts, ciggies put out in beer bottles, festering buckets of KFC and continual reeking dope pong.

When they came down to the bar I would watch them play pool, and engage in heartily faked camaraderie to establish myself as one of the team.

In the world of dangerous and remote workplaces, you are either one of the team or, one of the enemies. And you do not want to be an enemy of lunatics who find enjoyment in shooting the nail gun at each other, or throwing ice filled snowballs at you when you are hanging precariously on to the top of a 44-foot ladder.

I would then sit by the fire until I reached my limit of trying to be friendly and cool, then take off up to the room to recover.

An hour later they would stumble into the room, two incoherent Canadians clutching beers and dead set on tainting me by forcing me to go along to the strip club with them. I declined, faking exhaustion.

The strippers always made me sad. I would sadly stare at them and wonder about what led them to do it. I would spend their entire show, totally soft, fantasizing about how I could save them and get them cleaned up. These were not any sort of modern, upbeat "empowered" stripclubs, if such a thing exists,...where healthy feminists make 1000$ a night... these were outskirts-of-Ottawa-near-truck-stops ones...

After they had fueled up on dope and beers, they would be rambling back into the corridor by themselves and off to the strip club leaving me in peace.

There was another crazy factor to this trip—The mad French Canadian guys. My first run-in with such.

That crazy crew consisted of two supposedly "in charge" 50 or so-year-old weathered-looking, beaten-down roofers who wore denim, gold chains, rings, and cowboy boots when heading out on the town. And three young severely derelict-looking weasels, 18 or 19 years old, going on 30 they seemed. They wore mostly ragged hoodies, ragged shoes, and ragged jeans, they all had bad teeth and ragged beards as well. The only thing about them that didn't seem ragged was any new case of beer, as they carried it up the stairs to their room. But that too would be ragged as they ripped it to pieces to get to the liquid treasure within.

The Mad French Canadian guys were working on the shingle roof of the house in the forest that we were working on. I came to know the Mad French Canadian derelict work ethic.

The first day we were there they said it was "too wet" (It sprinkled in the morning, lightly for an hour) so they took off back to the hotel for some serious drinking and TV watching. The next day it was "too windy" (a gentle breeze and no more)... So, more drinking, bar hopping, and strip-club-going-to was in order for them.

The last day we were there they had no excuses left so they managed about four hours of stripping the roof of shingles with pitchforks before deciding that it was Good Friday, and a holiday, and the boss was gone, and they needed him to tell them what to do next so off they went.

What was really going on was that they were "Too hungover". The lady of the house had told me that they told her they all had food poisoning from some bad hotdogs, and that was the reason they hadn't gotten as much done as they wanted to.

I resisted the urge to say " Well they seemed healthy enough at three a.m. when they were scream-singing some sort of garbled French songs up and down the hotel hallway."

I made the mistake of going into their room to say Hi! Just for the whole "young French Canadian derelict traveling roofer experience". However, I realized that over the last few years I had changed as a person, through the diligent application of trying to do the right thing instead of things that fucked me up, and that I had abandoned much of my past twistedness.

Thus their mad behavior came as a bit of a shock to me!

So, as I walk in, the first thing I see is two of the young guys with their arms around each other, bottles in hand, singing a garbled Metallica song in heavily accented French.

The other beardy ragamuffin was standing on the bed, wobbling back and forth and reading the bible out loud to the other two.

Then I was accosted by a whisky-bottle-holding old timer, who proceeded to tell me how one of the blond girls at the strip bar could put her legs behind her head "Jesuschristfuckingchristallmaightjesus!!" he said as a way of emphasis... He also went on (complete with hand motions and air drawings) to describe various parts of her private anatomy that were on display while she did this.

I will spare you the details... and luckily I was also spared most of them, as in his excitement, he lapsed into French without knowing it, and I kept him at bay by nodding and smiling as I backed out the door then ran down the hall to the sanctuary of my room.

On the second night, Jim and Bruce brought a harried-looking skinny and drained, mid-30-something red-neck gal up to our room for drinks.

Her story was that she was hiding from a psycho ex. She went on a lot about how all her past boyfriends had treated her really badly and she drew a bunch of educational pictures of some ex's deformed penis.

I paraphrase her words here...but what I gathered from everything she said was:

She was a useless idiot whose dad owned a towing company and thus she was brought up rough, and was as rough as the rest of them, and she could drink like anyone, and had had a hard life. She explained that "All the ex's thought I was fat and ugly, and I think I'm fat and ugly, and I have a reputation for being a slut but I'm really not, and I don't know what I'm really doing with my life; I'm in a rut and I can't get out, and can I have another smoke? I'm so sorry, and I forget my bag everywhere; where is it? I think I left it in the bar, oh no there it is, What's this strange music you're listening to? Wow, where are you from? Oh, and I've had a hard life and all the guys say I'm fat but I'm not a slut no matter what anyone says.

Jim, the retired stripper, was a charmer, and laid on the compliments and the advice which of course were answered with "Do you really think so? ... Really?"

Bruce sat on the bed and chain-smoked with a stupid grin on his face. I smiled and nodded, filing it all away as material for the latest chapter of "The Adventures of the Cowboy Copper-smith".

They later gave her a lift home and she sat between them in the truck and with her hands out to the sides gave them both a hand job for being so nice to her. Because that is what good tow truck drivers' daughters from small towns on the outskirts of Ottawa, who aren't sluts, do.

Jim had to wake me up to tell me all about it for some reason, and now I'm telling you so this occurrence on planet earth will be recorded in your memory.

Friday afternoon we packed up all the gear into the truck" long ladders, 27 feet of guttering, all the tools, all of our stuff ... and ROARED off back to Toronto.

Roared back, while they listened to Shania Twain at full volume, sank beers, smoked joints, and Jim played the guitar in the middle between us.

Sometimes they would pause the CD, imitate Shania Twain, and then laugh so hard and long, bending themselves over and shutting their eyes, that I was sure that we were going to veer across the motorway into other cars and die.

For a terrifying half an hour, Bruce tried to keep pace with a flash new Pontiac at 150 ks. I was so scared I even said, "What are you doing bro?!"

And he said, "We're gonna make good time if I can pass this guy!"

I was so sure we were going to crash with the ladders and tools wobbling about in such a furious fashion, that I put my seat belt on...

Usually, I go for the "thrown clear of the burning wreckage while everyone else struggles with their flaming seat belts" theory". But this time terror overrode all my silly theories.

I survived.

They took the truck down Queen Street, Toronto with the ladders and guttering threatening to decapitate unwary pedestrians at every corner.

I got out near the movie theater and fled ... into the night...

The shakes stopped a few hours later.

THE JOKE

The Boss of the Copper Roofing company put together a crack squad to work on a quick, one-week, real good job for only the pros! I had them fully tricked into thinking I was a pro, as you have read. The only rules were don't talk to anyone at the house, and don't ever say anything about the job. And don't ask why the rules are the rules.

This particular job was doing the guttering of a gigantic mansion, and it was an extra 10$ an hour—so 35 an hour for me which was badass bucks back in 2003. It also sounded dodgy as fuck, so I of course agreed.

We saw some heavy-looking black leather jacket guys come and go in cool cars... they always looked stressed... We were kept busy by a hardcore foreman, so couldn't scope much more out than that.

I remembered a joke that this twisted skinny dude who worked with me on that job had told me. He was a weird, tall, skinny guy with bad teeth and a weasel face. He was pretty quiet, but after a few hours of working together with just me ranting away about crazy shit—as is my nature—there was a pause long enough for him to get out this joke...

And here it is—you have to imagine this twisted weasel-faced Canadian guy telling it to me as we put up guttering on that mansion in like -10°C.

THE JOKE.

So there's these two hobos eh? And they are starving and so they are walking round looking for food down by the railroad tracks eh?

And they get to a fork in the tracks. One says - "Let's split up Eh? You go that way and I'll go this way and we will meet back here in the morning and share whatever we find."

So they split up eh? They meet back in the morning and they both see they have found nothing, but one of the Hobos is really excited and he says "Hey I know we found nothing to eat, but oh wow I met the most amazing gal right by the tracks!

We got on so great and we had the most amazing sex all night long!"

The other hobo says "WOW! WOW! WOW! Well... tell me more about her! What did she look like? Was she a blond or brunette or what?"

The first hobo thinks for a second and says...

"Dunno... head was gone."

I have borne the pain of that joke for too long alone.

You share it with me now.

Oh, and it was of course... the Mansion of the head of the Toronto Russian Mob.

Weasel Face let me in on that little secret.

THE COPPER-SMITH KILLER: OPERATION UNDERCOVER COPPER-SMITH

The Toronto winter has kind of ended, and it's now a world of freezing slush and mud.

I go off to work with Bruce the Deevo and Jim the Retired stripper (Jim has gone fully evil and embraced the dark side from hanging out with Bruce too much). How demented is the scene now? Bruce keeps hounding Jim to print out bestiality pornography for him from his computer and bring it to him at work. It's that demented.

They put me over the other side of the worksite, so they could talk about how much of a bastard the boss is and steal diesel from the truckers' worksite tank, without me saying things like "I personally feel that stealing is a bad thing and I don't think you should be doing it".

They have stolen Diesel twice now. After the first time, I told the owner to lock his tank but he didn't. I told Bruce not to do it the first time, and the second time he did it he waited till I was down the other end of the site, but I spied and saw him ripping the diesel again. I took photos with my 400$ digital camera that you hook to your computer and upload the photos from because it is 2004.

They hate the boss too because he is "ripping them off" (by providing them with good work) so they "have to get their money back somehow." So they "fix" the hours by altering them by up to one, or one and a half hours extra per day, in the workbook.

Bruce puts our hours in at the end of the day and they are not the real hours we work. I sneak back in and change MY hours back to what they are supposed to be, and my receipt at the end of the week will reflect this. Soon the discrepancy will be noticed due to the fact that my receipt will be different from theirs, although I'm working at the same place. I will hopefully get called into the boss's office for one of our "special meetings". Where I give all the details of my undercover operation.

I don't want to say anything right now as I have to work with them 10-12 hours a day. They see this stuff as nothing, Bruce being a criminal and all. I don't like the picture of what would happen if they found out that I was ratting them out. I'm tough and carry knives and hammers... so it won't be nice for anyone if it gets ugly.

They both have kids and wives they are supporting, so I will feel pretty bad if they get fired. But not too bad, due to my Buddhist outlook that it's all Karma. Especially the Karma that I caused you by exposing your crimes.

I have mentioned at length my dissatisfaction with their crooked ways, yet they either ignore me and laugh it off, or do this stuff behind my back... So I have started documenting the stealing and keeping my proper hours, in an effort to distance myself from their criminal acts.

If you have read my other stories, then you would know my crooked past... But, I was reborn. And fully on the path of the Righteous Man. Beset on all sides by the tyrannies and wickedness of evil men of course....

Once on the way back from our job site they went into another guy's worksite to look for tools and such to steal. They didn't find any but they stole a hockey net that was left out, and then didn't stop for the Indian Sheik security guard as he took the license plate down. Almost running him down as they drove/fled out of there. I cowered down in the back seat of the truck.

I am thinking that on Tuesday I will have a little meeting with the boss. The fact that they call me "toes" (cause I'm so far up the boss's ass, that's all you can see of me!) does nothing to help their sorry plight.

Tuesday is the day I get to take off to London, Ontario to work on a big church spire with good, sane guys. So I can freely disclose my spying operation without fear of retribution from these guys. The boss is a really good guy who has worked hard to build this company, and takes care of the good dudes (like me with my free shed, heat, hot water, Internet, good pay, deal) so it is even worse that they are ripping the company off.

UPDATE!! THE BALLOON HAS GONE UP

It happened. On Friday... I was called into the boss's office to explain the discrepancy in our hour sheets and I fully ratted them out. I went FULL RAT-FINK. The stealing, the strippers, the drinking and drugs at work, the mucking about... getting the truck stuck in the mud for an hour a day, despite the boss telling them to park up by the road and walk to the site. I told on them for making me do all the work, and I backed it up with documents detailing the time and place of each crime along with the photos. I went full "detective undercover copper-smith debrief". I'm a talker... and I was amazing. The boss was blown away and very grateful. Also very angry!

He confessed to me that he knew Bruce was evil, and was pissed off that he had trusted him. You see, a few years back Bruce had been caught breaking into the office and stealing money, as well as a checkbook which he had then used to write himself checks.

"He's an old B&E man from way back..." the boss said....

He was arrested and jailed back then. However, in a fit of ex-alcoholic brain rot dementia, the boss got Bruce out of jail and had him working again—so Bruce could earn money to pay back what he had stolen. Great Idea! Not.

So now here we were.

I asked the boss to put off firing them until the night before I left for the new job in London, Ontario. I would take the light bulbs out of the shed, and stack up paint tins by the door... sleep in a different location, and arm myself with two hammers in case they came calling, in the night, for revenge.

He did so. He told me about how good it felt to "can those useless pricks". I was a powerful force of good in the world. No one came to kill me in the night, though I was ready.

The next day Bruce was found dead by the boss's wife, in the doorway to the office. Frozen and as stiff as a bread-stick, with a screwdriver in his hand. Lock half mangled. The police told us what they thought went down.

At around 3 a.m. at the coldest part of the night, and after a ton of hard, post "fired from the job drinking", Bruce decided to revenge rob the place. In a freak snap, it had dropped to -18°c. He got colder and colder and more stressed as he jiggled the lock. His unhealthy lifestyle, the booze, and the cold, brought on a stroke. He fell down and froze to death.

I went numb and blocked out the fact that my actions caused his death. If I didn't tell on him, then maybe he would be alive...?

But If he didn't do crimes and harrass me I wouldn't have told on him...?

But but but... back to GOD.

GOD KILLED BRUCE. BRUCE KILLED BRUCE. I KILLED BRUCE.

It was a team effort. And now the story is told.

STEEPLEBOSS

This is my steeple. There are many like it, but this one is mine.

The evil is done. That chapter is over. Bruce is Dead. I left Toronto for London, Ontario to work on the steeple. The world turned, and our hero learned his journey isn't always a happy one. I felt a triumphant surge within me though. I was with the GOOD GUYS!

They were regular people. Who weren't criminals. They were still hard-drinking working class, bitter and sour Canadians, but when they worked they worked. My over-the-top enthusiasm about everything was not grounds for attack. It was just grounds for mockery, but also begrudging respect. I was one of those guys who was in **Beast Mode** before it was a thing. I had so much energy and life force and was just always jacked.

It was the drug-free, spiritual zap pow, how ya doing man?!! I'm from New Zealand! Power of positive thought! Let's do 18-hour days! Who needs sleep? I'll sleep when I'm dead. No, I'm not on drugs, I'm high on life. Have you heard of spirulina?

I'm still like that, but just on the inside, because that amount of enthusiasm causes people pain, and drives them away. And I like to help people, not fuck them up. So I'm a bit less frantic... but I flow out the happiness like healing beams of non sexual rainbow light.

Revisiting this document I wrote over 20 years ago, I see the pride I had in myself and how I wanted to be like all my tough-guy role models. I wanted to be what was referred to in NZ and Auzzie as a "Hard Cunt." Something that is a bit lacking in today's world.

It could not be faked. It was a journey, and it can be created by working for a number of years in very physically demanding jobs. You must do it until you are warped and shaped by the elements. You cannot wear gloves. "Gloves are for people who want soft hands." And that's an exact quote from a Hard-Cunt demolition man called Robbo who I worked with at BAT Demolition. As detailed in the story "Peaches".

I worked with gloveless hands till I could put cigarettes out on my calluses and grab and crush wasp nests with one fast grabsquish. I was a true Hard Cunt.

So here we go. The new job. The new job is the 250-foot high steeple of St Andrews Church. It was a harsh job.

What is HARSH?

Harsh is this: Waking up at 5 a.m. to drive an hour to London, Ontario to start work at 6 a.m. in freezing rain which alternates with freezing snow. Always there is freezing wind. It is -8 again. Then you have to carry 14 x 30-kilo loads of tools and new copper up scaffolding steps, winding up and up and up a 250-foot church steeple. Then you have to climb to the very top of the steeple—a full 290 feet!!! People are ants and birds fly below you, and it is swaying in the freezing wind, and you wonder if it will fall down... it creaks. It is old... and you have to take off the ancient copper cladding, which weakens its structural integrity!

And why are you doing this? Why are you up at the top of the steeple, while the other guys are way below working on the lower copper cladding (under cover from the sleet and out of the freezing wind which burns your face and hands like acid) with the radio on, and you can hear occasional snatches of laughter and camaraderie on the wind?

And you work from 6 a.m. till 2 p.m. at which time you go halfway down to eat a cold hamburger one of the guys bought you... You have to piss into bottles, kept just for that purpose, because it takes about half an hour to climb all the way down and then about the same to climb back up.

The boss said we all need to piss in bottles and take our shits in the morning and night because he ain't paying for the hour it takes to get down and up.

Only I took the piss bottle order seriously. This was to SAVE THE DAY later in the month.

Back up you go after 20 minutes at the halfway platform for your cold burger, then back into: The wind, the stress, the cuts, the snow, the ice, the swaying of the steeple... YOU ROCK ON, WORKING TILL

10:30 PM! Why are you at the top of the steeple instead of down below? Why are you doing the harshest, most dangerous job on the site? You are doing it because when Mike said "Who's gonna be the Mad bastard who's gonna work the top of the steeple?" Everyone looked at you.

And you said, " **I will! I fucking live for this stuff!**" Even though you knew you would suffer every frigid moment of it, and the only reprieve you would get would be the smoking of the occasional clove cigarette, daring the wind and icy rain to put it out, and the relief as you got all your piss into the piss bottle without soaking yourself. Wide-mouth Gatorade bottles for the win. You did it for the respect and admiration of your fellows. You did it because when they said "Did that suck? " when you came down black with dust and shunt, you just nonchalantly said, "No it ruled".

You did it because you are one of the very few true "Hard Cunts" out there.

The last of a dying breed in a cushy automated world (Yip… the cushy world of 2004… if only I knew what was coming down the pipe…)

You did it so you can write about it at midnight, while everyone else sleeps exhausted sleeps around you. And as you type this with black, sweaty hands, you realize that in six hours you will be up there again, doing another round of work on top of the steeple, into it … for another 16 hour day.

They would expect no less from you now.

You have set your own standard.

You are a legend.

You are… **THE COWBOY COPPER-SMITH.**

And…you seem to have lapsed fully into the third person due to exhaustion and exposure-fueled dementia and should actually just have a shower and sleep instead of writing this out on your little laptop, plugged into the hotel's phone line…

Why aren't I tired? Because I fought the world and I won!

The world is yours, to create yourself as a legend in your own mind and that of those around you.

* * *

So I wrote that self-aggrandizing goodness and sent it out to my mates in an Email.

Why were we working such long days? Because the boss was a cheap bastard. The scaffolding cost a lot of money to keep up and was rented weekly. So we had to hammer it to get through. There was no overtime... It was salary with benefits on the books or CASH. I was on the CASH. 25$ an hour... which in today's money is $41.53. I was making great bucks and saving it all up!

CLIPS BOSS THE STEEPLE KING

After two months non stop on the steeple, 12 to 16 hour days, I had gone literally insane. Like a 1000-yard stare, laughing-and-talking-to-myself insane.

Over my lifetime, if you have been following my stories, you would know that I would often put myself through ordeals that would just blow parts of my mind. I would feel the fuses fizz and blow like failed firecrackers. This was one of those times.

I documented it, in email form, to send to my friends back in Australia and NZ. They had stopped replying to me a while back... so I was just emailing "the void"...

But now I have you, dear reader.

SO YOU WILL READ THIS demented email I wrote in 2003 that went unanswered!

I'm in *The Forest City*, London, Ontario.

Living in a hotel. For the last 63 days, my world has been small copper clips.

I am known as Clips Boss.

Here is my day:

- 6: 00am wake up and take a massive fortifying, healing, cleansing and awakening dump.
- Get gear on, get in car, and go to Tim Hortons to pick up an apple juice a coffee and a donut.
- 6:45am climb the stairs up the 200-foot scaffold that goes

up the side of the steeple. Load myself up with my tools and copper straps.
- Climb the ladders up the nearly 100-foot steeple tower.
- Cut little copper clips that will hold the copper panels onto the side of the steeple.
- Using a power drill, screw the little clips on.
- 4-8 clips on each panel side per 6 inches. 8 sides on the steeple. Steeple is 110 feet high.
- 8 clips x 6 inches into 110 feet x 8; 4 screws per clip (How many clips?
- How many screws?)
- 2:00pm go down for half an hour's lunch and take a big long piss. I got sick of pissing into bottles. I'm a grown up, I should not have to do such things.
- 2:30pm back up the steeple to resume being Clips Boss.
- 6:00pm Piss into bottle and put it into the bag with the other piss bottles of the day. Say to self "That's the last time I'm gonna do that, I'm definitely climbing down next time."
- 10:00pm Climb down and tell the guys that the yellow liquid in the Powerade bottles is NOT Powerade and should not be treated as such
- Go back to the hotel and dinner.
- 11: 00pm All showered and fed and feeling great.
- Jack in and write letters. (I used to call going online JACKING IN because I was a cyberpunk.)
- 12:00am Get drinks from the machine in the hall.
- 1 am. BLACK OUT.
- 6:00 a.m., wake up, get gear on, get in car....
- 4-8 clips on each panel side per 6 inches. 8 sides on the steeple.
- Steeple is 110 feet high.
- 8 clips x 6 inches into 110 feet x 8 (4 screws per clip. How many clips? How many screws?)
- When you are Clips Boss you cannot do maths.

Time went past...

Today I finished the entire steeple in clips!

I think I have put on more copper clips than anyone on earth.

I am a clips-putting-on master.

I am The Steeple King.

I am Clips Boss.

I just did nothing but put on clips for 63, 15-hour days.

With no radio. Alone. Up the top of the steeple. Tomorrow I am Panels Hammering Boss.

A few years ago I didn't know where I was, or who I was, or what I was doing with my life. I know now that I am **The Steeple King** and whatever I am doing will involve climbing stairs and ladders and working on a steeple.

I AM THE STEEPLE KING! I CAN DO ANYTHING!

END OF EMAIL.

At this point I had worked 97 straight days up the top of that steeple from, on average, 7 a.m. to 10 p.m. I was channeling those girder-walking New Yorkers from the 20s ... the ones that built the skyscrapers... I would sometimes smell pizza on the wind... 250 feet up there... blown from some pizza shop in the town below... the birds and the clouds were my friends...

The guys had started to worry about me, but of course, this only expressed itself in sideways glances... this was not a world where you gayly ask if someone's doing ok.

I had started skipping showers, sleeping on top of the bed in all my clothes some nights, and one night, I now only dimly remember, eating my entire dinner at the pub restaurant with my hands, like a monkey... I was the *son* of the steeple now.

The steeple doesn't care about cutlery. I was completely mentally and physically mashed. My diet was donuts, burgers, coffee, Gatorade, unfiltered clove cigarettes, and one huge pub meal at about 10:30 at night. All my bulked-up pretty boy home gym muscles were gone. I had dropped from 195 lbs of hard-won roofing work and Mega Mass 5000-fueled gains, to 168. I realized later, as I made yet another hole in my belt, that I had eaten away all my muscles working up on the steeple.

Around day 50 while bending a bit of copper with pliers over my head I felt a sharp electric pain down my arm. It went numb... I pushed on... In the morning my whole right side was pins and needles and I had so little strength in my right hand I literally couldn't crush a paper cup. I was, over a decade later (2016), to discover it was a partial dislocation of an upper vertebrae.

What I did was just switch the tools over to do everything left-handed! It only took twice the time!

Below is the final email I sent out into the Void back in 2003. I can't even remember writing it... but I seem to have lapsed fully into a dissociative third-person state, which we all know is fucking madness personified.

DAY OF THE PISS BOTTLE STEEPLE SAVIOR

Dear Friends,

It was the end of another grueling amber metal-filled, 15-hour day for the Copper-smith Cowboy.

He stood on the landing of the scaffold, lowering the boxes of tools and equipment down 200 feet to the ground below, using a little wheel and pulley system. This was his self-appointed job, always wanting to be the first one up and the last one down from the steeple. The feeling of the rope zizzing over his twisted leathery hands gave him a sense of pride in the day's work that no coin could purchase.

The other guys readied themselves for departure to the bar, where they would while away what was left of the night, and they leaned on the truck, waiting.

All of the boxes were down and packed away, and the men impatiently waited in the truck for the Copper-smith Cowboy to begin his mad scramble down the towering stairwell.

He started down the final section of stairs ... but then some inner power told him something was wrong.

He looked back at the steeple towering above him and saw SMOKE AND A FEW BRIGHT PAPERY EMBERS FLOATING IN THE WIND ABOUT HALFWAY UP THE STEEPLE!!!

He spun and was up the stairs and ladders before he realized what he was doing. Within seconds he was at the site of the fire! The sight greeted him with a nice cold shock.

Much black dry tar paper and wood chips from the refurbishment of the steeple had caught between the green plastic safety netting and the wooden decking of the scaffold and **WAS FULLY ON FIRE!** A carelessly biffed cigarette butt had nicely smoldered in this pile of tinder until the wind picked up and fanned it into foot-high flames as were greeting him now. It had started to ignite the wooden scaffold planking and had already melted a hole a meter square in the green netting. It was beyond the blowing or stamping-out stage and getting ready to kick into the "Burn down the hundred and seventy-year-old church, millions of dollars of damage, destruction of a heritage building" stage.

The Copper-smith Cowboy looked on in terror, yet with insight born of desperation he made an instant plan! He leaped down to the landing, snatched a big plastic bag up, and flew back to the conflagration.

An impatient horn sounded far below, yet he paid it no heed as he tore into the Santa sack, swiftly and carefully opening multiple Powerade piss bottles and fan spraying three days' worth of yellow liquid onto the fire.

Hissing and sputtering the fire gave up and was quelched, leaving only a horrid molten plastic and ammonia smell.

The horn and revving was heard again, far below, and rage rose up in the Cowboy. The others ...who had laughed at the pains he took to immerse his cigarette buts in pools of saliva and stash them in his pocket... The others... who had ignored the boss's orders to piss in a bottle when working up high on the scaffold instead of wasting half an hour climbing down from the steeple to the church toilet every time they needed a piss.

The others... who were now jokingly driving away as the Cowboy raced down the stairwell. His fury was uncharacteristic, a pent-up frothing of all the rage the fire ignited within him. The others looked at him in surprise... He was always so calm and happy...who was this strange, skinny, yellow-hard-hatted form ranting at them and proclaiming himself as the savior of the company and all of their jobs?

They finally realized what had happened! **The Steeple King was their Piss Bottle Savior!** A deep thanks was given, and an oath of silence then extracted some tentative gazes up at the steeple before they all piled off to the bar.

No mention was made of the horrendous pissy smell down one side of the scaffold, and all ciggie butts were destroyed and checked for fire from then on.

* * *

The Copper-smith Cowboy.
Guardian of the dome, Savior of the steeple.
A superhero-like protector of priceless heritage buildings since June 2002.
His powers were forged in the scorching heat of Australia's burning summers, and tempered in the frozen arctic blizzards of Northern Ontario.
He's growing his Danzig sideburns back and he cannot be stopped.
Look for him wherever a priceless heritage building is being restored to its former glory.

* * *

The job was done a day later.

I wrapped up with the company, gave the handshakes, and rolled out, never to return.

I was now just a story called: **"Remember that Crazy NZ guy that worked with us on that steeple, who put that fire out with his saved up piss?"**

I withdrew five grand in sweet hundys from the bank. I rolled up the bucks into a big gangsta roll, which then lived in the inside pocket of my leather jacket.

I had made over 30 grand. I celebrated by partying all night at Toronto goth club, when it closed I got a taxi to the airport to fly to America to get married.

I rolled into the airport with the make up only partially washed off... in my full leather Goth gear... reeking of booze.

CUSTOMS GUY : "You only have a one way ticket to the US.... why?"

ME: "Oh it's all good I'm marrying an American gal when I get there. We are engaged."

I was informed that I would not be entering the US, and if I tried I would be arrested. I would have to apply for a K1 Fiance Visa and wait the 6-9 months outside of the USA to get it.

I was escorted out of the Airport... out into the mean streets of Toronto. I called my gal.

She said "I just woke up, I'm getting ready to head to San Francisco to pick you up!"

I said "Well about that..."

So... after a tearful conversation I decided to go to Vancouver...

Chapter 56
THE GINGER MENACE
(The Coove Sucked, keeping it real in Victoria)

I FLEW THE *OVERNIGHT RED EYE* TO VANCOUVER. WHICH I called THE COOVE.

Calling it THE COOVE never caught on but I loved how it made the Canadians cringe; yet always too polite to say something. Put someone like me in a country where people are too polite to say things.. and it's just not fair on anyone.

I was waiting for my Fiance Visa, to get to the USA to marry my 90210 Barbie, who was waiting for me, while also not believing that I was actually going to come back. Now, what sort of twisted adventures shall I get into over in THE COOVE?

Vancouver was bullshit. I'm sorry. It wasn't a cool place like I thought.

It was not worth trying to stay there and make my nickname THE COOVE stick. It was a cold, impersonal, huge city. I felt lost and alone. Everyone had their own cool city-person thing going. I got an expensive craft beer at some hipster cafe... and looked out across the city... I could see people cooler than me snowboarding down the mountain from the cafe. This was too cool. I needed to get back into the *belly of the beast*. As I liked to call my adventures.

I enquired where the twisted hippy freaks were, and was told "Over In Victoria." That's on Vancouver Island. So that's where I went.

Two days later I had met a fat weed dealer who lived in a shitty hovel. He was so demented no one would live with him. I was a clean living high on life drug-free super boss... but I had blazed 7 years of trees and I understood that if you judge people and form walls around you, you will not only become smaller as a being but you may miss out on good things... like... cheap housing.

Perfect for me. I moved in for 50$ a week. All I needed was a phone line so I could "JACK IN". And write my emails sending them into TheVoid... long emails... few replies. This was going to be my BASE.

I bought a bike and started exploring. Talking to folks, finding the Goths, the freaks, the twisted hippies... my people. I was cashed up and fancied myself as a wise, helpful Shaman of sorts... I was looking for people who wanted to be experimented on in the name of personal growth.

So this guy I lived with... We will call him The Ginger Menace... seeing as *Star Wars the Phantom Menace* had just come out. He was a massively fat guy with a big Ginger Mop. He stank and he just sat on his couch all day smoking weed and blazing cigs playing Star Wars online. He would just sit on his couch in front of his computer getting more and more mashed as the day went by. People would come to the house and buy weed from him. He wouldn't leave the couch, except to get the delivery food or go do poos and wees. Friendly enough though.

My Idea was to find some pal and go on a four-day wilderness mission into the woods, with just some food and basic camping gear.

I had heard there was a water pipeline that you could walk along for days. It would take you way, way up into the bush. A straight shot.

I was gunna find some city guy who wants to go on an Adventure. Go on this adventure way, way up into the deep scary bush. And see what happens... probably a bear attack...

"Do you know there's Bears?" People asked, when I told them of my plan.

"Yes, I was born here. If a bear attacks me, and I can't kill it with my Rambo knife, then I don't deserve to live" That was my philosophy.

My goal was to find some suburban humans that wanted to be hardcore... and wanted to push it to the next level. I was going to be the spirit guide. My Idea was to find some pal and go on a four-day wilderness mission into the woods. With just some food and basic camping gear.

Chapter 57
PSUEDO-SHAMAN BUSH-MISSION - MONUMENTAL WIG-OUT ADVENTURE TIME (Winning Bear attacks)

I met a guy... He had a sort of fake mohawk thing where the hair was pushed up but not actually shaved on the sides... I met him "punking about" at a cafe and we started hanging out. Got to know him... let's call him Billy... He had strict parents, came from Toronto, and left home early to work as a chef... and "punk about" Toronto. He was chilling and leading a cushy chill life of weed-blazing, working 25 hours a week and sitting about on a couch watching *Seinfeld* DVDs. He wasn't particularly into self-improvement or pushing himself but, at my ranty dream-selling insistence, he was willing to drop the devil's lettuce for a bit and go on a four-day mission.

He needed a Jazz up! So off we went. We stocked up on supplies. Water, Banana chips, Dates, smoked sausages, and chocolate chips. That was to last us four days.

We rode out to the start of the pipeline, stashed our bikes, and started walking... It was just a big concrete pipe through the forest for miles and miles. We just walked and talked. When it got dark, we camped in our hammock tents. Sacks full of hopes and heads full of dreams.

So it seemed uneventful... we saw a snake and a huge slug... and ate all our food on the first day...We crashed out.... it was a bit boring really.... just lots of trees... but then... In the middle of the night... while wrapped up in my sleeping bag and hanging about 3 feet off the ground in the hammock tent... I suddenly woke.

Something MASSIVE came crashing through the bush towards us! It sounded like TREES were exploding. The ground shook.

It started sniffing huge sniffs and made a whiny noise. Was it a massive freaky Big Foot Monster? No. Just a massive bear that was going to eat us up. We couldn't run... dared not scream... and were nicely wrapped up like a bear burrito to eat. I have never been so scared. And still have not been as scared yet, but I can hope. My Rambo Knife was in my bag, out with the bear. So there would be no bear-stabbing *Legends of the Fall*-style knife fight.

I just had to hope it would eat Billy instead of me.

I took a photo of myself, stupidly forgetting the flash might cause it to come eat me... I did a thumbs up... I wanted my last photo to be a happy one... in case anyone found my camera one day. That's what happens... they always find the camera. Blair Witch Project taught me that. I was so fucked with terror, I thought I was smiling. But I actually had a frozen terror face... That face says "Yip... gonna die in the bush from a bear. But I'm sort of OK with that."

After the photo... I heard it sniffing around our stuff and pushing stuff about... I decided to explode out of my hammock tent, scream at it, make a run for my Rambo knife... blind it with the camera flash and stab it in the throat when it rushed me.

As I readied myself for my bear killing rush... it decided to just head out.

When the bush smashing noise of its departure faded... I said "Bro?"

Billy said, **"Fuck this shit man, we could have died."**

Me: "But we didn't and now we have a story to tell. Tomorrow we will just put our hammocks way up in the trees so bears can't get us."

Billy **"Bears can climb trees better than people bro, and we have no food"."**

Me: "Nah, we'll be fine. We will hunt and forage!"

Billy **"Fuck that shit. I'm out of here in the morning. You can die out here by yourself you crazy Kiwi."**

And so Billy rolled out first thing back to the soft, cushy human world of food and safety.

No judgment.

I slept in, and then hunted about my camp. I didn't know what berries were good or not, so I didn't risk it. I killed a small snake with a big whacking stick, cooked it, and ate it for dinner. From living in Australia I did know that all snakes were edible.

I read my book and felt strong and badass as fuck.

That night I put my hammock tent 50 feet up a tree, and slept with my knife on my chest so I could stab a bear's face if it tried to get me.

I didn't die from a bear. I went back to Victoria a legend (to myself) ... not because I met the bear and survived; but because I stayed on by myself, one more night, to show the wilderness who the boss was. I will admit that staying in the woods by yourself, a day's walk from anywhere, is so fucking scary that fuses blow in your brain. I highly recommend it. My record is 17 days alone in the bush. I got back to Victoria safely and was done with mind fucking bush missions for a bit.

It was time to start making a living playing Texas Holdem with stoners and blowing the winnings at seaside-restaurant seafood lunches, and fun filled nights spent in a shitty Victoria dive bar, listening to 80s music and pounding a Canadian beer called "Moose Piss".

All aboard the *Moose Piss Express*.

Next stop Badchoicesville and Miserytown.

Chapter 58
MOOSE PISS POKER NIGHTS: HEAVY METAL IMPLOSION (I live, I die, I live again)

I WAS IN THE LOUNGE ON THE COUCH ACROSS FROM THE Ginger Menace's couch, where he sat Jabba-like, playing his online *Star Wars* game.

I was watching VHS tapes of UFC fights; slowly dying from the ciggie smoke, and slowly getting easy baked by the weed smoke. Dual couches facing each other; a trash-covered table in the middle. A mainstay of any shit-hole dwelling of the grunge lower-class bottom feeder.

This was how I grew up. I was born to the ciggie and weed smoke fog. Raised by it.

Surrounded by the stench of stale, spilled beer and something rotting in the overfull rubbish bin.

I was recovering. Having a wee rest from going fully astray over the last few weeks.

After my wilderness bear experience, I went to a kind of metal/alternative dive bar and made a friend. One of those bad example friends that you allow to lead you astray. Because FUN. Both his father and grandfather had been Carnies. In the game, we call this "Of Carnie from Carnie". I was a Carnie. And it is over this connection we bonded.

The chronic positivity and enthusiasm I had arrived to Victoria with, had become a bit much for me to maintain. Getting up early and making a good breakfast of eggs, organic toast and spinach... getting on my bike and riding about town happy and chatty.

Organizing wilderness missions...

The insane happy grin was starting to hurt my face.

The decline started out with poker. The Devil's in the cards...

Because we would stay straight and sober, and the rest of the players would drink and blaze weed, we would take in about 100$ a night each. Four nights a week.

We were good. Well...We were good compared to totally baked dudes. I would just drink pineapple juice... trying to be like the guys from *Rounders* with a little signal system... then wasting the gambling money on late-night feeds and booze and becoming unhealthy and numb.

Once we had our poker winnings, we would dress up like black-metal whack jobs and head to the bar, where we would drink, dance and rant till close.

Gals would hit on me often... and invite me back to their place, but I was celibate and engaged, waiting for my Visa. I was determined not to fuck up my ticket to the promised land. I never had gals approach me in such numbers till I was an engaged celibate. That's how it works—it's a twisted backward universe.

So after I let them hit on me for a while, just as I felt my soul was starting to become in danger... usually after the third touch and fifth hair flip, I would say "Do you see that very available, very happy and disease-free gentleman dancing over there? He's a great guy and would love you to dance with him. I made him promise that for every girl I referred to him, he had to dedicate the first 10 thrusts to me. He had to imagine it was my dick. The First 10, the good best 10, and each one had to go all the way in, to the bag.

If he ever didn't make it to 10, it resets, and he would have to owe. 2003 was a simpler time. This system actually helped me remain celibate. We would party all night, then sleep all day and do it again.

This was very normal Canadian 24-year-old Metal Head Nihilism.

It was a dark, Moose-Piss and rum-fueled two weeks, which came to the brutal climax of spewing 50/50 rum and coke, foam-power barf sprays off the wharf at 3 am, followed by a two-day hangover.

The rum was Captain Morgan.
We called it "Tiny Sexual Organ" (Carnie Rhyming slang)
I was fucking done with this shit.

I told Buzzy that I was out. I started a recovery week, hanging with the Ginger Menace... on the couch, in the healing fog... as we were, at the start of the story....

So, two healing weeks rolled by and I started to feel almost healthy again.

SUDDENLY THE DOOR FLEW OPEN!!!

In strode two WIZARDS! With actual wizard staffs! Long hair, beards, homespun clothes, and wearing fucking moccasins man! I sat up! I could feel shamanic power actually emanating from them! My salvation had arrived!

Chapter 59
THE FIRE RISES FULL WOO WOO (The healing Shaman friendship begins)

THE TWO BEARDED WIZARDS WERE ACTUALLY TWO GUYS IN their early 20s. They had recently returned from Guatemala! Where they had been for almost a year. They had been back a few days and were doing the rounds, saying hi to old school friends. The Ginger Menace was one such friend. I needed *in* on this friendship, as I was also a wizard —a fact they soon discovered!

We became great mates and started hanging out and having deep spiritual and philosophical chats. Let's call them Raven and Bear. Revealed to me, over the next few weeks, was their story. They were hippy as fuck guys, trained as much as possible in new age shamanism as is easy to do in BC.

Fed up with suburban materialistic life, bullshit jobs, druggy friends, and pressure from their wealthy middle-class parents to aspire to something, they fled their hometown... to Guatemala to go into the wilderness and learn about sacred things. The real deal. No more shrooms around the backyard fire pit, sage smudges, crystals, and dream catchers... No... Welcome to the Jungle baby!

They traveled about as tourists for a bit but then started staying in the jungle and camping out near sacred sites. The old pyramids where the human sacrifices went down. You can study up on all that, it's some scary stuff. They wanted to communicate with the spirits and be guided in the tribal ways. Well, one night they were heading up a pyramid to hopefully have a freaky spiritual experience, when they got caught by a park ranger.

He thought at first they were just idiot tourists, but when he saw their tribal outfits and talked to them, he realized they were *actually* trying to *really* learn some deep shamanistic stuff, *and* thought the spirits of the old pyramids would help them out.

The ranger happened to be the big boss shaman of the whole area. He explained that the pyramids are sacred but also very dangerous due to the tremendous amount of human sacrifices over hundreds of years. A vortex of dark energy that could make you very sick or even kill you. Which is why many of them are totally off-limits.

He took them to his Village and they stayed there. They lived there and trained in Mayan shamanism with him, and other people, for months. Now they were back! And they had the FIRE. So we hung out and I saw them quite a bit over the next few weeks...

However... Anyone who has lived up in the rarefied air of the spirit world and then returns to the human world, soon learns about **The Crash.**

Let me tell you about **THE CRASH.**

When you come back to town, from the Ashram, Mt Olympus, the Monastery, Vipassana retreat, or the four-day empowerment "love yourself and let go" seminar, and you're verily humming with spiritual energy and ready to drive out the swines and walk on water... an interesting phenomenon occurs.

Sometimes the state can be maintained for a week sometimes three sometimes the high can be maintained for months, but the crash always comes... (well I lie... there are ways to not crash, but this is not a discourse on spirituality, its a story about twisted shit going down).

For those of you who have never sought out high and authentic spiritual states, I recommend It. I also recommend **The Crash.** Both are equally valid learning experiences. One moment you have people coming up to you in the street bursting into tears and telling you their problems... and with a benediction and a wave of your hand they walk away smiling and healed.

The next moment you find yourself about as spiritually powerful as a kitten born dead, and suddenly think that going to raves with a vape and goatee is a good idea. There is a reason the monks have vows and stay in the Temple and don't fuck and pound beers.

Anyway... Bear and Raven were new to the game and I wasn't going to kill their buzz. I was born to the crash... raised by it...So Raven lasted three weeks, and Bear lasted two.

Bear started hanging with some of his old pals and was back on the Devil's lettuce within a week. Then he hooked up with a skinny, twisted but hot and blond pixie-looking gal who was an ex from before he went away.

They went to a bush rave, she took ecstasy and cheated on him. That was him done.

He put on a hoodie and shoes and started talking about hockey again.

Raven did better... he wasn't as good-looking. Bear looked like a young Chuck Norris, super outgoing and loving. He was a target for the evil.

Raven was pretty sly. Intelligent, quiet. Cunning. We got on well, sharing tales of scams and tricks we had pulled. My Spirit Animal is the Raven. He was wise enough to recognize I had been around the block. I judge people **entirely** based on how cool they think I am.

But... It was two things that took him down. The first one was his parents ragging on him to do something with his life. They were both doctors and were smashing him daily. He was back living in his old bedroom. Surrounded by his old Star Wars toys, the hidden porno mags, the school photos, the shame, the sadness.

He was pretty depressed at one point and I asked...

"When was the exact moment you felt you lost your shamanic powers"

Raven: *"When I went to the grocery store with my mum and carried groceries in and stocked up the fridge with utter shit chemical poison food. Then got hungry and ate some of the shit sugar poison food. Then I had a shit molson beer with my dad while he ranted to me about doing something with my life. Then I got a call from Guatemala and found out that the gal that I was dating just wanted to let me know that she was pregnant."*

My Shaman Brothers were being straight-up fucked. All their power was gone. They were miserable, sorry, furtive-eyed, sad bastards now. Raven was being fucked by THE MAN, as represented by the well-meaning conversations with his concerned middle-class parents, and the fridge full of shitty chemical-filled food.

Bear was being fucked by THE FORCES OF DARKNESS in the form of sweet sweet weedy oblivion and the hootchie coochy ass-shaking lure of his cheating pixie gal.

I know all about The MAN and how he tries to crush the dreams of the shaman . I liked to think of myself as a reverse "De-Programmer". The guy that fights to KEEP you AT the weird commune. I'm there for every person who asks if they should hitchhike across the country instead of going to college. I'm there for every person who hates their job, their boss and thinks they should quit but doesn't know how they will live (the answer is always dumpsters).

Move in the Direction of The Madness, with a Clear Body, a Clear Mind, and an open heart. Do what you want. All other cunts can get fucked. When your head hits the pillow, you are the only one who has to live with you. So if you want to keep the baby at 16, fucking keep the baby and let the chips fall where they may. Let your life become "**An affirmation of freedom so reckless and unqualified, that it amounts to a total denial of every kind of restraint and limitation**". And for good measure "**The only way to deal with an unfree world is to become so absolutely free that your very existence is an act of rebellion.**"

Because fuck it. Live free man! Don't live as a slave to others. Blah Blah Blah. This attitude got me in a WORLD of shit of course, as I've led armies of kids off the paths of others and onto their own. I had to move about a lot...fleeing angry parents.

I digressed into freedom rantspace there for a second... bear with me.

I knew as a team we had the power to salvage the situation and get our power back! I had the know-how; I just had to find the right time to tell them my plan.

That time came quickly... We were out the back of the Ginger

Menace's place late at night, he had a small party going on. Total dingus fest.

We had fled to the kitchen which stank so bad we moved out onto the back patio.

Bear was trying to keep himself away from the weed and was outside taking deep breaths and trying not to think about the chick which occupied about 97% of all his thoughts...

Raven was morosely drinking a bottle of cider and had lapsed into a sullen silence. Suddenly he looked at the bottle of booze and said "THIS IS BULLSHIT" And threw it into the wall of the house. Boom SMASH!

In the silence that followed... I coolly said

"It's Grade A Bullshit bro. But I have a plan to get all our powers back! We are gonna call it Operation Get all the Magic Powers back and Re-Enter the Spirit world!

Are you Fuckin READY!" They looked at me with hope... because enthusing sad MFs is my business.

Yes, they were fucking ready.

Chapter 60
OPERATION GET ALL THE MAGIC POWERS BACK AND RE-ENTER THE SPIRIT WORLD (Exiting the middle classes' shitty gravity)

OK, THE PLAN! I ALWAYS HAD A PLAN. HERE'S THE FUCKIN plan man!

I discovered early in my Fool/Jester training that if you looked someone dead in the eye and spoke with powerful intention, focusing your communications directly into the center of their head...maybe AT the pineal... and what you said seemed mostly correct, and if you stood in a kind of mini power stance, commanding but not hostile... you could convince people of shit. If they didn't quite believe you and asked "Really though?"

A wide-eyed incredulously confused face at their doubt, along with a "FUCK YEAH MAN!" often pushed it over the edge. If you were also RIGHT in what you said...well ...you could change lives and create miracles.

I turned to Bear, pulled the shame hood down off his hoodie, looked him in the eyes, and said the magic spell.

"**Bear, you are a great and powerful Shaman, indoctrinated into the deep mysteries of the Mayans. We have been led astray by the evils of civilization. We need you to lead us up and out of the darkness like the tribal leader and spirit warrior you are. You are going to guide us on the greatest of healing spirit quests earth has ever seen.**

We all need to prepare and purify ourselves. No sex, No whacking it, no booze, no drugs, good sleep, enough water, exercise, and only organic food! Starting it all with a cleansing cold shower.

The Summer Solstice is in two weeks and that is when we will have the great ceremony, which you will guide us through, and we will be reborn into the best and truest most complete versions of ourselves."

I turned to Raven... altered the power stance slightly...

"Raven! You're in a fucking world of shit, and the only way out is going to be taking total responsibility and being a man about things. There is a village girl back in Guatemala with your baby in her belly. You know you want to do the right thing and go and get her and bring her here. You're going to go home and tell your parents that you're going to pick up your new wife and their new grand-kid. You're gonna fly to her on the next plane and be back for the ceremony which she will help us with and your child will be born blessed and powerful."

Raven broke down, emotionally folding up like a cheap plastic deck chair.

Then Bear grabbed us both in a big healing bear hug and we all broke down in power-bonding young tribal spirit warrior man tears under the weight of our own... I don't know "FREE SPIRITS TOGETHER TELLING THE MAN TO GET FUCKED POWER VIBES!!"

"What kind of gayness is going on out here!"

The Ginger Menace had wandered out...

We laughed tears of freedom streaming down our faces and just missioned off to walk on the beach and make our plans.

And plan we did. We were totally revitalized, humming with THE FIRE.

Raven practiced what he was going to tell his parents, and how he was going to hit them up for the money. We drilled every possible thing that two wealthy doctors who suddenly find out that their hippy 22-year-old son with no job has made a baby with a Guatemalan village girl and is flying there tomorrow to pick her up... and we created perfect responses and practiced them.

It was going to happen. All the Mayan and Norse Gods were on our side.

The godless Doctors were shit out of luck.

Bear Nokia text messaged ecstasy pixie girl.

"I love you and I let you free. Be a free little bird and fly free."

He got back "WTF are you on about?"

He had to send "We are through, I'm moving on."

Her: "OK Bye :)."

And like that he was free.

And so it was that Raven DID fly straight to Guatemala to see the village girl. He went straight to the Village and to the house. Her dad was on the porch cleaning his guns... when whitey gringo beardy long-hair mini shaman Raven rolled up.

He smiles ignoring the man's frown and gives him the power handshake, looking him right in the eye as we had practiced... and with powerful intention, focusing his communications directly into the center of the man's head... maybe AT the pineal... standing in a kind of mini power stance, commanding but not hostile.... says:

"Señor, estoy aquí para preguntarle si puedo casarme con su hija y llevarla conmigo para tener el bebé en Canadá."

And it FUCKING WORKED!

Chapter 61
TRIBAL SOLSTICE SHAMAN LED HEALUPS
(The real deal. No crystals, no dream catchers)

BEAR DRIVES, RAVEN RIDES WING-MAN. I AM IN THE MIDDLE of the backseat as we head to the sacred site. The sacred site chosen was "The Cabin". Ravens' parents had a bush cabin! 30 minutes north of Victoria in the deep woods, on the shores of Lake Cowichan. For a younger, and less wise Raven and crew, this cabin was of course used for all kinds of off-the-rails hedonistic shenanigans. But we were wise shamans now and totally done with dead-end druggie time waste.

We assembled the tribe. Bear, Raven, Ravens pregnant Guatemalan missus, a half First Nations Canadian girl with a big mop of curly hair, let's call her Summer... and Random drifter blow-in Me. We drove up together in Bear's little beater car he bought for 333 dollars, and already we were out of our minds with the power and spirituality of the event.

Non-stop boost rants the whole way from us—silent power and reflection on the coming event from Bear. His entire demeanor changed. He took on a Jesus-like aspect, super loving and powerful...we had total faith that he was going to heal us all and lead us out of the darkness!

We set to work setting it up for the Ceremony which was to take place in two days. Bear guided us through, Raven was his wing-man. I acted solemn and focused and did what I was told. Clearing the brush around the river and building the sweat lodge out of curved branches and blankets. We were all pretty chill, we worked hard, and I learned about some edible plants. One was some wild licorice root that would go in the water in the sweat lodge.

There was lots to do. The gals were preparing food and we were chopping firewood and building the sacred site. That night we had a fire and sang songs. No electricity, no booze, just the stars and pure caring for each other as spiritual beings on a journey…

The Guatemalan gal couldn't speak a word of English, the half-native gal was too sexy for me to even look at or really talk to. She was also… a bit wild… I was engaged and celibate and being super pure and not being led into any kind of temptation, mental or physical.

The morning of the Summer Solstice day I woke from where I slept on the floor of the cabin to everyone making and eating breakfast bare arse naked.

OK. Was this part of the thing?… I guess it was… pregnant, naked, big-butt gal, half-native gal, bare-ass, big-perky-tits-and-hairy-box-out, Raven—bare skinny assed, and Daddy Bear striding about, big dick a-swingin. All young healthy bodies… with no sexual vibe. Now that was weird.

A note on that: A few times in my life I have been a momentary nudist, but generally in our "society," anyone who takes their clothes off is just nuts, a stripper, about to have a shower or have sex. In New Zealand, we would sometimes get hammered enough to get all our clothes off and go skinny dipping, but it was always a drunken thing and always had a cringey sexual, checking-each-other-out vibe.

This was just totally different. We were in a very spiritual space and there were no embarrassing hard-ons or weirdness. **Yet I will caution you.** If you are ever in a tribal all-clothes-off solstice celebration, go for the high fives, not the hugs.

Because you will touch cocks, and you will never, ever be able to block that experience out.

Well, I was 25, strong, good-looking, and had zero shame, so I got up and got naked like it was something I did all the time and we got to work… It was freeing and I will likely never be in a situation where I can do it again… but may the gods bless that glorious naked day.

It was a quiet day of reflection and Bear led us through the prayers in the morning, calling in the gods and spirits and such... and then the funniest shit ever, went down around lunchtime. Bear and I were carrying the blankets that were to cover the sweat lodge we had built and we heard loud house/trance music bleeping and farting and coming closer up the drive.

Into the clearing in front of the cabin roared a big black twin cab truck blaring the music. The back seemed loaded with coolers, and party stuff. Inside the truck were two cool, tanned, frosted-tips, gold-chain guys and two good looking makeup-wearing, hairspray, gum-chewing, cig held out window gals. I hope you get the picture here.

I could see our tribal women looking at the arrivals from the window of the cabin, with deep concern. Their faces like smacked bums.

I thought... this ... is ... interesting...What I correctly guessed was that they were Bear and Raven's old mates from their party days in the cabin times of the off-the-rails hedonistic shenanigans. They had heard from Bear's parents that "The Boys are up at the Cabin for the weekend."

Which obviously meant off-the-rails hedonistic shenanigans and **absolutely not** solemn drug-free, naked-asses-in-the-woods, tribal-solstice, shaman-led forest healups. So they rolled up with their beers, their whiskey and wine, with weed and trance music and tons of meat to barbecue, plus bags of chips and big bright lanterns and air mattresses.

Bear did not miss a beat.

He opened his arms wide and long, schlong a swinging, strode over to the truck FULL JESUS with SPARKLY EYES TECHNIQUE on full blast.

"Welcome Brothers and Sisters!"

I just stood there grinning like a spaz. Fuck you should have seen their faces. The gals' mouths were wide Os of shock and I lip read "What... The... Fuck," with eyes right to his dong.

So Bear is over there at the door of the truck and catching them up about his trip to Guatemala and what's going on here. He's got the fire.

He tells them we are having a tribal solstice ceremony. We are purifying ourselves. No sex, no whacking it, no booze, no drugs, good sleep, enough water, exercise, and only organic food! All the love, all the time, bare assed in the woods, all crammed into the sweat lodge together for hours, naked and chanting and drumming and wigging in the darkness, followed by going off into the woods by yourself to sleep and pray for guidance from the great spirit.

He makes the pitch: looking them right in the eyes... and with powerful intention, focusing his communications directly into the center of the head...maybe AT the pineal... standing in a kind of mini power stance, commanding but not hostile... says: "JOIN US!"

There is a pained silence... the glassy-eyed city folk stare. One of the guys has the audacity to look back at the girls and I lip-read "Whaddya think?" I could hear the loud response. "Get fucked, no Fucking way." The other gal was just a full frowny face and was projecting a pissed-off/disgusted combo-vibe.

I waved, to no response as they reversed on out of there silently. It was the intersection of two worlds for a moment. Perfume vrs essential oils, tribal drums vrs Techno... No one got out of that car and got their clothes off to do nonsexual naked hugs followed by ceremony madness. It just wasn't in them.

I said to Bear "It would have been pretty crazy if they joined us anyway bro"

He said, "It would have been a great blessing."

He was so badass, with so much love. So we got the ceremony going and it was awesome. We all crammed into the sweat lodge together for hours, chanting and drumming and wigging in the darkness, followed by going off into the woods by ourselves to sleep.

One of the most amazing things was the deep cold river pool next to the sweat lodge. When you came out absolutely twisted, you got a rock and waded in and let the rock take you down to the black midnight bottom, where you lay like a fetus in a black void. Man o Man. It was like being a unit of out-of-body consciousness in outer space.

When you remembered you were a human and wanted to live, you would drop the rock and swim up. At one point I almost didn't make it out... and burst up gasping. But Raven and Bear were there. "We've got you brother!" they said. They saved me and carried me to the shore... where... the half-native girl was crouching about 15 feet away doing long super massive loud healing power screams!

It was a bit much for me at that point and I just lay on the ground looking at the stars.

The ceremony was amazing, Bear was a great Shaman and we got all the goodness.

I will share one powerful and healing spiritual thing.

As you know, there was a bad man in my life called Jan who treated me badly when I was six, and I had decided to really hurt him when I was older, and big and strong. I had previously decided that after this ceremony, I was going to pay him this revenge visit.

It was in the ceremony while led by Bear, that I fully forgave Bad Man Jan. When I went to his place a few weeks later and saw him, there was no hate there. It was gone, washed away in the purifying black waters.

We went out into the woods alone after the ceremony and asked the spirit world for guidance. I tell you it worked. I went on to become a great healer of broken beings; Bear and Raven went on to do very well in life, and primal-scream girl became a stripper and, not long after that, a disease-ridden hooker working the BC truck stops. A "Lot Lizard" as they call them. Just kidding, I have no idea what happened to her but I'm sure she's rocking too.

And so ends the tale.

Chapter 62
MY DAD'S SECRET HARD PARTYING LIFE OF THE 70's (As told to me by an old logger I met randomly)

My late-70s childhood was a pretty normal lower-class, redneck Canadian one. My Dad was young (27) and he was off working up on forested islands north of Vancouver, cutting down thousand-year-old, old-growth forests, to be pulped into toilet paper and newspapers. These were the ways of the big Canadian Logging camps. It was an earth-rapey boom time.

I have photos of my young and ripped father, standing proudly next to redwood tree trunks nearly 30 feet across. There was backlash against loggers back then, to the degree that he would tell people he was a helicopter pilot.

The pay was massive. And they would fly into the logging camps by sea plane, work for three weeks or so, and then fly out to see their families for a week. I heard him tell many intense and nostalgic stories to friends as they boozed and blazed about the kitchen table in New Zealand, when I was a young teen. Often he didn't know I was listening in the lounge, calmly baked on second hand weed smoke .

Apparently if you chose NOT to take the time off, the company would fly in a "hooker and coke weekend" for you… a good way to incentivize productivity I guess… but I don't think it would work these days… He would tell stories of a guy called Animal, who never spoke and just ate with his hands… Another time they found a guy who had wandered off to sleep off a hangover, in the bush, on a break between falling trees, and a bear came along and literally ripped his head off. They found the badly chewed head about 20 yards from the body.

Tales of alcoholics who felled trees while chugging on bottles of whiskey and then were eventually found dead in the snow. The wife leaving them and taking the kids was often a prior incident to this.

I asked once why no one said anything or got these guys help. People just being allowed to drink themselves to death in the bush without intervention, or gobbled up by bears or eating with their hands and never speaking, boggled my mind. He and his pals just laughed at me. "A man's business is his own" they would say. It's almost impossible for the modern mind to grasp the grit of the 70s logger.

There are still receding pockets of this grit and mindset in places I'm sure... but I think one day it will be gone, until we open up space, at which point it will be born again in the lives of rough asteroid miners or something...

Anyway... That's the scene set... Here's the story...

I had been living large on my massive gangsta roll, earned by working doing roofing in the Toronto snow. Many months had gone by, drinking with maniacs or partying with hippies, and I had frittered almost all of it away.

I got a bizarre job through a friend. It was to travel with an electrician around Vancouver Island, living in hotels, eating out of restaurants and just run back and forth to the van, getting him the tools he needed, as we installed Keno Machines in almost every bar on the island.

Keno is a bingo type game, where you buy tickets and stare at a screen, praying your numbers come up and you win enough to buy a jug of beer. So I was working in this bar, way up northern Vancouver Island, and I was chatting away to the boss as I was handing him tools so he could wire up this keno machine.

There was a big, old and grizzled, logger-looking guy at the bar drinking whiskeys...

He said "**Are you from New Zealand?**"
Yes I am sir.

"I once knew a guy from New Zealand... you sound just like him."

What was his name...? New Zealand is a small place. I probably know him...

GIVES NAME OF MY DAD.

OK ... here we go...

"Oh wow... I want to hear all about that!"

And so here is the story within a story...

This is what this old, grizzled logger told me...

Location Vancouver. 1979, Canada is booming.

This guy and my dad used to log together, working the logging camps and then on their time off, flew in to Vancouver to party for a straight week. I always wondered why my dad was gone for MONTHS at a time.

My three-year-old self, my one-year-old sister and my mother were on Gabriola island, which was in between Vancouver Island and the mainland. We always thought he was working for months on end, often telling us he was snowed in... or the seaplane broke down... and he was stuck at the camp... I realized now, that he wasn't coming to see us when he got off every three weeks; he was partying in Vancouver.

I don't blame him. Fly out to see his 33 year old wife and two kids for a boring week at home...? Or booze, coke and girls in party town Vancouver 79?

This old guy told me of one incident of intense late 70s partying... He said that my Dad was a bit younger than them and partied harder than them all. It was a heavy snowy winter.... The crew had brought a CASE of whiskey, and a big bag of good coke for the week, and they would get a head start on this during the day before hitting the bars.

My 27 year old dad was hitting it so hard that on the way to the bars, that he went down on the icy sidewalk, went into convulsions and spewed. They picked him up, walked him along a bit and he came right!

So they headed to the bar. At the bar they were playing pool and my dad was talking but no one could understand him.

What had happened is that his upper teeth were false, because he had knocked them out in a motorbike accident in his teens, and so when he had fallen down and spewed, he had lost his denture in the street.

Two of the guys ("city-folk" the guy said) in the bar were mocking him, one, because he wasn't making any sense when he talked and two, because he actually only had two fingers and a thumb on his right hand. He was born that way.

Now, my old man was an absolute beast of a fighter. Even in his later years. He would brook no insults from anyone ever. He was also polite and would never give any insults back when insulted. He would just act. Growing up in rural New Zealand with only two fingers and a thumb on one hand was a serious "Boy Named Sue Situation". The old man grew wistful as he told me of this fight... looking down the years to that happy time...

It was like something out of a movie, he got real quiet and went around closer to these guys and pretended to be looking for a shot to take at the table... but I knew he was just lining them up.

He flipped the pool cue round and spun, smashing it directly into the face of one the guys and then, as that guy dropped, he kicked the other guy square in the nuts. Following up with a massive battering of punches with his big, strong hand, using his little two fingered hand to hold the guy in place by his jacket.

As soon as that guy was out, he spun on the other guy and similarly beat him to the ground. We grabbed him and pulled him out of there after he had stomped on each of that guy's hands breaking his fingers.

I can imagine them fleeing, laughing, from the bar. Just rolling down the road to another joint to keep the party going. They picked up some girls, who I'm sure were of similar, awesome quality to this crew, and headed back to the hotel.

On the way back my dad found his false teeth frozen in a spew pile in the snow on the sidewalk where he had collapsed from partying too hard earlier that evening.

He picked up the frozen spew disk and took it back to the hotel. The party continued in the hotel room, and my dad got a pot of water on the stove and put the frozen spew disk in the pot to melt. Then he "coma-ed out" on the sofa.

The party continued until the most foul reek emanated from the kitchen. The spew water mixture had boiled over and gone into the elements, roasting up and sending plumes of rancid burning barf gas through the hotel room. The smell was so horrendous it drove the girls off and killed the party.

One of the guys turned the stove top off and they called it a night.

And that was the tale.

I thanked him... and we rolled out... job done... Keno machine up on the wall...

I was reeling from this new information about my dad.

I thought over my life, and despite what I thought were our tremendous differences, I realized I was indeed my father's son. I had also fallen down and spewed in the streets from partying too hard. I had bashed people's heads in with nun-chucks and kicked assailants as hard as I fucking could, square in the nuts.

I had recently worked for weeks on end in the snows of Northern Ontario, followed by a week of staying in a cheap hostel, working through a bottle of Finlandia Vodka a day, and hard raving in Toronto's Gothic nightclubs.

I did this cycle for about 5 months. Spending about 1500$ every time I had a week off, from four weeks on. Instead of spending it on whiskey, coke and fun-time gals, I spent it on expensive restaurants, CDs, movies, and entry to goth clubs.

I was engaged... to my future wife who was in the USA... and I didn't have two kids and a wife living on an island that I was avoiding... so I guess the similarity only goes so far...

But to some degree I might have been channeling my Dad. The snowy cold, and the booze, activating cellular memories...

OK I'm losing track here...What I wanted to say was, of all the things in my life, it was *that* conversation with that grizzled old logger in that bar that enabled me to understand and love my dad more than anything else had up to that point.

I had left home at 16, and we were more or less estranged, mostly due to the fact that I was off doing my own thing as you have read...

But right there in that stinking dive bar. Right at the part of the world, which was my young dads stomping grounds... he reached through the ether and gave me a firm handshake.

Partying wastrel to partying wastrel. RIP Dad. Thank You for teaching me how to be a tough bastard. The best lessons are the hard ones.

Chapter 63
ARRIVAL TO 'MERICA: PROMISED LAND (I get engaged to the first woman that could stand me)

I WOULD UP, AND MOVE TO VICTORIA AS YOU HAVE READ. I managed to get my fiance out twice to see me for 5 days at a time of pressure-releasing goodness.

Since leaving the US, I had wound up seeing her 11 days in 11 months. But I never cheated (though I was kissed twice by bad girls who thought they could break me with surprise attacks!) We chatted over MSN messenger and kept the dream alive!

When I finally got the Visa, I was too scared to take the plane down, in case I got stopped again, so I took the Bus. Wow... the bus from Vancouver to Sacramento was quite a trip.

But I got to see what I was getting into, by looking out the window, and talking to people at gas stations.

When I finally got to the Sacramento bus station... I realized I had almost forgotten what my Fiance looked like... I went up to the wrong gal and heard someone calling me from across the way... I found her, and it all worked out.

We were married a week later. And from there I crawled into the belly of the beast that was suburban Merica life. I had made it... my new wife supported me as I studied to become a counselor and I had many more adventures, which continue to this day.

Yet none have been, nor will be as dangerous as the ones that came prior, as I was no longer just living for myself. It was important that I didn't die. I became fast friends with her son who was now 8. I was the new pseudo father. His old father was once again in the downtown jail.

As we drove past it I used to say

"Hey! Look! I think I can see your Dad trying to wave to you from that window!"

He would desperately look for some sign of his Dad.

"Oh no you just missed him..."

The new wife would say nothing... united as we were in our new life, with no place for the druggie, deadbeat dad of her old life.

I was a good new Dad and raised him as my own, harshly with lots of intense kiwi life lessons for which he thanks me often, in the form of exasperated angry reminiscences.

So that's how my Mercia life started.

I embraced Bevmo, Starbucks, Red Lobster, In and Out, Malls, Netflix, a mini van, snowboarding trips to Tahoe, Christmases, trips to LA and San Fran, Movie Theaters and Barbecued meat. I went all out and became fat and listless.

The inner freedom part of me going crazy as I sold out to The Man. Outwardly hating on all things Middle Class and Merica. Inwardly shamefully consuming it all. Over eating and over drinking.

I became fat and beardy, and became "Weird New Zealand Guy". I was staying up till 4 am, drinking from my home bar and watching DVDs like a boss.

So I learned I don't do well without brutality and privation to keep me sharp.

I did my counselor studies and worked on the road as a Rug Selling Carnie...

I finally snapped in 2008, when my wife caught me pocketing a muffin someone had left behind on their plate at a restaurant. Following this was a huge fight in the parking lot, about how I needn't live like I'm on the streets anymore, because I'm safe now with people who love me.

This caring truth bomb caused me to throw the muffin across the parking lot in a rage, where, by some miracle, it hit the pastor of our church in the back of the head, as he was heading into the restaurant.

We fled...

And, consequently I made plans to move my family into the outback of Australia to harden us all up.

Letter to a NZ mate in 2004

I had been living in the USA for about 2 months with my new wife...

I was all about the emails to mates back home... documenting the strangeness of the USA... I saved these emails... like a person of old would save letters.. :)

MAAAAAAATE,

I have been daydreaming of camping in my hammock tent in the bush. This city is stifling me. It was (NEW WIFE'S) birthday yesterday and I had found a very very nice bag on the side of the road that would retail for about 60 $ in the shops here. Someone had obviously stolen it, taken its contents and then threw it away . When I found it, all it contained was a neck brace and some cough drops (which I kept, ya never know when your gunna need a neck brace eh, and the cough drops which were a nice herbal type I am still getting through.)

Anyway she really liked it and was thrilled. I excitedly told her where I got it and how it had not cost us a cent. She liked it less when she got to work and showed a few of her friends there and they gave her their opinions. She came home pretty sad.

Well after a long talk, I learned that a bag found on the side of the road is NOT a suitable gift in America no matter how nice it is. I tried to explain the cultural differences and the reason why I HONESTLY thought she would be thrilled.

I tried to explain this from the viewpoint of a poor N.Zer.

In N.Z that bag would have been worth at least 120 $ and an import-far in excess of any gift that a young couple (such as ourselves) would buy one another.

The money that would have been spent on the bag would now be able to be spent on vital survival goods - like food, rent, gas and oven cleaner - thus conserving money and making life easier as you grovel it out in a freezing 150 per week Auckland flat room, when you earn 370 $ for a 44 hour week painting the houses of corporate executives.

The man's resourcefulness and good scavenging skills would be applauded.

Generally the woman would be very happy as she would be able to boast about the new bag and how much it DIDN'T cost as opposed to how much something DID COST!... As seems to be the way over here.

I am beginning to understand how it is here.

You buy a HUGE expensive gas guzzling truck on credit so that people will pay attention to you and so you can try to fill the huge empty hole of spiritual bankruptcy inside you with STUFF. It can be summed up in this command.

Buy things you don't need, with money you don't have, to impress people you don't like.

Also at work I was horrified that the health center buys little single use plastic vitamin baggies for clients instead of using an old vitamin container that can be reused. I was told to throw away the little baggies after ONE USE!

When I was caught saving them and told to throw them out, I said " You could use these again - you could put old screws in them or something."

The person said "Why would you want to save old screws?"

To Quote Mugato of Zoolander "I feel like Im taking crazy pills!!!"

Well I've said my bit.

I'm off to straighten old nails.

Best WEZ

PS- I looked this sort of stuff up online to see if I actually WAS crazy... and apparently I'm not.

Attitudes

The remoteness of many parts of New Zealand and the distance of the country from much of the developed world meant that things that were easily obtainable in other parts of the world were often not readily available locally. This has given rise to a culture of saving things, in case they will be needed later and to the attitude "She'll be right, mate". "She'll be right, mate" is the attitude that the situation, repairs, or whatever has been done is adequate or sufficient for what is needed. This is often perceived as carelessness, especially when a failure occurs.

Chapter 64
THE BAZZINATOR (Your chosen son returns)

I'M ON GREAT BARRIER ISLAND, NEW ZEALAND. IT'S 2008 It is a bastion of untainted old-timey wilderness at the end of the world.

I have come from urban Sacramento, California. Living on the fat-lined artery of the Schwarzenegger-fueled heart of the sixth biggest economy on the planet.

Fat of the land. Eating the fat. Becoming The Fat. Six long years of urban blob out.

I was soiled from the taint. I once felt so strong as to liken my body to have been carved out of wood. I was now made of cookie dough. And not wholesome organic cookie dough either, but the nasty cheap chocolate-chip-filled stuff that you squeeze directly into your mouth while beached on the couch in front of the TV. But now I'm here at my Dad's house, and I'm working myself over. Punishment for blobbing.

A week of fishing and carting concrete and bricks about as well as diving in the sea and the occasional mini jog down to the wharf readied me for the big mission.

I'm going to hike to the top of the nearest but biggest mountain and I'm gunna harsh it out through the night. As you know, I consider going into the wilderness to be purifying... I used to do days on end... Now one night seems to be enough... getting weak?...No... EFFICENT!

Yesterday I packed my swag, which consisted of a Moro bar, a bottle of water, a thermos of Tibetan tea (genus Camels Breath); two thick vegemite, cheese, and onion sandwiches; two carrots, three bananas, a bottle of Monteith's stout beer, and an apple.

I had my hammock tent to sleep in and a little grey blanket for warmth. As it was summer I thought I wouldn't need much.

The utter purpose of the one-night journey was to fully blow away any parts of the American blobness that had infiltrated me while I was living in the States, on my couch at home, cocktail in hand watching TV at 3 am... Or sitting hunched and dribbling over a bucket of fried clam strips and calamari rings, in a fake leather-clad booth at Red Blobster; and to give me back the long and near-forgotten feeling that I am a true Conan-like, wilderness warrior.

In a moment of past hard man bravado, I had made the grandiose claim that I was forged in the fires of Australia's blistering outback sun and tempered in the 14-foot snow drifts of northern Ontario.

I had to live up to my own self-created reputation. I had to walk the walk and use my ass to cash the check that my mouth had written. The warrior is within. The spirit controls the body. I don't care how high that mountain is or how brutal the trip is, I shall drive myself up there bleeding and screaming.

In bare feet.

And so I set out in the early afternoon along the gravel road to the farm that I had to cross to get to the bush track. Immediately I regretted packing too much stuff. I was so weak. My muscles had suffered deep atrophy in my four year USA Blob fest. I was nearly exhausted before I got to the bush. Staggering through the overgrown fields I saw a big brown cow lying in the grass and it gave me a glance from 10 feet away. It had big wicked horns and it knew it could take care of me if I suddenly saw red and charged.

I climbed over a style and entered the native forest—hoofing it up the trail with self-manufactured gusto.

The rugged path wound through and up the ridge of the mountain—a good 45 degrees in some parts and actually downhill in others.

All the old friends were there—Rimu, Rata, grabby Bush Lawyer, Pohutakawa and many stands of small iron wooded Kauri. I counted ten in one cluster, and pounded upon their rock-like trunks... "Back to nature" I mouthed.

After about half an hour of trying to just blaze up the trail hardcore bushman style, I was so sweating and burned out I was starting to fall over and my eyes were beginning to sting. I had to rest but that would go against everything I had told others was the true way.

So I got into a good head-down, knees-up, drunken-pirate stagger. When the dry red dirt skidded out from under my stinging, bare and dough-soft feet, I would try to turn the fall into a forward motion and come bursting up.

When it was really hard to breathe, and my lungs were burning, I would focus on things... a tree, a leaf, a stone, the shrill cry of some endangered bird on this island sanctuary.

About halfway up, and an hour and a half after I had begun, my legs gave out utterly and I lay there spinning with a strange dusty taste in my mouth, and feet that throbbed from harsh rock and stick jabs. I wasn't actually bleeding yet. But I had achieved my goal—I had gone till the body gave up and fell down.

I was the master again.

I picked it up and made it mission up the path again and it didn't like that. But I'm the fuckin boss and it will now do everything I say.

So I now had my second wind and was blazing up the trail. The body had given up trying to fall over and I almost skipped lightheadedly along with only two calm, little rests for the rest of the way.

Almost six hours after I began, I finally emerged at the top of the mountain. There was no lookout—nothing but a burned out half-rotted old survey station—obsolete with the advent of handheld Global positioning systems and Google Earth.

I had found a piece of obsidian and, with this Stone Age tool, gouged my moniker into the side of the survey station, to rest there with all the names of people who will probably never come back.

I missioned out to the high rock which overlooked the harbor and the valley on one side and the islands, sunset, and open sea on the other.

I used my Stone Age tool to open my Monteith's beer and while peeling back this malty beverage I reveled in the majesty of the vista.

The healing had begun.

I gazed out over the slopes and watched the native birds chase each other and shriek. I finished my beverage and tried to think deep and ponderous thoughts. The result of this was realizing that I had figured everything that needed figuring out, long ago and knowing that, I had the power to figure out anything that was to come.

I'm basically a Pirate-Yoda, I thought.

I made the most of the dying light, having purposely forgotten my flashlight so I could squeeze a little bit more roughing it into my hard man bush mish. I set up the hammock tent before the light fully died and then went back to the rock to crouch, and slap at mosquitoes until darkness engulfed the land and the stars came out. I stared at them for a bit and listened to the night calls of the Moreporks. (Nz Native Owls)

It had been almost 5 years since I actually slept in the bush alone and in that time I had become mentally and physically weak...

Getting slightly scared of the darkness and fully alone in the freaky bushness, as well as being cold from the wind that had sprung up, I cocooned myself into my hammock tent—for erroneously conceived safety. That's when things got really bad.

The wind picked up and began to howl through the mesh, freezing me. Rolled into a ball and wrapped in the scratchy wool blanket did not help to warm me. Worse, the blanket I had foraged out of an old plastic bag off my dad's boat, was SO dusty and spore-covered that my eyes started to burn and I began sneezing, sometimes in a series of up to eight sneezes in a row. The sneezing was accompanied as well, by brutal coughing.

My throat began to hurt so bad that when I sneezed it was like a small glass-filled grenade going off at the back of my throat. I started to dread the sneezes. I would hold my breath for long periods of time hoping to just black out and sink into unconsciousness. Merciful darkness would not embrace me.

More coughing and sneezing. I shivered in tears-streaming, breath-holding misery, forgetting entirely that the purpose of the bush/mountain mission was to harden myself up... I wished only for a shower and a soft warm bed.

I was surely getting sicker by the moment and was getting a brutal cold that was going to leave me stuffed up, weak, and headachy for days.

I also desperately had to take a piss. I had been in my hammock tent for only 15 minutes. It was pitch black and wasn't going to be light for a long time yet.

I crawled out of the hammock tent in the darkness, groped along the path, and relieved myself. I had stopped coughing and sneezing and, now that I wasn't lying down in a miserable ball, I wasn't cold. I thought I would creep along the path like an animal and crouch on that lookout rock again. And there... like a half-crazed wild man, I would gaze down upon the humans miles below in their comfortable warm man-dens and snort in animalistic derision.

I decided to walk along no longer feeling my way, but instead sneaking in the dark like a wild beast, using only my powerful animal senses.

I slipped down the rock on which I was supposed to crouch pensively,, and for lack of better words, TOTALLY ATE SHIT down the side of it.

I screamed a high-pitched, cowardly scream as I fell, because I had seen the sharp-stick-filled abyss and knew that if I went fully over the edge I would be crawling back to civilization... bleeding and screaming at best, or would die, impaled and twitching at worst.

However, I managed to slam into the little grassy ledge at the bottom of the rock and grab on. I only bruised and scraped myself kind of badly, taking skin off my knees and palms. But as I was filled with terror and pumping with adrenaline, I instantly free climbed up the rock, to the top, and perched.

There, on that rock, with my brain baking in its own primeval self-created drugs, I gazed down upon the humans a mile below in their comfortable, warm man-dens and, not unlike a half-crazed wild man, snorted in animalistic derision.

I looked out upon the stars, upon the boat lights on the secluded bay; I listened to the wind and the noises of the bush and awakened the warrior within. All I needed to do in order to find "the warrior" was to fall down a bank in total darkness, get scraped up, and have a small one-second look at my own possible death.

It started to rain on me. I headed back to the Hammock tent and drew the waterproof fly over it before crawling in. I found I could keep the respiratory distress to a minimum if I lay face-down, breathing through the Velcro-lined hole in the bottom. The mosquitoes made a pin cushion of my face, but I could sort of sleep.

I was woken!

The moon streamed its bright but eerie light down through the trees. There was a heavy crashing going on, it sounded like the Blair Witch, and If I had seen the branches form into anything resembling a weird macramé of pure evil I would have started screaming and never stopped. I was scared again.

The crashing continued and I heard a snuff chuuf snoof. Just a pig? I'm safe... or am I? ... Is it after the food in my bag? Shouldn't my sweaty pissy stench scare it away? I wasn't going to risk it and hauled my bag into the hammock tent with me, setting off another big cloud of dust and spores.

Now, with my face pressed against the open entrance hole of my hammock tent, I could hear slow crashing about 15 paces ahead of me, just creeping off the path. It no longer sounded like a pig at all... It was definitely a freaky Blair Witchy, angry, female Maori spirit, hairy-faced, alien-eyed Sasquatch with six erect black animal teats running down its hairy chest!

Soon it would just appear in the moonlight with its face upraised and looking at me. I would be too scared to scream and would just lie there paralyzed and weeing my pants. In the morning the search party would find nothing but a little bundle of sticks bound with a strip of my shirt. Inside the little bundle of sticks would be a small number of my bloody, freshly pulled teeth.

The crashing moved on, I unclenched my buttocks and eventually blacked out for a bit.

I would wake now and always with the same insane thought going around in my head:

CARGO CULT. Pacific islanders on remote islands seeing planes and ships for the first time. Worshiping these planes and big cargo ships. Making wooden sculptures of these strange cargo-carrying gods. I don't know, but images of this shit began kicking me in the head. Visions of dark-skinned dudes leaping up and down on beaches and pointing and gibbering at planes. Why was this?

I have no idea, but I hated it, and as soon as it got light enough to see, I crawled out of the hammock, went to my rock, ate a sandwich, and then missioned back down the mountain.

The roots and slips didn't bother me now.

Although my legs screamed, I made the occasional little leap over the odd obstacle and even jogged down some slopes. I was the boss again! And now I was only a small mission away from a shower and a little mini blackout on a nice-smelling bed in the healing mosquito-free daylight.

I belted this story out on the laptop with a Jim Beam and Coke next to me, sitting at the breakfast bar of my father's Mansion batch on the waterfront. The sun was going down behind the mountain in the distance. The Crayfish and Snapper dinner is almost done. I am fully safe, just slightly more of a man, and getting ready to tuck into the NZ Seafood feast.

But.. if you go out onto the deck and gaze across the river and up into the bush, with the right kind of ears you can hear the petrifying warble of the Blair Witchy, angry female Maori spirit, hairy-faced, Alien-eyed Sasquatch, with six erect black animal teats running down its hairy chest; as it creeps through the scrub searching for lone wilderness missioners to terrify.

Chapter 65
SHORT TALE ABOUT HAPPINESS IN SCHOOLS
(Why kids today are soft)

I WAS AT MY KID'S SCHOOL LAST YEAR, AND EVERYWHERE there were quotes of positivity and bright colors...

"Be the best you can be"

"You are Loved"

"You choose your feelings and today you choose HAPPINESS!

And many other great messages... Warmed me heart, it did. It made me think back to my school. And I searched my memory for something similar... among the rainy cold walkways, the beatings, and the teasing...

This is the best I came up with...

In the playground, we had a super dangerous high tower that was walled in at the top. It was two stories tall and a ladder led up to the second floor.

One day everyone was laughing and happy. I had never seen such merriment at my school!

A line of kids stretched down the ladder and across the playground...

What was it up there in the tower making these kids laugh and change them from dour urchins to happy cheerful kids!??

I took my place in line and climbed up into the tower... and what I saw DID make me laugh and it brightened my day—just as much as the brightly painted affirmations at my kid's school...

Some genius had dropped a massive duce right in the middle of the floor of the tower room and, with thick, black sharpie, written MR RUSH (that was our school principal) with an arrow pointing to the proud turd.

It stayed there for weeks and even after it was gone, if I was ever feeling down... all I had to do to cheer myself up, was climb that ladder and look at the MR RUSH sign, with the little brown stain that it pointed to..

Chapter 66
I HEART NY (Lady Liberty kicking me square in the nuts and laughing)

I FELT NEW YORK DRAWING ME TO HER. AS A YOUNG BOY growing up in New Zealand I'd watched all the movies set there. *Ghostbusters, Coming to America, Desperately Seeking Susan, Trading* Places, *Wall Street, Big*, and all the rest. I've watched them all.

But the movie that really grabbed me was Crocodile Dundee. In this movie Mick, a croc hunter from the outback of Australia, goes to New York and has many exciting adventures.

I was a bush-raised NZ hick, and in my early 20s I moved to Australia and became a crocodile hunter, among other things. So I know I would fit in with the socialites of New York as did Crocodile Dundee.

I just needed that chance.

That chance came in 07 when I had the opportunity to work with the NYPD and NYFD on a special medical project connected to 911 syndrome. The medical center was just off Wall Street and the bosses had got me a place to stay in the spare room of one of the clinic's staff members in Jersey. This was over an hour commute.

I wasn't having any of that bridge and tunnel bullshit. I needed to be the number 1 worm in the rotten core of the BIG APPLE!

I got an air bed and made myself a space in the storage room of the clinic, and there it was where I lived for Dec, Jan and Feb. I had my own Wall Street apartment!

I was told that, because of rules and zoning, I could not stay in the storage cupboard. I told them I would rather get on the plane back to California than live in Jersey. This was a pretty hard core project and my role in it had to be filled by someone who could be more intense and crazy than a NY first responder if needed.

Which was why I was flown out for the position. When regular New Yorkers have to fly an insane Kiwi in to do a job... you know it's gotta be fucking mental. So, they conceded to me living in the storage closet. This is another proud moment where everyone who never thought I would make it could kiss my arse! I'm living In Manhattan bitches!

I made many great friends among the cops and firemen, heard a lot of crazy stories about insane shit going down in the five boroughs, and was even given a special card to show any NY cop if I got in trouble with the cops... I dove deep into the NY first responder life and it was awesome. Just like in the movies.

However this story is not about that. This story is about having too much fun and getting up to mischief in New York.

I was 29 and had been drug free for 9 years and very, very temperate with alcohol.

I had to work from 2pm–10pm mon-sat. Which meant I could explore NY from 10pm–5am.

JUST LIKE BAT MAN! Retiring to my cave near dawn to sleep through the day.

I had made a cool NY uniform for myself: Leather "Wild Ones" Jacket, Polyester disco shirt, black beanie with Ernie on it, Big black Ugboots. Black band pants with a red stripe down the side, and my Huge hand made copper wallet chain.

I roamed and talked to all the people. Ate at all the restaurants, walked central park from end to end. Hid in the woods, watched all the street performers, went up all the buildings, but that's all boring.

NY was peak hipster at that time and I was determined to be the cringiest metal guy in the hipster bars of Park Slope, and Williamsburg. One particular one was called Barbes. I would get the subway almost directly there from Wall Street and sit at the bar ranting, telling stories, drinking Ricard, Raki, and Whiskey and having fun till close. Then I would stagger back to my Manhattan apartment like a boss.

ME: WERE SO BACK!

NY: I'M GOING TO KILL YOU, YOU KNOW THAT RIGHT?

ME: NO! I'M TOO TOUGH.

NY: WE WILL SEE.

I partied like a younger man. Nothing held back. Admirable... but mistaken. I hit peak burn on New Year's night, where I left the bar early to go to a Brooklyn party. I'd been invited by the hostess who I'd been chatting with for a few hours, at the bar.

Within minutes I was drinking absinthe with my new best friends.

At one point a bunch of us fled the lameness of the crowded lounge and piled in this gal's room... shit started to get a bit too wild... and the young New Yorkers started hooking up with each other on her bed.

The hostess jumped on me and started kissing me. This was the first kiss I had had from someone other than my wife, since meeting her. I freaked. She knew I was married. I pulled her off me and lamely told her I can't do this. Not even in NY, hammered at a New Year's party in a state of total reckless abandon.

She was sad, and embarrassed. I told her not to throw her love away, as "she was such an amazing girl with so much to offer". I had started my counsellor training at that point and pulled some on her, right there in that weed-smoke-filled bedroom, with people getting it on, on the bed. She started crying.

I fled into the night fearing for my soul. I had a close call...

While sitting on the train back home, thinking about my bad choices, I considered easing back the throttle... maybe just go out once a week... but then... I ran into a guy on the subway train and started chatting, as you do at 1 am New Year's morning heading back into the city. He was 23 with a 35 year old girlfriend who was a rich banker chick and he was going to this rich banker people's party. Of course I would be coming with. It had food and more high end booze and all was well in the world.

I chilled in the lounge, alternating between lying on a bean bag and drinking and eating till everyone was kicked out at about 4am.

* * *

To paraphrase a friend ...

"New York in the middle 2000s was a very special time and place to be a part of. Maybe it meant something. Maybe not, in the long run . . . but no explanation, no mix of words or music or memories can touch that sense of knowing that you were there and alive in that corner of time and the world. Whatever it meant."

* * *

I realized I was losing myself. I was becoming something new. I was tapping into the old and evil. New York and its twisted way was worming into my guts, and I loved it. I was shedding my healthy, tanned skin, like a snake and emerging as NEW YORK ME. I was living on a diet of cigarettes, quad shot espressos, car fumes, fluorescent light, and bodega food. The boozing and nonstop NY-scene-essence-soak was taking its fee. I started tapping into my old, still-functioning addict skills. Taking deep breaths and looking fellow co-workers in the eyes. Acting upbeat. Moving quickly.

Four Emergen Cs a day. Liters of water. Gatorade...B-complex... magnesium...

I had been in the detox and drug rehab field for years. Now I was using those skills on myself to keep my body going so I could keep up with New York and its twisted children.

I realized I was just doing a deep dive into ONE Slice of NY. Just the boozy hipster scene of Williamsburg, Park Slope and Mid-town. Once a week Central park to reconnect with "nature"...Walking the streets and riding the subways. I know living there is actually a huge and whole experience. I didn't give a shit about that. I was not involved in regular human NY life. I was involved in the bars and the people at those bars, who wanted to listen to my stories while I blazed smokes, drank, ranted and sang from my bar stool throne.

I had become a caricature of Bukowski. A Kiwi Metal Goth Poet.

That no one knew what to do with. Least of all me. I was popular and I fed on every handshake, hug, arrival cheer, and smile.

I feared that I had finally turned into what they've always said I would turn into? A Court Jester.

I couldn't quit my beloved New York though. So night after night I went out. I spent every cent I made. I lived a double life. Downplaying everything to my loving wife, back in California. Connected to her only through texts and a few weekly phone calls. She was oblivious. Everything finally came crashing down when an old friend from my bad old days in NZ was visiting NY and wanted to hang out. He was one of the many close friends I had abandoned when I went clean and fled NZ.

That this guy would randomly reach out to me and connect up with me in NY is very interesting... It was so, because of "Vibrational Rates of Connected Souls".

Prior to this NY trip I was properly on my way up and out of the darkness... engaged for almost a decade in clean living and on a deep and intense path of training in spiritual counselling and self improvement. I had worked in medical detox and addiction services... and had fully broken from my old tribe of dreadlocked mushroom elves.

I was up in the rarified pure spiritual weet grass air... But then... New York.

Within 48 hours of arrival, I was outside a bar standing in foot deep snow in Williamsburg drinking a 35 year old scotch from a brandy balloon, blazing my first clove cigarette in 5 years, screaming FREEEEEEDOOOOOM!

This insane drunken freedom-call unlocked lines of energy from me. Shooting through time and space it called to my old Team. Team Destruction.

So I met up with my old Kiwi friend and fell immediately into my old role as guide, into all things dark and crazy. But this time... New York! I was showing him I was her chosen son, loved and embraced.

I bought a 160$ bottle of Jade Edouard Absinthe for the occasion. It's an exact replica of the original french recipe. Esprit Edouard® is a fabulously faithful reproduction of the famous pre-ban 72° absinthe that was highly regarded during the Belle Époque. Esprit Edouard® is absolutely correct to the original, from its delicate tint, to its refined texture and delightfully aromatic finish.

First stop was a house party in Park slope. Hipster Central.

Main Show: Crazy NZ guy and his friend.

I did not wake for work the next day at 2.

The boss found me by smelling a strong anise smell coming from the hallway.

I was on my little bed face down, in all my clothes, in the exact position I collapsed, when I got in. Sweating straight absinthe into the room all night long

I was yelled at as only a NY boss can yell.

I promised to reform and clean up.

"No more drinking... no more I promise."

It was not a hard promise to keep.

It took me about a week to detox and come back to full life.

I focused on work, went out to restaurants with the other staff, stopped all booze, smokes, crazy stories, wild dancing, and instead walked round central park in the snow. I ate better, took my vitamins and got my shit together.

My contract finished and I had my 30th birthday in the clinic surrounded by great guys.

I demonstrated that I could once again function as a respectable individual before heading back to my family in California, who were none the wiser.

Like a wild romance with an insane redhead, NY is something I will always love deep in my heart. It was mine for those three winter months of 07. I fucking lived my Kiwi Jester Truth, and I pushed it till I just about died, then eased back.

That's how I roll.

No one I met will forget "Crazy NZ Guy". I channeled Crocodile Dundee.

New York. I am yours. You are Mine.

I salute you.

* * *

Latimer Redlance

Take it away Alicia...
> *In New York (ayy, aha)*
> *Concrete jungle (yeah) where dreams are made of*
> *There's nothin' you can't do (yeah)*
> *Now you're in New York (aha, aha, aha)*
> *These streets will make you feel brand-new (new)*
> *Big lights will inspire you (come on)*
> *Let's hear it for New York (you're welcome, OG)*
> *New York, New York*

Chapter 67
MY ONE CRAZIER SYSTEM (How to win life using mashed potatoes)

YOU ARE NOW AWARE THAT I HAVE NOT LED A BORING existence. Once I was a homeless druggie raggamuffin grinding it out on the mean streets of New Zealand, as well as a logger, a demolition man, a roofer and an all round Try Hard.

I developed many systems over the years to help me survive the various insane situations that I found myself in. The following are my bullshit systems, which you can use to make your life more exciting.

Note I did not say better.

The ONE CRAZIER System is the first one I will detail, and here it is.

Here is the premise.

As a student of people and systems, and an untrained social scientist, who has been booted about on the winds of fate, I have learned that all social systems and functioning systems of law and order are based around violence at the end of the day.

The fact that many pay taxes or obey the law is because at the end of the line there are men with guns to make sure you do so. This is how governments work. You pay for a dog license, because at the end of the line, if you buck the system too much, and don't pay the fines, eventually someone may show up at your house to take the dog. And when you try to stop them with force, they will use greater force to shoot you and that dog. So you pay the license...

Anyone thinking that they hold any kind of power without violence at the end to enforce their will, is merely play acting.

All political power originates in Violence. I don't make the news... I just report it.

Growing up in the 90s in the rugged social systems of NZ and Australia, and for many years living very rurally, many uncertain social situations were rapidly resolved with the question "Do you wanna punch in the head, cunt?"

The person could then ask themselves if they wanted to fight to be right about what stupid action they had done or stupid statement or insult they had made, or blisteringly apologize. I had said NO a few times to that question myself...

So... as I graduated out of the working class and being punched in the head or punching others in the head for infractions on our social, code I saw that in the realm of the moderately educated and ostensibly sane middle class, people controlled each other with social systems. Systems that did not rely on violence.

These middle class systems seemed to be based on being mean, sarcastic comments, not inviting people to parties, backstabbing and other mostly incomprehensible-to-me-at-the-time bullshit. The result of which meant as a rough country worker guy I often didn't know where I stood with people. I had a hell of a time integrating with "Polite Society".

I'm sure SOME of you readers grew up as a penniless white trash hicks somehow crawled into the middle class by mimicry.... and reading.

Well... what has this got to do with my ONE CRAZIER SYSTEM...?

Well it was an outgrowth of growing up in a rough rural area...

It was embodied by this quote by one of my mentors.

"Civilized men are more discourteous than savages because they know they can be impolite without having their skulls split, as a general thing."

When I read that, I was quite rocked... as I had experienced it at a dinner party.

Gutter to the Stars

I was a 23 year old East End Boy and at a nice dinner of the parents of a high class West End girl, in Remuera Auckland NZ. It may as well have been the Hamptons for how flash this was to me at the time.

Her uncle, a chubby rich real estate agent kept making smart ass remarks to me about my job in demolition and scummy sexual innuendo to my gal. His sister (the gals mother) would laugh nervously at these remarks... her father, an insipid drunk milquetoast of a man, pretended not to hear. This behavior was apparently normal and tolerated.

The Uncle had money and was an emotional bully. I wasn't as smart back then as I am now but I saw the scene for what it was and did not care for it. I got up from the table and went over to him. I calmly said "One more mean word out of you and you will find out how hard I can punch." I was sinister and he could feel how much I wanted to beat him out of his boat shoes.

But despite this... he laughed at me and said "Piss off little man." Before he could get the full word of "man" out, I scooped up a full handful of mashed potatoes from his plate and slapped him as hard as I could in the face with it.

The slap is the best way to start the monkey dance.

The monkey dance is not the song by The Wiggles, it is the chest puffed posturing and shouting that untrained fighters do in front of each other in order to attempt to assert dominance. Sometimes it goes on forever, with no fight eventuating.

I was taught by tougher bastards than me about the slap. When I worked in demolition we had a bag in the bedroom (see the story PEACHES) and we would practice delivering devastating slaps to the bag. The slap is humiliating and soul destroying. It signals the brain to fight or cower almost instantly.

One trick we would practice was to throw the left hand in the air, glance at it and say "SEE THIS HAND?" And at the same time as saying HAND deliver the brutal slap with the right. The slap immediately either enrages the person to fight or to cower and apologize. The *slap* was delivered after the threat.

The system that was always followed in the NZ and Aussie red neck world I worked in was this.

1. Rudeness. Someone was rude or pissed you off. Discourtesy.
2. The Threat:
3. "Do you want to see how hard I can punch?"
4. "Do you want a punch in the head?"
5. "One more word out of you and I will throw you off this fucking roof."
6. "If you pull some shit like that again, we will be going outside."
7. If the person did not cower or apologize and kept misbehaving... then the SLAP or the warning push that sends them sprawling was enacted.
8. If the person did not get the message and cower... they would often try 5.
9. The monkey dance. This is where the untrained fighter would posture with chest puffing and insults, but would not dare attack.
10. At this point things would progress to a beating, followed by piteous cries for mercy.
11. It's a rough thing to see a grown man beg off a fight because of being too bashed about. As a trauma counselor working with the NYPD and NYFD I encountered the male trauma caused by losing fights and being badly beaten. It's a rough one, and brings to mind a lot of ego stuff and ideas about one's self worth. A man is never the same after a few bad beats.
12. Many men never get to the point of getting punched... such is our wondrous society where we just call the cops on each other so they can take turns tasing our butt holes...
13. I decided long ago that I would either fight to the death or never get into a fight I couldn't win. I badly lost one fight when I was 16 and had to ashamedly back away apologizing. My friends were embarrassed and ashamed for me and It fucked me up mentally for a few months.
14. Never in all my years did I see the above 1-6 happen with two evenly matched super hard tough guys. They just

respected each other and were not disrespectful with mean comments.
15. I had seen shit blow up between two fake tough guys who start fighting right at 2. One not giving the other any warning or chance to back down. They did not use the formal system. But their lack of skill and fitness prevented them from seriously hurting each other anyway.
16. The above system was only used when there was one hard as nails guy and someone who was misbehaving, and whom the tough guy wanted to sort out.
17. Maybe this is just a NZ and Australian thing ... (possibly Irish as well) of pre- 2000...
18. I can't comment about what sort of scene is in NZ or Austria these days...
19. America where I live now has a totally different system, it's called the PEW PEW PEW!
20. A note on PEW PEW PEW:
21. When I moved to the USA I just kept my mouth shut and was very careful to be aware of my surroundings and polite to everyone. Because... guns.
22. I made sure I got guns right away. I lived in a rough as fuck ghetto and gun shots were common, one stray bullet going through our front window one night.
23. The cops would never come by when you called and I decided it would be best to just shoot baddies at a distance as they tried to smash in my door... I was not going to get into a punch up with enraged tweakers.

I digress... back to mashed potatoes uncle face slap.
KASLAPPPP!!! Mash potatoes to the face.
I was in uncharted territory.... Was he going to monkey dance...? Was he going to try to fight me...?
Yes monkey dance. He staggered out of the chair and screamed insults at me while cleaning his bright red face off... The screamed insults continued...

1. As cool as I could, imitating Michael Madsen from Reservoir dogs, I said
2. "Are you going to bark all day little doggie, or are you going to bite?"
3. This is called "the taunt"... where you use more and more degrading emasculating comments to push the slapped guy to attack you.
4. If he does, you beat him into the dust.
5. There is one more trick... the fake rush.
6. If the taunts don't work, you ball up your fists and put on the warrior face and fake rush the guy. If he attacks... it's on!
7. I did the fake rush and he shit himself and backpedaled so quick he fell onto the floor waving his arms about to ward me off. My gals mother screamed "STOP! GET OUT! JUST GET OUT!" finally woken up from her boozy middle class slumber, and about to see her mash potatoes covered brother stomped into the 40$ a foot Kauri floorboards.

I rolled out with her grinning daughter.

Cue intense and wonderful testosterone filled Victory Bang.

So this "One Crazier System" that I came up with was born out of that night.

Antisocial and Narcissistic people will be rude until some badass says NO.

They will push it as far as they can. They get away with it because few people are willing to fight. These nuts, and emotional bullies only understand violence. Reasoning does not work. They will not behave until forced to behave.

SO! The system is Thus: **When someone is being a crazy arsehole and does not respond to discussion, reason or logic, GO ONE CRAZIER.**

There will be a point at which they realize that their anti-social behavior —say, pulling their girlfriend along by the hair through the produce aisle, while the rest of the Californians pretend not to see—is not ok. It may be after you have thrown them through a cat food display in the bougie supermarket and they are upside down pissing their pants in shock, that they realize, in all of Sierra Oaks Sacramento, that there was one Kiwi, ready to go ONE CRAZIER.

In order to use this system it helps if you have had about ten years of martial arts training, and are fine with being punched.

But I think you should just try it anyway.

What's hilarious is that by dint of hard work and diligent hustle, I entered a very comfortable life in the USA. A few months ago in my back yard training my 13 year old son, he actually got a few good punches in on me. I spun a roundhouse kick to his head to sort him out, missed and almost threw my back out.

I realized peace had cost me my strength... "victory" had defeated me... I was fighting as if I were a younger man... nothing held back... admirable... but mistaken.

I had a little spiritual crisis that I'm sure any aging fighter gets...

And watching the Mike Tyson's "geriatric comeback" fight DID NOT FUCKING HELP AT ALL.

So what I've been doing to fix this is:

1. Daily Van Damme Movies.
2. Workouts and stretching.
3. Daily fight training.

When I was 25 in an argument with my father we both realized that it was *his* turn to back down from threats like taking me outside and beating me. I could beat him if it came to it. I know this is insane... but this is rural NZ.

I threatened to kick his ass across his dining room if he even tried a shot at the title.

He said "I still have the equalizer." And pointed to his gun cabinet.

Man, I guess my upbringing was nuts. My Dad threatened to bash me so I said I would kick his ass, so he said he would just shoot me. Super sane.

BUT NOW I GET IT... so step 4 of my program... is most importantly... getting back to the gun range making sure I'm a good shot with my pistolas!

Latimer Redlance

PEW PEW PEW! If I can't pull off a good Patrick Swayze, *Road-House* level roundhouse at 48, I'm going to be shit out of luck at 60.

Chapter 68
THE DECIDE NOW! SYSTEM (Use this to win life)

THIS SYSTEM WAS VERY LIKELY BORN IN ME BY THE INSANITY and chaos of my upbringing. Despite my seeming craziness... I love structure.

This system goes hand in hand with my ONE CRAZIER SYSTEM.

Early 90s....I was PUSHING, DRIVING and SMASHING to SURVIVE in life. The DECIDE NOW system is what made me who I am and got me where I am now.

Which is: **Winning in Florida on my Farm surrounded by my Guns and Gold bars.**

Despite the side effects of shock and misery it has caused some, this is a great system.

It was forged one day at the Skate Ramp in my home town in rural NZ. I was 15. I had been training in Martial arts for two years three times a week, but few knew this. I was still a skinny, glasses-wearing crazy kid. But under my baggy Vision Street Wear jacket I was ripped. I was bullied and would just take it... up until this moment.

One day one of the older, bigger and tougher kids decided to grab my skateboard and, using a sharp stone, scratched the absolute shit out of the awesome graphics of my brand new board—with SANTA

CRUZ SPEED WHEELS! I had saved up for months for these wheels and they were my pride and joy. For the first few weeks I even WASHED them when I got home each night. The thing to do in rural NZ is destroy other kids' nice things. If you had nice things it was wise to hide them.

As I limply watched him destroy one of my prized possessions, the voice of my Sensei echoed in my head.

The ancient Samurai would always choose death before dishonor.

I realized that I needed to DECIDE NOW, iif I was going to be a Samurai or a fucking maggot.

The technique I chose was the Shuto-Uchi Knife hand strike to the neck.

A **knife-hand strike** is a strike using the part of the hand opposite the thumb (from the little finger to the wrist), familiar to many people as the **karate chop** (in Japanese, *shutō-uchi*). Suitable targets for the knife-hand strike include the artery at the base of the neck (which can cause unconsciousness), mastoid muscles of the neck, the jugular, the throat, the collar bones, ribs, sides of the head, temple, jaw, the third vertebra (key stone of the spinal column), the upper arm, the wrist (knife-hand block), the elbow (outside knife-hand block), and the knee cap (leg throw).

He got the knife-hand to the base of the neck with everything I had.

He screamed and half fell down, grabbing his neck. I wasn't strong enough to put him all the way down, but It had caused some kind of nerve damage, to the point where all it took was me advancing on him to cause him to jog off, panicked. I heard he was telling people his left arm didn't work right, and his heart felt fucked after the strike. Those Japs know a thing or two about fucking up their enemies, I tell ya.

The news spread through my school that I had taken him down with one Karate Chop to the neck, but now he had recovered and was going to bash me. I informed all that I don't take shit anymore and if he wants a fight, I will be fighting to the death. I literally said "I will die on the battlefield before I take any more shit."

This bonkers statement, coupled with my years of erratic behavior precipitated the complete end of me ever being hassled at school and my status of even more of a maniac secured.

SO.... This is my system.

I hated not knowing things, I hated people not being able to decide.

When faced with threat, confusion, doubt, insecurity, maybe's or multiple choices I would DECIDE NOW! LIVE OR DIE! YES OR NO. Many Many Many times I used this in life to impinge my will on others and myself.

I became more certain, and that reputation has helped stabilize those in my environment. It also fucked them up. I would calmly discuss the options on the table and then YELL!!! "DECIDE NOW!!"

And any excuse they said was met with "I DON'T CARE!!! - DECIDE NOW!"

Here are some uses.

1. Relationships: In a number of relationships some ditz would say "I'm just not sure..."
2. I would tell them to "DECIDE NOW. IN OR OUT! We are together and it's awesome or I fucking roll and call your friend Cindy who's a badass and wants me cause I make decisions and pay for the nice dinners!
3. I never *ever* in my life have sat around in a state of indecision about relationships with women. Just awesome times or calm endings.
4. Friendships: A friend starts acting up. Starts deciding they want to start stealing, doing drugs, cheating on his wife with hookers, or being a victim or a cunt to people. I tell them to DECIDE NOW. The behavior stops or they exit my circle. No waiting around to see if they get better. They rarely do.
5. Running businesses: A staff member acts up. Starts moving away from being a part of my rocking tribe of awesomeness. I pull them into the office and ask
6. "Do you want to be here? DECIDE NOW". We don't keep them on.
7. I pride myself in knowing that the employee wants to quit a month before they do. Just as productivity starts to falter.

8. Bosses: "I think we will have a talk about this later".
9. NO. NOW. NOPE... NOW!
10. "I'm quitting at the end of your sentence unless we talk about this now and handle this NOW." You sure cut through a lot of worry about whether you're getting canned or not this way.
11. People being rude or misbehaving at parties or events: "Apologize or be thrown out by the head. DECIDE NOW." Works in tandem with the ONE CRAZIER SYSTEM. No waiting about to endure more bullshit while everyone gets more uncomfortable and your family gatherings disintegrate.
12. Stepson starting to act up as a young man: DECIDE NOW. You have until I book you a flight to go and live with your dad in his trailer and suck down weed smoke while living on ramen, to DECIDE if you want a good productive life with me and your mother. He made the right choice as soon as I opened the flight website.
13. This is harsh. But It's how I run my life because I'm a DRIVEN MF and my life is awesome. I have worked for 20 years in Drug and Criminal Reform.
14. DECIDE LATER OR NEVER doesn't work.

When you put things off—like the intervention, or the arrest, or the deserved beating, or the dishes, or the leaky roof, or the good diet, or the shitty worker, or the exit from the toxic relationship—all you do is waste your time. and prevent the learning of lessons which life would teach one day anyhow.

The person who sucks, who you keep on in your business, just gets more and more non productive and hateful until, one day, they are taking 4 one-hour fake shits a day while playing *Clash of Clans* in the dunny.

That shit friend, just sucks more of your time which you could be spending with awesome friends. People don't like pulling the trigger because it's painful, and they fear conflict.

Well, my other motto is "MOVE IN THE DIRECTION OF THE BEATINGS."

You can front load the pain that's going to happen anyway by DECIDING NOW and CHOOSING AWESOMENESS.

THE "DECIDE NOW!" SYSTEM Is the first part.

The "FUCK YA THEN!" SYSTEM is the second part.

You will get your life back. Simple and nuts. But there it is.

Chapter 69
GUIDED LEAF (The ultimate life guidance system)

LET ME SET THE SCENE...

As a young man I was a proponent of Prime Causation. The philosophical principles I strongly held to were:

1. If It happened to me I caused it somehow.
2. If it exists without my knowledge it exists without my permission.
3. I am the absolute boss of everything in my life.
4. The ONE CRAZIER SYSTEM.
5. The DECIDE NOW SYSTEM.

These systems had got me a certain distance in life. But shit was sure hard, when you can never back down, won't admit your wrong and you assume you automatically know best in every situation...

I had become friends with Raven, a 23 year old hippy wanderer detailed in The Shaman series of stories you read prior.

He probably thought I was nuts, but being a Canadian hippy, was far too polite and tolerant to let me know this. I had buddied up with him for the summer because he was a survivor and always had some good money-making scam running. He also needed my guidance. He had recently returned from Guatemala with a pregnant village girl and needed to show his rich doctor parents that he was playing their game. Making money and working so they would love him and help him.

There is nothing more batshit than driven young men in their early 20s, who have given up drugs and embraced spirituality. Still not healed or detoxed from the weed, mescaline, mushroom and LSD brain fungus/crystal damage... yet forging ahead in life despite, and with this damage.

There is nothing more meat-hook brutal than wholly believing reality is an illusion, yet declining to continually mash yourself into hallucinatory numbness with drugs to soften the beatings that reality deals out.

It's all fine and dandy to trip balls and blaze weed, go to raves and live in your brother's basement while believing your actions don't matter... and when you get a sneaking suspicion that your actions might actually be influencing your life, just hit the bong again... However, try to "raw-dog" life, drug free, while eating well, trying to make money, dealing with all the people in the world; thinking about, working towards and planning your future and also going to Vegan Yoga Potlucks where people talk about injustice and the environment for hours at a stretch. You wind up in the corner of these potlucks wanting to peel your skin off like a mandarin.

Indeed, Raven and I were grappling with exactly those above things. And so we had fled to an Island off the coast of Vancouver to work a job for a rich guy he knew. We were both roofers and Raven had scored us this job putting a new sheet metal roof on this guy's house while living in his Catamaran. Through the balmy summer days we slowly worked on the roof and ranted philosophically back and forth.

After a slow and chill day of work we would skate to the top of the hill, up to the center of the Island and eat at a pub. It was a special and awesome time, of politely chatting with pretty girls (both of us were engaged and celibate) and listening to live music. At the end of the night doing the downhill run lying on our skateboards all the way back to our Catamaran bedrooms.

Bliss.

. . .

I borrowed a rifle from our employer and shot a small deer on our fourth day there. Showing Raven how to butcher it, we stored it in our employer's shed freezer.

His wife was rude and posh, she would not let us into the house or talk to us. They would not feed us... so the deer meat is all we had after we ran out of the meager rations we had brought. We barbecued deer meat chunks for breakfast and lunch every day. Eating so much of it, after a few weeks we started shaking and feeling ghostly and fucking wak. The only thing that stopped the shaking was eating a huge burger and fries at the pub each night. Later when I got back to Civilization, I Net Searched "TOO MUCH DEER MEAT HANDS SHAKING FEEL WEIRD".

Fat starvation or Rabbit starvation was the verdict.

Rabbit starvation, also known as protein poisoning, occurs when a person consumes a diet that is excessively high in lean protein, like rabbit meat, without enough fat or carbohydrates. This can lead to malnutrition and serious health issues due to the body's inability to process the excess protein effectively.

Raven also had the genius idea to use the deer head on a string to catch crabs off the side of the wharf. So we feasted on crabs for two days till it was picked clean.

OK... so that's the scene...

So...**GUIDED LEAF.**

Raven's philosophy was that one was just a leaf being blown on the winds of fate! There was nothing one could do to influence this. It was all preordained by some great cosmic rhythm. He even had BALANCE tattooed on his back. That tattoo is what got me started. I had a tattoo of a circle with a triangle on my shoulder. This means *will* over the universe. We were opposites.

"BALANCE! Fuck Balance man! You will get nothing done if you seek Balance!

Seek AWESOMENESS!"

Seeking AWESOMENESS, I was to discover, was not a thing to crow about in hippy Canada at the start of the Iraq war. Seeking

AWESOMENESS is what Yanks do with Bombs apparently. I learned to keep that one to myself after a while.

Yet, I tore his arguments to pieces. I explained all my choices had led me to this roof having this discussion with him, and one could not only control one's destiny, but one's own will was ALL there was in the UNIVERSE. One's own will, all the time, non stop through time and space for eternity. He mellowly came back with "What about babies that die randomly ? What about the effects of Karma and past lives? What about the spirit world, your higher self, God's will and all the rest of it?"

Well I honestly couldn't discount those things...

He had been raised by wealthy doctors who had controlled every inch of his life from birth until very recently. I liked to think he was hanging out with me because he liked the freedom, personal direction and certainty I espoused. But his mindset was of course, as it was, due to the overwhelming control his parents and Canadian Society had mashed into him.

I was raised by wolves in rural New Zealand and then fled into the wild world at 16 to kill and win on my own. If you have been paying attention you now know how it all started for me at the age of 6 being babysat by a retarded kid. I have detailed my experience of trying to carve a life out for myself as the entire world tries to kick me in the nuts and then stand on my neck until I expire, while I try to scam food, money, sex and friendship from other humans.

Anyway....

Round and round we went...

We were not studied enough at that time to know we were engaging in the ancient Greek Dialectic method. We were just two young hairy-arse roofers... on Galiano Island off the coast of Canada in the summer of 2003. But we were indeed channeling Socrates and he would have been proud of us.

The dialectical method, refers originally to dialogue between people holding different points of view about a subject but wishing to arrive at the truth through reasoned argument. The concept excludes elements such as emotional appeal. It has its origins in ancient philosophy and continued to be developed in the Middle Ages.

A dialogue of arguments and counter-arguments, advocating *propositions* (theses) and *counter-propositions* (anti-theses). The outcome of such a dialectic might be a synthesis, a combination of the opposing assertions.

Well after three weeks of non stop ranting about free will and individual power on my part, or hopeless other-determinism, on his part, we came to the resolution.

GUIDED LEAF.

The SYNTHESIS.

We were both right.

HERE IS: GUIDED LEAF.

One is a LEAF blowing on the winds of fate, BUT if you push like a motherfucker with your drive and will, you can GUIDE the leaf.

You may go into puddles, and down drains, hit cars and get sucked into gutters, shat on, torn and smashed... but if you keep pushing you can get that leaf going in the direction you want.

I use GUIDED LEAF to this day.

We completed this rich boomers roof and the dude tried to STIFF US. Raven had not fully negotiated the price of our job before we started, as he did not enforce his divine will on people. The rich island boomer tried to give us 250$ each. Obviously stuck in some deranged 70s illusion. It had taken us three weeks... we did work kind of slow but we did a good job.

Well... this was a time for me to shine. Cracking this old boomer cunts illusions right there on his porch. I used a trifecta of Systems. CROSSING THE STREAMS!

The GUIDED part of GUIDED LEAF, followed by ONE CRAZIER followed by DECIDE NOW! To win the day. Here's how it went down.

"Here you go guys, I think 500$ for the job is fair"

Raven looked a bit shocked and sad.... but started to put the money away.

ME: "No sir. A job like this would cost you at least 5000$. You are giving us 1000$ each, and that's us giving you a fucking great deal."

Initiate: STARING SPARKLY CRAZY EYES TECHNIQUE.

Raven perked up.

DERANGED BOOMER: "No, this is all I'm paying".

ME: Without hesitation. "You are giving us $1000 each or I'm going to climb right back up there, undo all the roofing screws and start throwing the sheets right back on the ground bending the fuck out of them!"

Raven laughs nervously.

DERANGED BOOMER: Mouth open like a hooked bass... thinks I'm not serious....pauses too long.

I see I have to go ONE CRAZIER.

"ME: Then if you still don't pay, I'm going to take that axe over there and chop through the hull of your Catamaran, before disappearing into the bush. I'll be down 1000 dollars and on the run, but you will have no roof and a sunk boat."

I paused for a second before yelling "DECIDE NOW!!!"

The realization that he's dealing with a crazy man wakes him up. He goes pale and stiffly says "I'll go get the money".

By some miracle this boomer had $2000 cash. His face was like a smacked bum as he handed it over. We fled to the Ferry. Sure he was going to call the Mounties on us... I was slightly pooing because I heard "They always get their man". He didn't call them. I fucking won.

On the Ferry looking back at the island, Raven was thoughtful and silent. staring down at his mini Gangsta roll of crisp Hundys... which only an hour ago was going to be a paltry $250...

He said...

"You know, I now think you are right, that we forge our own destiny...."

I said "Fuck man... I thought we agreed on Guided Leaf!"

Chapter 70
DEMENTED GAMES (A Favorite New Zealand Pastime)

MY 13 YEAR OLD SON CAME BACK FROM A SCOUT TRIP FIRING off a cap revolver. Kablam!

There are no screens at Scouts, so the kids rapidly revert to their naturally feral *Lord of the Flies* state. This manifests itself in crazy games that they sneak off and play.

This cap gun had a chamber that you could spin. He gleefully told me of a demented game he devised involving this cap gun. It had something to do with Uno Cards and Russian Roulette. If you lost or pulled the wrong card you had to put the gun against your head and pull the trigger, with a two in six chance of half deafening yourself.

Many kids were deafened that weekend. I was so proud.

I proceeded to tell him about demented games I played when I was young in Rural New Zealand. Without screens to pacify and hypnotize us, us gen X kids made up all sorts of demented games. I will detail a few of my favorites here.

THE JELLYBEAN OR THE PAPER

This game was invented while being slowly gassed from petrol fumes, riding back from the big city for three hours in the covered back tray of my friend's dad's truck. I was there with my two friends, brothers they were. We were poor but somehow I had scored a large bag of the most amazing new thing to hit NZ ever. These things blew up so big it was totally mental.

"Jelly Belly Jelly Beans" had just hit. We were about 9 years old.

I explained that I would give them one each, but after that I was not going to share. But when that sweet American corn syrup and Red #40 hit them they were jonesing BAD and their begging was incessant.

I came up with an idea to try to dissuade them. Ripping a small square of newspaper from a bundle that was in the back of the truck with us, I hid it in one hand and a jelly bean in the other. Holding them out I said "You have to eat whichever you choose."

And it was on. They chose and ate NON STOP. Until my entire bag was gone. And they each had eaten a large sheet of newspaper. Watching them eat squares of newspaper was hilarious. The JOY of choosing correctly! The SCREAM when my hand would open revealing the newspaper. Soon their mouths were black with ink.

Later they were to tell me that they pooed almost straight newspaper and could even read the words.

HANDMASH

I have no idea which demented Sadist invented this game—for one to four mentally sick players—but it was popular for a few days before being banned at my boarding school.

We were being beaten so badly by the housemaster, that inflicting pain on each other seemed like the next logical step...

It was played by getting a pack of cards. Each player chooses one Ace to be their "Stop Card."

Each player lays their hand on the table and takes turns flipping cards, and delivering punishments to the other player's hand of a type and severity equaling the card flipped.

HEART = A POUND DOWN ON THE HAND WITH THE FIST.

DIAMOND = A VICIOUS PINCH TO THE HAND

CLUBS = A RAKE ACROSS THE FINGERS WITH THE KNUCKLES

SPADES = A SLAP TO THE HAND.

The intensity of the punish was determined by the card. A 2 (two) being the lowest...and very, very mild and not to be painful, all the way to an ACE, being bone crushing or blood drawing. If you drew your ace you got to smash the opponents hand with everything you had. If they drew yours, they got to smash your hand... but then you were out and continued to smash without being smashed.

I remember kids keeping their horribly cut bruised and smashed hands in their pockets to stop being found out. I played twice, but quit after a particularly vicious long nailed pinch scooped out a chunk of flesh... which my opponent then ate.

A few days later, four kids were caught playing by the house master and all were taken downstairs and caned for hurting each other.

Hurting them will teach them not to hurt each other I guess.

SHITCAKE

I learned about this game at the Purangi Winery. It was at a party with guys and gals from our school, getting mashed. Ace of base, and Cypress Hill was playing.

I do not know the origin of this game but once it hit the scene it was played at every single house party from then on. The rules were simple. Everyone sat around a table; a large jar was placed in the middle; dice is rolled...

On a 1 (one), the person must pour some of their drink into the jar.

The dice is then rolled again.

If it's a 1 again, something from the fridge goes into the jar: ketchup... Worcestershire sauce... mayonnaise... you get the idea.

The dice is rolled again, If it's a 1 the roller must drink the WHOLE JAR!

If it's a 6, the roller can nominate another to drink the WHOLE JAR!

On a 3, the roller must take a small sip from the jar and the dice is rolled again. If it's another 3 the roller can nominate someone to have a sip from the Jar.

This builds the suspense as the sipper can describe how gross the drink is.

A roll of a 6, everyone takes a drink of *their* drink and pours some of it into the Jar.

The dice is rolled again. On another 6, the roller gets to wear the Immunity Hat. This protects them from drinking from the Jar, until someone else rolls a 6 twice.

So...

Everyone would be drinking different things... and within minutes the jar would be a lava lamp-like potion of beer, rum, Kahlua, wine, Baileys, cider and whatever else.

Soon things from the fridge would be added... and the jar would become... SHITCAKE.

A fucking rank as fuck layered chunky brownish creamy witches brew. I never saw anyone drink the Shitcake and not spew.

The contents of the Shitcake would be discussed throughout the next week at school.

"Bro, at Jesse's party the Shitcake had sardines in it..."

"Bro, at Gavins party I heard that their Shitcake had part of a rotten crayfish in it."

"Bro remember that time the Shitcake had a whole thing of green food coloring in it and then Amanda spewed in the lounge and they could never get the massive green stain out of the carpet."

It was a simple better time for sure.

SHOCKY

I'm 18. I live in a flat in the city. I work in Demolition now. My friend had a machine that was for stimulating the muscles of the body with powerful electric shocks. We called it SHOCKY.

We were seeing who was the toughest—which of course was determined by who could endure the hardest shocks for the longest. We would hook up the special pads to various parts of the body and then crank on the Juice. When the dude either started screaming or started ripping the pads off, we would stop the flow of current.

But sometimes we would hold the guy down and shock the hell out of him. We screamed in glee, while he screamed in terror. After receiving a bunch of shocks to the chest and neck, I was shaking so bad that I pissed myself a little bit and got really, really terrified of SHOCKY and stopped playing.

It was as if SHOCKY was an evil living thing.

One of my friends took the safety pads off SHOCKY and taped SHOCKY's wires to his temples. Despite his insistence that he be the one to shock himself—and only lightly—we cranked the juice to MAX. There was a POP! And a loud scream accompanied by the smell of burning flesh. He ripped off the wires yelling obscenities. There were harsh burn marks from where the wires were. He said his memory never was right after that.

We stopped playing SHOCKY after that.

Chapter 71
THE FLORIDA STATE FAIR AS A SPIRITUAL EXPERIENCE (The Greatest Carnival on the Planet)

I'M NO STRANGER TO SPIRITUALITY OR AWAKENED STATES OF consciousness...

I was talking with a friend about people going to sacred sites, to get magic crystals, or India or wherever, so they can find themselves or learn something... and all locations and objects are bullshit. It's just the fluff. I have in front of me pieces of the Basilica of St John, The Temple of Artemis and the Tomb of Mary mother of Jesus. They are just rocks. I have lived in the Outback with Australian First Nation tribes, spent months with the Maori, the Hawaiian Kahuna and Native Americans... I spent most of 2023 living full time in a retreat in the wilds of South Africa. I've done all the things.

I'll tell you the secrets right now, and you can save yourself the hassle and plane tickets. All the love for your fellow man and the love for yourself is already inside you. And it's always been there. That's what you learn in India at the Ashram, In the sweat lodge, or in the desert while covered in mescaline and dream catchers.

You're welcome.

On that note... NOTHING could have prepared me for the raw spiritually awakening power of the Florida State Fair.

As you well know, as a young man I was a deranged hippie. Full of rage at the destroyers of Our Mother Earth. Which was everyone in the world except me and about 8 friends...

I touched no plastic, I used no money if I could help it, and I was sour and very unhappy. I was so busy hating on everyone not living up to my demented Gaia approved standards, that I was dying inside. I was vegan, and wore no shoes.... my survival system was that the energy from the earth flowed up through my bare feet, into my body, through the chakras and out through the crown chakra, then back through the beaver tail dreadlock and down to the earth, and then up and around me in a cycle, forming a powerful energy shield around me that kept all the evil out.

In 1997 I had a devastating hippy wig out one day in a bar (La Luna) in downtown Wellington. I got overwhelmed with the perfume, the boozy smell, the cigarettes, the yelling, the crazed laughter, the weird looks and the pure beer drinking planet killing normie-ness of it all. I staggered outside to get some air... outside the bar was a fat gal puking into the gutter while holding a bag of McDonald's.

A car full of drunk young men drove past and screamed "FAG-GOT!!!", at long haired me. I was hit by the petrol fumes and then the barf whiff...

I snapped, and took off running straight up into the park.

There is a massive park in the middle of Wellington NZ. A large botanical garden. Anytime I had to go to a city, I would immediately go directly to the biggest and best park or garden in that city and connect with all the nature spirits. I would give them my allegiance and they would give me protection. Then I could function for a few hours at a time in the concrete hell of the city.

Well, this wig out found me alternating between running and sneaking about on all fours through the bush of the gardens like a wolf for an hour or so. Breathing in the healing spores and rapturous energies of the woods and drinking the cool mossy waters of the fish pond... I came right and headed back to the bar, catching my friends just as they were leaving...

"Bro, Why are you covered in dirt and sticks?"

"Oh I was just having a little bush walk..." I kept these monumental wig outs secret.

Just between me and the moss... Anyway, I was reminded of the above wig out because today I saw a fat gal puking up rancid fair food into a rubbish bin, at the Florida State Fair. I caught a good whiff of it... and combined with the gas smell of the generators, it sent me right back to that time.

Instead of running into the woods and racing about like a wolf in tie dyed pants, I just chilled. Now, if there is anything on this planet that is the opposite of living on Organic Food and Rainwater, on a commune in the deep bush of New Zealand—like I used to—it's The Florida State Fair.

Working as an educator in drug and chemical detox over the years, I have sent the following data to trainees:

Signs of Heavy Metal Toxicity: affected patients are drawn to man-made, artificial environments. Such prefer Disneyland or Vegas over a trip to the ocean or forests and prefer loud repetitive beats over melodic music. When patients have detoxed from heavy metals, the change of entertainment and music preferences is sometimes startling.

Well, I would go as far as to say that the humans of the Florida State Fair are not the healthiest folk, bless their massive, clotted hearts. The bright lights, the loud music, the toxic food, the booze, the spinning terrifying rides... It's quite something.

I was not ready for the powerful spiritual experience of the State fair.

I felt good that I was with my people, the Carnies... I am a Carine, and worked the mean shows of West US for many years, and I spent much time bonding with them, which is why I always go to the fairs. Being a Carnie is like being Goth. If you "***Were*** a Carnie... then you never really were a Carnie"

I am OF Carnie and From Carnie. as we say with our slang and our stories... but what was a shock at this fair... was that the people partaking of the fair... looked ROUGHER than the Carnies. That fucking threw me...

The people at the fair were ... ROUGHER than the Carnies. My world was upside down. I always thought I was down there with the Carnies looking out, at the high class marks.

I started to get a bit judgy and cynical... I almost went into a "decay of modern values, health and society, everyone and everything is fucked, rabbit hole spiral".

But then in a flash—part of one of my favorite prayers came to me...

May all beings be at ease!
Let none deceive another,
Or despise any being in any state
Let none through anger or ill-will
Wish harm upon another

I rallied! I started chatting to them and loving them. I started smiling and projecting love into all of them, and seeing perfection in each and every one of them. No one needed to change to be more acceptable to me.

They were all perfect and beautiful.

First there was a guy and gal hammered drunk dancing to Cotton Eye Joe. When I was 17 I remember dancing to this song in a barn in rural NZ, mashed on Southern Comfort. I danced with them! We did cowboy dances, let out excited cowboy screams while people smiled and laughed... We were in love with the world.

Then there was a young redneck mom who was dancing with her tiny baby, to Kid Rock—that "I'm a Cowboy baby" song... The baby stared at me smiling as they danced; I smiled and danced looking at this baby. Till I felt so much love for humanity I cried. Tears streaming down my face like a total spaz.

This scared the gal a bit and she smiled nervously and headed off.

I saw a fat mom smoking a cigarette next to her baby in the stroller. LOVE and LIGHT TO YOU.

There was the lady parked on the mobility scooter filming her daughter dancing. BLISS

I took my boy to the Gravatron and, in the cue, I noticed a girl and guy displaying so much love and tenderness for each other that it made my heart soar. She looked amazing. Short, brown pixie cut, tattoo of an ornate heart on her chest, and what blew my mind was a low down crotch tattoo of some kind. I first thought that the black triangle that started under her bellybutton was some sort of underpants. It wasn't. I doubt she was wearing any. It was some massive intricate tattoo.

She was a work of art. I hope they have ten kids.

I then saw these two tubby rocking Goth girls, strutting past the fried Oreo Hut, and I sent them the LOVE AND THE LIGHT. They did not know that I'm so Goth I fart dead bats. I was wearing a trucker hat, a totally hippy shirt and German sandals WITH SOCKS, and khaki shorts. We call this CRINGEMAXXING in the industry.

Well I couldn't just rock over and schmooze them into a TGT... thats a Tubby Goth Threeway, for the uninitiated... cause it's not 2002; I'm not that guy anymore...

It's 2025 and I'm a 48 year old suburban dad... sigh... Still could have pulled it off though... Just sayin.

What I love about Florida is that you can literally wear anything. No one cares. As a person who has cringed out so many people with my demented outfits, I love it. You can dress down or dress up! It's all good here.

I saw a young guy who looked so flash. His jeans had sparkly diamonds all over the front and his jacket had amazing designs of birds and trees. His shoes were so white and clean they hurt my eyes.

I was spiraling out of control with my love for all beings. I almost went up to this guy and told him he was beautiful and tried to hug him. But I checked myself... and went and got a meal that embodied and personified the fair to help ground me.

I got THE PLATTER. It's 3 Barbecue Battered Ribs, a pile of Pulled Pork, Baked beans with bacon, fries, and a big chunk of smoked chicken. I'd been on my farm for months, living out of my garden on blended green drinks, salads, and omelets from my wonderful chickens. Drinking only the purest water, and breathing the purest air...

In one hit, I balanced all that out. It shut down the crazy spiritual high I was on and chilled me the fuck out. The meat sweats and dry horrors hit hard so I got a huge ice tea and we went to the Ferris Wheel to wrap up the night. I knew a few rotations of that magic ride would soothe my black guts.

All is well in the world.

One of my mentors once told me:

"In the icy peaks of the Himalayas, we see the perfection of it all in the evolutionary journey of beings. And at the same moment, the caring part of us is like the bleeding heart of Jesus, and we look down and see the blood on the snow. We keep both of those in mind at every moment so we can help beings who are suffering in the way they need to be helped. If we are really going to help them get out of the illusion, we ourselves must not get lost in the illusion."

Chapter 72
THE CRUISE SHIP AS A SPIRITUAL EXPERIENCE
(Nothing says enlightened like lining up for a beer and a pizza slice at 10 PM)

I GROW ALMOST ALL MY OWN FOOD ON MY MINI FARM, HAVE 9 chickens, eat all organic, my house is free of all scented and toxic non-earth friendly products, and I bake my own bread. I don't have a phone. I don't wear shoes unless forced to.

I don't shame people for their bad food or life choices, but when I go to peoples houses, parties or barbecues, I calmly refuse all food and drinks except water, without saying why. When they weirdly apologize, I say "There is no judgment here."

And there really isn't. They don't know what's what.

To my shame I once made a visitor to my house eat his McDonald's in his car.

I was once way worse than I am now. If that's even possible.

Peak hippie spaz was achieved when I had fallen in with a crew of hardcore tree huggers in Victoria Canada. All it took was one vegan potluck for me to code switch from the life of a redneck roofer, who lived on Filter-less Clove Cigarettes, Vodka and Tim Horton's, to my old hippy Kiwi self—veteran of the Mid 90s commune scene.

What I'm more into than subcultures, and ideological onanism, is SURVIVAL... and having interesting times while trying to help people live a better life in their own estimation.

I have been and done so many things, I will just adapt to whatever is going down. On last count I had done 37 different jobs.

If you cannot BE like those you want to hang with, you will not be hanging with them long. At my hippy peak in BC Canada, 2003, me and the crew tried to live only on what we could forage, hunt or dumpster dive. #freegan

On the rare chance we had to buy something, no packaging was allowed. Many of them carried their own glass jars and string bags with them at all times.

I once mistakenly asked if going to restaurants was allowed? The type of boho farm to table—paper straw, super-eco sustainable eatery that exists now, barely existed back then... so the answer was a definite NO! Followed by a punishing lecture about the waste generation and planet killing antics of the restaurant industrial complex.

I held these ideals as long as I could. I remember the day they shattered.

February the 14th 2004.

My wife's boss had bought us a cheap ass honeymoon trip to Vegas. To stay in the Pirate themed mega hotel, Treasure Island.

It was on the strip that day where the last shreds of hippieness I had, went into the giant garbage trucks that continuously circled the strip, and expired.

It was a three stage mental collapse for Kiwi hippie me. Never in my life had I seen such a bloated Baal, Mammon, Consumerism confluence.

First stage: seeing thousands of little cards on the streets with hooker pictures on them.

Prostitution is Legal in NZ. I grew up with it as part of life. And regulated with taxes and health check ups, and there is a modicum of class. It's tucked away, but has been a real part of our society from its beginning... it's still a demented job... but Sex is not the garish economic beast I have seen it displayed as, in the USA.

This Vegas hooker card thing was a horrendous invasion of plastic tits and asses scattered in the gutter and being pushed into my newlywed face...

Second stage: was seeing hordes of poor Mexicans, old mamas, young girls, teenage boys and old men handing out these hooker cards to tourists! Who would then throw them on the ground. I had never seen anything like that. Even littering shocked me.

I had been sheltered, by living in socialist countries with welfare safety nets and closed borders that up till now, prevented me from experiencing this grimness.

My new wife explained the entire concept of illegal immigration, Mexicans, their struggle and hustle. Also talking to me about the trials of her own Portuguese grandfather, jumping off a whaling ship in California in 1910, at 15 years old.

I had been stuck in Canada waiting 11 months for a Fiancé visa, paying 8K to get in legally... I could see now how my "struggle" wasn't even an option for these people.

As I was reeling from the above mental implosion I was hit by the third stage.

Third Stage: Bloated fat pasty and sick looking Americans staggering, screaming and drunk down the strip with giant plastic, rainbow booze filled Margarita goblets, adorned with flashing lights, pinwheels and spiral straws. To be consumed and then the remaining planet destroying plastic ensemble to be thrown onto or near an overflowing rubbish bin.

Now I saw why there were so many garbage trucks circling the strip.

They were just taking all this trash and riding it out of town to be hurled into a massive pit somewhere. Fuses blew in my brain. For the last 8 months, I had been carefully recycling everything and not buying anything that had any wrapping or packaging of any kind. I was washing jars and saving them... composting. Picking up trash off the beaches and streets... I had been hanging with vegans so vegan they composted in their pockets and didn't eat anything that cast a shadow.

I realized that if me and my hippy mates did all we could to reduce, reuse and recycle for the next 10,000 years we wouldn't even make a dent in the trash that Vegas and its demented beast-children produced in one second.

I just gave up right then and there. BAM. I was out. I went directly to the Caesars Palace Bacchanal Buffet and over ate every day.

I gamified getting free drinks while grinding it out at the low stakes

Holdem tables like a demented Kiwi Matt Damon. One night I had 14 Martinis and left up 280$.

Is that winning or what?

I bought shit that came in plastic packets. Drank from plastic water bottles and then threw them at the overflowing bins. I just utterly gave up. The beast won.

Over the next few years I evolved into a 210 lb blob. When we got back home to Sacramento I discovered the joys of Dining out in America. Red Lobster, TGI Fridays, Thai food, Indian food, PF Chang's... three of four times a week for years.

That will do it. I finally got myself back under control on a trip back to Australia and New Zealand which then precipitated moving my entire family into the Outback and living on roo, goat and rabbit for months on end. I started gardening and stopped worrying about it all so much and became the change. The book "Building a better world in your own backyard" helped a lot.

One of my mentors said....

"Together we are all on a journey called life. We are a little broken and a little shattered inside. Each one of us is aspiring to make it to the end. None is deprived of pain here, and we have all suffered in our own ways. I think our journey is all about healing ourselves and healing each other in our own special ways. Let's just help each other put all those pieces back together and make it to the end more beautifully. Let us help each other survive."

I talk to everyone I can, interact... bring joy... Vibe and love. I now seek out and purposely crawl into the belly of the beast.

Always a proponent of our boy Byron. **"The road of excess leads to the palace of wisdom...You never know what is enough until you know what is more than enough."**

So... THE CRUISE !!!

A low budget cruise is a bit more intense than the state fair, and thus able to give one more wisdom.

The Cruise. What I learned... from my deep dive of friendly prying.

It's mostly overweight lower middle class grinders from the Midwest and Southern states and Canadians. Asking around I learned that many people saved up for the trip and it was a special occasion. They hunted for the best deal they could. They bring their families and often their crew of friends and go all out. Many of them are in debt, paid for the cruise on a credit card and give no fucks.

A lot of people joked that due to the inflation and prices of food/restaurants, they have fully stopped going to restaurants and now instead just go crazy on the cruises. Going on a cruise so they can eat at restaurants... there's some sort of logic there somewhere...

I would say it's about 30% overweight, 30 % badly overweight and 20% obese (like waddling, or using a scooter thing). Also 10 % healthy gym people. 30% tattooed... but no piercing people, punks, goths or metal heads.

The white people were like country-music-loving people mostly. And it was 20% black, 10% indian, 10% spanish/latin's/mexicans.

And of course one Kiwi hippy in shorts and socks and sandals smiling at everyone like a beatific spaz. It was a melting pot of happiness. I saw not one harsh word or raised voice.

Perfect manners all round. Friendliness and kindness shown to and by all.

It did not seem like a high class thing full of super educated people... I doubt many of them spent much time reflecting on social issues... I didn't see anyone reading...

I wasn't there to talk to over-educated, opinionated know-it-alls anyway. I was there to soak in the essence of America's chosen sons and daughters.

So, we are on this gigantic floating entertainment center being served by an army of slim brown people, who are super happy to have their job. It's weird how happy they are, and they are indeed happy. They make 500$ a week, but with all board, food and flights home paid at the end of their punishing 11 month contracts. I tip my room guy 200$ at the START of the Trip. This really messes with his head. It cuts through so much stress and anticipation for the poor dude. You have never seen more joy and relaxation hit someone, than a 33 year old Indonesian cruise ship room cleaner, with three kids that he sees 2 months a year, getting high fived with two crisp benjamins on day 1.

I talk to every single one of the staff about themselves and their lives until they start getting a hunted look and start glancing about to see if their masters are watching them, to push them to get back to serving or cleaning. I have interrogated them at length to see if they are really happy with their jobs... and I found that every single one of them was.

The shows are good, the food is good. People are happy... Well... as happy as people slowly dying in the matrix tanks can be...

I love being a hippy and living on my farm, but you can't lose track of humanity and just stay working in the garden all day and reading all night. You have to get in there and connect.

I learn just as much on spiritual retreats as I do in the belly of the beast.

So.... 5 days on that cruise ship pounding down a breakfast, brunch and lunch buffet topped off with a high end fine dining meal at night. On day 2 I started waddling down from my room to line up with the fatties for a couple of pizza slices, a beer and a bit of cake at 10 pm. No shame. No judgment. Just eating pizza and cake at 10pm like a team of bloated bosses.

The food is the diametric opposite of my normal diet. All non organic, a sea of GMOs, battery-farm and feed-lot rage meats. The vegetables screaming with pesticides and all of it slathered in sugary sauces. The mixing of all the seafood and meats... as well as the rich desserts, churning away in my pure guts like an unholy brew.

We would normally eat what I grow in my massive organic garden and only organic or wild meat or seafood....

My body went into total shock after the first meal. I think it's good to shock it now and then. Show it who's boss. Stop it craving Kale and Avocados and smack it about a bit.

Within 8 hours my wife and I started farting almost constantly.

When these farts started we actually thought there was something wrong with the ship's sewer plumbing, I even went into the bathroom and sniffed about... only realizing to my horror that it was us, on reentering the bedroom.

I told my wife that her new name is Sally Sewerpipe—so much like septic sewer gas were these farts. Surprisingly she did not like her new name...

We opened up the balcony door and it stayed open for the rest of the trip. The hang time of these farts was incredible. Like 20-30 minutes. I tried to handle the farts with herbal bitters and peppermint tea, but they were way beyond simple herbal remedies. Usually a person loves their own brand… but not this. This chuff was actually burning my eyes and nostrils and I started visibly flinching at olfactory contact.

We couldn't even tell who's farts were who's after a while. It seeped into our clothes and the bedding… it was horrific… Every hour we had to go for a walk to give the room time to air out… I would desperately try not to fart around people too much. This was almost impossible. I felt like the quality control section of a Bagpipe Factory.

I farted in the elevator once, just before a family got in and we fucking ran out in shame as soon as the door opened and hid down the back of the boat helping propel the ship along with our incessant farts.

I'm better, wiser and enriched with experiences and life from getting in there amongst it with my fellow cruise ship humans. I implore you to go out there and fart it up.

Afterword

I am 48 at the conclusion of this book, which means that stopping the crazy antics early and switching from drugs, hard booze and bad food, to clean living, all organic food and herb tea over the last 20 years have caught any rot early and I wont die of liver failure, brain cancer, or madness and suicide.

Which is what happens to people who don't chill the fuck out.

OR... maybe not... and any moment now I will burst open like one of those late and left over rancid Halloween pumpkins, spilling moldy spore covered guts all over the steps.

We are the sum of all we have experienced thought and done. So make sure you are living the life you want, so in the future you will have the life you love. I hope my story inspires you to greatness, and if not greatness at least the idea that getting out there and doing things is senior to watching things.

Acknowledgments

I started my story writing career with the discovery of Email, on buying a laptop in 2002.

Emails of interesting times I was experiencing became stories sent to friends. This quickly became stories written in Word, and sent out in bulk. A number of them made it into this book..

My friends Bianca and Ian were the first to see that I had a WordPress blog where these stories could live, and have given me valuable advice and encouragement along the way.

It was from there to Substack, which got me an audience and fueled my desire to entertain with my writing.

Substack put me in touch with Fleur Hull of The Substack Bookstore who was the catalyst for getting it DONE.

My good friends Matt and Taliesin were my fantastic proofreaders and editors.

And my wonderful wife who has been waiting 20 years for this to become a huge success and a massive pay out.

About the Author

Latimer Redlance is a survival consultant, for businesses and life. He currently lives on a farm in West Florida, surrounded by snakes and crocodiles.

www.ingramcontent.com/pod-product-compliance
Lightning Source LLC
Chambersburg PA
CBHW030229100526
44583CB00013BA/585